HIGHER EDUCATION AND
INTERNATIONAL STUDENT MOBILITY IN
THE GLOBAL KNOWLEDGE ECONOMY

HIGHER EDUCATION AND INTERNATIONAL STUDENT MOBILITY IN THE GLOBAL KNOWLEDGE ECONOMY

Revised and Updated Second Edition

KEMAL GÜRÜZ

FOREWORD BY
CHANCELLOR NANCY L. ZIMPHER

STATE UNIVERSITY OF NEW YORK PRESS

Published by
STATE UNIVERSITY OF NEW YORK PRESS, ALBANY

For information, contact
State University of New York Press, Albany, NY
www.sunypress.edu

Production, Laurie Searl
Marketing, Michael Campochiaro

Library of Congress Cataloging-in-Publication Data

Gürüz, Kemal.
  Higher education and international student mobility in the global knowledge economy /
Kemal Gürüz. — Rev. and updated 2nd ed.
     p. cm.
  Includes bibliographical references and index.
  ISBN 978-1-4384-3569-5 (hardcover : alk. paper)
  ISBN 978-1-4384-3568-8 (pbk. : alk. paper)
  1. Education, Higher.   2. Student mobility.   3. Foreign study.   4. Knowledge
management.   5. Education and globalization.   I. Title.
  LB2322.2.G87 2011
  378—dc22
                                                                              2010031950

10 9 8 7 6 5 4 3 2 1

CONTENTS

ILLUSTRATIONS

FIGURES

TABLES

ACKNOWLEDGMENTS

My interest in higher education governance as a scholarly pursuit in itself started twenty-five years ago, when I was appointed as the dean of the graduate school at Middle East Technical University. Since then, I served at nearly all levels of the Turkish higher education system, and represented my country in a number of international organizations. The last position I held was president of the Higher Education Council, national board of governors at the top of the system, where I served for two terms from 1995 to 2003. I take this opportunity to express my heartfelt gratitude to Süleyman Demirel, the ninth president of the Republic of Turkey, who appointed me to that position, and put his unwavering support behind the Council in its efforts to internationalize the Turkish higher education system. A believer in an interdependent, global world, in which nations coexist in harmony and peace, advancing humanity in all fronts, President Demirel also acted as the intellectual leader of the Turkish higher education system.

It was in my capacity as president of the Council that my association with the State University of New York (SUNY) system started, when in summer 2000 I met former Chancellor John W. Ryan and Robert Gosende, associate vice-chancellor for International Programs of SUNY at an international meeting on higher education. It was during this meeting that the current dual-diploma program between Turkish universities and the SUNY system was hatched; enrollment in the program currently stands at 1,800 students and 750 students have graduated since its start.

When I stepped down from my position as president of the Council, I was accepted to participate in the Fellows Program at the Weatherhead Center (WCFIA) for International Affairs at Harvard University for the 2004–2005 academic year. On December 2, 2004, I was awarded the first "Chancellor John W. Ryan Fellowship in International Education" by SUNY. The first draft of this book was written during that academic year, which I spent at WCFIA, while at the same time lecturing at various campuses of the SUNY system on several aspects of international higher education. This book was thus made possible with the generous support provided by the central administration of the SUNY system and the WCFIA. My deep gratitude goes to John W. Ryan, whose name I now proudly carry in my title as the first recipient of the fellowship named after him, Thomas Egan, chairman of the Board of Trustees of the SUNY system, Robert King and John Ryan, succeeding chancellors, and John O'Connor, vice chancellor and secretary general of the SUNY system, Jorge Dominguez, the then director of WCFIA, and the current vice president of Harvard University for International Education, Steve Bloomfield, assistant director of WCFIA, and Kathleen Molony, director of the Fellows Program at WCFIA.

It was during those lectures at the SUNY campuses where I had the chance to interact with leaders in the field of international higher education, Bruce Johnstone, Dan Levy, and Stephen Dunnett, and in the intellectually invigorating atmosphere at WCFIA, that the contents of the present book began to take shape. No less were the contributions that my friend John Ryder made during the times we drove around upstate New York, speaking in various languages, some of which we created. John also kindly edited the first draft of the book.

I thank James Peltz, associate director of the SUNY Press, and Lisa Chesnel, my editor there, without whose efforts this book would not have been possible.

My vocabulary fails me in thanking Robert and MaryBeth Gosende, with whom I start thanking family members, for my wife Güniz and I have come to consider them as brother and sister. Many a time, I wonder what I have done to deserve friends like Bob and MB.

Last, but not least, I thank my beloved wife Güniz for so unselfishly putting up with and supporting me, and our son, Murat, who has made us proud. As someone with his ancestral roots in today's Greece, Bulgaria, Cyprus, and Turkey, with a Turkish and American education, and currently a knowledge worker traveling between San Jose, Mexico, and the Philippines, Murat possibly epitomizes the title and the content of this book.

ABBREVIATIONS

AAU: American Association of Universities

ACA: Academic Cooperation Association

ACE: American Council on Education

AEI: Australian Education International

AIEA: Association of International Education Administrators

AUCC: Association of Universities and Colleges of Canada

BCCIE: British Columbia Center for International Education

BCCIHE: Boston College Center for International Higher Education

BFUG: Bologna Follow-Up Group

CBIE: Canadian Bureau of International Education

CEPES: European Centre for Higher Education (UNESCO, Bucharest)

CHEA: Council for Higher Education Accreditation

CIC: Citizenship and Immigration Canada

CNE: National Committee for Evaluation (*Comité National d'Evaluation*)

CRE: Conference of Rectors, Presidents and Vice-Chancellors of European Universities (*Conférence des Recteurs Européens*)

DAAD: *Deutscher Akademischer Austausch Dienst*

DETC: Distance Education and Training Council

DS: Diploma Supplement

EC: European Commission

ECTS: European Credit Transfer and Accumulation System

EHEA: European Higher Education Area

ENIC: European Network of Information Centers

ENQA: European Network of Quality Assurance

EQAR: European Quality Assurance Register

ERA: European Research Area

ESIB: International Union of Students in Europe

EU: European Union

EUA: European Universities Association

FE: Further education (in the United Kingdom)

FEE-HELP: Higher Education Loan Program (Australia)

GATS: General Agreement on Trade in Services

GDP: Gross domestic product

GER: Gross enrollment ratio

GNI: Gross national income

GNP: Gross national product

GPI: Gender parity index

HECS: Higher Education Contribution Scheme

HEFCE: Higher Education Funding Council for England

HEFW: Higher Education Funding Council for Wales

HESA: Higher Education Statistics Agency (in the United Kingdom)

IAU: International Association of Universities

ICHEFAP: International Comparative Higher Education and Accessibility Project

ICT: Information and communication technologies

IDP:International Development Program (IDP Education Australia)

IIE: Institute of International Education

IIM: Indian Institute of Management

IIT: Indian Institute of Technology

ISCED: International Standard Classification of Education

IUFM: *Institut Universitaire de Formation des Maitres*

IUT: *Institut Universitaire de Technologie*

LLL: Life-long Learning

NAFSA: National Association of Foreign Student Advisors

NARIC: National Academic Recognition Information Centers

NASULGC: National Association of State Universities and Land-Grant Colleges

NCAA: National Council for Academic Awards

NCES: National Center for Education Statistics

NIAD-UE: National Institute for Academic Degrees and University Evaluation (Japan)

NICA: National Accreditation Agency of the Russian Federation

NIS: National Innovation system

NPEC: National Postsecondary Education Cooperative

NZQA: New Zealand Quality Agency

OBHE: Observatory on Borderless Higher Education

OBHE-A: OBHE Articles

OBHE-BN: OBHE Breaking News

OBHE-BNA: OBHE Breaking News Article

OBHE-BfN: OBHE Briefing Note

OBHE-KI: OBHE Key Issue

OECD: Organization for Economic Cooperation and Development

OUW: Open University Worldwide

PCFC: Polytechnics and Colleges Funding Council

PTE: Private training establishment (New Zealand)

QAA: Quality Assurance Agency (United Kingdom)

SHEFC: Scottish Higher Education Funding Council

SIU: *Senter for Internasjonalisering av Hoyere Utdanning* (Norway)

STS: *Section de Technicien Supérieur*

TAFE: Technical and further education (in Australia)

UFC: Universities Funding Council

UGC: University Grants Committee

UKCOSA: The Council for International Education (United Kingdom)

UNESCO: United Nations Educational Scientific and Cultural Organization

USDE: U.S. Department of Education

WTO: World Trade Organization

FOREWORD

Professor Kemal Gürüz brings to his study of higher education mobility a perspective garnered in part by his service as the leading higher education policymaker in his country of Turkey. During his tenure as president of the Turkish Higher Education Council, his commitment to international educational exchange was prominent. He was one of the main architects of the innovative and highly successful dual-diploma programs linking leading Turkish universities with many campuses of my own institution, the State University of New York (SUNY). These programs account for the mobility of more than five hundred students each year.

In this edition of *Higher Education and International Student Mobility in the Global Knowledge Economy*, Professor Gürüz provides a well-documented, current, and scholarly analysis of the impact of the mobility of students, scholars, and knowledge in a rapidly evolving global economy. He incorporates data from a wide range of sources in discussing historic and future trends in the internationalization of higher education. His excellent review of this topic is, of course, informed by his own experience as an international student and scholar, and as the first recipient of the John W. Ryan Fellowship in International Education at SUNY.

Higher Education and International Student Mobility in the Global Knowledge Economy is an important scholarly contribution to the field of international education, and should serve as a valued resource for scholars, higher education policymakers, and university administrators.

Chancellor Nancy L. Zimpher
State University of New York

PREFACE TO THE REVISED
AND UPDATED SECOND EDITION

Both higher education and international student mobility are dynamic topics. This is why I had ended the introductory chapter of the hardcover
edition of this book with the following words: "Given the increasingly rapid
pace of change and developments occurring in this area, those remarks, and
possibly some of the material presented in the previous chapters, may be
irrelevant and obsolete by the time this book is published." Indeed, so much
new data became available since the first edition that it would have been
an incomplete task to print a second edition without incorporating them.

I have incorporated all the new UNESCO and OECD data on national enrollments and financial indicators into Chapters 2 and 3, as well as the
new developments in governance and quality assurance. The changes occurring in the area of new providers are so rapid that it is nearly impossible to
keep up with them in the book format. I did my best to include the major
developments in that area as of April 2009. There are relatively few new
additions to the material in Chapter 5 other than the recent developments
related to the Bologna Process.

All of the figures and tables in Chapter 6 have been updated to include
new data on international student mobility as of April 2009. The term *international student mobility*, of course, covers students at all levels. The focus
of both the hardcover and the revised updated second editions of this book
is, however, at the higher education level. No international standards yet
exist in data reporting by countries even in that relatively narrower area.
Different countries include different categories of students when reporting
data on foreign students. In this edition of the book, I tried to clarify this
issue by supporting figures with tables that show time-series of the numbers
of different categories of students at the postsecondary level for the major
host countries. As for the nomenclature concerning the different categories
of students, I have stuck to those used by the individual countries in reporting data on foreign students. These revisions and updating have resulted
in nearly completely new sets of tables and figures. I do hope that, while
trying to clarify, I have not ended up being more confusing.

I believe that the concluding remarks in the hardcover edition are still largely valid. I have, therefore, left them essentially unchanged. I did, however, intentionally refrain from elaborating too much on the potential effects of the recent global economic crisis, as no data yet exist from which to draw conclusions concerning student mobility. One possibility is that such uncertainty will make parents and students to look toward perceived "safe havens" in a seemingly paradoxical manner similar to the case of the recently strengthened U.S. dollar in the face of a weakening U.S. economy. In that case, we may see increased student flows to the so-called major English-speaking destination countries, in particular, to the United States. Another possibility is that the demand for foreign-provided higher education will keep increasing, but parents will find it increasingly difficult to afford the costs of educating their children abroad. In such a case, we are likely to see increased activity in different forms of offshore provision, in particular, in various forms of joint degrees.

There also were a few typographical errors in the hardcover edition, small in number, irritating nevertheless, such as showing Blair in power in 1992 (p.41), and confusing Kluwer Academic Publishers with Kluwer Law International (p. 314). The function of the second stage of the new degree structure required by the Bologna Process was misrepresented in the first edition as being "more professionally oriented" (p. 147), which I have hopefully clarified in the second edition. I take full responsibility for these and any other such errors that may exist in the second edition, too.

I thank Chancellor Nancy L. Zimpher for her continued support and kind words.

Finally, I am gratefully indebted to Gary Dunham, former executive director of SUNY Press, and Laurie Searl, senior production editor of SUNY Press without whose support and efforts this revised and updated second edition would not have been possible, and to the excellent editorial and production staff of SUNY Press with whom it has been a delight to work.

ONE

THE GLOBAL KNOWLEDGE ECONOMY

AND HIGHER EDUCATION

1.1. INTRODUCTION

Global refers to worldwide in scope and substance and de-emphasizes the concept of nation, but without negating it. Globalization, in general, is the flow of technology, knowledge, people, values, ideas, capital, goods, and services across national borders, and affects each country in a different way due to the nation's individual history, traditions, culture, and priorities (Knight 2004). Economists define globalization more narrowly as the integration of commodity, capital, and labor markets.

In any case, globalization involves the coming together and interaction of human beings. Thus, the process of globalization began with the genesis of human beings. It has always been driven by the human desire for economic and political gains, a zeal for spreading faith, ideology, and culture, and a quest for new knowledge. It has been made possible by advances in transportation and communication technologies. Globalization clearly is a continuous process that is dependent on and intertwined with technological progress.

Until about two centuries ago, it was possible to identify different civilizations as distinct from one another, simply because transportation and communication technologies were not as developed and widely available as they are today. This meant that different communities could not interact sufficiently to influence each other in a manner that would lead to new socioeconomic and cultural syntheses. Since then, and especially in the previous century, however, a single global civilization has emerged that like a marble or an amalgam, consists of the "higher outputs" of different cultures, political, scientific, technological, socioeconomic, artistic, and literary that

1

are now shared by the masses worldwide. McNeill and McNeill (2003, 325), describe this process as follows:

> Civilizations engulfed originally independent human communities, creating new, more powerful bodies politic, economic and cultural; and being more powerful, they persistently spread to geographically favorable new ground. Moreover, their spread meant that across the past millennium, as communications intensified, what began as separate civilizations followed a familiar path by blending into an ever more powerful, global, cosmopolitan web that now prevails among us—a huge web of cooperation and competition sustained by flows of information and energy.

At the very core of this single global civilization is rational, critical human thought and reasoning, which originated in the Hellenic world in the first half of the sixth century BC.[1] From there, it followed a tortuous path over a vast area extending from China to Spain before eventually reaching the West to form the core of today's global civilization. Scholars, polymaths, philosophers, and students wandering from one place to another throughout centuries played a key role in spreading ideas, knowledge, know-how, and civilization.

This book is about how the international mobility of students, scholars, programs, and institutions of higher education evolved over time, and the ways in which it is occurring in today's global knowledge economy.

Students and scholars leaving their homes on a quest for education and knowledge is not a new phenomenon; neither are the transplantation of educational institutions, and the transfer of the epistemic knowledge base of curricula and textbooks from one culture to another. In medieval Europe, for example, there were times when foreigners accounted for about 10 percent of the student enrollment across the continent. This figure is much higher than the share of foreign students in higher education enrollment worldwide today, which is about 2 percent. However, the number of foreign students today is a staggering 2.75 million worldwide, compared with a few hundred in medieval Europe. At that time, students traveled to other places simply because there were no institutions where they lived. Today, there are more than seventeen thousand institutions of higher education in 184 countries and territories in the world, and opportunities for access have been vastly improved for masses since then. This is what makes the relatively smaller number of foreign students in higher education today much more significant. The question then is what has caused this expansion? In other words, what are the rationales, on the part of students and their families, the governments of their countries of origin, and the institutions and countries hosting them, that are driving this expansion? Furthermore, student mobility, although the biggest part, is just one component of the international higher education scene in today's world. More than one rationale is at work, and a multitude of modalities and opportunities exist, which are expanding academic mobility today, and they are all interdependent.

This book is an attempt to survey the literature on these complex phenomena. Academic mobility, in its various forms, is and has been an important aspect of the process of globalization throughout history. Rapid technological developments have made and are making it much easier and faster today. However, this is only part of the picture, even when analyzed in a historical perspective. Any attempt to study academic mobility without linking it to the evolution of institutions, structures, systems, functions, governance, administration, and financing of higher education throughout history would be incomplete. Developments in higher education worldwide that have taken place in the second half of the twentieth century, particularly those that have been paralleling the onset of the global knowledge economy, are particularly pertinent to the topic at hand.

1.2. GLOBALIZATION AND THE KNOWLEDGE ECONOMY

Throughout history, knowledge, as both technical expertise and any kind of information, has been important to humankind for improving the quality of life. What have changed over centuries, however, are the characteristics and the quality of knowledge, the relative importance of science as its source, the methods by which it is created, stored, accessed, transmitted, acquired and retrieved, its relative importance as a production factor, and the level of education and training required in the workforce.

1.2.1. The Industrial Society

Until the late nineteenth century, technology was developed independently of science; technological developments, in general, preceded scientific developments.[2] The Industrial Revolution that took place between 1760 and 1830 began with the invention and commercialization of the steam engine by James Watt (1736–1819), long before the formulation of the laws of thermodynamics that govern the relationships between heat and mechanical energy and the limitation imposed by nature on the conversion of the former to the latter.

Based on the educational backgrounds of the technological leaders of the Industrial Revolution, it can also be argued that the university as an institution made little, if any, contribution to the Industrial Revolution.[3] Mokyr (2002, 37–41), on the other hand, argues that the Scientific

Revolution and the Enlightenment, both of which owed indirectly to universities and other institutions of higher education, resulted in what he refers to as "Industrial Enlightenment." He cites the associations of technical and scientific knowledge, whose number in England had reached 1,020 by the end of the nineteenth century with a total membership of about 200,000, as a major contributor to the Industrial Enlightenment.[4] It should, however, be pointed out that chairs and professorships in various branches of natural sciences had been established in Oxford and Cambridge as early as the beginning of the seventeenth century, and by the end of that century, Scottish universities, St. Andrews (f. 1411), Glasgow (f. 1451), Aberdeen (f. 1495) and Edinburgh (f. 1589), together with the Dutch universities, Leiden (f. 1575), Groningen (f. 1612) and Utrecht (f. 1636), had emerged as the leading scientific and intellectual centers in Europe. It is inconceivable that the scholarship of the Scottish universities did not permeate the neighboring northern England, the cradle of the Industrial Revolution. Furthermore, the dissenting academies, where such great scientists as Joseph Priestley (1733–1804) and John Dalton (1766–1844) gave public lectures, were concentrated in the new commercial and industrial centers, Manchester, Liverpool and Birmingham, where rich merchants and industrialists sponsored and supported them. Many of the mechanical institutes affiliated to the Royal Institution[5] also were located in this region. The role that universities and other institutions of higher education played in the Industrial Revolution was obviously indirect; nevertheless, it should not be underestimated.

However, owing mainly to the German research universities (see Section 5.1.4), an entirely different picture started to emerge in the nineteenth century. Scientific breakthroughs achieved in laboratories led to new technologies, which, in turn, formed the bases of new industries. The chemical industry and electrical technologies are generally considered the first science-based industries.[6]

The period from about the middle of the eighteenth century to the beginning of the twentieth century marks the advent of the industrial society, which is characterized by technologies and industries based on the results of scientific research, replacement of inventions and inventors by innovations and organized research and development (R&D) activity, and the appearance of large-scale, smoke-stack factories mass-producing goods.

In the preindustrial society, individual scientists and scholars worked in isolation, even away from the universities where some of them were employed. With the advent of industrial society came the university research laboratories, and public research institutes. *Physikalisch-Technische Reichsanstalt* (f. 1887), the *Kaiser Wilhelm Gessellchaft* (f. 1911, renamed Max Planck institutes in 1948), the industrial R&D laboratories, such as those of the German chemical giant *Badische Aniline und Soda-Fabrik* (BASF, f. 1865)[7] were the first ones in Germany. Research laboratories of General Electric and Bell Telephone, and Edison's laboratory/shop in Menlo Park were the pioneers in the United States.

To channel public funds more effectively and to organize R&D activities toward national goals, institutions were established as early as the first quarter of the twentieth century. In this manner, national R&D systems began to emerge, comprising universities, public research institutions, and private-sector research departments, each with distinct, but partially overlapping and complementary functions.[8]

Technological progress financed by credits and sustained by innovations resulting from organized R&D activity was identified by Joseph Schumpeter (1883–1950) as the main driver of capitalist growth as early as 1934 (Mokyr 1990, 8). Such progress and growth effectively led to new scientific discoveries, which, in turn, formed the bases for new technologies, and opened up entirely new vistas for the humankind.[9]

Since then, the precursor–follower type of linear relationship between science and technology has been transformed into a much more intertwined, complex, and fuzzier relationship, where a science-based technology opens up a new scientific field that, in turn, forms the bases for a new set of technologies, and so on. The last quarter of the twentieth century especially was a period where distinctions between basic research, applied research and technological research, and development and industrial applications, and even marketing (e.g., e-commerce) and financing (e.g., venture capital) were increasingly blurred.

1.2.2. Transformation to the Knowledge Society and the Global Knowledge Economy

Out of this complex historical process in which many factors interacted over a period spanning more than one hundred years, but especially in the last quarter of the previous century, technologies emerged, which have started to change our lives profoundly, chief among which are the information and communication technologies.

Information and communication technologies involve innovations in microelectronics, computing (hardware and software), and telecommunications, in an integrated and interactive manner. Thus, these technologies, collectively abbreviated as ICT, enable the processing, storage, and transmission of and access to enormous amounts of data through communication networks. The Internet has grown exponentially, from 16 million users in 1995 to more than 1 billion users in 2005, with the number of users currently approaching 2 billion.

The ICT revolution is transforming the "industrial society" into the "knowledge society." A number of other factors, some of which are in fact byproducts of the complex interactive process I outlined above, also have contributed to this transformation. However, it is not possible to assign a specific date to this transformation. Bill Gates (2006) points out that it was in the last twenty years that the word *knowledge* became an adjective. The widespread availability of the Internet through personal computers equipped with browsers and the establishment of the World Wide Web in the early 1990s, have indeed revolutionized the way we live, and thus, in the eyes of many, epitomize the transition to the knowledge society and the global knowledge economy.[10]

At the beginning of the nineteenth century, "the global economic world" comprised only North America and western Europe that is the so-called Atlantic economy. The sociopolitical changes coupled with and driven by the ICT revolution, which made it possible for people to become aware of and informed about events and developments in other parts of the world, radically transformed the world economy and led to dramatic policy changes around the world. In 1978, Deng Xiaoping began to pave China's way toward capitalism. The Berlin Wall fell on November 9, 1989, which symbolized the implosion of the Soviet system. In 1991, with her model no longer intact, India abandoned the autarkic socialist system, and starting with her telecom industry, opened her economy to foreign investment and competition. These were paralleled by the consolidation of civilian rule in Latin America, and a much more improved sociopolitical landscape in Africa. In summary, the proportion of the world's countries practicing some form of democratic governance rose from 40 percent in 1988 to 61 percent in 1998 (The World Bank 2002, 19). The global world now comprises more than 6 billion people, nearly all of the global population.[11]

Privatization rather than central planning, and export competitiveness rather than import substitution, rapidly began to unify world markets. This process, referred to as "economic globalization," is intertwined with technological transformations. New tools of information and communication technologies make the world's financial and scientific resources more accessible and unify the markets into a single marketplace, where intense competition further drives scientific and technological progress (UNDP 2001, 30–31).

The convergent and mutually reinforcing impacts of globalization and the ICT revolution have radically changed not only the methods and structures of production, but also the relative importance of the factors of production. The transformation from an industrial society to a knowledge society and the global knowledge economy is characterized by the increased importance of knowledge, both know-how and information, and a well trained workforce that not only can apply know-how, but also is capable of analysis and decision making based on information. Just as the steam engine and electricity harnessed inanimate power to make possible the Industrial Revolution, digital breakthroughs are channeling brainpower to form the basis of the knowledge economy (UNDP 2001, 4).

In summary, knowledge and people with knowledge are the key factors of development, the main drivers of growth, and the major determinants of competitiveness in the global knowledge economy. In his seminal work on competitive advantage, M. Porter (1990) had already pointed out a decade and a half ago that a nation could no longer rely on abundant natural resources and cheap labor, and that comparative advantage would increasingly be based on combinations of technical innovations and creative use of knowledge.

These complex interactions are now driving the science, and technology-based global knowledge economy, where R&D and production are horizontally integrated in the form of networks covering production sites and laboratories in a number of countries, making it possible to outsource knowledge, labor, and other factors of production globally. Thus, the transformation from an industrial to a knowledge economy has been accompanied by the emergence of a worldwide labor market and global networks for production of both goods and services (World Bank 2002, 17–19).

This has been paralleled, and possibly brought about, by another type of transformation. The particular organization of R&D effort outlined earlier, which served industrial society very well, gradually evolved into the "national innovation system" (NIS), which now functions as the heart of the knowledge society, continually pumping knowledge to its organs through complex information and communication networks, of which the Internet is the prime example. The World Bank (2002, 24–26) defines the NIS as follows: "An NIS is a web of: (i) knowledge producing organizations in the education and training system; together with (ii) the appropriate macroeconomic and regulatory framework, including trade policies that affect technology diffusion; (iii) innovative firms and networks of enterprises; (iv) adequate communication infrastructures; and other selected factors, such as access to the global knowledge or certain market conditions that favor innovations."

M. Porter (1990) appropriately referred to the components comprising a fully developed NIS as "advanced and specialized factors of production." These can be summarized as follows: (1) the national R&D system; (2) modern infrastructure, particularly the ICT infrastructure; (3) an innovation- and business-friendly legal and regulatory environment; and (4) the education and training system, in particular, the higher education system.

Tables 1.1 to 1.3 show recent data available from the World Bank (2006a, 20–22, 88–91, and 302–9),[12] which determine in part the level of

Table 1.1. Demographic, National Income, and Educational Data for Selected Countries

Country or Country Group	GDP, Current $Billion, 2004	GNI per Capita, Current $ (Atlas Mthd.), 2004	Population, Million, 2004	Annual Population Growth Rate, % 2004	Gross Enrollment Ratio, % 2004		
					Primary	Secondary	Tertiary
Low-income	1,200.0	507	2,343.0	1.7	100[a]	46[a]	9[a]
Middle-income	7,200.0	2,274	3,017.8	0.8	111[a]	75[a]	24[a]
High-income	32,900.0	32,112	1,004.2	0.4	100[a]	105[a]	67[a]
World	41,290.0	6,329	6,365.0	1.1	106	65	24
U.S.	11,712.0	41,440	293.7	0.9	100	95	82
Europe[b]	9,500.0	27,921	309.3	0.1	104[a]	108[a]	57[a]
Sub-Saharan Africa	523.0	601	725.8	2.2	90	30	5
UK	2,124.0	33,630	59.9	0.3	101	170	60
Germany	2,741.0	30,690	82.5	0.0	99	100	48
France	2,046.0	30,370	60.4	0.3	105	110	56
Australia	637.0	27,070	20.1	0.9	102	154	72
Japan	4,623.0	37,050	127.8	-0.1	100	102	54
Russia	581.0	3,400	143.8	-0.5	118	93	68
Canada	978.0	28,310	32.0	0.8	101	105	57
New Zealand	98.9	19,990	4.1	0.5	102	119	72
China	1,932.0	1,500	1,296.2	0.6	118	73	19
India	691.0	620	1,079.7	1.4	107	52	11
Korea	680.0	14,000	48.1	0.5	105	91	89
Turkey	303.0	3,750	71.7	1.2	95	85	37
Morocco	50.0	1,570	25.8	1.6	106	47	11
Greece	205.0	16,730	11.1	0.1	100	96	72

Malaysia	118.0	4,520	24.9	1.5	93	70	29
Hong Kong	163.0	26,660	6.9	1.0	108	85	32
Indonesia	258.0	1,140	217.6	1.0	116	62	26
Bulgaria	24.0	2,750	7.8	-0.8	105	99	41
Thailand	162.0	2,490	61.4	0.7	99	77	41
Mexico	677.0	6,790	103.8	1.1	109	79	22
Singapore	107.0	24,760	4.2	1.3	nd	nd	46
Vietnam	45.0	540	82.2	1.2	98	73	10

ªDemographic and income data and enrollment data are for 2003 from World Development Indicators. The World Bank (2006a, 20–22, and 88–91), and can be accessed at http://devdata.worldbank.org/wdi2006/contents/Table1_1.htm, and http://devdata.worldbank.org/wdi2006/contents/Table2_11.htm. Other enrollment data are from UNESCO (2006).

ᵇEurope includes only those countries in the European monetary union.

GDP, gross domestic product; GNI, gross national income

Table 1.2. National Innovation Systems: R&D Indicators

Country or Country Group	R&D Personnel per Million	R&D Spending, % of GDP, 1996–2003	Scientific and Technical Publications, 2001	High-Technology Exports, $Million, 2004	Royalty and License Fee Income, $Million, 2004	Patent Applications Filed, 2002 Residents	Patent Applications Filed, 2002 Nonresidents
Low-income	nd	0.73	13,147	0	59	1,469	3,003,874
Middle-income	851	0.87	83,927	266,410	2,447	81,493	4,789,712
High-income	3,558	2.54	551,426	1,170,986	107,302	853,868	5,088,479
World	nd	2.36	648,500	1,296,586	109,808	936,630	12,882,065
U.S.	4,484	2.60	200,870	216,016	52,643	198,339	183,398
Europe[a]	2,607	2.20	148,619	361,128	17,110	129,155	2,448,271
Sub-Saharan Africa	nd	nd	3,500	nd	17	220	181,463
UK	2,706	1.89	47,660	64,295	12,019	33,671	251,239
Germany	3,261	2.50	43,623	131,838	5,103	80,661	230,066
France	3,213	2.19	31,317	64,871	5,070	21,959	160,056
Australia	3,670	1.63	14,788	3,128	472	10,823	96,434
Japan	5,287	3.15	57,420	124,045	15,701	371,495	115,411
Russia	3,319	1.28	15,846	3,432	227	24,049	96,315
Canada	3,597	1.94	22,626	25,625	3,019	5,934	102,418
New Zealand	3,405	1.17	2,903	858	98	2,137	91,240
China	663	1.31	20,978	161,603	236	40,346	140,910
India	119	0.85	11,076	2,840	25	220	91,704
Korea	3,187	2.64	11,037	75,742	1,790	76,860	126,836
Turkey	341	0.66	4,098	1,064	0	550	250,492
Morocco	782	0.62	469	696	16	0	89,300
Greece	1,413	0.65	3,329	1,031	32	614	162,387

Malaysia	299	0.69	494	52,868	782	nd	nd
Hong Kong	1,564	0.60	1,817	80,109	341	112	9,018
Indonesia	nd	nd	207	5,809	221	0	90,922
Bulgaria	1,263	0.50	784	247	7	306	158,051
Thailand	286	0.24	727	18,203	14	1,117	4,548
Mexico	268	0.42	3,209	31,382	92	627	94,116
Singapore	4,745	2.15	2,603	87,742	224	511	93,748
Vietnam	nd	nd	158	594	nd	2	90,135

Source: World Development Indicators 2006. The World Bank (2006a, 306–09). http://devdata.worldbank.org/wdi2006/contents/Table5_11.htm.

Note: Data for a period beginning and ending in different years is for the most recently available year in that period.

aEurope includes only those countries that are in the European monetary union.

nd, no data available; R&D, research and development.

Table 1.3. National Innovation Systems: ICT Indicators

Country or Country Group	No. of Personal Computers per 1,000 People, 2004	No. of Internet Users per 1,000 People, 2004	Schools Connected to Internet, % 2004	International Internet Bandwidth, bits per Capita, 2004	Secure Internet Servers per Million People, 2004	Price Basket for Internet, $ per Month, 2003
Low-income	11	24	nd	10	0	45.5
Middle-income	61	92	nd	91	4	22.3
High-income	574	549	98	4,545	384	20.9
World	130	140	nd	816	65	25.8
U.S.	749	630	99	3,305	783	14.9
Europe[a]	421	443	94	5,785	149	22.5
Sub-Saharan Africa	15	19	nd	6	2	51.2
UK	599	628	99	13,055	466	23.9
Germany	561	500	99	6,860	274	14.1
France	487	414	97	3,312	79	14.1
Australia	682	646	97	1,097	500	18.1
Japan	542	587	99	1,038	257	21.1
Russia	132	111	65	100	2	10.0
Canada	700	626	98	6,803	570	12.7
New Zealand	474	788	99	1,127	493	12.9
China	41	73	nd	57	0	10.1
India	12	32	nd	11	1	8.7
Korea	545	657	100	1,485	20	9.7
Turkey	52	142	40	124	17	19.8
Morocco	21	117	nd	26	1	25.3
Greece	89	177	59	589	31	37.6

Malaysia	197	nd	397	128	15	8.4
Hong Kong	608	100	506	4,793	159	3.8
Indonesia	14	nd	67	10	0	22.3
Bulgaria	59	60	283	80	9	12.4
Thailand	58	37	109	47	5	7.0
Mexico	108	60	135	108	8	22.6
Singapore	763	100	571	5,826	270	11.0
Vietnam	13	nd	71	23	0	19.9

Source: World Development Indicators 2006. The World Bank (2006a, 302–305).

http://devdata.worldbank.org/wdi2006/contents/Table5_10.htm.

[a] Europe includes only those countries that are in the European monetary union.

ICT, information and communication technology; nd, no data available

development of NIS in a number of selected countries that currently are key players in international student mobility (see Chapter 6). The countries selected include the major host (destination) countries for foreign students, the United States, the United Kingdom, Germany, France, Australia (see Table 6.1 and Figure 6.2, and Table A.6 in Appendix A). Japan is both a major host and a major country of origin (source country) of foreign students. There also are emerging destinations like Canada and New Zealand; Russia is still both a major host country and an emerging country of origin.[13] Other major countries of origin of foreign students are China, India, Korea, Turkey, Morocco, Greece, Malaysia, Hong Kong, Indonesia, and Mexico (see Figure 6.5 and Table 6.2, and Table A.6). Recently emerging countries of origin are Bulgaria, Thailand, and Vietnam. Singapore, a major country of origin until recently, is aspiring to become a regional hub for international education.

Table 1.1 shows the data on national income, demographics, and enrollment at the three levels of education. It is interesting to note that the six major host countries with only 10 percent of the world's population generate 58 percent of the global income. The United States, the United Kingdom, Australia, Canada, and New Zealand, collectively referred to as the major English-speaking destination countries (MESDCs) for foreign students (Bohm et al. 2004), which have 6 percent of the world's population, produce 38 percent of the global wealth. The second point to note in Table 1.1 is that the differences in per capita income between the United States, the leading host country, and China and India, currently by far the leading first and second countries of origin of foreign students, are more than twenty-seven- and sixty-six-fold, respectively. Third, all of the countries shown in Table 1.1 are able to provide primary education to the full age cohort in their countries, and most are able to do it at the secondary level as well. Large differences exist at the tertiary level between host countries and countries of origin. It is thus clear that enrollment at the tertiary level is a key factor in determining the participative power of a country in the global knowledge economy (see Figure 2.4).

Table 1.2 shows the data on R&D indicators as they pertain to the degree of development of NIS in selected countries. The six major host countries on the average spend 2.3 percent of their gross domestic product (GDP) on R&D, and produce 61 percent of the scientific and technical publications, account for 47 percent of the high-technology exports, and receive 83 percent of the annual royalty and license fee income. The corresponding figures for the MESDCs are 45, 24, and 62 percent, respectively, and 31, 17 and 48 percent, respectively, for the United States alone. A key indicator is the ratio of patents filed by nonresidents to that by residents. This ratio is 0.98 for the United States, 1.4 for the six major host countries, 2.9 for the MESDCs, and 12.4 for the major countries of origin, including Russia and Singapore.

Table 1.3 shows ICT indicators as they pertain to the degree of development of NIS in selected countries. The ratio of personal computers per one thousand people in the six major host countries to that in the major countries of origin is 8.4, when Korea, Hong Kong, and Singapore are excluded. This ratio becomes 9.7 for the MESDCs, and 9.5 for the United States. The corresponding ratios for Internet users per one thousand people are 5.0, 5.2, and 4.9, respectively. When expressed in terms of the number of secure Internet servers per 1 million people, the ratios become 48, 56, and 87, respectively. Furthermore, although nearly all schools in the major host countries and Canada and New Zealand are connected to the Internet, major countries of origin other than Korea, Singapore, and Hong Kong still have a long way to go.

A very important characteristic of a fully developed NIS is the share of the private sector in the R&D activities. In the recent past, countries such as India (before the transformation in 1991), Brazil, and especially the former USSR failed to gain significant returns on their investment in R&D, mainly because the outputs were "locked" in public institutes, academies, and universities, or in defense industries with no civilian spin-offs. In the global knowledge economy, the private sector has much of the finance, knowledge, and personnel for technological innovation. Among industrialized nations, the share of the private sector in the national R&D activities is above 50 percent, both in terms of financing and in carrying out. Universities typically undertake 15 to 20 percent, and public institutions on the average account for 10 to 15 percent of the activities (UNDP 2001, 37).

Thus, the data reported in the World Development Indicators 2006 allow cross-country comparisons to be made that show the relative degree of development of NIS in selected countries.[14] Such comparisons clearly show that most of the countries in the West and Japan, Korea, Singapore, Hong Kong, and Israel have succeeded in transforming their national R&D systems, fully or partially, into NIS. These also are among the richest and humanly most developed countries, as indicated by the Human Development Index.

The statistics given in Tables 1.1 to 1.3 clearly point to the concentration of technological capacity in today's globalized world in the hands of the few. In fact, the capacity to generate knowledge and innovate is more than ever, "the lever of the riches" (Mokyr 1990). The United States is the undisputed leader in scientific knowledge production with 31 percent of the scientific and technical articles originating from there; Japan (8.9 percent), the United Kingdom (7.3 percent), Germany (6.7 percent), and France (4.8 percent) are far behind. The share of the United States in terms of most frequently cited articles is even greater with 44 percent (Friedman 2006). In a survey entitled "Brains Business" in *The Economist* of September 8, 2005, it is reported that 70 percent of the Nobel laureates are presently employed in American universities. On the other hand, according to an article in *The Wall Street Journal* of May 16, 2006 (p. 11 in the European edition), Europeans won 19 percent of the Nobel prizes between 1995 and 2004, down from 73 percent in the period from 1901 to 1950.

Developed countries are taking advantage of low-cost labor abroad to improve their competitiveness in the global markets, but are also experiencing the repercussions of job loss and displacement at home. Outsourcing of manufacturing and services is now an established feature of the global knowledge economy. China has emerged as the manufacturing hub of the global knowledge economy, followed by Thailand, Malaysia, Indonesia, the Philippines, Vietnam and Mexico.

Scardino et al. (2004) forecasted that by the year 2008, total spending on ICT services via global outsourcing would surpass $50 billion per year. More than thirty countries in varying degrees of development are presently competing in this subsector. India is presently the leader, but Indian companies are being challenged by companies in Canada, Russia, Ireland, China, Singapore, Malaysia, the Philippines, and Bulgaria, to name but a few.

Capitalism in the global knowledge economy is now driving the virtuous cycle of innovation, reward, reinvestment, and more innovation. It appears that the world is moving in a direction where there are three groups of countries. The first group, largely led by the United States, comprises the countries that create knowledge and knowledge-based technologies; these are the "knowledge producers." China is emerging as the manufacturing hub, and India as the service hub of the global knowledge economy, both countries taking on increasingly central roles in the global supply chains. China and India are currently leading the so-called knowledge users. The third group includes countries that either are passive users of knowledge or "technologically disconnected."

Not only manufacturing and services are being globalized. Technology increasingly is being developed and commercialized in locations where critical masses exist with respect to the capacity to generate new scientific knowledge, and where human resources with the requisite skills profile exist. In other words, innovation, too, is being globalized. Many of the tasks formerly performed in the integrated R&D centers of multinationals are now being outsourced to India, China, and Russia. In March 1986, Deng Xiaoping announced the so-called 863 Program, which aimed to make China a world power in science and technology; today there are some seven hundred multinational R&D centers in China (Liu 2006). In other words, economic activity is moving to wherever it can be performed in the cheapest and most effective manner. The large number of English-speaking, well-educated Indian technicians, engineers, and software scientists played a key role in overcoming the Y2K bug. The technicians are the graduates of hundreds of technical colleges in India. The software engineers are the graduates of the prestigious Indian Institutes of Technology (IITs), which date back to 1951. A well-educated workforce with connections to networks in knowledge-producing countries is a key asset in the global knowledge economy.

It is thus quite clear that countries with fully developed NIS are the knowledge producers with the capacity to convert the knowledge produced into goods and services that can be traded in the global markets, and that these also are the countries that are attracting foreign students from all over the world. The general direction of international student mobility is clearly from "knowledge-user" countries to "knowledge producers" (see Sections 6.4 and 6.5.)

Nearly two decades ago, M. Porter (1990) pointed out the importance of "clusters," where start-up companies, research labs, financiers, and corporations converge; creating a dynamic and conducive environment that brings together knowledge, finance, and opportunity. At the beginning of the new century, forty-seven such "global hubs of innovation" existed around the world. The United States has thirteen hubs. Europe has seventeen: four in the United Kingdom; three in Germany; two each in Finland, Sweden, and France; and one each in the Netherlands, Austria, Norway, and Ireland. Japan, Brazil, and Australia have two each, China has three, and there is one hub in each of Canada, Singapore, Korea, New Zealand, Israel, India, South Africa, and Tunisia (UNDP 2001, 45). Many multinational companies are moving parts of their in-house R&D activities to countries where such hubs, qualified workforce, and a business- and innovation-friendly environment exist.

According to an article entitled "China Becomes Magnet for R&D," in the March 14, 2006 (European edition) issue of The Wall Street Journal, the huge and inexpensive talent pool in China is drawing multinationals to that country. Furthermore, China is pouring money into R&D, which promises to broaden the country's big role in the global economy. China is currently spending close to $30 billion on R&D annually, up from just over $10 billion in 2000. The corresponding figures for India are $4 billion and $3 billion, respectively. China, the United States and India, in that order, are now at the top of the list of most attractive R&D locations, with Japan as a distant fourth, and followed by the United Kingdom, Russia, France, and Germany. As seen in the following parts of this book, with the exception of Russia, these also are among the most active countries in international student mobility, and Russia, too, is reemerging, both as a host for and a source of foreign students.

China has already overtaken Russia as a knowledge-producing country. Scientific and technical publications from China accounted for 3.2 percent of the global total in 2001, as opposed to 2.4 percent from Russia, and 1.7 percent from India. Chinese royalty and license fee income was $236 million in 2004, compared to $227 million for Russia and $25 million for

India. With a 12.5 percent share of the global high-technology exports in 2004, China was way ahead of Russia (0.3 percent) and India (0.2 percent). These are reflected in the increased average income of the Chinese and the Indians; the per capita GDP growth rate from 2003 to 2004 was 8.8 percent in China, and 5.4 percent in India (World Bank 2006b, 292).

China and India have emerged as by far the first and the second leading countries of origin of foreign students within a few decades. Although there are, as of the date of the writing of this book, no quantitative studies on the relationship between outward student mobility from and economic development in these countries, sufficient indirect evidence exist, such as those I have reported, to conclude that China and India are benefiting from this phenomenon. According to *The Economist* ("Brains Business," September 8, 2005):

> Few highly skilled migrants cut their links with their home countries completely. Most keep in touch, sending remittances (and, if they are successful, venture capital), circulating ideas and connections, and even returning home as successful entrepreneurs. A growing number of Indian and Chinese students go home after a spell abroad to take advantage of the hot labour markets in Shanghai or Mumbai. And a growing number of expatriate businessmen invest back home.

(See Section 6.5 and Concluding Remarks.)

1.3. THE GLOBAL HIGHER EDUCATION AGENDA

The foregoing analysis shows that a country's capacity to take advantage of the global knowledge economy, not necessarily as a technology creator or developer but even as a user, adapter, and diffuser of technologies developed by others, clearly depends on its capacity to participate, at least to some extent, in the processes of generating, accessing, and sharing knowledge. If no such capacities exist, then that country is technologically disconnected and excluded from the global knowledge economy. National developmental efforts worldwide currently are focused on acquiring, maintaining, and improving such capacities. Among the minimum requirements are (1) a national education and training system catering to the masses, rather than to a handful of elites, and producing a workforce with a relevant skill profile; (2) the essentials of an R&D system with the potential to evolve into a fully developed NIS; and (3) a reasonably developed ICT infrastructure.

Higher education plays a dual role as the key component of both the education and training system and the R&D system of a national economy.

Its contributions to developing human resources and knowledge creation are vital. Jobs in the knowledge economy are increasingly requiring a tertiary-level degree. In a survey entitled "The Knowledge Factory," *The Economist*, October 4, 1997 (p. 4), the university has aptly been referred to as "not just a creator of knowledge, a trainer of young minds and a transmitter of culture, but also as major agent of economic growth: the knowledge factory, as it were, at the centre of the knowledge economy."

The brief survey and analysis of the developments in the past few decades presented in the section above indicate that globalization, transformation from the industrial into the global knowledge economy, and international student mobility are mutually reinforcing one another and changing the higher education landscape worldwide.

The seventh Transatlantic Dialogue was held in July 2001 at the Universite Laval in Quebec, Canada, and was focused on this particular theme. Thirty presidents, vice chancellors, and rectors from the United States, Canada, the United Kingdom, and Continental Europe participated in the meeting. The essay that emerged from this meeting was published with the title "The Brave New (and Smaller) World of Higher Education: A Transatlantic View" (Green, Eckel, and Barblan 2002). It is indeed a smaller world driven by rapid technological changes, which make it easier for people, goods, services, capital, and ideas to move around the globe.

Nye (2004) defines globalization as follows: "Globalism is a state of the world involving networks of interdependence-networks of connections and multiple relations at multi-continental distances." This definition has been made in the context of international relations and governance, but is obviously equally pertinent to the global knowledge economy, for production of goods and services in global supply chains and the functioning of international capital markets clearly depend on people who can communicate with each other. This, in turn, requires a common language, a common base of skills, and the capacity to work in intercultural environments. These are factors driving internationalization of higher education worldwide.

The same factors are also motivating young people to seek the best education they can afford anywhere in the world so that they can compete in the global labor market, and, in the process, also make friends and meet future business partners. The outcome is internationalization of higher education as an end in itself, and a historically unprecedented number of students attending institutions of higher education in foreign countries.

Internationalization of higher education is a multifaceted topic. It includes elements that pertain to curricula, such as teaching of foreign languages and cultures, as well as those that have to do with scientists and scholars carrying out research and teaching in other countries, and students studying abroad for a full degree or as part of their degree requirements back home. The latter component is referred to as "academic mobility," and until recently has essentially involved the movement of persons and, to a much smaller extent, institutions across borders. Transnational movement of institutions is not a new phenomenon: It dates back to centuries ago when the university, then a distinctly western European institution, was transplanted to other continents, and more recently to the classical branch campuses. International mobility of students and scholars is an even older phenomenon. It dates back to the origins of the medieval European university when it was difficult to distinguish students from teachers. What have changed in the second half of the past century, however, are the numbers involved and the modes of delivery made possible by developments in transportation, information, and communication technologies. Educational services can now be provided across borders and over intercontinental distances (distance education, e-learning, online provision). Branch campuses are no longer the small outfits they were, many now are operated by local partners, and higher education increasingly is being provided in many parts of the world in organizational forms derived from the world of business (franchises, offshore provision). Thus, internationalization of higher education in today's global knowledge economy includes, in addition to increased international content in curricula, movement of students, scholars, programs, and institutions across borders. These are collectively referred to as "transnational" or "cross-border" higher education (see Section 4.5).

International student mobility refers to students studying in a foreign country. It is just one component of transnational higher education, but one with the greatest socioeconomic, cultural, and political implications.

A global higher education market has thus emerged, with annual revenue estimated at tens of billions of dollars. Services provided in this market range from publishing, testing, and counseling to the provision of education in one transnational form or another. This market is characterized by intense competition among traditional institutions as well as new types of providers, which were made possible by advanced educational technologies based on ICT. International student mobility is again just one of the components of this market, but at the present, financially, its largest segment.

Rapid technological progress is creating new types of jobs, which require different and, usually, more advanced skills. At the same time, other types of jobs are becoming obsolete and disappearing. Reeducation and retraining of already highly educated adults is a major challenge faced by many nations (World Bank 2003). Lifelong learning is increasingly becoming a key component of education and training systems in advanced economies, especially in those countries with aging populations. The World Bank (2003) has recently put a priority on the establishment of national systems of lifelong learning in order for developing countries to reap the benefits of the global knowledge economy. This has led to the emergence of new types of students in addition to those in the relevant age cohort. To meet the demand for lifelong learning, traditional institutions have developed new programs and structures, and new types of providers have emerged that heavily rely on ICT. Many such programs and new providers are transnational in nature and operate for profit.

Parallel and in response to the emergence of the global knowledge economy, higher education institutions worldwide are increasingly being scrutinized and called on to change in the following directions:

1. Institutions should not be insular to the world of business and academic research should produce commercial activities.

2. Access should be broadened and teaching should produce a workforce with an entrepreneurial attitude, capacity to learn, intercultural skills, and the skills that are necessary to adapt to the new ways of using knowledge and organizing work to produce goods and services internationally.

3. Traditional institutions should change the way they are organized so that they can efficiently, effectively, and preferrably profitably, compete with each other and the new providers of postsecondary education for students, scholars, and resources in the global higher education market.

The socioeconomic developments that have taken place over the last few decades have thus set a global agenda for higher education, which can be analyzed under the following subheadings: (1) increasing demand; (2) demographic shift and nontraditional students; (3) the rise of market forces; (4) impact of technology; (5) new providers and increasing competition; and (6) globalization/internationalization.

To understand international student mobility in today's global knowledge economy, this global higher education agenda needs to be analyzed in its entirety and with a historical perspective, as the six agenda items are intertwined, and all have historical roots. Not only would the global picture be incomplete, but it would also be difficult to analyze international student mobility in today's knowledge-driven economy without understanding the changing nature of higher education worldwide. For example, answers to the following questions are crucial to understanding international academic mobility:

- Why has demand for some form of postsecondary education increased over time, but especially in the second half of the twentieth century?

- Would it have been possible to increase access to and massify higher education worldwide if the traditional, Humboldtian type of university were the only type of higher education institution available to humankind?

- If higher education institutions were completely financed from public sources, and were governed by academics alone according to rules and regulations prepared by state bureaucracies, would there be any incentive for them to expand their range of activities, to diversify their revenue base, and to increase student intake, both nationally and internationally?

- Why are increasing numbers of students worldwide attending higher education institutions abroad or some form of foreign-provided higher education at home, while cheaper local opportunities also are increasing? Is the demand increasing for a particular type of higher education, or just any type?

- Why is demand for foreign-provided higher education more in some countries and less or nonexistent in others? Why are some countries being preferred as destinations? Why are countries interested in hosting foreign students, even when there is unmet local demand?

Clearly, these questions cannot be answered in isolation, and are interlinked with the global higher education agenda items I summarized. An answer to the first question posed is provided in the previous section. Chapter 2 deals with issues related to demand and supply. Chapter 3 deals with questions related to finance, administration, governance, and the emergence of national systems. A clear understanding of these aspects of higher education in a historical perspective is central to the topic at hand, and at the same time provides answers to many of the questions posed. Chapter 4 is an attempt to summarize the literature and information on technology-driven developments in higher education worldwide. This is an area that is currently growing at such a pace that any article written on it is faced with the prospect of being obsolete shortly after its release. Chapter 5 is an analysis of the internationalization of higher education, and attempts to identify the dynamics embedded in historical antecedents of academic mobility and the historical developments presented in the previous chapters, which may have possibly led to today's global higher education scene. Chapter 6 is concerned with the major host countries for and the countries of origin of foreign students, and in particular, the rationales for and the drivers of international student mobility that are specific to these countries.

The concluding remarks are simply musings by the author on the topic at hand. Given the increasingly rapid pace of change and developments occurring in this area, those remarks, and possibly some of the material presented in the previous chapters, may be irrelevant and obsolete by the time this book is published.

TWO

ENROLLMENT AND INCREASING DEMAND

2.1. INCREASING DEMAND

Trow (1972, 2006) classified national higher education systems according to gross enrollment ratio (GER) into three groups as elitist (GER less than 15 percent), mass (GER between 15 and 50 percent), and universal (GER above 50 percent).[1] According to Perkin (2006), in 1860, the GER was only 0.46 percent in Europe, and 1.1 percent in the United States. The corresponding values for 1900 were 0.88 percent and 2.3 percent, respectively, which heralded the beginning of the growth in enrollment and the transformation of what was until then a highly elitist system.

In the period from 1860 to 1930, the number of university students increased from 3,385 to 37,255 in Britain, from 12,188 to 97,692 in Germany, and from 5,000 to 43,600 in Russia. Nonuniversity enrollment, including teacher training, increased from 2,129 to 28,954 in Britain, from 5,797 to 37,199 in Germany, and from 3,750 to 247,300 in Russia. Enrollment ratios, although still quite low even in 1930, 1.9 percent in Britain, 2.6 percent in Germany, and 4.3 percent in Russia, nevertheless marked the beginnings of massification of higher education. On the other hand, total enrollment in higher education institutions in the United States had increased from 24,464 students in 1860 to 783,100 students in 1930, with a corresponding increase in the GER from 3.1 percent to 15 percent (Jarausch 1983; Ringer 2004).[2] Thus by 1930, higher education already had been massified in the United States, while it was still elitist in Europe according to Trow's classification.

In 1955, GER averaged only 4.5 percent in western Europe, and it increased to 10.3 percent in 1965, 19.5 percent in 1975, and 24.3 percent in 1985. The corresponding values averaged for the United States, Canada, Australia, and New Zealand taken together were 12.5 percent, 24.3 percent, 36.6 percent, and 46.8 percent, respectively (Ramirez and Riddle 1991). Thus, higher education in western Europe was massified in the late 1960s and early 1970s, about three decades after the United States.

The explosive growth in student numbers worldwide occurred after World War II. In the period from 1955 to 1994, student numbers increased by a factor of thirty-two in Norway; twenty-four in Spain; fifteen in Portugal; fourteen in Greece; twelve in Austria, Finland, Italy, and the United Kingdom; eleven in France, Germany, and Ireland; ten in Denmark and Sweden; nine in Switzerland; eight in Belgium; and seven in the Netherlands (Eicher 1998). In 1950, there were 2,296,000 students in the United States, 1,247,000 in the USSR, 391,000 in Japan, 262,000 in India, and 139,000 in China, and these five countries accounted for 69 percent of the global enrollment (UNESCO 1970). In 1970, enrollment in the United States had increased to 8,498,000, to 4,580,000 in the USSR, 1,819,000 in Japan, and 2,009,000 in India (UNESCO 1972). Enrollment in China, on the other hand, had grown to 500,993 in 1975–1976. In 1990–1991, 3,822,371 students were enrolled in Chinese institutions of higher education; the numbers for the USSR, India, and Japan were 5,100,000, 4,950,974, and 2,899,143, respectively (UNESCO 1999).

In 1955, there were 30,792 higher education students in Australia; the number in 1975 was 273,137, and in 1985 it was 370,016 (Marginson 2002). In the period from 1970 to 1990, the number of students in higher education institutions increased from 201,436 to 1,529,244 in Korea, from 10,995 to 75,178 in Malaysia, from 13,683 to 50,742 in Singapore, and from 203,473 to 535,064 in Taiwan, corresponding to annual growth rates averaging as high as 20 percent in Korea and Malaysia in the 1970s (Singh 1991). The GER in Taiwan was 15 percent in 1977; it had risen to 85 percent in 2008.[3] Between 1955 and 1986, enrollments multiplied by 112 in Nigeria, 103 in Kenya, 87 in Madagascar, 63 in Venezuela, 60 in Congo, 36 in Indonesia, and 33 in Thailand (Eicher and Chevaillier 2002). In the period from 1974 to 2009, enrollment in the Turkish higher education system increased from 262,000 to 2,532,622, and the GER, which was only 4 percent in 1965 and 6 percent in 1980, increased to 36.8 percent in 2005 (Barblan, Ergüder, and Gürüz 2008, 69; Gürüz 2001, 315). Since 1960, enrollment in Africa has grown at an average annual rate of 9 percent. Africa now has more than 300 public and more than one thousand private institutions of higher education, enrolling close to 5 million students (Teferra 2005).[4]

Ramirez and Riddle (1991) and Scott (1998, 2000) estimate that of the 1,854 universities founded between 1200 and 1985, 75 percent were established since 1900, and 59 percent were founded between 1950 and 1985. However, universities met only part of the increasing demand. New types of tertiary-level institutions, generally referred to as nonuniversity institutions were founded in order to meet the demand from students with increasingly diverse backgrounds, motives, and career prospects in a cost-effective manner. These generally were more vocationally oriented, and of shorter duration.

The Open University, founded in the United Kingdom in 1969, represented a new type of institution of higher education. It served as a model for the distance education institutions that followed in many countries.

Thus, national higher education systems came into being that included, in addition to universities, distance education institutions and short-cycle vocational institutions. The latter are collectively designated as non-university institutions, where the term *university* is traditionally, but not necessarily and increasingly less so, reserved for institutions with significant research activity and the power to award doctoral-level degrees. By about the 1970s, national higher education systems in developed countries, in general, comprised (1) research universities, both public and private; (2) mass education universities, generally public; (3) various types of two- and four-year nonuniversity institutions offering degree programs at bachelor- and associate-levels in vocational fields, generally public; and (4) distance education institutions, almost exclusively public at the time.

Thus, the terms *higher education, tertiary education,* and *postsecondary education* came to encompass all of the above. According to the latest figure available from UNESCO-IAU, there are presently 9,760 university-level institutions plus nearly 8,000 institutions of higher education in 184 countries and territories around the world.[5] However, in fully developed national systems, institutions are stratified according to their mission, research-oriented or mass education, and so on, and differentiated according to their type as public or private.

In many countries, including the United States and western Europe, nonuniversity institutions met a large portion of the increasing demand; in some cases they accounted for more than half the national enrollment (Eicher and Chevaillier 2002; Gellert 1997; Scott 1996; Teichler 1991, 1996, 1997, 2001; Trow 1984).

The GER, which averaged 2.1 percent in 1955 (Ramirez and Riddle 1991) worldwide, increased to 7.7 percent in 1965 (UNESCO 1980), 10.7 percent in 1975, and 12.9 percent in 1985 (UNESCO 1999). The corresponding numbers for developed countries in the same years were 6 (Ramirez and Riddle 1991), 19.2 (UNESCO 1985), 33.5 (UNESCO 1999), and 38.6 percent (UNESCO 1999); and 0.9 (Ramirez and Riddle 1991), 2.8, 3.9, and 6.6 percent (UNESCO 1999) for the developing countries, respectively. Thus, higher education enrollment was rapidly becoming an indicator of development.

Figure 2.1, adapted from UNESCO statistics, shows that global higher education enrollment, which was 6,317,000 in 1950, increased to 28,084,000 in 1970, 68,613,000 in 1990, and 88,156,000 in 1997. The increase in developing countries was even more dramatic: from 2,200,000 students in 1960, to 6,955,000 in 1970, and to 43,358,000 in 1997, which accounted for more than half the global total in 1997. Increasing enrollments in higher

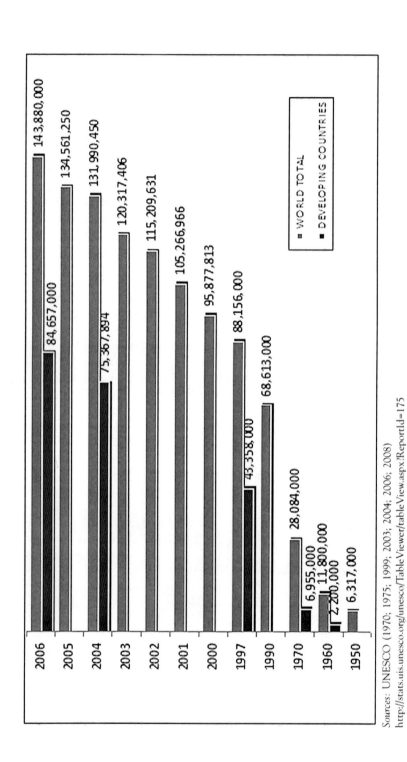

Sources: UNESCO (1970; 1975; 1999; 2003; 2004; 2006; 2008)
http://stats.uis.unesco.org/unesco/TableViewer/tableView.aspx?ReportId=175

Fig. 2.1. Global Enrollment in Higher Education

education is now an established global trend. UNESCO (2003a) reported that the historic threshold of 100 million was passed in 2001. The most recent UNESCO data puts the global enrollment in 2006 at 143,880,000 students (UNESCO 2008).

Table 2.1 shows the breakdown of the global enrollment according to regions. East Asia and the Pacific region together with North America and western Europe account for more than half the global enrollment—54 percent in 2002–2006. Also shown in Table 2.1 are the average annual growth rates for the period from 1991 to 2004. All regions showed significant growth in enrollment, and the world average was an impressive 5.1 percent. East Asia and the Pacific region, driven by the explosive growth in enrollment in China, experienced the highest growth in enrollment with an average annual growth rate of 8.1 percent. The increase in the higher education enrollment in this region was 25 million students in 1999–2006, and 33 million in 1991–2006. The average annual growth rate in this region was a staggering 11 percent between 1996 and 1999. Such growth rates that surpassed population growth rates led to a more than threefold increase in the gross enrollment ratio, from 7 percent in 1991 to 25 percent in 2006. The enrollment growth in South and West Asia was driven by the growth in India, which resulted in nearly doubling the GER from 6 percent in 1991 to 12 percent in 2006. The growth in enrollment in Sub-Saharan Africa averaged an impressive 7.2 percent in 1991–2004, but was just not able to cope with the growth in the population of the tertiary-age cohort. Central Asia was the only region that did not experience a significant growth in tertiary enrollment.

Gender parity, as measured by the Gender Parity Index, seems to have been achieved in the world as a whole, but Arab States, East Asia, the Pacific, South and West Asia, and Sub-Saharan Africa still need to do significantly more in this area.

Also shown in Table 2.1 are the numbers of teaching staff in various regions. The world average of the student–teaching staff ratio was 15.7 in 2006. North America and western Europe and Latin America and the Caribbean regions had the lowest ratios with 13 each, and Arab States and Sub-Saharan Africa regions had the highest with 25.1 and 24.3, respectively.

Table A.1 shows data on the enrollment characteristics of national higher education systems of a large number of countries. Figure 2.2, based on this table, shows the top twenty countries with respect to enrollment. China, the United States, India, Russia, and Japan—the top five countries—now account for just under half the global enrollment—46 percent. UNESCO (2003a) draws attention to the impressive achievements of China and India in the recent past. Enrollment in China has almost tripled over a relatively short period, whereas that in India more than doubled from 6.2 million in

Table 2.1. Breakdown of the Global Enrollment by Regions

Region	Enrollment			GPI	Growth Rate, % 1991–2004	Teaching Staff, 2006	Gross Enrollment Ratio, %				
	2002	2004	2006				1991	1999	2002	2004	2006
Arab states	5,939,658	6,517,436	7,038,000	1.00	7.9	280,000	11	19	20	21	22
Central and eastern Europe	16,224,692	18,509,355	20,125,000	1.25	5.0	1,255,000	33	39	48	54	66
Central Asia	1,627,339	1,883,736	1,974,000	1.10	0.4	142,000	29	19	23	25	26
East Asia and the Pacific	30,812,401	38,852,387	43,777,000	0.95	8.1	2,710,000	7	13	19	23	24
Latin America and the Caribbean	13,094,561	14,601,908	16,247,000	1.16	5.1	1,249,000	17	21	26	28	34
North America and western Europe	31,180,813	32,818,944	33,752,000	1.33	1.9	2,600,000	52	61	67	70	80
South and west Asia	13,582,983	15,465,266	17,253,000	0.76	6.8	777,197ª	6	nd	9	11	9
Sub-Saharan Africa	2,747,184	3,300,418	3,723,000	0.67	7.2	153,000	3	4	4	5	4
World	115,209,631	131,999,450	143,899,000	1.06	5.1	9,165,000	14	18	nd	24	25

Sources: UNESCO (2004, 2006, 21–23 and 120–9, 2008). http://stats.uis.unesco.org/unesco/TableViewer/tableView.aspx?ReportId=175

ª2004 data.

GPI, Gender Parity Index.

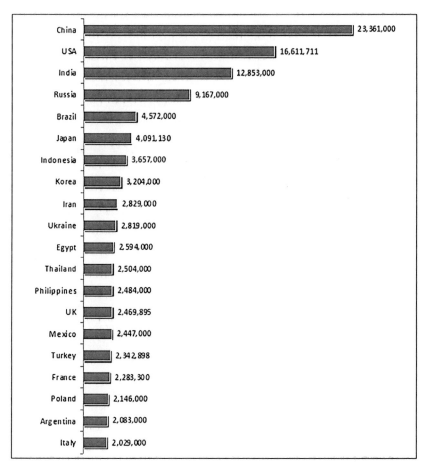

Source: Table A.1 in appendix A

Fig. 2.2. Top Twenty Countries in National Enrollment in Higher Education, 2006

1993 to 12.9 million students in 2006. These two countries accounted for more than 28 percent of the global enrollment in 2006.

In 1950, there were only 139,200 students in Chinese institutions of higher education, and the GER was only 0.26 percent. In 1978, when China abandoned Mao Zedong's version of communism and opened up to the global economy, enrollment was 1,321,900 students and the GER was still a dismal 1.56 percent; the corresponding numbers in 1985 were 3,558,700 students and a GER of 2.84 percent (Xie and Huang 2005). Following the sweeping reforms in the 1990s, current Chinese higher education institutions can now be categorized into three major types: regular, adult, and private institutions. There were 1,683 regular institutions in 2004, comprising regular universities, four-year colleges, junior colleges (*Zhuangke Xuexiao* in Chinese), colleges of higher vocational education, and independent colleges; by 2007, that number had increased to 1,792 (Fazackerley and Worthington 2007). All of the regular institutions are financed by and administratively supervised by the Ministry of Education, or another central ministry or agency, or provinces and province-level municipalities. The 528 adult institutions in 2004 comprised workers' colleges, peasants' colleges, colleges of administrative cadres, and various types of distance education institutions. The majority of adult institutions are administered and financed by local authorities, and a few by central ministries, and there are only two private ones (F. Huang 2005). Students comprise full-time undergraduate and postgraduate students in regular institutions, students in adult institutions, and self-directed learners in distance education institutions (Xie and Huang 2005).

On May 4, 1998, when then President Jian Zeming unveiled Project 985, aimed at advancing the creation of a knowledge economy by building universities and colleges, there were 8,156,500 students in the Chinese higher education system, including self-directed learners, and the GER was 8.62 percent. Without the latter group of students, enrollment was 6,429,900 and the GER was 6.80 percent. The number of full-time students, including postgraduate students, which was then 3,610,000, had increased by more than threefold to 11,736,000 in 2003, and the number of students of all types to 22,525,000,[6] corresponding to an average annual growth rate of about 25 percent. The number of full-time instructors in regular institutions, on the other hand, increased from 410,000 to 724,700 in the same period, corresponding to an average annual growth rate of 12.1 percent.

Projections by Xie and Huang (2005) for China are staggering; their estimations for total enrollment in 2020 vary from 23.55 million to 30.90 million students, with a GER between 36.3 percent and 47.7 percent. As enrollment was already more than 23 million in 2006, it is quite likely that the number of students in the Chinese higher education system will be well above 30 million by the year 2020.

Figures 2.3 and 2.4, however, point to a dark side of the global picture. Figure 2.3 shows that the GER, which averaged 6 percent for developed countries in 1955, had increased to 51.6 percent in 1997, and was 70 percent in 2006. This meant that developed countries had succeeded in making the transition from mass to universal enrollment (Trow 1972) just before the turn of the twentieth century.

On the other hand, the average GER for developing countries was only 10.3 percent in 1997, significantly below the world average of 17.4

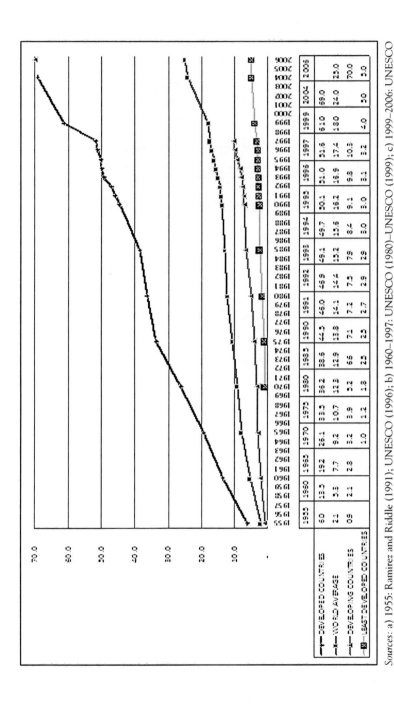

Fig. 2.3. Gross Enrollment Ratios in Selected Country Groups

Sources: a) 1955: Ramirez and Riddle (1991); UNESCO (1996); b) 1960–1997: UNESCO (1980)–UNESCO (1999); c) 1999–2006: UNESCO (2006; 2008); d) http://stats.uis.unesco.org/unesco/TableViewer/tableView.aspx?ReportId=167

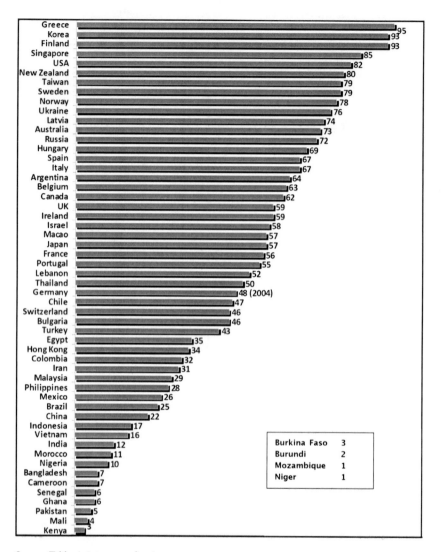

Source: Table A.1 in appendix A

Fig. 2.4. Gross Enrollment Ratio in Selected Countries, %, 2006

percent in that year. The picture becomes much bleaker when one looks at the least developed countries. The average GER, which was 1 percent for that particular group of countries in 1970, had increased to a meager 3.2 percent in 1997, and in 2006 was only 5 percent in Sub-Saharan Africa.

As seen in Table 2.1, the period 1991–2006 witnessed significant increases in GER worldwide as well as regionally. The global average, which was 14 percent in 1991, increased to 25 percent in 2006. The regional average for North America and western Europe increased from 52 to 70 percent, that for central and eastern Europe from 33 to 66 percent, that for Latin America and the Caribbean from 17 to 34 percent, and that for East Asia and Pacific from 7 to 24 percent, with the GER for South and West Asia averaging 11 percent in 2004, down to 9 percent in 2006, but up from 6 percent in 1991. An increase, although at a much lower level, also was observed in Sub-Saharan Africa, from 3 to 5 percent. Central Asia appears to be the only region that has seen a downturn in higher education enrollment. The GER in this region fell from 29 to 19 percent immediately after the collapse of the Soviet regime, and started to recover after 1999, reaching 26 percent in 2006, still considerably below what it was back in 1991.

Figure 2.4, based on Table A.1, shows the GERs in selected countries. There clearly is a great variation among countries, from dismally low values such as 5 percent for Pakistan, 3 percent for Burkina Faso and 4 percent for Mali, 2 percent for Burundi, and 1 percent for Mozambique and Niger, to values of 90 percent for Greece, Korea, and Finland and above 80 percent for the United States and New Zealand.

Figure 2.4 also points to another important feature of the global higher education scene. There seems to be a threshold corresponding to a GER value of about 40 percent, which has been pointed out by UNESCO (2003a, 7) with the following statement: "Current estimates indicate that enrollment rates around 40 to 50 percent of the relevant population group are needed in order to allow for a country to function well in a globalized, competitive world."

Viewed from this perspective, the situation in many African countries is indeed bleak; even China and India, despite their tremendous achievements in increasing enrollments in the recent past, have a very long way to go. It is for this reason that UNESCO (2003a) is now advocating a global program for development and cooperation in higher education based on strong commitments by national governments and the international community. It is recommended that such a program should have clear targets and priorities, which are similar to those in the Education for All program for basic education. Following the publication of the report by the Task Force on Higher Education and Society (World Bank 2000), the World Bank has started to put more emphasis on higher education, whereas in the past its lending policy, which was based on rate-of-return analysis, was geared toward lower levels of national education systems (Post et al. 2004).

According to a recent survey by the *Financial Times* ("Gearing Up for a New Battle of the Bulge," January 25, 2006), and Longman (2004), the world is faced with a "youth bulge." Presently, 2.8 billion people are under twenty-five years old. By 2015, the global youth population will reach 3 billion, with 2.5 billion of them living in developing countries. Educating the youth to be productive citizens employable in the knowledge-driven global economy is now a major global challenge.

Figure 2.5 shows various projections for global demand for higher education. Values projected for the year 2025 vary from 125 to 263 million students. Since the former value has already been surpassed, it is quite likely that the second historic threshold of 200 million students will be surpassed by 2025. What is now certain is that the demand for some form of postsecondary education will continue to increase in the conceivably near future. IDP Education Australia (Australian Universities International Development Program)[7] predicts that in the year 2025, 56 percent of the global demand for higher education will come from China, India, Malaysia and Korea (IDP 2002).[8] Data I presented earlier on China clearly confirm this general trend in the composition of the future global demand for higher education. Furthermore, this particular feature of the projected global demand is currently one of the major drivers of the developments in international education in general, and in international student mobility at the tertiary level in particular, with countries in the East and the South Asia regions having emerged as major countries of origin of international

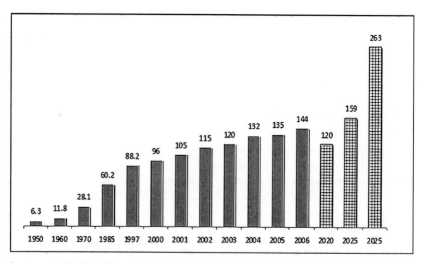

Sources: a) 1950-2006: Figure 2.1; b) 2020: Altbach and Teichler (2001); c) 2025: IDP (2002) quoted in Davis (2003), Olsen (2003), and Pearman (2004)

Fig. 2.5. Projected Global Demand for Higher Education

students, and some like Malaysia, Singapore, and Thailand now aspiring to "regional hub" status, and China recently emerging as a major host country for international students.

2.2. DEMOGRAPHIC SHIFT AND NONTRADITIONAL STUDENTS

The increasing demand for higher education has different demographic implications for developed and developing countries. The relevant age cohort and possibly adults who missed out before make up most of the enrollment in the latter case, and this is likely to continue in the near future. On the other hand, in the case of developed countries with knowledge-driven economies, not only are higher skills required in the workforce, but also continuous updating is needed to adapt to changing demand and creation of new knowledge. Outsourcing and especially offshoring are increasing the number of displaced workers in manufacturing industries in developed countries. Those who lose their jobs as a result need to be retrained if they are to be reemployed in other jobs.

Furthermore, many of the developed countries that have made the transition from an industrial to a knowledge-driven economy are faced with the problem of aging populations, increasing the load on the workforce and straining the resources for social security systems.[9]

The need for lifelong learning (LLL) is thus expanding. This is leading to a blurring between initial degrees and continuing education certificates and between institutions at the secondary and the tertiary levels. The further education sector in the United Kingdom and the technical and further education sector in Australia are two of the many similar systems that exist in most of the developed countries.[10] Such systems comprise diverse institutions that enroll students in a wide range of ages.

Clearly, tertiary-level institutions, including universities in most cases, especially in developed countries, increasingly are coming under pressure to serve a more diverse clientele, including, in addition to the relevant age cohort, working students, mature students, part-time students, day students, students enrolled in degree programs, students taking courses that lead to new vocational qualifications, and so on (Hore 1992). In other words, part-time students in full-time employment are now part of the higher education scene, and an "earning and learning" market is emerging in many countries (van der Wende 2002).

Older working and commuting students are now the majority in U.S. institutions (The Futures Project 2000a, 2000b, 2000c; Morey 2004). According to the figures quoted in "Brains Business" (The Economist, September 8, 2005), the majority of the undergraduates in U.S. institutions are female, 33 percent come from racial minorities, more than 40 percent are aged twenty-five and over, 50 percent attend part time, and 80 percent of students work to help support themselves. Enrollment of older students is on the rise in the United Kingdom (Woodley and Wilson 2002) and Australia (Dobson 2001), as well as in Austria, Canada, Germany, Ireland, Japan, New Zealand, and Sweden (Schuetze and Slowey 2002). The latter two studies also clearly show that the majority of the nontraditional students tend to be enrolled in nonuniversity institutions or programs, rather than traditional universities. Furthermore, evidence from all of the countries mentioned indicate that the more elite research universities often are reluctant to engage in the types of programs favored by nontraditional students.

Data are presented in Table A.1, which also show the distribution of students between ISCED 5A (bachelor-level and above) and ISCED 5B (below bachelor-level) programs. Most of the nonuniversity institutions where ISCED 5B-type programs are offered were created as mainly public institutions in the 1960s and the 1970s to meet the increasing demand from growing cohorts in the tertiary-level age. There are now private nonuniversity institutions, both nonprofit and for-profit in many countries. Such stratification and differentiation is now a desirable feature of national higher education systems in order to simultaneously address the issues of increased access, social mobility, quality, knowledge creation, LLL, and the skill profile required in the workforce of a knowledge-driven economy (Osborne 2003; Schuetze and Slowey 2002; World Bank 2000).

It is quite likely that the fastest growing service sector in any developed country will be the continuing education of already well-educated adults. Countries with differentiated and stratified national systems of postsecondary education will obviously be better positioned in that respect. Governments in Australia, Canada, and the United Kingdom are attempting to expand and diversify higher education to meet student demand and labor market needs by resorting to private and vocational providers to offer degree programs at the tertiary level (OBHE-BN September 2003, February 2004).[11]

The populations of Europe and Japan are aging; even the United States, which has a comparatively younger population, will be faced with 5 percent fewer working people by 2015 ("New Working Models," *Financial Times*, September 27, 2004). The aging population of developed countries is increasing the need for immigration. It now looks certain that there will be increased immigration of foreigners with different nationalities, languages, cultures and creeds to advanced countries, including Japan, a country not yet culturally attuned to this phenomenon. The United States, Australia, Canada, and New Zealand now have "selective" immigration policies, which aim to attract "skilled immigrants." Germany, France, and the United Kingdom also have changed their immigration and citizenship laws and started campaigns to attract young people from all over the world to study in their universities (see Section 6.5).

According to an article entitled "Globalisation Creates Its Own Workforce," published in *Financial Times*, October 6, 2005, an estimated 200 million presently live and work outside of their countries of birth, double the number of such migrants twenty-five years ago.[12] Formal transfers of remittances by migrant workers amounted to about $150 billion in 2004. The general question is the impact of migration on countries of origin and destination countries, and the specific issues involved are the following (Chellaraj, Maskus, and Mattoo 2006; Docquier and Marfouk 2006; Ozden 2006; Ozden and Schiff, 2006; Schiff 2006; see also Section 6.5):

1. Educational attainments of emigrants and the proportion of the well-educated, skilled emigrants to workforce in countries of origin;

2. The value of education and qualifications received in countries of origin in entering job markets in destination countries;

3. Education of immigrants' children and their integration into societies in destination countries;

4. The establishment of a "fair balance" between direct (e.g., remittances) and indirect (e.g, the general positive diaspora effect) economic gains that accrue to countries of origin and the negative effects of "brain drain."[13]

The United States, too, is already facing some of these issues. Minority students are projected to make up 80 percent of the growth in tertiary enrollment. Thus, minority students will account for 37 percent of the higher education enrollment in the United States (The Futures Project 2000a; Newman and Couturier 2001).[14] Eighty percent of the prospective higher education students in the United States between 2000 and 2015 will be non-white and almost 50 percent will be Hispanic, the majority of whose parents have low educational attainments and have never been to an American school (Newman, Couturier, and Scurry 2004, 165).

2.3. INCREASING DEMAND AND INTERNATIONAL STUDENT MOBILITY

An overview and the drivers of the transformation from an industrial to a global knowledge economy and the way these have influenced the higher education agenda worldwide was presented in Chapter 1. This chapter is concerned with the first item of that agenda, namely, increasing demand for higher education all over the world

The population of the world was 2.557 billion in 1950; today it is 6.329 billion, which corresponds to a 2.5-fold increase since then. On the other hand, enrollment in institutions of higher education worldwide increased from 6 million students to 144 million, which corresponds to a twenty-four-fold increase in the same period. Thus, the increase in the world's population alone cannot explain the increasing demand for higher education worldwide.

The world potential labor force defined as the population age twenty-five and older including retirees, increased from 2.6 billion in 1990 to 3.2 billion in 2000. In this period, the share of workers with a tertiary-level education increased by 2.2 percentage points, whereas the share of low-skilled workers decreased by 2.5 percentage points (Docquier and Marfouk 2006).[15] On the average, labor and capital costs presently account for 70 and 30 percent, respectively, of the total cost of production in a typical business enterprise in a developed country ("New Working Models," *Financial Times*, September 27, 2004). The best companies are now devoting one third of their investment to knowledge-intensive activities such as R&D, licensing, and marketing ("Brains Business," *The Economist*, September 8, 2005).

The answer thus lies in the skill requirements and the wage structure of the new economy. Most jobs in the global knowledge economy not only increasingly require an education at the tertiary level, but also continuous upgrading of skills and acquiring of new skills. Thus, demand for higher education is originating from both the tertiary-age cohort, traditional students, and the already well-educated adults, the nontraditional students. The latter category of students is increasingly encompassing female students, children of immigrants, and students from all sections of society. Many countries are finding it difficult to cope with the increasing demand for higher education. There also is the issue of unmet demand in certain types of tertiary education even where overall national enrollment targets are achieved. Unmet local demand in general, and for particular types of higher education, has thus emerged as one of the major drivers of international student mobility.

The next chapter is concerned with the ways the global socioeconomic dynamics and increasing demand have reshaped the governance, institutional structures, and financing of higher education over time. As seen in Chapter 6, the ways institutions of higher education are governed and financed in a given country bear directly on the position of that country in international student mobility and the global higher education market.

THREE

THE RISE OF MARKET FORCES

3.1. HISTORICAL BACKGROUND

Bologna University, considered the first university in the world, traces its origins to 1088, when the famous jurist Irnerius probably started teaching Roman law in Bologna. What is pertinent to the topic at hand, however, is not the chronology of the medieval university, but the fact that Irnerius was teaching for a fee. In other words, the university in its origins was a demand-driven institution structured by market forces.[1] It was centuries later that universities became creations of the state, and following the massification of higher education in the period after 1945, they increasingly came under the power and the influence of the state (Scott 1998). By the 1970s, in many countries, even in continental Europe, they were in fact effectively absorbed within the state bureaucracy.

Beginning with the Reagan administration in the United States and the Thatcher government in the United Kingdom, the role of the state in the economy started to diminish. Socioeconomic policies increasingly became predicated on market forces, and these developments affected the governance and financing of higher education worldwide (Hira 2003). Newman and Couturier (2001) described the results of this shift as "the invasion of the academy by market forces."

Higher education thus entered an era in which processes were started in many countries to transform it from a public sector structured principally by government regulation into a semipublic sector responsive to demand and competition, and the process is continuing at the present. This came at a time when demand for some form of postsecondary education was taking off in response to the skill requirements of the new economy, and public resources were shrinking. Governments started pressuring higher education institutions to do more with less. It was becoming clear that no country could afford to provide higher education of the most expensive kind free of charge to whoever demanded it, and that those who personally benefited from that service, including students and employers, had to contribute to its costs (OECD 1990). The result has been, in the words of Newman et al. (2004, 32) "a shift from dependence on regulation and oversight (by the state and on funds from the public purse)[2] to using the market as a means of ensuring public purposes."

Two developments in the 1980s, one in the United Kingdom and the other in the United States, had a profound influence on higher education policy formulation throughout the world. The report issued by the Committee of Vice-Chancellors and Principals (CVCP 1985), known as the Jarrat Report, after its chairman, Sir Alex Jarrat, made the following recommendations:

1. Universities must be responsive to the market.

2. The university head should assume the role of the chief executive.

3. Managerial techniques must be introduced in university administration.

4. Unit costs and efficiency of resource utilization should be among the key concerns.

5. Evaluation of university performance must be based on qualitative and quantitative performance indicators.

The recommendations of the committee were so radical for the time that they were severely criticized by academia, which referred to them as "Jarratian Measures"; their implementation was commonly ridiculed as "Jarratization," and the period following the report was dubbed the "post-Jarrat" period.

In 1980, the U.S. Congress passed the Bayh-Dole Act,[3] which allowed universities to patent and commercialize the results of federally funded research conducted within the university. Thus, not only was a new source of income created for the universities, but the ties with corporations grew stronger, and the university came to be viewed as the place that supplies "commercially valuable" initiatives, and corporate giving to universities increased considerably (Newman et al. 2004, 61–62). Perhaps as important, the traditional view of the products and outputs of the activities of the university as public goods started to change.[4]

To the Jarrat Report and the Bayh-Dole Act must be added the literature that emerged (Johnstone 1986, 1991, 1992, 1993; Johnstone and Arora 1998; Leslie and Brinkman 1988; OECD 1990; Paulsen and Smart 2001; Psacharopoulos 1992; Tilak 1989; UNESCO 1998a; World Bank 1994,

1995). The various reports by the World Bank, United Nations Educational Scientific and Cultural Organization (UNESCO), and the Organization for Economic Cooperation and Development (OECD), which portrayed higher education as a semi-public good with a private and a social return, rather than a purely public good, were particularly influential. This meant that the costs of higher education had to be borne partly by those who benefited from it. This argument provided a rationale for and gave legitimacy to tuition fees that was in line with social equity concerns. As I summarize in the next subsection, by the mid-1990s, the level of tuition fees as a proportion of recurrent expenditures in public institutions had significantly increased even in formerly Communist countries like Vietnam and China, where they were well above 10 and 20 percent, respectively (World Bank 1994, 42).

The introduction of tuition fees and calls for revenue diversification were accompanied by a new look at governance structures. Additionally, many governments encouraged the development of private institutions to meet the increased demand in a manner that did not put pressure on the public purse. Thus, the rise of market forces in higher education manifested itself in the form of: (1) tuition fees; (2) private institutions; and (3) new governance patterns and structures.

3.2. PUBLIC SPENDING AND TUITION FEES

Table A.2 shows institutional expenditures per student in all types of institutions, both public and private, in OECD countries as well as partner countries in the years between 1990 and 2006.[5] In most countries, per-student expenditure has increased by more than 50 percent in the past two decades, clearly showing the increasing cost of providing higher education. Figure 3.1 shows expenditure per student in 2006. United States and Switzerland lead the pack by a wide margin, with average per-student expenditures of $24,370 and $21,734, respectively whereas Uruguay, Romania, and Paraguay are at the bottom with $2,852, $2,655, and $2,662, respectively.[6]

There are generally two sources of institutional income from which these expenditures are made: public and private. The latter includes the expenditures made by students and/or their parents, referred to as household expenditure, in the form of various fees, and other private sources, such as donations made by charitable organizations and various forms of corporate giving.

Table A.3 shows the change from 1995 to 2005 in the share of private sources in the per-student expenditures shown in Table A.2 and Figure 3.1. Figure 3.2 shows the values of this indicator for various countries in 2005. At the top of the list are Chile, Korea, Philippines, Japan, and the United States, with 84.1 percent, 75.7 percent, 66.9 percent, 66.3 percent, and 65.3

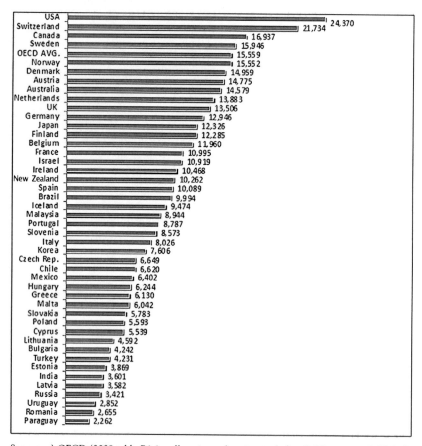

Sources: a) OECD (2008 table B1.1a; all tertiary education including R&D activities); b) India (2004) and Malaysia (2007) are from UNESCO (2008).

Fig. 3.1. Expenditure on Tertiary Level Institutions per Student, U.S. $ (PPP), 2005

percent share of private sources, respectively. These countries have large shares of private institutions in their higher education systems, and tuition fees in public institutions. In Korea, for example, private institutions are 95 percent dependent on tuition fees, and fees make up 40 percent of the revenues of state institutions (Chevaillier and Eicher 2002).

Table A.4, which shows the change in the contribution of households in per-student expenditures in the period 1995–2005, and Figure 3.3, which shows the value of this indicator in 2005, bring this point more clearly to the fore. Chile 83 percent, Philippines 66.9 percent, Japan 53.4 percent, and Korea 52.1 percent are again at the top. This time, however, the United

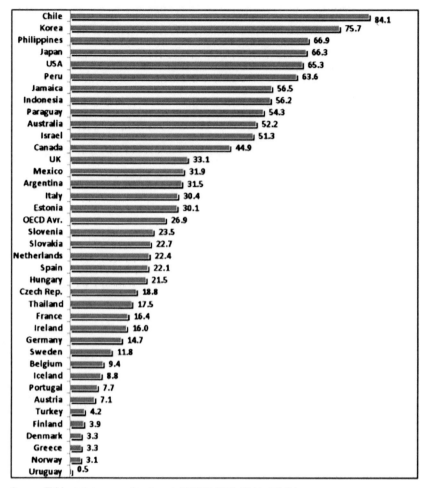

Chile 84.1
Korea 75.7
Philippines 66.9
Japan 66.3
USA 65.3
Peru 63.6
Jamaica 56.5
Indonesia 56.2
Paraguay 54.3
Australia 52.2
Israel 51.3
Canada 44.9
UK 33.1
Mexico 31.9
Argentina 31.5
Italy 30.4
Estonia 30.1
OECD Avr. 26.9
Slovenia 23.5
Slovakia 22.7
Netherlands 22.4
Spain 22.1
Hungary 21.5
Czech Rep. 18.8
Thailand 17.5
France 16.4
Ireland 16.0
Germany 14.7
Sweden 11.8
Belgium 9.4
Iceland 8.8
Portugal 7.7
Austria 7.1
Turkey 4.2
Finland 3.9
Denmark 3.3
Greece 3.3
Norway 3.1
Uruguay 0.5

Source: Table A.3 in appendix A and (OECD 2008, Table B3.2b).

Fig. 3.2. Private Expenditure on Tertiary Education, % of Total Expenditure, 2005

States has dropped to the twelfth position among the countries shown with a 36.1 percent share of households. The reason for this is the large amount of donations to U.S. institutions from charitable organizations and private donors, which, according to the survey "Brains Business" (*The Economist,* September 8, 2005) totaled $24.4 billion in 2004—a value that is many times the public higher education budget in a large number of countries. Thus, the share of contributions from private sources other than households is much higher in the United States compared with other countries.

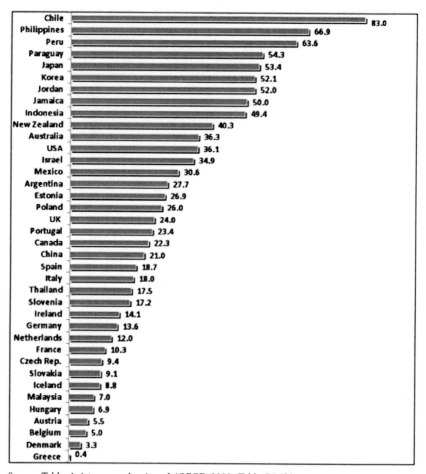

Source: Table A.4 in appendix A and (OECD 2008, Table B3.2b).

Fig. 3.3. Share of Households in Expenditures on Tertiary Education, % of Total, 2005

Continental western European countries, in general, are at the bottom of both figures. The conventional view in Continental western Europe is that higher education is a public good. Higher education in this region is thus characterized by a relatively low share of private institutions,[7] relatively low tuition fees, and high state subsidies even for students' living expenses (Schwarz and Rehburg 2004; Vossensteyn 1999). Johnstone (2004) characterizes Europe as "the last bastion of generally 'free' higher education."

Values in Table A.4 clearly show that the contribution of households to the expenditures for higher education has increased in all countries in the period 1995–2005, including western Europe, and have remained high where they were already high as in the Asia-Pacific rim, Latin America, and the United States. Johnstone (2004, 2006, 39–41) refers to this worldwide trend as increased "cost sharing," which he defines as:

> a shift of the higher educational cost burden from exclusive or near exclusive reliance on government, or tax payers, to some financial reliance upon parents and/or students, either in the form of tuition fees or of "user charges" to cover the costs of formerly governmentally- or institutionally-provided room and board.

According to Johnstone (2004), cost sharing has occurred in a number of ways, including (a) introduction of tuition fees in public institutions where they did not exist before or sharp rises in countries where there were tuition fees already; (b) the imposition of "user charges" for student services such as lodging and meals, which were heavily subsidized or free available before; (c) elimination or reduction of student grants and scholarships, and introduction of more effective ways of cost recovery on student loans; and (d) shifting the burden of meeting increased demand to private institutions. In this subsection, I summarize developments concerning tuition fees, whereas the focus of the next subsection is private institutions.

United States, Canada, Japan, and Korea are countries where tuition fees already existed in public institutions. In the United States, starting in the 1980s, subsidies from state budgets to public institutions were significantly reduced. As a result, the share of tuition fees in the income of public institutions rose from 18.9 percent in 1980 to 24.9 percent in 1998 (Newman et al. 2004, 42).

Chile, Australia, the United Kingdom, and China are countries where tuition fees were introduced starting in the 1980s. Tuition fees were introduced and institutions were forced to diversify their revenue sources as part of a comprehensive series of structural and financial reforms launched in Chile in 1981 (Brunner 1993; Schiefelbein 1990; World Bank 2002). Students pay tuition fees in all types of institutions. Typical annual tuition fees are $ 2,500 in a private autonomous university, and $1,650 in a traditional public university ($9,670 and $5,270 on a purchasing power parity [PPP] basis; see Table A.5). The university entrance examination plays a triple role in Chile: It places students in institutions and programs; it is used in distributing the indirect public support funds among both private and public institutions; and it is used to select students eligible for loans and scholarships. Students must obtain a minimum score to be eligible to enter a public university or an autonomous private university, and about 6 percent higher than that to be eligible for loans and scholarships, which are means-tested. This student support scheme is administered by each university separately as a university-specific fund. Repayment has been a chronically major problem. Since 2004, a parallel scheme has been put in place, which is open to all students and managed through the banking system. The top 27,500 students in the university entrance examination carry with themselves a per-student entitlement, which is paid to the institutions in which they are placed, both public and private (Brunner and Tillett 2006). These awards range in value, depending on how high the individual's test score is. The highest value awards represent a significant share of the total cost of one year of study at a typical institution.[8] Since 1981, private institutions have expanded, enrollments have significantly increased, and the share of fees and income from services have come to account for nearly 60 percent of the revenues of higher education institutions, public and private taken together (Espinoza 2000; Gonzalez 1999). The result is clearly seen in Table A.4 and Figure 3.3, where Chile is at the top by a wide margin with a household share of 83 percent in per-student expenditure in higher education in 2005.[9]

In Australia, students paid fees in the 1950s and the 1960s, but fees were kept low, and were waived in many cases to increase access. They were abolished by the Labor government in 1974 (Duckett 2004; Marginson 2002). In 1988, the Higher Education Contribution Scheme (HECS) was introduced by another Labor government, whereby students started paying a portion of the full cost, either upfront at a discount, or through the tax system after they graduate and start earning above a certain annual salary. In 1996, a three-tiered fee structure was incorporated into the HECS, where different fees were charged to students in different programs according to the future income-earning potential of the graduates. The Australian system moved closer to a market-driven system in 2003, when (a) universities were permitted to charge up to 25 percent higher fees, and HECS repayments by students were moved closer to full-cost recovery; (b) universities were authorized to admit students up to 35 percent of the domestic students enrolled in each undergraduate course and charge direct tuition fees at any level; and (c) fee-paying students in both private and public universities were made eligible for a new system of income-contingent loans entitled FEE-HELP (Higher Education Loan Program; OBHE-BN, March 2004). Since the mid-1990s, the ratio of fees to public spending in Australian universities has increased from about 30 percent to more than 55 percent (Gamage and Mininberg 2003). Comparison of the share of households in per-student expenditure in Australian institutions of higher education for the years 1995 and 2005, shown in Table A.4, reflects the results of the fee policies adopted in this country, where the share of households increased from 20 to 36.3 percent in the period indicated. The so-called Commonwealth-supported places are allocated to students on the basis of their secondary school performance as measured by various examinations. Only citizens of Australia and New Zealand and some Australian permanent residents are entitled to the Commonwealth-supported places where the government pays part of the cost up to seven years for full-time students and sixteen years for part-time students. Thus, the new scheme provides additional incentive to Australian universities to recruit more foreign students. However, tuition fees became a hotly debated election issue in 2007. The new Labor Government's campaign promises included across-the-board cuts in HECS charges, an increase in the number or size of targeted scholarships to students from disadvantaged backgrounds, cancelling the HECS debt of graduates in fields such as nursing and teaching that have a relatively lower future income potential, and boosting student income support to those from poor families.[10]

Until the 1980s, the only fees that students paid in continental European countries were of an administrative nature, and were very low. Otherwise, tuition fees were taboo throughout the Continent. Since the 1980s, however, tuition fees have been introduced or greatly increased in public institutions in a majority of continental European countries and in the United Kingdom (Chevaillier and Eicher 2002; Johnstone 2006, 11–23, 55–74). In the 1980s, universities in the United Kingdom started charging full fees to students from outside the European Union (EU) and considerably lower partial fees to students from within the EU. Then in 1998, a flat fee of 1,000 pounds was introduced by the Labor Government of Prime Minister Blair on a means-tested basis. Scotland, however, chose to split off from the rest of the United Kingdom in 2001 and adopted a system of deferred-payment tuition fees like in Australia. The Graduate Endowment Scheme was created in 2001 for this purpose (Chevaillier and Eicher 2002; Johnstone 2006, 62). Starting in 2007, universities in the United Kingdom are allowed to determine the fees to be charged up to a maximum of 3,000 pounds, more than double the amount that students paid up to that time.[11] The bill also allows institutions to charge non-EU foreign students up to five times the fee paid by British students. Most of the higher education institutions opted for the highest rate (Labi 2005a). Welsh students in universities in Wales, on the other hand, were exempted from the new arrangement and continue to pay the previous flat fee of 1,200 pounds per academic year on a means-tested basis (Johnstone 2006, 64).

In 1998, the *Land* of Baden-Württemberg imposed fees on students who took longer than the six years normally required to complete undergraduate studies. The fee was about $550 per semester, but the federal government discontinued it in 2002. In January 2005, however, the Federal Constitutional Court overruled the tuition ban imposed in 2002. There is now a fee of 500 euros per semester for students who stay on beyond normal periods in Germany (Labi 2005c). Like in Germany, legislations enacted in the Czech Republic and Hungary[12] in 1998 also allow institutions to charge fees to students who fail to graduate in time (Johnstone 2006, 69).

Tuition fees were introduced in Austrian universities and *Fachhochschulen* starting in October 2001. Tuition fee was set at the relatively modest level of 363 euros per semester. In September 2008, however, the ruling left-of-center coalition government caved in to students' protests and abolished tuition fees, depriving Austrian institutions of a revenue source as the government had simply reduced public subsidies to university budgets by a corresponding amount when fees were first introduced.[13]

Presently, tuition fees do not exist in public institutions in Greece, Denmark, Norway, Sweden, and Finland. Where they exist, fees in continental Europe, are either less than 10 percent of the average living costs (Schwarz and Rehburg 2004; Vossensteyn 1999), or are restricted to some graduate-level programs as in Greece, or to students who remain beyond normal periods of study, as in Germany and the Czech Republic. Ireland charges no tuition fees, but students are required to pay a service of 750 euros per year.

"Dual-track fees" or "selective fees," which target certain groups of students are becoming increasingly common. Students are targeted either on the basis of their secondary school performance as measured by their grades in various tests, or on the basis of their nationality. Examples of selective fees on the basis of student performance are found in former Communist countries of central and eastern Europe and in African countries formerly ruled by Marxist regimes. Two types of students are admitted to higher education institutions in these countries: those who pass an entrance examination or have sufficiently high grades at the secondary level and become eligible for state support, and others, including foreigners, who pay fees. Russian universities, for example, from 1996 on, are allowed to enroll fee-paying students to the extent that in the 2001–2002 academic year, the ratio of full-fee-paying students had risen from 25 to more than 50 percent of the total enrollment (Chevaillier and Eicher 2002; Johnstone 2006, 65–66); fees now make up about half of the revenues of public universities in Russia (Tilak 2005). Scott (2002) refers to this as "privatization of higher education in central and eastern European countries from within." Australia is the only non-African or non-former Communist country that implements such a dual-track fee scheme to her own citizens from. Other counties that have such schemes are Egypt, Ethiopia, Hungary, Kenya, Poland, Romania, Tanzania, Uganda, and Vietnam.

According to many, China, like Chile, is another success story in implementing higher education governance and finance reforms. Starting with the Decision of the Central Committee of Chinese Communist Party on Reform of the Education System issued on May 29, 1985, higher education in China has undergone major structural changes (Cai 2004; Garrett 2004; Hewitt and Liu 2006; F. Huang 2005; J. Huang 2005; Johnstone 2006, 68; Mohrman 2005; Mok 1999; OECD 1990, 2003a; Yang 2000). These include a shift from an elite system to emphasis on increased access, decentralization and devolution of power from central to provincial and municipal authorities and institutions, allowance for and facilitation of private higher education, and introduction of a cost-sharing approach through greater reliance on tuition and other fees to finance higher education costs. Tuition fees charged in public universities were $25 per year in 1989 and had reached $100 in 1995, when fees in public institutions accounted for 13.5 percent of the revenues. Tuition fees were increased to $250 in 1996, $375 in 1997, and $ 500 in 2000, when the share of fees had increased to 22.2 percent, whereas the share of public subsidies had decreased from 70 to 56 percent. In 2001, the breakdown of the revenue sources of regular institutions was as follows: appropriations from the state budget, 52 percent; tuition and other fees, 25 percent; other sources, 23 percent. Since 1997, all institutions charge fees according to centrally determined criteria, which correspond on the average to around 25 percent of the unit cost. In 2004, tuition fees in public universities were the equivalent of $625 per year. Fees are relatively quite high in world-class institutions such as the Tsinghua, Beijing, Shanghai, and Jiao Tong universities (Feng and Gong 2006; Hayhoe and Zha 2006).

Xie and Huang (2005) underline the rapidly rising student-to-staff ratios, and the significantly diminished teaching facilities and library resources per student as negative aspects of the staggering expansion of the Chinese higher education system in the last decade. J. Huang (2005) and Hewitt and Liu (2006), on the other hand, point to a different aspect of the impressive growth in the Chinese higher education system. In J. Huang's view, Chinese higher education is currently exhibiting the characteristics of a "seller's market," which means that there is a shortage of supply of higher education services, and a big demand for higher education despite significantly increased tuition fees. However, what the buyers seek to purchase is a diploma to be used for promoting their career and to ensure further promotion, not scholarship. Cutting classes and hiring others to attend classes in their place to avoid punishment by teachers is not uncommon. Hewitt and Liu refer to this situation as the "stuffed duck" system, whereby they liken students educated by pervasive rote learning in Chinese institutions to force-fed Peking ducks, fattened for the dinner table. Nevertheless, recent Chinese reforms are generally viewed as impressively successful, both quantitatively and qualitatively.

The New Zealand experience clearly shows how the introduction of fees and forcing institutions to diversify their revenue bases transform universities into active players in the global higher education market. In New Zealand, the 1989 Education Act established the Students Allowance Scheme in a manner similar to the HECS in Australia, and empowered the institutions of higher education to set fees. This has forced institutions of higher education to start recruiting foreign students aggressively in order to make up for lost state subsidies.

The government of India, on the other hand, tried to do just the opposite in order to attract foreign students. Tuition fees in the prestigious IITs and institutes of management in India are more than $3,000. In 2005, the Supreme Court of India overturned a move by the government to slash fees in IITs to below $700 in order to increase their international competitiveness (Gupta 2005). In some Indian public institutions where tuition fees are low, revenues from other types of charges to students now account for up to 50 percent of the annual institutional income (Tilak 2005).

As part of the sweeping reforms introduced in Japan in spring 2004, national universities are now allowed to set their own fees up to 10 percent higher than the ministry's designated standard fee, which is presently about $5,000 regardless of the field of study (Maruyama 2005).

Fees were introduced in Turkey as part of the new governance structure legislated in 1981. Later in the 1980s, fees were redefined as student contributions to costs of tuition and student services. A special fee-paying track was introduced in 1992, for which student contributions are considerably higher. Students in the regular track attend classes during the day and students in the second track in the evenings. However, admission to both tracks is through the central admission system, which is based on a central examination and high school performance. Thus, the present fee structure in Turkey is a combination of tuition fees and user charges. Parental contributions that appear in budgets of state universities in Turkey essentially reflect the student contributions in both tracks, which cover tuition-related contributions as well as contributions toward the costs of highly subsidized meals, lodging, medical care, and extracurricular activities. Fee levels are determined each year by the government and vary from one discipline to another based on standardized, rather than normative unit costs. Standardized unit costs are calculated essentially by using budget figures. By law, contributions to be paid by students in the second track cannot be less than half of the unit costs. Universities have the authority to increase fees by up to 20 percent, and to admit or not to admit students in the second track; most research-intensive public universities and private universities have chosen not to admit students in the second track. Students who remain beyond normal periods of study pay 50 percent more for the first year, and twice the regular fee in any subsequent year they remain. The so-called contributions to be paid by students in the normal track in the 2007–2008 academic year varied from $55 for distance education programs to $140 in the two-year programs, and $425 in faculties of medicine, depending on the program in public universities. Contributions to be paid by students in the second track varied from $440 in the two-year programs to $750 in business and economics and $1,000 in engineering. Tuition fees in private universities can be more than $10,000. Tuition-related expenditures from this source account for about 20 percent of the total payment by students.

Detailed information and data are available on the Web site of International Comparative Higher Education Finance and Accessibility Project (ICHEFAP) at the State University of New York (SUNY) at Buffalo on tuition fees, total costs of higher education to parents and students (household expenditures), and the various mechanisms that the governments use to aid and subsidize students in various countries. Table A.5 summarizes the ICHEFAP data on tuition fees in various countries in public and institutions. Data presented in Table A.5 show that tuition fees, all expressed in U.S. dollars on PPP basis, in public institutions vary from 128 dollars in Ethiopia to 12,000 dollars in some U.S. state universities.

According to OECD (2007, Table 5.1), tuition fees in 2004–2005 in member countries expressed in U.S. dollars on PPP basis (2005 PPP) were as follows:

- $5,000 and above: United States
- $3,500–$4,000: Australia, Japan, Korea, Canada
- $3,000–$3,500: Israel
- $1,500–$2,000: United Kingdom, New Zealand, Netherlands
- $1,000–$1,500: Italy
- $500–$1,000: Turkey, France
- Free: Czech Republic, Finland, Ireland,[14] Iceland, Norway, Poland, Sweden

Outside of continental Europe, the general tendency is to increase fees, particularly in Latin America and the Asia-Pacific region (Chevaillier and Eicher 2002; Tilak 2005). A study by Psacharopoulos and Patrinos (2002) shows that private returns to higher education are increasing worldwide, which provides further justification for tuition fees. However, the fact that the bills on fees were enacted with only the slimmest of margins in parliaments in both Australia and the United Kingdom, and the rejection of fees in Austria and Hungary in 2008 clearly shows that although no longer taboo, tuition fees in public institutions remain a controversial issue. The introduction of tuition fees in countries where higher education used to be free, and increase in fees where they existed, is now a major global trend. There are few countries left where there are no fees in public institutions. In those countries where public institutions do not charge tuition fees, such as in Brazil, private institutions account for a large portion of the enrollment. Johnstone (2006, 31–49) refers to this approach as another form of cost-sharing.

A final note on tuition fees concerns the differential charged to foreign students. Countries in which higher fees are charged to foreign students are Australia, Austria, Canada, Ireland, the Netherlands, New Zealand, the Slovak Republic, Switzerland, Turkey, the United Kingdom, and the United States. In the EU, students from other member countries are treated as home students.[15] Countries that charge the same fees to all foreign students include France, Greece, Hungary, Iceland, Italy, Japan, Korea, Portugal, and Spain. On the other hand, until recently, the Czech Republic, Denmark, Finland, Germany, Norway, Poland, and Sweden did not charge fees in public institutions; this, however, is changing in Germany (OECD 2004b, 26), the Czech Republic, Sweden, and Finland.

3.3. PRIVATE INSTITUTIONS

Market forces in higher education are interacting in such a way that the differences between public and private, and for-profit private and nonprofit private institutions are becoming increasingly blurred. On the two ends of the spectrum lie the 100 percent privately funded and the 100 percent publicly funded institutions (Levy 1986; Newman et al. 2004, 108). A typical private institution receives some revenue from public sources directly or indirectly, and a typical public institution generates some of its revenues from private sources such as tuition fees, donations, and services performed. The traditional private–public dividing line is now replaced by a new one, which would separate for-profit from nonprofit institutions. Even that line tends to be blurred because a number of public and nonprofit institutions are engaged in for-profit undertakings, especially in transnational education (Levy 2009; UNESCO 2003a; see Section 4.3.1)

The OECD (2004a, p.11 in Glossary) and UNESCO (2006, 30) define a private institution as one "controlled and managed by a non-governmental organization (e.g., a Church, Trade Union, or business enterprise), or if its Governing Board consists mostly of members not selected by a public agency," and distinguishes between government-dependent and independent private institutions. A former type of institution is one that "receives more than fifty percent of its core funding from government agencies or one whose teaching personnel are paid by a government agency." Thus, church-affiliated universities such as those encountered in France, Spain, Belgium, and the Netherlands are government-dependent private institutions, and there is little difference between them and the state institutions in their respective countries. The real distinction at the present, however, is between nonprofit and for-profit institutions. To keep the discussion in this section simple, no such distinctions will be made, and the simple definitions of public and private institutions given by the OECD will be adhered to.

With these caveats, Figure 3.4, prepared by using the data shown in Table A.1 in Appendix A, shows the share of private institutions of all types in higher education systems of selected countries, based on enrollments. At the top of the figure are Israel, 82 percent; Japan, 80 percent; Korea 78, percent; Chile, 76 percent; Brazil, 72 percent; and Taiwan 70 percent.[16] However, the older private universities in Israel, like the church-affiliated private universities in Belgium and the Netherlands, are of the government-dependent type, and there are few differences between them and the state universities. UNESCO (2006) reports the share of private universities in the Netherlands as 100 percent.

Israel currently has eighteen public colleges and universities and nine private ones. Private universities are of the government-dependent type, receiving financial aid through the Council of Higher Education (Iram 2006). Applications to open eleven new private colleges, about half of which are branch campuses of private institutions, have been on hold due to resistance from public institutions, which have cited unfair competition.[17]

There is only one truly private university in the United Kingdom, the University of Buckingham. Many, however, view the British universities, especially the pre-1992 ones, in particular the red brick civic universities, as government-dependent private institutions that have charters of their own. In Levy's (1986) typology, the United Kingdom system is public-autonomous. It is for this reason that UNESCO (2006) regards the United Kingdom higher education system as 100 percent private, while the share of the University of Buckingham in the British system is insignificant.[18]

Students in private higher education institutions make up significant percentages of the national enrollments in Asia-Pacific countries and in Latin America. In a number of countries such as Korea, Japan, Taiwan, the Philippines, Indonesia, Macao, Cambodia, Chile, Colombia, India, Paraguay, Peru, and Brazil, private institutions of higher education make up more than half the total enrollment, and more than one fourth of the enrollments in Armenia, Jamaica, Jordan, Oman, Malaysia, Mexico, and Venezuela. Tilak (1991) and Altbach (1999a) attribute the growth in private higher educa-tion in relatively poorer countries to the inability of governments to fund

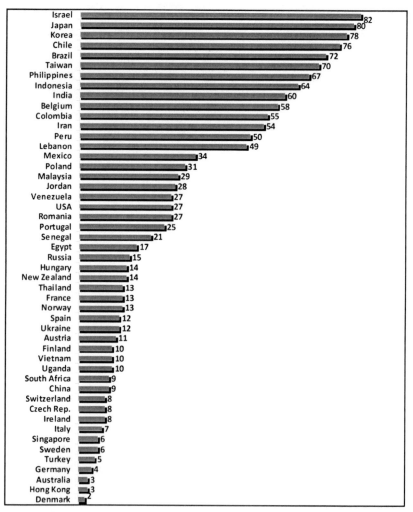

Source: Table A.1 in appendix A

Fig. 3.4. Share of Private Institutions in National Systems, % of Total Enrollment, 2006

expansion. Johnstone (2004, 2006, 41) views this growth as another form of cost-sharing policy by governments. Private higher education has more than half a century of history in countries like Japan, Korea, and Colombia, but the growth of the private sector has accelerated since the 1980s.

Brazil has 195 state-funded higher education institutions, including 78 universities, and there are no tuition fees in these institutions. The private higher education sector, on the other hand, comprises some 1,442 private providers, including 84 universities, which charge tuition fees ranging from $5,490 to $10,720 per year (OBHE-BNA, June 27, 2006).

The historical roots of Japanese higher education go back to the Meiji Restoration of 1868. The University of Tokyo was founded as a public institution in 1877 under the Ministry of Education. But by then Japan had a centuries-old tradition of private schools, which later evolved into the so-called miscellaneous schools (*kakushu gakko*). Thus, Japanese higher education from its very beginning was a differentiated system with a public–private mix, and at the end of World War I, a law was passed that enabled some of the private specialized schools to be upgraded to university status (Kaneko 1997).

The higher education systems of Japan, Taiwan, Korea, the Philippines, and Malaysia are classified as majority-private in Levy's (1986) typology. On the other hand, until 2000, there were no private universities in Singapore.[19] The private institutions and colleges in Singapore, in general, do not have the power to award degrees themselves, but many of them award degrees of foreign universities in various types of franchise arrangements, including brand-name institutions from Australia, China, France, Germany, Japan, Netherlands, United Kingdom, and United States. Recently, the Singaporean government expanded the degree-awarding power beyond the three public universities in the country (OBHE-BN, September 2003, January 2005). The Singapore Institute of Management (SIM) was founded in 1964 as a nonprofit nonuniversity institution. Currently, SIM awards degrees in partnership with a number of leading institutions in the United States, the United Kingdom, Australia, and China (see Section 4.4.8). In 2005, its degree-awarding powers were expanded by establishing UniSIM, which largely caters to working adults. Both SMU and UniSIM now receive financial support from the Singaporean government, and can thus be regarded as government-dependent type. It is estimated that the share of private enrollment in Singapore is 6 percent.

Most undergraduate education in India is provided by privately managed colleges, which are affiliated with public universities and financed largely by public funds (Altbach 1999a). According to the Indian government statistics (Government of India 2003), only a few of the 272 Indian universities are private. On the other hand, of the 11,146 colleges two thirds to three fourths are private. Most of these colleges are given financial assistance by the state, and are hence called "private-aided" institutions. Recent government approaches, however, seem to favor self-financing colleges (Tilak 1999). Gupta (2004) points out that the lack of a restraining centralized national government has led to the current growth in private higher education motivated by monetary gains.

As of 1990, private institutions did not exist in China. As part of the reforms of the 1990s, private higher education was allowed to develop. In 2002, the Law for the Promotion of Private education was enacted, which allows private investors to make "a reasonable return on their investment" (Lin 2004; OBHE-BfN 12, July 2003; OBHE-BfN 13; September 2003). By 2003, some two thousand nongovernmental colleges and universities had been founded. These are called *Minban* or *Shehui Liliang Banxue* in Chinese, meaning institutions run by the nongovernmental sector or by social forces. However, only about one hundred of these are recognized, but some of them are accredited to offer bachelor-level degrees. Additionally, certain disciplines in some public universities are allowed to operate as private or quasi-private units, somewhat similar to the "privatization within" in the formerly Communist countries of central and eastern Europe. Presently, there are some three hundred of these so-called second-tier colleges, or independent colleges, enrolling almost one third of the undergraduate students in regular institutions (F. Huang 2005; Lin 2004). These institutions, together with the 909 colleges of higher vocational education offering short-cycle programs at the subbachelor level, have made major contributions to the growth in enrollment, rather than the prestigious research universities.

Chinese universities have been allowed to cooperate with foreign partners and institutions to offer joint programs leading to foreign degrees (see Section 4.4.8). Such programs now involve institutions and organizations from various countries, including the United States, the United Kingdom, Australia, Singapore, and Hong Kong. Adequate data are not available on the scale of foreign activity in China; the information available indicates that in 2002, there were 712 "approved" jointly run educational programs in China, which encompassed a range of typologies, including co-developed new institutions, a foreign degree franchised to an existing Chinese university, and many nondegree courses and programs (Garrett 2004). Joint programs that were authorized to award foreign degrees numbered 137 in 2003, up from 97 in 2002 (F. Huang, 2005). Full British degrees are offered both at the undergraduate and the graduate levels at the University of Nottingham's Ningbo branch campus established in 2003. All courses are taught in English by staff sent from the main campus in the United Kingdom (Hewitt and Liu 2006).

In September 2003, new regulations on foreign providers in China came into force, which require hundreds of Sino-foreign partners to apply retroactively or face closure (OBHE-BfN 13; September 2003; OBHE-BN, November 2003). In February 2004, two American for-profit higher education institutions (Western International University and ITT Educational Services) were approved by the Beijing Municipal Education Commission to offer undergraduate programs in partnership with the Canadian Institute of Business and Technology, a development firm already well established in the Chinese market, and Beijing Polytechnic University. These are the first foreign bachelor-level programs and the first example of for-profit providers securing approval to offer programs in China (OBHE-BN, February 2004).

The share of private enrollment in China increased from 0.7 percent of the total in 1998 to 4.3 percent in 2003 (F. Huang 2005), and as of 2004 stood at 9 percent as seen in Figure 3.4. Privately funded colleges of various types now number at least 1,300, with 45,000 students enrolled in Shanghai alone (Hewitt and Liu 2006). However, private institutions have made a relatively little contribution to the massification of Chinese higher education so far, and it is believed that public institutions will carry the major burden of any future expansion (F. Huang 2005). Furthermore, there is a heated debate in China on the balance between autonomy and control in private higher education, with government officials accusing private universities of profit seeking, and the private institutions complaining about excessive government interference (Lin 2004).

Vietnam, like China, has introduced a flexible policy of mobilizing resources to develop capacity in her higher education system. Tuition fees were introduced and private institutions were permitted in 1986 as part of sweeping economic reforms known as *doi moi* (P. Huang and Fry 2004; Le and Ashwill 2004). In 1989, a group of intellectuals founded the first nonpublic higher education institution, Thang Long University, on an experimental basis. By 2002–2003, the number of nonpublic institutions of higher education had increased to twenty-three, the largest one being Van Lang University with an enrollment of forty-seven hundred students. Presently, there are two types of private institutions in Vietnam. Semipublic institutions are owned and operated by the state and a public authority at the central, provincial, district, or communal levels. Nongovernmental organizations (NGOs), or private associations such as trade unions, cooperatives, youth organizations, and women's associations own and operate the so-called people-founded institutions. Although presently there are no institutions owned by private individuals, Vietnam allows foreign providers. In 2003, the first foreign-owned university campus was established by the Royal Melbourne Institute of Technology in Ho Chi Minh City. This is a typical Australian offshore operation (see Section 4.4.8). On December 30, 2004, plans to inaugurate the first American university in Vietnam, the American Pacific University, a branch campus of the U.S. Roger Williams University, were announced as well as the opening of four new private universities (OBHE-BN, January 2005). After more than two decades of policies of "change" (*doi moi* in Vietnamese), the share of private institutions in enrollment presently stands at 10 percent as seen in Figure 3.4. The plans are to increase the share of private institutions to 30 percent by 2010 (Overland 2006).[20]

Many regard the United States as the bastion of free enterprise. According to the latest statistics reported in the Almanac 2008–2009 issue of the *Chronicle of Higher Education*, the total number of degree-granting higher education institutions in the United States is 4,314.[21] Of these, 643 are four-year public, 1,045 are two-year public, 1,533 are four-year nonprofit private (up from 1,387 in 1980), 107 are two-year nonprofit private (down from 182 in 1980), 453 are four-year for-profit (up from 18 in 1980 and 297 in 2003–2004), and 533 are two-year for-profit (up from 147 in 1980 and 494 in 2003–2004). Thus, private institutions of all types make up 61 percent of the institutions in the U.S. higher education system. Yet, with a total private share of only 27 percent of the enrollment, the United States does not figure prominently in Figure 3.4. The major difference between public and nonprofit private institutions in the United States is the higher level of fees and the higher share of fees in total revenues in the latter. Thus, nonprofit private institutions in the United States also can be viewed as government-dependent.

The national higher education systems of Australia, New Zealand, and Canada are characterized by low shares of private institutions in enrollment. Private institutions in these countries are more active in the nonuniversity sector, with a few private universities only in Australia. There are presently two private universities in Australia and two U.S. branch campuses, Notre Dame and Carnegie Mellon Heinz School. Public universities in all three countries, especially in Australia and New Zealand, have considerable freedom in setting tuition fees and allocating their resources as they see fit.

An interesting model that was emerging in Australia was the Melbourne University Private (MUP), the for-profit arm of Melbourne University, a public institution (OBHE-BN, September 2003; August 2004). However, the MUP incurred a loss, rather than being a source of additional revenue, and was absorbed into the profitable Melbourne Enterprises International; the new entity retained the name Melbourne University Private (Ryan and Stedman 2002). Furthermore, MUP has been denied membership in the Australian Vice-Chancellors Committee, the representative body of Australian universities. The Association of Universities and Colleges of Canada, too, has closed its doors to new members (OBHE-BN, August 2004). Both moves can be interpreted as manifestations of traditional institutions' reactions to the emergence of new types of providers, especially to for-profit providers.

Europe has a long tradition of private higher education. The Dutch Constitution of 1848 and the French legislation of 1875 both allowed private institutions. Public higher education is even more dominant in western Europe than in the United States, especially if the government-dependent nature of the church-affiliated universities in Belgium and the Netherlands is taken into account. Altbach (1999b) estimates that more than 95 percent of the students in western Europe attend public institutions. According to OECD figures, 76.6 percent of all students in Europe study in a public institution; 18.5 percent are enrolled in a government-dependent private institution, and only 4.8 percent study in a truly private institution (OECD 2004b, 127), which confirm Altbach's estimate.

The Greek constitution explicitly bans private institutions of higher education. On the other hand, Greek legislation permits private companies offering postsecondary education to exist as "laboratories of liberal studies" (*EES* in Greek), registered with the Ministry of Commerce, rather than the Hellenic Ministry of Education and Religious Affairs. As of 2005, thirty-five thousand students were enrolled in the "laboratories," paying an average of $5,166 per year in a wide range of academic and vocational programs extending from floriculture and hairdressing to information technology (IT), finance, and business management. Altogether, courses are offered in 214 areas of specialization, more than 40 percent of which are in business and commerce. As businesses, the so-called laboratories are free to establish partnerships with foreign providers. There were sixty-two such partnerships with one hundred foreign providers; fifty-three of them were based in the United Kingdom, twenty-three in France, and fifteen in the United States. However, the peculiarity of the situation in Greece is that the qualifications awarded by foreign institutions on the basis of a program of study or any part of a program at an *EES* are not recognized for employment in the Greek public sector (OBHE-A, April 20, 2005). In response to pressures from Brussels instigated by foreign providers, the Greek government drafted a law that would in effect recognize these so-called laboratories as bona fide higher education institutions. The law has not been enacted as of March 2009 due to fierce public opposition to private higher education in Greece.[22]

The private higher education sector in Germany consists of private *Fachhochschulen*, business schools, and theological institutions. There are only two private universities, and together with the thirty-three private *Fachhochschulen* and the forty-four church-affiliated institutions, private institutions in Germany number about fifty, but account for 4 percent of the enrollment in programs leading to degrees. International University of Bremen was founded in 1999 by the city of Bremen in partnership with Rice University (Hochstettler 2004).

France has two types of private institutions: church-affiliated universities similar to the ones in the Netherlands and Belgium, and private *grandes écoles*. The latter, although classified as nonuniversity institutions, are in the majority of cases more prestigious than universities. Private institutions account for 26 percent of the students in the *grandes écoles*, and 41 percent of the enrollment in the *Section de Technicien Supérieur* (STS). Spain, too, like France, has government-dependent universities that are church-affiliated. There also are private business schools in Italy, Spain, and France. Private enrollment accounts for 7, 12, and 13 percent of the national enrollment in Italy, Spain, and France, respectively (see Figure 3.4).

There are no private universities in Switzerland, Norway, and Finland, but numerous private, vocational nonuniversity institutions operate in all these countries; students in such institutions make up a relatively higher share of the national enrollment, 8 percent in Switzerland, 10 percent in Finland, and 13 percent in Norway. Until 1994, the only private institution in Sweden was the Stockholm Business School (*Handelshogskolan i Stockholm*), founded in 1909 by royal decree. The present-day Chalmers Technological University was founded in 1829 as a private institution, but was transformed in to a state institution in the 1960s. The conservative government that came to power in 1991 privatized this institution by retransforming it into a nonprofit university, governed by a board with no government-appointed members. Private institutions presently account for 6 percent of the Swedish enrollment at the tertiary level.

Portugal, with a private share of 25 percent in the national enrollment, is truly an exception in western Europe.

The Turkish Constitution only allows nonprofit private institutions of higher education. As of March 2009, of the 132 universities in Turkey, 38 are private, but, together with the 4 independent private vocational schools, they account for only 5 percent of the national enrollment.

Private higher education in the formerly communist countries of central and eastern Europe have developed rapidly in the 1990s along a path that is radically different from that in western Europe. Following the collapse of the communist regime, the term *nonstate education* appeared for the first time in the 1992 federal law on education in Russia. This led to a flurry of private institutions, which now account for 15 percent of the national enrollment.[23] According to Smolentseva (2003), private institutions in Russia are all for-profit, and very few of them are characterized by high standards. Developments in other formerly Communist countries have been similar, where the shares of private institutions are significantly higher than those generally encountered in western Europe. Slantcheva (2005) draws attention to the concerns about the legitimacy of, and Stetar, Panych, and Bin (2005) express concern about corruption in private institutions in the former Communist countries.[24]

Teferra (2005) estimates that there are more than one thousand private institutions in Africa, where the number of public institutions is slightly more than three hundred. Private institutions account for significant shares of national enrollments in a number of African countries, such as 32 percent in Burundi and Mozambique, 25 percent in Niger, and 23 percent in Ethiopia.

Since the World Conference on Higher Education, convened by UNESCO in Paris in 1998, the number of public institutions in the world has remained essentially unchanged, whereaas that of private institutions has continued to grow. UNESCO (2003a) estimates that 31.5 percent of students worldwide are enrolled in private institutions. It does appear that private higher education will grow worldwide. UNESCO (2003a, 18) draws attention to the difficulties of starting private institutions, and cautions that: "many of the new private institutions lack both material and intellectual resources. Often they fail to resist increasing competition in an emerging market that does not always show concern for quality standards and established practices in the respective national systems."

3.4. CHANGING PATTERNS OF GOVERNANCE

3.4.1. Historical Background

The roots of the actors presently involved in university governance can be traced to the beginnings of the medieval university when guilds of students and/or teachers (*universitas scholarium, universitas magistrorum, or universitas magistrorum et scholarium*), mostly from foreign countries, needed protection from the townsmen and local authorities. In general, this involved ceilings imposed on exorbitant rents charged to students and teachers, but in other instances, it could be a matter of life and death. The *Authentica Habita* of the Emperor Frederick I in 1155, which he proclaimed during his crowning in Bologna after hearing the grievances of the students, was the first privilege given to universities. Many, however, agree that it was the bull of Pope Gregory IX in 1231, known as the *Parens Scientiarium*, the founding charter of the University of Paris, which authorized the university to make its own statutes and punish the breach of them by expulsion from the *universitas* that established the newly emerging institution as a body corporate.[25]

The universities in Bologna (f. 1088), Paris (f. 1160), Oxford (f. 1167), Cambridge (f. 1209), Montpellier (f. 1220), Padua (f. 1222), and Orleans (f. 1235) spontaneously came into being in the period dating from the late twelfth to the early thirteenth centuries. These universities in time acquired a prestige and a reputation of their own, such that they could grant teaching licenses that were respected throughout Christendom. Thus, authorizing universities to grant teaching licenses that would be valid everywhere without further examination subsequently became the basis for founding charters by popes, emperors, and kings.

All of these bulls and charters addressed issues such as meals and lodging for students and teachers, libraries, and rights and responsibilities of teachers and students regarding matters of discipline. They also included requirements by the higher authority that pertained to academic matters, such as admission and graduation criteria, length of studies, and, in some cases, even syllabi, course contents, and books that were allowed. Nevertheless, such charters and bulls did protect the university as an institution against interference by local administrations and ecclesiastical authorities, and laid the foundations of university governance and autonomy. This point can be taken one step further by positing that these royal and papal documents also were the first examples of licensing and quality assurance schemes, a salient feature of higher education governance today, which I discuss in Subsection 3.4.3.

The university thus emerged as a uniquely western European institution, and took its place as the third, and possibly the most potent, transformative power in Christendom, *studium*, in addition to the spiritual power represented by the church (*sacerdotium*), and the temporal power exercised by the emperor, king or the prince (*imperium, regnum*). The number of universities in Europe, which was thirty-one in 1400, had increased to sixty-three in 1500, and it had diffused to all parts of Europe, except Russia and the Balkans.

Altbach and Teichler (2001) and Altbach (2004a) have defined the medieval university as an international institution, supervised by the international authority of the Roman Catholic Church that used a common language, Latin, to provide training to students from many countries by internationally recruited teachers who used an international knowledge base comprising books translated from Arabic and Greek. However, in time the Roman Catholic Church was replaced as the external authority by the temporal authorities as represented by the emperor, king, prince, or local government, which increasingly became the major source of funding (see Section 5.1.1).

With the Protestant Reformation, universities started teaching in vernacular languages, and they were soon linked with the emerging nation-states. Over a period from the beginning of the nineteenth century to the 1980s, continental European universities became increasingly absorbed within the central state bureaucracies. The latter took on a "regulatory" role that involved issuing rules and regulations pertaining to nearly every aspect of university activities. The state bureaucracy regulated the appointment of professors, academic and administrative structures, curricula, graduation requirements, salaries of staff, and matters related to expenditures and budgets (Charle 2004; de Groof, Neave, and Svec 1998, 5–157; Gerbod 2004; Ruegg 2004a; Veld, Fussel, and Neave 1996, 17–89).

De Groof et al. (1998, 16) and Neave (2003) refer to this stage as a "bureaucratic revolution," when the *Universite de France* (f. 1806–1808), sometimes called the Napoleonic University, and Berlin University (f. 1810), were placed under the tutelage of the ministries of education, and served as referential models for continental European universities. In this period, teachers were transformed from being members of the *universitas*, the guild, a collegial community of scholars, into civil servants. Higher education institutions, universities in particular, became the main sources of human power for the emerging bureaucracies of the nation-states. The period 1860–1930 in particular saw the transformation, professionalization, expansion, and diversification of higher education itself, as well as its role in nation building and as an agent for social change and mobility (de Groof et al. 1998, 5–157; Jarausch 1983; Reed, Meek, and Jones 2002; Veld et al. 1996, 17–89).

Thus, higher education in continental Europe came to be viewed as a purely public service to be financed exclusively from the public purse. In the Netherlands, for example, the law enacted in 1876 provided for public financing for all institutions, including private ones (de Boer, Maassen, and de Weert 1999). In return, the state assumed full control of the administration of institutions by appointing a civil servant as the head of administration, called the *Kanzler* in Germany, *Secrétaire Général* in France, and *Secretaris* in the Netherlands, who was not subordinate to the rector. Neave (1986, 1988a) and de Groof et al. (1998, 18–19) have referred to such power sharing as a "bicephalous" arrangement.

A very subtle aspect of the Humboldtian model was the way in which academic freedom was safeguarded against both political incursions and narrow guild-like interests within academia itself. To that end, Humboldt insisted that the professors of the new University of Berlin be appointed by the state and not by the university (Wittrock 1993).

In Germany, the *Kaiser* appointed full professors, and the minister of education made the appointments at the associate professor level; about 25 percent of such appointments made in Germany between 1817 and 1900 were from outside the short lists proposed by the universities (Cowley 1980, 26). In this manner, what is generally referred to as the continental European model of governance emerged and took shape along an axis with the state bureaucracy at one end and the academia, or in Clark's (1983) terminology, the "academic oligarchy" on the other.

The classical continental European model does not include lay members other than the government-appointed heads of administration, although bodies made up of interested citizens had been put in charge of many Italian universities by local governments, and by princes in some German universities as early as the mid-fourteenth century. Furthermore, the rector, who is elected by peers from their own ranks, is *primus inter pares* with mostly ceremonial, rather than executive, powers at the head of the institution.

On the other hand, a lay board governed the Calvinist Academy (*Academia Geneviensis*), founded by John Calvin in 1559 in Geneva. This was in accordance with the Calvinist creed that the church and schools were too important to be administered by the clergy or the teachers alone. This served as the prototype first for the governance of the Protestant universities in Holland and Scotland and for Trinity College founded in Dublin in 1593, and later for the colonial-era American colleges (Kerr and Gade 1985). For example, lay boards (*college van curatoren*) governed Dutch universities, whose members were appointed by the government (de Boer et al. 1999).

Oxford and Cambridge, from the start, had been organized as confederations of colleges. They are often cited as examples of the fully autonomous, collegial institution. However, Oxford and Cambridge were not taken as prototypes or referential models either for Durham (f. 1832) and London (f. 1836) or for the "civic universities" that were founded in the late nineteenth and the early twentieth centuries in the newly industrialized urban centers. Rather, it was, although short-lived, the dissenting academies,[26] in particular the statutes of Owens College in Manchester adopted in 1880 that served as the prototype for what would emerge as the British model of governance. This includes a court as the highest policymaking organ of the university, the council as the executive branch of the court, and the senate as the academic organ. The chancellor, who always is a prominent layman, is the nominal head of the university and chairs the court. The vice-chancellor, not necessarily an academic, appointed by the court, is the executive head, and in that capacity chairs the council and the senate. It was stipulated in the charters of the civic universities that the majority of the members in the court and the council were to be lay, and this continues to be a central element of the British governance system. A second layer was added to this system in 1919, when the University Grants Committee (UGC) was established to advise the government on grants to be made to universities from the public purse.[27]

Governance structures of the early colonial colleges in America, all of which were founded by Protestant immigrants, were naturally modeled according to Calvinist tenets (Kerr and Gade 1985). Trow (2003; see also Neave 2003) argues that the early colleges were also influenced by dissenting academies, and incorporated many of their features such as closer relations with the society and with occupations. He also notes the positive effect of the failure of efforts to found a national university of the United States as a federal institution that would inevitably be a referential model, stifling diversity and competition. The second historic event that shaped the present-day American system of governance was the Supreme Court decision in 1816 that prevented the state of New Hampshire from appointing public representatives to the board of trustees of Dartmouth College. A decision by the Supreme Court in Michigan in 1869 affirmed the power of the board of regents of Michigan State University. A similar decision by the Illinois

Supreme Court in 1943 affirmed the legal status of the state university as a public corporation. These decisions provided the legal framework for lay governance in both private and state institutions in the United States (Carnegie Foundation 1982, 10–11).

According to Kerr and Gade (1985), the American system emerged from these roots as "a gift of history." It differs from the British system in that the governing board at the top of the institution has no internal academic members. In the majority of cases, the board also has no student members. The American system is characterized by a strong president appointed by the board—as opposed to the elected rectors in continental Europe with essentially no managerial powers—and its responsiveness to the market, a fundamental social institution in the American society from the beginning.

3.4.2. The State, the Academia, and the Society as Actors in Governance

The foregoing brief summary of the history of university governance can be summarized as follows. The evolution of the British system, and especially the American system of governance from the nineteenth century on, introduced the society and the market as a third group of actors in the governance of higher education systems in addition to the state and academia. Lay members, increasingly referred to as stakeholders; represent the former in institutional governing boards and intermediary bodies. The "triangle of coordination" with the three groups of actors placed in each apex of the triangle proposed by Clark (1983, 143) in his seminal work on comparative higher education systems provides a framework for analysis with such a perspective.[28]

Figure 3.5 shows Clark's triangle of coordination. In his original work, Clark (1983, 143) identified the then USSR and Italy as the epitomes of systems dominated by state authority and the academic oligarchy, respectively. He had cited the American system as "what comes closest to a market of freely interacting and competitive institutions," and had placed the said countries at the three apexes of the triangle of coordination as prototypes. In terms of their internal decision-making structures and their relations with the Ministry of Education, Japanese universities were quite similar to classical continental European institutions. However, because of the large share of private institutions in the system, Clark placed Japan next to the United States in market-responsiveness. Canadian universities, much like British institutions, are quasi-private, nonprofit corporations, chartered by provincial legislatures rather than by the federal parliament. The Canadian higher education system is characterized by somewhat weaker state control compared with the British system (Jones 2002). Thus, Clark placed Canada

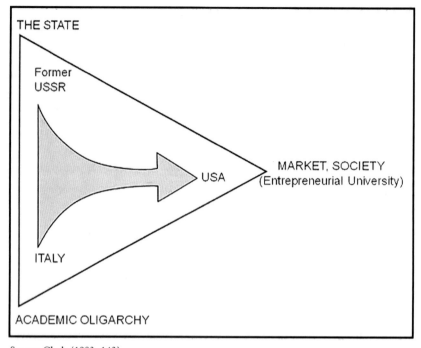

THE STATE

Former
USSR

USA

MARKET, SOCIETY
(Entrepreneurial University)

ITALY

ACADEMIC OLIGARCHY

Source: Clark (1983, 143).
Note: The (Enterpreneurial university) phrase on the "MARKET, SOCIETY" apex is the author's interpretation.

Fig. 3.5. The Depiction of the Rise of Market Force in the Triangle of Coordination

behind Japan, followed by Britain. As examples of continental European systems, Clark put Sweden and France on the state–academic oligarchy axis. Neave and van Vught (1994) share Clark's analysis, and point out that the continental European model is configured on the state–academic oligarchy axis of the triangle, while the British and the American models, with limited, in the case of the United States very limited, government regulation, are close to the market/society apex.

Massification of higher education in Europe led to differentiation within the national systems, increased regulation by ministries, and centralization of decision making in Europe (Beckmeier and Neusel 1990; Neave 1986). This is reflected in laws enacted by parliaments between the late 1960s and the early 1980s, such as in France (*Loi d'Orientation sur l'Enseignment Supérieur*), in 1968 and 1984, the Netherlands (*Wet op de Universitaire*

Bestuurleiding) in 1970, Ireland in 1971, Germany (Hochschulrahmengesetz) in 1976 and 1982, Austria (Universitatsorganisationgesetz) in 1975, Sweden in 1977, and Spain (Ley de Reforma Universitario) in 1970 and 1983. Neave (1998) refers to this process of enacting legislation as a means of enforcing practice and implementing policy as the "juridification" of higher education in Europe, whereby nearly all aspects of higher education, ranging from admission and access, curricular content, and internal governance to expenditures, was indeed regulated in detail (de Groof et al. 1998, 5–157; Veld et al. 1996, 17-89).

In response to the student demonstrations and campus unrest of the 1960s, these laws designated "internal constituencies," such as representatives of administrative staff and students to share power with the academics in the various boards and councils of universities under the banner of democratization.

It is interesting, however, to note that the French and the Spanish legislation included lay members in the higher decision-making bodies of universities as stakeholders who represent the interests of the society in consejo sociales in Spain, and in all of the three university councils in France, including the senate, conseil scientifique. The Swedish legislation, on the other hand, established the Board of Universities and Colleges (Universitetsoch Högskoleambetet) as the central governing and coordinating body for all of higher education in the country. Thus, the Swedish system was the first unified higher education system in Europe.

Clearly, this was a period in continental Europe when universities were transformed into public agencies regulated by ministries of education at the central level as in France, or at the Land-level as in Germany (Beckmeier and Neusel 1990). A survey was commissioned by the Institutional Management in Higher Education program of the OECD in the early 1980s to determine the relative degree of autonomy of institutions of higher education in a number of European countries. Questions asked in the survey covered the authority of the institutions themselves to make decisions on matters such as the distribution of posts among academic units, purchasing of computers, making changes in syllabi and curricula, moving equipment from one laboratory to another, appointment of professors and staff, moving funds from one line or chapter of the institution's budget to another, acceptance of research projects, allocation of consumables between research and teaching, and so forth. Based on the answers to such questions, a "relative index of autonomy" was developed. This showed that where British universities, governed by predominantly lay boards and appointed vice chancellors, scored 100, French and German universities with elected rectors and presidents scored 42 and 29, respectively (Jadot 1980, 1984).

3.4.3. Transformation from the Regulatory to the Evaluative State

Starting in the mid-1980s, patterns of higher education governance, too, started to change radically (de Groof et al. 1998, 5–157; Veld et al. 1996). The main drivers of this transformation were the following:

1. The changing view of higher education from a purely public service to be financed from the public purse to a semipublic service, the costs of which should be borne by all stakeholders, that is, by all of those who benefit from its outputs.

2. A "financial crisis" resulting from increasing demand coupled with increasing costs (Eicher and Chevaillier 2002; Johnstone 1993; Neave 1997, 1998).

3. The political discourse on what the role of state in general should be in an advanced participatory democracy.

The basic elements of this change included the changing role of the state; new funding arrangements coupled with resource diversification, and increased managerialism in the administration of institutions. Neave (1988b, 1998) and de Groof et al. (1998, 61) refer to these changes as the transformation from the "regulatory" to the "evaluative state." This transformation was accompanied by the introduction of the market as the supreme regulating principle of higher education.

The regulatory state prescribes the processes by which institutions function to produce outputs through an array of detailed legal instruments including laws, line-item budgets, guidelines, and rules. The evaluative state, on the other hand, sets forth institutional missions, qualitative and quantitative input and output targets and confines itself to evaluating achievements, while allowing institutions to determine their own ways of achieving those missions and targets. Among the major changes were lump-sum budgets, resource diversification through the introduction of or increase in tuition fees, and provision of incentives for income generation, increased institutional powers, including professorial appointments and discretion in financial matters.

There was little change in the United States when compared with the changes in Europe, Australia, and Japan. The major noticeable trend was a general shift toward more discretionary powers to public institutions in financial matters. Otherwise, the basic governance structures were left unchanged (Newman et al. 2004, 31–34).

In the United Kingdom, too, the basic structure of governance remained essentially unchanged. However, the Education Reform Act of

1988 replaced the UGC with two funding councils: the Universities Funding Council (UFC) for the university sector, and the Polytechnics and Colleges Funding Council for the remaining part of the binary system. The radical change, however, was the abolition of tenure and the defining of academic freedom in one article of the legislation. The UFC was authorized to enter into contractual agreements with universities and to evaluate their performance for funding purposes. The first research assessment exercise was carried out by the UFC by using quantitative performance indicators, such as numbers of publications, citations, patents, degrees awarded, and funding from external sources. This was in line with the recommendations of the Jarrat Commission. Universities and departments were ranked on this basis, and the findings of the exercise were made public.

The research exercise carried out by the UFC marked the beginning of an entirely new era in evaluation, academic assessment and quality assurance in Europe.[29] But even in the United Kingdom, evaluation had never reached the level of institutionalization and formalization it had in the United States.

The roots of the present-day structure of accreditation in the United States can be traced back to 1905, when the newly founded Carnegie Foundation for the Advancement of Teaching set forth the requirements it would seek in the institutions of higher education to which it would provide funding. The first list of accredited institutions was, however, prepared by the American Association of Universities (AAU) in 1914, when Berlin University made it clear that it would accept students to its doctoral programs only from those institutions that were recognized as universities by the AAU (Carnegie Foundation 1982, 21–37). Regional accreditation boards were established by universities and colleges and their number increased rapidly. Professional organizations, too, joined the process in the early twentieth century. This was led by the American Medical Association, which started accrediting medical schools in 1910.

The G.I. Bill of Rights enacted in 1944, stipulated that to be eligible for financial support under that federal law veterans had to enroll in "accredited" institutions of higher education. From these roots, the present U.S. accreditation system evolved, which consists of two parts. Specialized accreditation is discipline-specific, and is carried out by professional organizations. Institutional accreditation, on the other hand, evaluates the institution as a whole in terms of the compatibility and the sustainability of its activities and resources with its mission. Since 1949, institutional accreditation is carried out by six regional associations, which were founded by the institutions themselves. Reauthorization of the Higher Education Act of 1992 set the standards and procedures for institutional accreditation, and authorized the U.S. Department of Education (USDE) to supervise the regional accreditation boards, and the state higher education boards for the opening of new programs in public institutions. The law also established a "state postsecondary review entity" in each state to monitor the pay back of student loans.

Accreditors in the United States are "recognized" following periodical reviews by the Council for Higher Education Accreditation (CHEA), a private, nongovernmental national coordinating body for national, regional and specialized accreditation or the USDE. As of 2002–2003, nineteen institutional and sixty-one specialized accreditors were in operation, which had been recognized by either CHEA or the USDE or both (OECD 2004b, 63–74).[30]

Clearly, accreditation in the United States is based on academic assessment carried out by NGOs; neither the federal government nor the state governments play a significant role. Academics, on the other hand, do play a very significant role, but the process itself is not dominated by the academic oligarchy; rather, it is inherently market-responsive. Recognition of an accreditor by CHEA confers an academic legitimacy. On the other hand, USDE recognition is required for accreditors whose institutions and programs seek eligibility for federal student aid funds.[31] A very strong incentive thus exists for institutions to seek accreditation. Furthermore, a culture has developed in time that does not reject such an evaluation as an infringement on either institutional autonomy or academic freedom.

At the beginning of the transformation from the regulatory to the evaluative state in the mid-1980s, neither the structures and mechanisms nor the culture existed in continental Europe for academic evaluation and assessment. The prevailing view was that universities were self-governing institutions, and that they needed no steering by external agents, especially in academic matters. Neave (1998) argues that a form of evaluation did exist, but that it essentially involved routine institutional reporting on expenditures, student numbers, and the number of degrees awarded, which was part of the state control. This started to change in Europe from the mid-1980s, when powerful specialist bodies emerged at the national level, which were charged with evaluating the performance of higher education institutions.

It is interesting to note that the first such body was established not in the United Kingdom, but in France, where the *Comité National d'Évaluation* (CNÉ) and the *Conseil National de l'Enseignement Superiéur et de la Recherche* were established in 1985. The first of these two bodies evaluates the performance of higher education institutions every four years and reports its findings to the president of the republic. The latter, on the other hand, is chaired by the minister of education, and advises the minister on the new programs leading to national diplomas, appointments to be made to institution, and general coordination. The *CNÉ* evaluates institutions in the areas corresponding to the public service mission of higher education, which includes education and continuing education, R&D activities at the regional, national, and the international levels. It also examines the governance, policies, and management practices of institutions. The recommendations of the CNÉ are not binding on the institutions. It is not an accreditation body, nor are its findings related in any way to the allocation of public resources to institutions

In 1997, the Quality Assurance Agency for Higher Education (QAA) was established in the United Kingdom "to safeguard the public interest in sound standards of higher education qualifications, and to encourage continuous improvement in the management of the quality of higher education." Each institution of higher education is responsible for the standards and quality of its academic awards and programs. Each has its own internal procedures for attaining appropriate standards and assuring and enhancing the quality of its provision, mainly through the assessment of students and the institutional procedures for the design, approval and monitoring, and review of programs. Periodic reviews typically are carried out every five years and normally involve external examiners drawn from other institutions, or from areas of relevant professional practice. The QAA is an independent body funded by subscriptions from universities and colleges of higher education in the United Kingdom, and through contracts with the UK funding bodies mentioned earlier. It carries out its role by reviewing academic standards and quality, and providing nationally agreed reference points that help to define clear and explicit standards. It achieves its mission through a peer-review process of audits and reviews conducted by teams, most of whom are academics but with some members drawn, where appropriate, from industry and the professions. Quality assurance in research, on the other hand, is achieved through the research assessment exercise, which is carried out by the funding councils mentioned previously. It differs in its aim from the activities of the QAA in that it has a direct bearing on the distribution of public funds for research selectively based on quality.

The Bologna Process (see Section 5.4) has added momentum to external evaluation in continental Europe. Quality assurance and accreditation agencies have been established, and evaluation and assessment schemes have been put in place in all of the European countries. To facilitate and encourage institutions and authorities to cooperate and exchange best practices, the European Commission supported the establishment of the European Network of Quality Assurance (ENQA), which became operational in 2000. As of March 2009, ENQA had forty full and nine candidate members from twenty-five countries.

Some of the national quality assessment agencies in Europe are set up by governments. These include the National Accreditation Agency of the Russian Federation (NICA), the Danish Evaluation Institute, the Center for Accreditation and Quality Assurance of the Swiss Universities, the Norwegian Agency for Quality Assurance in Higher Education, the State Accreditation Committee of Poland, Hungarian Accreditation Committee, Accreditation Commission of the Czech Republic, the National Committee for the Evaluation of the University System in Italy, the Swedish National Agency for Higher Education (Hogskoleverket), and the Hellenic Quality Assurance Agency.[32] The CNÉ in France, the QAA in the United Kingdom, and the Finnish Higher Education Evaluation Council, on the other hand, are independently constituted, but financed by the state. The recently established Netherlands-Flemish Accreditation Organization (Nederlands-Vlaamse Accreditatie Organisatie, NVAO) is binational. It accredits all existing and new bachelor- and master-level programs in the Netherlands and Flanders, where accreditation is now a precondition for government funding of the programs. Programs are assessed by visiting and assessment bodies (Visiterende en Beoordelende Instanties) that are recognized by the NVAO; as of January 2004, six such bodies were recognized. Currently, there are separate visiting and assessment bodies for the university and the nonuniversity (HBO) subsectors, both established in 2004. Quality Assurance Netherlands Universities is for the university subsector, and Netherlands Quality Agency is for the nonuniversity subsector. Their memberships comprise the institutions in the two subsectors, which also own the organizations.

In countries with a federal structure, such as Germany and Spain, there are agencies at the local level in addition to the ones at the national level. Like in the Netherlands, there are different agencies for the university sector and the nonuniversity sector in Austria, Belgium, Ireland, and Poland. In Ireland, the Higher Education Authority functions as both an intermediary body charged with funding and steering and a quality assessment agency. Some of the agencies focus on institutional assessment, others focus on programs and departments; in most cases agencies evaluate both the institutions and the programs and departments within the institutions. The European University Association (EUA) has been implementing an institutional evaluation program on a voluntary basis that focuses on improving institutional management. The program has been in existence for more than a decade.

With all signatory countries of the Bologna Declaration now switching to some form of bachelor- and master-level degree structure (one plus four, or three plus two years), there seems to be a convergence toward linking institution or program approval to some kind of evaluation, assessment, and accreditation procedure throughout continental Europe, and there are clear signs that a common framework is developing. Yet, Europe is nowhere near the United States in terms of the enforcement power of such agencies and schemes (Billing 2004; OECD 2004c, 75–106). All of the bodies established at the national level are essentially evaluating and assessment agencies; their accreditation powers are effectively restricted to recognizing/licensing evaluation and assessment panels, institutions, and organizations.

Thus, quality assurance and accreditation in continental Europe, also largely in the United Kingdom, is essentially a part of the general accountability and reporting process. That is, in general, there are neither direct financial rewards nor penalties associated with the outcomes of the processes as are there in the United States. The recent Dutch and Flanders practice of linking accreditation to funding and the British practice of selective distribution of public funds for research based on the outcomes of the research assessment exercise probably come closest to the American practice. Nevertheless, in an environment where quality is assumed the natural outcome of self-governance and any external influence is still regarded by many in the academia as an infringement on institutional autonomy and academic freedom, and hence detrimental to core academic values, Europe has come a long way. Westerheijden (2003), on the other hand, argues that a level of transparency is required in Europe that can only be achieved by more strict procedures that establish fixed quality thresholds below which accreditation is denied.

Australia has a relatively short history in higher education. In the late 1980s, funding was linked to "institutional profiles," and this, combined with the introduction of fees, meant that a weak relationship had been established between student numbers in various disciplines and public funding. These also meant a shift in the cost from the state to the individual, national, and international competition for students and research income, and resource diversification accompanied by greater deregulation through the collection and retention of student fees and the right to borrow money for capital works (Meek 2002).

A very important policy change in Australia in the late 1980s was the deregulation of the foreign student market. Until 1985, the education of overseas students was seen as a form of aid to developing countries; governments established aid programs to subsidize students, and fees were not paid directly to institutions. In the late 1980s, however, Australian government changed its policy from "aid" to "trade," and full-fee paying foreign students became an important source of revenue for the universities, starting a fierce competition to recruit overseas students (Gamage and Mininberg 2003; Marginson 2002; Meek 2002).

Greater emphasis on accountability and the move toward performance-based funding was accompanied by increased emphasis on assessment and evaluation. In the late 1980s, universities started their own evaluation schemes, which were modeled after the institutional procedures in the

United Kingdom and affected by total quality management practice in the business community. In 1992, the government established the Committee for Quality Assurance in Higher Education.

By the mid-1990s, Australia had emerged as a major host for foreign students and a key player in the global higher education market. Many of her public universities had offshore operations and online programs, and some of them were partners with foreign institutions in consortia, providing higher education globally. Two of her major competitors, the United Kingdom and New Zealand[33] had established quality assurance bodies at the national level. To address the need to maintain the standard and assure the quality of the "Australian brand" in higher education as a key element of international competitiveness, the Australian University Quality Agency was established in March 2000 (Mollis and Marginson 2002; OECD 2004c, 107–117). It is authorized to conduct audits of quality in self-accrediting universities every five years, monitor quality assurance processes, and advise the states on accreditation requirements for nonuniversity providers of higher education.

In terms of Clark's triangle of coordination, the changes introduced in Australian higher education from the early 1980s on clearly imply a shift in balance of power from academia to the state and a move toward the market apex. The process of change is continuing in Australia. In 2004, the government unveiled a plan to abolish the system of nationwide wage bargaining and tenure, allowing instead each institution to establish its own system of tenure and negotiate pay (Cohen 2004a).

The Japanese higher education system was heavily influenced by the classical German model in its inception during the Meiji Restoration and by the American model during its reformation after World War II (Murasawa 2002; Ogawa 2002; Okada 2005; Osaki 1997; Yonezawa 2002). Although postwar reforms significantly curbed the powers of the Ministry of Education, the system remained highly centralized under direct ministerial control. Until April 2004, Japanese universities did not have corporate status. Administratively, national universities were extensions of the ministry, and local public universities belonged to the local governments, which founded them. In the case of private universities and colleges, the corporate status of the institution was vested in the head of the board of trustees of the school corporation that founded the institution. Buildings and facilities belonged to the "founder," that is, the ministry or the local government in the case of public institutions, or the school corporation in the case of a private institution. Likewise, educational and research programs were operations of the founder, which had direct responsibility and authority for the administration of the institution. Budgets of public universities were under the ministry or the local government budget. Academic and administrative positions were also under the ministry or the local government, which meant that the founder rather than the institution employed the staff. Professors in national universities were full-time civil servants with tenure. The president of a national university was elected by the senior professors from among themselves, subject to ratification by the minister, and had somewhat stronger powers than the rector had in the classical continental European model. The head of administration, on the other hand, was a civil servant who reported to the ministry, not the president.

The University Establishment Standards, which were issued as a ministerial decree, determined the forms, organizational structures, and curricula of Japanese higher education institutions. Thus the standards, in a way, defined quality and served as the basis for both chartering and accreditation (Amano 1997; Doyon 2001).[34]

The government determined the salaries of the academic and the administrative staff, tuition fees, and the numbers of students admitted to national universities (Murasawa 2002). The professors' council (*kyojukai shihai*), however, controlled most academic matters in national universities (Goodman 2005). Thus, national universities in Japan could be placed on either the "state" or the "academic oligarchy" apex in Clark's triangle of coordination, depending on whether one looked at the administrative and financial aspects or the academic side of the institution, but certainly nowhere near the "market" apex.[35]

In the mid-1990s, Japan faced the phenomenon of decreasing population of the eighteen-year-old cohort, which was projected to fall from its peak value of 2.05 million in 1992 to 1.2 million in 2010. This meant a loss of 850,000 potential students in higher education, and implied that, despite increasing demand for higher education in general, some institutions would not be viable in terms of student numbers. There was growing concern about the quality of Japanese higher education in both teaching and research. Although Japanese secondary education was renowned for its strictness and its quality in mathematics and sciences, universities were strongly criticized for their slackness and "leisure-land mentality." Of particular concern was the weakness of research and education at the graduate level. The fact that Japan had only 8 Nobel laureates against 182 Americans was considered a source of embarrassment for the world's second largest economy with a GDP that is nearly 40 percent of that of the United States. The World Competitiveness Report of 2001 placed Japan at the bottom of the list of forty-nine nations examined in terms of the contribution of the share of her higher education system to her competitiveness (Goodman 2005).

In 1998, a law was enacted, which made it a requirement for junior faculty members to publish articles based on their research before they are promoted to tenure-track positions (Doyon 2001). In 2000, the National Institute for Academic Degrees (NIAD, *Gakui-juyo Kiko*), which had been established in 1991 to validate degrees awarded by nonuniversity institutions, was reorganized to carry out evaluation in universities; its name in

Japanese was changed to *Daigaku-hyoka Gakui-juyo Kiko*. In 2003, its English abbreviation was changed to NIAD-UE to include university evaluation as one of its two main activities, and in 2004, NIAD-UE acquired statutory powers by legislation.

The sweeping reform process that was started in 1999 aimed to transform national universities into "independent administrative institutions" (*dokuritsu gyosei hojin*) by April 2004, through a process referred to as "incorporation." The process aims to increase efficiency by decreasing government regulation. It involves decreased funding from public sources and increased powers to institutions to manage their affairs and diversify their revenue base with a particular focus on enhancement of research capabilities. Basic features of the reforms include the following (Asonumo 2002; Brender 2004a; Goodman 2005; Hatakenaka 2005; Itoh 2002; Murasawa 2002; Ogawa 2002; Yonezawa 2002):

1. Incorporation of national universities as independent administrative units with their own budgets and staff positions;

2. Merging of institutions that are no longer viable in terms of student numbers;

3. Establishment of graduate schools independent of undergraduate schools;

4. Establishment of research professorships and merging of chairs to form "enlarged chairs";

5. Introduction of managerial techniques in university administration;

6. Establishment of administrative councils similar to lay governing boards;

7. Introduction of a new selection process for university presidents that gives a say to the administrative council together with the senate;

8. Strengthening of the discretionary powers of university presidents in financial matters;

9. Establishment of vice presidencies to which laypersons can be appointed;

10. Competitive funding for research and financial resource allocation based partly on the outcomes of evaluation by the NIAD-UE.

As part of the reform process, the number of national universities has been reduced from ninety-nine to eighty-nine, and consolidation has started in the local university subsector, too (Hatakenaka 2005). Japanese reforms also include recognition and regulation of foreign universities operating in Japan as well as Japanese offshore provision, and allow for-profit providers (Brender 2004b; OBHE-BN, April 2004; Ohmori 2004a, 2004b; see Section 4.4.8).

Korea, with 50 national and 160 private universities and 158 two-year colleges has one of the largest higher education systems in the world. It also is one of the major countries of origin of foreign students (see Tables A.1 and A.6). The present governance system, much like the pre-reform system in Japan, is a tightly controlled one, with the Ministry of Education and Human Resource Development in charge of budgets and personnel of public institutions. The country, like Japan, has entered a period of declining higher education-age population. In response, the ministry has recently announced plans to transform national universities to self-governing institutions and abolish tenure. The intended outcome is institutions consolidated in enrollment size by mergers, which are more competitive (Brender 2006).

As part of the sweeping reforms in China, assessment of the quality of teaching was started as early as 1990. This was emphasized in the Higher Education Act of 1995, and such evaluations were carried out in more than two hundred institutions by 2003. The Center for Assessment of Higher Education Teaching was established on October 26, 2004. The center is mandated to carry out academic evaluation of teaching in each institution of higher education every five years, and to report its findings to the Ministry of Education. The center will rank institutions as excellent, good, pass, and failure. In addition, every institution is now required to report data on its teaching activities to the ministry every year (F. Huang 2005).

With more than 12 million students, the Indian higher education system is currently the third largest in the world, and is quite likely to surpass the United States in the near future. The system currently comprises more than 250 universities and close to 11,000 colleges. In excess of 70 percent of these colleges are privately run. Those established before 1980 are called "grant-in-aid colleges," which get most of their funding from the state, whereas the rest are self-financing institutions that run on student fees. According to Stella (2002), the Indian higher education system is modeled after the classical British system, and it has inherited the funding structures of that model through the University Grants Commission (UGC), along with the classical British quality control mechanisms. The latter involves the affiliation of colleges to universities. This is a mechanism by which a connection is established between a college and an affiliating university. The college follows the syllabi set by the university, which also holds central examinations for all affiliated colleges. Some of the larger affiliating universities have more than four hundred affiliated colleges. In other words, the affiliating university in the Indian case plays the roles Oxford and Cambridge universities traditionally play for their constituent colleges, and the validation that Durham and London universities exercise for the institutions placed under their academic tutelage. Over time, as the system grew enormously, this led to many substandard institutions, with the possibility of many more to come, and hence the need for an effective mechanism for quality assurance. Accreditation by an autonomous body was seen as an appropriate strategy for quality assurance. Consequently, after a number of studies and reports in the late 1980s, as a part of its responsibility for the maintenance and promotion of standards of education, the UGC established the National Assessment and Accreditation Council (NAAC) in 1994 (Stella 2002) "to make quality the defining element of higher education in India through a combination of self and external quality evaluation, promotion and sustenance initiatives."

As of March 2009, NAAC had accredited 140 universities and 3,492 colleges.[36] Accreditation by the NAAC is not mandatory for institutions of higher education, and does not carry direct penalties or rewards, such as reduced or extra funding through the UGC. Furthermore, in a country like India, which still has a long way to go before achieving massification in higher education, linking accreditation and funding is not felt to be appropriate. However, the Indian system is unique in the sense that the chairperson of the UGC also chairs the General Committee of the NAAC, conjoining, in a manner of speaking, the functions of the judge and the prosecutor in the same corporate personality. Thus, NAAC is effectively an advisory body to the UGC. Nevertheless, NAAC has been successful in infusing a "quality culture" to Indian higher education, which has led to many curricular and managerial improvements. Stella (2002), however, also draws attention to an unintended consequence of academic evaluation and assessment that seems to have inflicted the Indian system. According to Stella, many institutions have started to copy top-level institutions leading to uniformity in the system. Such loss of diversity may indeed work against functional differentiation and stratification in national systems, with all institutions aspiring to research university status, which is neither desirable nor attainable.

Other countries in Southeast Asia that have a quality assurance framework are the following (Lee 2006):

• Cambodia: the Accreditation Committee of Cambodia, established in 2000.

- Malaysia: the National Accreditation Board (*Lembaga Akreditasi Negara, LAN*) established in 1996.

- Philippines: the Accrediting Agency of Chartered Colleges and Universities in the Philippines, established in 1989, and the Philippines Association of Schools, Colleges and Universities, established in 1957.

- Thailand: the National Educational Standards and Quality Assurance, established in 2000.

- Vietnam: The Quality Assurance Unit, established in 2002.

In her drive to be an international education hub, Singapore started implementing the Education Excellence Framework in 2004. As part of this framework, CASE Trust for Education (CTE) and Singapore Quality Class for Private Education Organizations (SQC-PEO) schemes were established by the Consumer Association of Singapore (CASE). To enroll international students, all private education organizations (PEOs) must obtain the CTE certificate. If, in addition a PEO obtains the SQC-PEO certificate, it can receive financial support form the government to promote itself internationally, and its international students' visa applications are processed with priority.[37]

Evaluation and assessment schemes were introduced in the 1990s in Latin America. In Argentina, the National Committee for University Assessment and Accrediting was established in 1995 (Fanelli 2006). As part of the sweeping reforms in Chile that I have outlined earlier, *Consejo Superior de Educacion* was founded in 1990 to accredit private universities and professional institutes. Later, two commissions were set up by the ministry in 1999 to evaluate undergraduate and graduate programs of public and private universities on a voluntary basis (Brunner and Tillett 2006). In Mexico, the Higher Education Evaluation Commission was established in 1989. This was followed by the Interinstitutional Committees for Higher Education Evaluation in 1991, the National Center for Higher Education Evaluation in 1994, and the Council for Higher Education Accreditation in 2000. The last one is a meta-accreditation body for both public and private institutions (Casanova-Cardiel 2006). Although aiming to link their results in some way to funding, the various bodies set up in the three countries are characterized by an understanding of licensing as equivalent to accreditation and quality assurance, and results have so far been mixed (Alvarez-Mendiola and de Vries 2005; Ceaser 2004; Mollis 2006; Mollis and Marginson 2002).

In June 2006, a new higher education law was enacted in Brazil. Among the provisions of the new legislation are a new agency and new guidelines for quality assurance, increased autonomy for public institutions in setting their curricula and managing their financial affairs, and a new procedure for appointing university heads where the president of Brazil will make appointments from a list of candidates submitted by the academic community (OBHE-BNA, June 27, 2006).

The emergence of national quality assessment agencies and the switch from line-item to lump-sum budgets accompanied by a strengthened role of the university head and the increased discretionary powers of the central institutional administration are basic features that characterize the transformation from the regulatory to the evaluative state.[38]

However, as I have pointed out previously, other than the United States, assessment and evaluation worldwide are largely in the form of a new way of regulation by the state and a source of information rather than a basis for funding decisions (OECD 2003b, 2004c).

3.4.4. Spread of Lay Governance, Strengthened Institutional Leadership, and a Redefinition of Autonomy

The summary of the changes introduced in Australian higher education in the 1990s provided by Meek (2002) and cited in the previous section arguably can be generalized to describe the structural changes introduced in many countries as the role of the state changed from a regulatory one to an evaluative one. These changes also can be depicted on the triangle of coordination as a sweeping move from the state–academic oligarchy axis to the market–society apex as shown in Figure 3.5. Clark himself refers to these changes as the emergence of a new model of institutional behavior, which he calls "the entrepreneurial university" (Clark 1998, 2001). He defines it as an institution that:

1. Has a diversified revenue base, which includes mainline institutional support from a governmental ministry, funds from governmental research councils and all other sources lumped together as "third-stream" income;

2. Relies on all three sources rather than on the first one alone;

3. Has the legal means to raise money and spend it at its discretion.

In the third-stream income category, Clark (1998, 2001) lists income from other governmental sources, private organized sources including industrial firms, professional and civic associations that promote continuing education for their members, and philanthropic foundations, and university-generated income. Potential sources for the last subcategory include earned income from campus services ranging from the hospital to the bookstore and commercialization of physical campus assets like residence halls and sports facilities for external use; student tuition and fees, increasingly including fees from continuing education and LLL in various forms, and from foreign students enrolled on campus or offshore or in e-learning programs or in franchise arrangements; industry-related contract research and consultancy services; income from technology transfer and royalty income from patented intellectual property collectively owned by the institution and specific faculty members; and alumni fund-raising.

The entrepreneurial university is predicated on an institutional culture that is different from the traditional or, according to some, the utopian collegial model of institutional behavior. Whereas the head of the institution in the latter case is elected by his peers and is *primus inter pares* within the community of scholars that in the former case has a leading role to play both academically and administratively. Clark (1998, 2001) underlines the crucial importance to the creation of an entrepreneurial institutional culture of what he calls the "strengthened steering core" as a philosophy/style/manner of administration/management/coordination, whereby the central administration encourages, promotes, and rewards creative initiatives by the various units and members of the institution without infringing on the core values of the academia. Clark defends this type of approach to university administration as a more effective form of collegiality that is more appropriate to the changed nexus of higher education than the passive collegial model of the past.

There are many, on the other hand, who argue that the collegial spirit is disappearing in entrepreneurial universities. They refer to the changes outlined previously as "marketization of higher education," "corporatization of university governance" (Jongbloed 2003; Mollis and Marginson 2002), and "managerialism" (Reed 2002).[39] Jeliazkova and Westerheijden (2002) describe these changes as a new and more sophisticated control mechanism based on accountability and academic excellence rather than on one-to-one control. Niklasson (1996) and Calero (1998) refer to the results of these changes as the emergence of "quasi-markets in higher education." Chevaillier (2002) describes two methods of creating quasi-markets. In the first method, the state funds institutions on the basis of the number of students, paying a "price" for each student enrolled. In the second method, the state provides "purchasing power" to students in the form of vouchers that students are able to spend on the institution of their choice. The two methods would be identical were the students completely free to choose institutions. Karmel (2003) describes the changing role of the state as one from a provider of subsidies to a provider of a pool of funds without really giving autonomy to market participants, that is, institutions and students. Hence, the term *quasi-market* rather than market is used as a more appropriate description of the current state of affairs in higher education in many countries.

It is clear that a complex relationship has developed in the past quarter of a century that now has more to do with the interaction between the state and the "market," however, one defines the latter, rather than the balance between the state and the academic oligarchy, as the case was in the past. This change has been accompanied by a devolution of decision-making power from the central government level to the local and the institutional level, the spread of lay governance, strengthening of the executive powers at the central institutional level at the expense of senates, councils, and assemblies with elected members (Amaral and Magalhes 2002; de Boer 2002; OECD 2003b).

The term *lay member* in the context of university governance is synonymous with the term *external stakeholder*. Amaral and Magalhes (2002, 2) cite the following general definition of stakeholder as "any group or individual who can affect or is affected by the achievement of the organization's objectives," and on this basis, define external stakeholders as representatives of the interests of the "outside world" in university governance.

French reforms of the last two decades have not stemmed from neoliberal ideologies as the case has been in many countries, but also have resulted in strengthened university leadership, allowed for the development of strategic plans and increased discretionary powers at the institutional level (Chevaillier 2002; Mignot-Gerard 2003; Musselin and Mignot-Gerard 2002). France has a tradition of bureaucratic centralism at the national level, weak management structure at the central institutional level, and strong faculties led by powerful deans. The traditional culture had led presidents and the three central bodies of the universities to view themselves with symbolic decision-making powers, in most cases rubber-stamping decisions made at the faculty levels. This is what changed in the last decade after the introduction of the "planning contracts" (*contracts de plan*) in 1990, which required each university to prepare a strategic development plan that describes its priorities and main objectives for the next four years based on an analysis of institutional strengths and weaknesses. The operational budget of the institution is then based on this plan and, in effect, it becomes an agreement between the Ministry of National Education and the individual institution. Additionally, at the beginning of the 1990s local authorities were given a role in the planning of new facilities and the improvement and upgrading of existing ones. Thus, these medium-term contracts rather than the market became the central tool of higher education policy in France. The French higher education system still exhibits most of the distinctive characteristics of a bureaucratic system. Decisions to invest in a new building or to create a new chair or to hire new clerical staff are still made by the ministry. Nevertheless, the changes introduced in the last two decades have led to the emergence of a new generation of university presidents that do not shy away from a stronger executive role, the three central councils have taken on more responsibility, and the roles of deans and department heads have been significantly altered.

The University Reform Act (*Ley de Reforma Universitario*) of 1983 established the social council (*Consejo Social*) in Spanish universities, which was patterned after the boards of trustees in the American system. With 60 percent of its members drawn from outside of academia, the council has the authority to approve the institution's budget, and is intended to represent the wider interests of the society in the university (Amaral and Magalhes 2002). Mora and Vidal (2000) argue that the role of the social council in Spanish universities has remained limited due to lack of tradition and the unclear definition of its role. Recent changes have given a wider role to the local governments and have allowed universities to set up their "own program." These programs do not require validation by the Council of Universities (*Consejo de Universidados*).[40] They do not lead to national diplomas, and are offered to students who already have a degree from a "regular program." They are not financed through public funds; students pay full costs. Faculty members teaching in these programs receive additional remuneration. Mora and Vidal (2000) regard the increased role of local governments and the offering of "own programs" as positive steps that have made Spanish universities more responsive to the market and local needs. Villareal (2001), on the other hand, argues that there have been no significant structural changes in Spanish higher education since 1983, and the system has remained on the state–academic oligarchy axis of Clark's triangle of coordination with a heavy dependence on the government for funding.

In Italy, too, the Council of Social Institutions was recently established with membership and functions similar to its Spanish counterpart. In both cases, the rationale is to increase the universities' responsiveness to societal demands and to the needs of the labor market (Amaral and Magalhes 2002).

From the late 1980s on, the Italian higher education system has been undergoing a reform process aiming to change the curricular, organizational and governance structures in the quintessentially academic oligarchy-dominated system that resisted or marginalized former attempts at reform (Vaira 2003). Following the removal of higher education from the ambit of the Ministry of Public Education and its placement under the newly established Ministry of University and Scientific Research, the centralized budget system was replaced by lump-sum budgets and increased discretion for the universities in 1993. The National Committee for the Evaluation of the University System was established in 1999. On the other hand, university regional committees have been established to coordinate and plan university development to meet the needs of local clients. Additionally, short-cycle vocational and technical tracks have been established within the universities. These reforms aimed at making Italian universities more responsive to the needs of a national economy that can compete in the global market have the support of *Confindustria*, the major employers' association, but Vaira (2003) argues that their success ultimately depends on how willing academia is to adopt the new entrepreneurial culture.

Portuguese legislation, The University Autonomy Act of 1988, allows for the participation of external members up to a maximum of 15 percent of the membership in the senates of the universities. Although it is mandatory for the polytechnics to have external members in their governing bodies, it is up to the universities to opt for that. So far, six old universities with deeply rooted traditions have not allowed external participation in their senates (Amaral and Magalhes 2002).

Several conclusions can be reached from the foregoing analysis that concern the relative roles that the state, the academic oligarchy, and the market and society play in the governance of national higher education systems. The French, the Spanish, the Italian, and the Portuguese higher education systems, despite the presence of nonacademic lay members in councils at the national level and in some of the institutional boards, are still very closely located to the state–academic oligarchy axis in Clark's triangle of coordination. Lay members play no role in the Greek system, which is therefore strictly located on the said axis. The Turkish system moved slightly away from that axis with the legislation enacted in 1981, which, in principle, allows lay members in the Council of Higher Education. Nevertheless, the Turkish system is still under the financial yoke of the state bureaucracy on the one hand, and the guild-like interests of the academic oligarchy on the other.

Elsewhere, lay governance is on the rise. Where it has been in existence, it has been enhanced, or it has been introduced in a number of countries where it did not exist before. The establishment of quality assessment agencies by legislation and the presence of nonacademics in such bodies in itself is a manifestation of the spread of lay governance as a global phenomenon.

After the changes in Australia in 1988, in the words of Mollis and Marginson (2002, 322):

> Universities were urged to reduce governing councils to boards of directors. Though internal representation survived, council sizes were reduced, and traditional collegial bodies became marginal, supervising academic standards, but losing involvement in resource matters. By the second half of the 1990s, corporate organization

had been secured in every Australian university, coexisting uneasily with academic cultures. The decisive element was the power of the executive leaders, drawn mostly from academic ranks, but imbued with a new spirit of enterprise.

The new universities in the United Kingdom that were established by the transformation of the former polytechnics by the Higher and Further Education Act of 1992 have a more streamlined governance structure. The highest decision-making organ in the new universities is the board of governors rather than the council. The law authorizes the secretary of state for education, rather than the Privy Council, to approve the governance structures of the new universities and stipulates that the number of members of governing boards cannot be less than twelve and more than twenty-four, and that at least half of them must be drawn from outside academia. The chairperson of the board must be a layperson, and the number of board members appointed by the senate and those elected by the students is restricted to a maximum of two each. Sizer and Howells (2000) contrast the "managerial model" of governance in the new universities with the "collegial model" of the old universities. Reed (2002), on the other hand, points out the increasing managerial and bureaucratic control that has permeated UK universities, both old and new, and the emergence of "manager academics." Reed's description of the changes in UK higher education is strikingly similar to that of Mollis and Marginson concerning Australian higher education. Fulton (2002) underlines another striking feature of rising lay governance in British higher education, where the funding councils now require all governing bodies to set up committees controlled by or made up of external members for audit, remuneration of senior staff, and nomination of new governors—a model of governance drawn directly from "good practice" recommended for private sector corporations.

The ultimate responsibility for decision making in the incorporated national university in Japan rests with the university president, who will control internal appointments with the power to fire when necessary, budget, and even pay scales. The minister appoints the president nominated as a candidate by a selection committee consisting of both internal and external members, that is, nonacademic, lay members (Goodman 2005; Hatakenaka 2005; OECD 2003b). However, Japanese reforms have been criticized for not going more in the direction of lay governance. The majority of the members in the newly formed management councils (*keiei kyogikai*) in national universities are external, but these councils are advisory to the presidents together with the research councils (*kyoiku kenkyu kyogikai*), which comprise senior academics only, and presidents do not report to these councils. The board of directors (*yakuinkai*), on the other hand, includes vice presidents appointed by the president, and is essentially an internal management organ (Hatakenaka 2005).

With respect to the presence of external members in the governance of higher education, the picture that has emerged in northern Europe is completely different from that in southern Europe. In 1993, the previously mentioned Board of Universities and Colleges was abolished in Sweden, and universities were transformed into entities that are now, legally, agencies under the government, but independent from direct ministerial interference. A governing board is established in each university, comprising nine members directly appointed by the government, two elected by the academic staff, and three student representatives. The rector is appointed by the government from outside the institution on the recommendation of the board after consultation with the academic staff. Initially, the rector chaired the board and acted as the chief executive officer of the institution. Since 1997, the board is chaired by a "well-qualified and experienced external personality," who is not employed at the institution and is appointed by the government. It is up to the board to decide on the inner structure of the institution. Institutions sign contracts with the government that include specific numbers of students in each program in each university, which are determined according to labor market forecasts. Funding from public sources is based on formulae that include student numbers as well as output parameters, and is in the form of lump sums in five areas corresponding to teaching disciplines. Research funding is almost entirely competitive. Academic evaluation and assessment is carried out by the *Hoghskoleverket*, which was created to replace the Board of Universities and Colleges, and which comprises eleven members appointed by the government. However, funding is not linked to the outcomes of assessment and evaluation. As institutions were given more discretionary powers, the academic staff expected that this would be accompanied by a similar devolution of power within the institution. What emerged, however, were a strengthened central administration, rectors with more executive powers and a move away from collegial decision making (Askling 2001; OECD 2003b).

The current Dutch legislation (*Het Bestuur en de Intrichting van de operbare Universiteiten*) was enacted in 1997. According to the new law, the minister of education appoints a "supervisory board" (*raad van toezicht*) for each institution comprising five members all drawn from outside academia. The board, in turn, appoints an institutional executive board (*college van bestuur*), which now comprises the rector and two external members. The senate (*universiteitsraad*), which formerly had considerable decision-making powers, is now a consultative organ to the board (de Boer 2002; de Boer and Goodegebuure 2001; Maassen 2000, 2002; OECD 2003b).

Funding from public sources in the Netherlands is also in the form of a lump-sum budget, but based on a simpler formula than the one used in Sweden. Additionally, students pay fees, which make the student demand much more cost-conscious. Research funding is, like Sweden, almost completely competitive. As opposed to Sweden, funding is increasingly being linked to the outcomes of assessment and evaluation. Niklasson (1996) has compared the new governance arrangements in Sweden and the Netherlands with those in the United Kingdom and Australia, as examples of introduction of market mechanisms, and has concluded that all of the four cases correspond to "quasi-markets." Furthermore, Niklasson has also underlined the move toward more powerful institutional heads in all four countries, and concluded that the difference between the British and the Continental models of university governance is diminishing.

In Denmark, governing boards with a majority of external members have been established and given the authority to appoint rectors and deans (Rektorkollegiate 2003), and nonacademic members are now being appointed to institutional governing boards in growing numbers in Norway (Norwegian Council for Higher Education 2002).

The Austrian reform process, which started in 1993, has produced a radical restructuring of higher education in a country that had what could possibly be characterized as the epitome of a classical continental European governance system. The law enacted in 2002 established a university council in each university as its highest governing body comprising only external members, and with the power to appoint and dismiss rectors. The new law also terminates the status of academic and administrative staff as civil servants. Funding arrangements are changed from line-item budgets to lump-sum budgets based on input and output parameters specified in target agreements between the ministry and the institutions. Universities are allowed to set up foundations, companies, and other business enterprises (Federal Ministry of Education Science and Culture, 2002).

In Germany in 1998, the Lander were given more freedom in structuring their institutions of higher education. The Lower Saxony University Reform Act of June 24, 2002, gives universities the choice of remaining a state institution or being transformed into a foundation as a legally self-governing body financially supported by the state. The financial support to be provided by the state is based on the achievement of specific targets laid out in a contract signed between the state and the institution, and built into the budget approved by the parliament. A supervisory board replaces ministerial control, which in the past included the appointment of professors from a short list of three candidates proposed by the university. Board members are appointed by the minister of education of Lower Saxony on the advice of the senate of the university concerned. The change into this status requires a two-thirds majority vote in the university senate; so far, five universities, including Göttingen, have opted for the new status (Palandt 2003).

In January 2004, the Social Democrat-Greens coalition government of Chancellor Schroder announced its intention to transform at least ten universities into "elite" institutions that can compete in the "global premiere league of higher education" with the likes of Harvard and Stanford. German higher education is considered to be under-funded, inefficient, overly dependent on the state and not competitive with rivals in the United States, the United Kingdom and France (Hochstettler 2004; Labi 2005b; OBHE-BN, January 2004). The so-called Excellence Initiative aims to improve the research performance and international competitiveness of German universities by injecting $2.3 billion into a small number of institutions over five years. The project includes competitive proposals to establish graduate schools in and research clusters comprising research institutes, companies, and government agencies around universities. The project has been continued under the present coalition, and the preliminary round of competitive bidding was concluded in January 2006 (Labi 2006a).

The foregoing discussion and the analysis of Amaral, Jones, and Karseth (2002) indicate that there is a worldwide trend toward convergence of the continental European, the British, and the American models of governance. In the author's opinion, the trend is in the direction of the former two models to become more like the American model. According to Marginson (1996), in the current globalizing environment institutions worldwide are overshadowed by the American system, and are under pressure to shape their developments according to the model of the global university, which is generally perceived to be the American model. Mora (2001) characterizes recent developments in higher education governance as the emergence of what he refers to as the "universal university model"—the birth of a third model after the medieval university and the modern university system. Neave (2005) argues that the "commodification" of higher education, that is, higher education conceived as a tradable and purchasable good, is the major strategic change that is shaping all aspects of higher education worldwide. Given this fact, the American system, by far and away the most enduring example of higher education driven by market forces, is now serving as the "world referential model" in a manner somewhat similar to the Napoleonic, the Humboldtian and the British models in the nineteenth and the twentieth centuries.

One can argue that this stems from the generally perceived superiority of the American model. McDaniel's (1996) work on comparative governance systems shows that American public institutions have clear advantages over their European counterparts, including those in the United Kingdom. These advantages manifest themselves in the areas of less earmarked funds in institutional budgets provided by legislatures, authority to borrow money in the capital market, determination of salaries and admission of students. *The Economist*, in a supplement entitled "The Knowledge Factory," October 4, 1997 (22), had this to say about American higher education:

> The unique advantages of America's universities go beyond the hybrid vigor of a system in which private and state institutions have all been allowed to seek out their competitive advantage. Much of the system's success derives from the readiness of American academics to let market forces work. In contrast to most countries, where pay is centrally negotiated, competing American campuses strive to outbid one another for talent. How ready are academics in Continental Europe and Japan to accept such a free-for-all?

Shanghai Jiao Tong University has been ranking world universities regularly since 2003 (academic ranking of world universities, ARWU).[41] Results of the last four years are summarized in Table 3.1. The United States has been consistently at the top by a wide margin, followed by the United Kingdom. Seventeen of the top 20, 54 of the top 100, and 159 of the top 500 universities were U.S. institutions in 2008. The corresponding numbers for UK institutions were 2, 11, and 42, respectively. Cambridge, Oxford, and Tokyo universities were the three non-U.S. institutions in the top twenty. It also is interesting to note that nearly half of the universities in the top 500 are in the United States, the United Kingdom, Australia, Canada, and New Zealand, collectively designated as the MESDCs for foreign students.

The *Times Higher Education Supplement* (THES) rankings of universities are based on five indicators that reflect strength in teaching, research, and international reputation. Results from 2006 to 2008 are shown in Table 3.2. In 2008, of the first ten institutions, six were in the United States and four in the United Kingdom. Of the 200 universities ranked, 58 were American, 29 British, 13 Canadian, 11 Japanese, 10 Dutch, and 9 each Australian and German institutions. The MESDCs collectively accounted for 58 percent of the top two hundred universities in the world.

In a comprehensive recent survey of higher education worldwide by *The Economist* ("Brains Business," September 8 2005), the state of Europe's higher education is described as a "threat to its competitiveness." The remedy recommended is a radical move from a state-dominated toward a market-oriented system with tuition fees, a diversified revenue base and changed hiring practices. Institutions in Spain and France hire 95 and 50 percent of

Table 3.1. International Classification of Universities, Shanghai Jiao Tong

Country	2008			2007			2006			2005		
	20	100	500	20	100	500	20	100	500	20	100	500
U.S.	17	54	159	17	54	166	17	54	167	17	53	168
UK	2	11	42	2	11	42	2	11	43	2	11	40
Japan	1	4	31	1	6	33	1	6	32	1	5	34
Germany	—	6	40	—	6	41	—	5	40	—	5	40
Canada	—	4	21	—	4	22	—	4	22	—	4	23
France	—	4	23	—	4	23	—	4	21	—	4	21
Sweden	—	3	11	—	4	11	—	4	11	—	4	11
Switzerland	—	2	8	—	3	8	—	3	8	—	3	8
Netherlands	—	2	12	—	2	12	—	2	12	—	2	12
Australia	—	3	15	—	2	17	—	2	16	—	2	14
China	—	—	30	—	—	25	—	3	19	—	—	18
Italy	—	—	22	—	—	20	—	1	23	—	1	23
Spain	—	—	9	—	—	9	—	1	9	—	—	9
Korea	—	—	8	—	—	8	—	1	9	—	—	8
Austria	—	—	7	—	—	7	—	1	7	—	1	6
Israel	—	1	6	—	1	7	—	1	7	—	1	7
Denmark	—	2	4	—	1	4	—	1	5	—	1	5
Norway	—	1	4	—	1	4	—	1	4	—	1	4
Finland	—	1	6	—	1	5	—	1	5	—	1	5
Russia	—	1	2	—	1	2	—	1	2	—	1	2
Belgium	—	—	7	—	—	7	—	4	7	—	1	7
Brazil	—	—	6	—	—	5	—	1	4	—	—	4
Singapore	—	—	2	—	—	2	—	1	2	—	—	2

Argentina	1	—	1	—	1	1	—	1
Mexico	1	—	1	—	1	1	—	1
New Zealand	5	—	5	—	5	—	—	5
South Africa	3	—	4	—	4	—	—	4
Ireland	3	—	3	—	3	—	—	3
Czech Republic	1	—	1	—	1	—	—	1
Greece	2	—	2	—	2	—	—	2
Hungary	2	—	2	—	2	—	—	2
Poland	2	—	2	—	2	—	—	3
India	2	—	2	—	2	—	—	3
Chile	2	—	2	—	1	—	—	1
Slovenia	1	—	1	—	1	—	—	1
Egypt	—	—	1	—	1	—	—	—
Turkey	1	—	1	—	1	—	—	2
Portugal	2	—	2	—	2	—	—	1

Sources: http://ed.sjtu.edu.cn/rank/2005/ARWU2008Statistics.htm; http://ed.sjtu.edu.cn/rank/2006/ARWU2007Statistics.htm; http://ed.sjtu.edu.cn/rank/2005/ARWU2006Statistics.htm; http://ed.sjtu.edu.cn/rank/2005/ARWU2005Statistics.htm.

Table 3.2. The Times Higher Education Supplement Classification

Country	2008				2007				2006			
	10	50	100	200	10	50	100	200	10	50	100	200
U.S.	6	20	37	58	6	21	38	59	7	22	33	55
UK	4	8	17	29	4	8	19	32	3	8	15	29
Australia	—	6	7	9	—	6	8	12	—	6	7	13
Canada	—	3	5	12	—	3	6	11	—	3	3	7
Japan	—	3	4	10	—	2	3	10	—	2	3	11
Hong Kong	—	3	3	4	—	2	3	4	—	1	3	4
Netherlands	—	—	4	11	—	1	4	11	—	—	7	11
Germany	—	—	3	11	—	—	3	11	—	—	3	10
Switzerland	—	2	3	6	—	1	1	4	—	2	5	7
China	—	—	2	6	—	2	3	5	—	2	2	6
France	—	2	2	4	—	2	2	5	—	2	5	7
Sweden	—	—	2	4	—	—	1	4	—	—	—	4
New Zealand	—	—	1	3	—	1	1	3	—	—	2	2
Denmark	—	1	2	3	—	—	1	3	—	—	1	3
Korea	—	1	2	3	—	—	1	2	—	—	1	3
Belgium	—	—	1	5	—	—	1	5	—	—	2	5
Israel	—	—	1	3	—	—	—	2	—	—	—	3
Singapore	—	1	2	2	—	1	2	2	—	1	2	2
Ireland	—	1	1	2	—	1	1	2	—	—	1	1
Finland	—	—	1	1	—	—	1	2	—	—	—	1
India	—	—	—	1	—	—	—	—	—	—	2	3
Austria	—	—	—	1	—	—	1	2	—	—	1	3
Russia	—	—	—	1	—	—	—	—	—	—	1	2

Spain	—	—	—	1	—	—	—	—	1
Norway	—	—	—	1	—	—	—	—	1
Taiwan	—	—	—	1	—	—	—	—	1
Mexico	—	—	—	1	—	1	—	—	1
Greece	—	—	—	1	—	—	—	—	—
Thailand	—	—	—	1	2	—	—	1	1
Brazil	—	—	—	1	—	—	—	—	—
South Africa	—	—	—	1	2	—	—	—	1
Italy	—	—	—	—	2	—	—	—	1
Malaysia	—	—	—	—	—	—	—	—	2

Source: www.timeshighereducation.co.uk.

their faculty members from among their own alumni, respectively, compared with 7 percent in the United States, and only 2 percent of the academic staff in France is foreign-born.

Salmi (2009) recently redefined national higher education systems to include a new category of institutions, which he labels as "world-class," "elite," or "flagship" universities. Salmi relies on the ARWU and the THES ranking to identify the characteristics of these "globally competitive universities," and points out that these institutions are concentrated in a small number of Anglo-Saxon (United States, United Kingdom, Australia, Canada, and New Zealand) and western European (Netherlands, Finland, Norway, Sweden, Denmark, Switzerland, France, and Germany)[42] countries, with Japan, China, Hong Kong, and Singapore as the only exceptions.[43] According to Salmi (2009, 7), the success of these institutions result from the following three sets of factors:

> (a) a high concentration of talent (faculty and students), (b) abundant resources to offer a rich learning environment and to conduct advanced research, and (c) favorable governance features that encourage strategic vision, innovation, and flexibility and that enable institutions to make decisions and to manage resources without being encumbered by bureaucracy.

An OECD survey (2003b) concludes that governments in many OECD countries have reformed their governance structures well beyond what one would expect the prevailing academic cultures would have allowed them to do. Consequently, university autonomy has been redefined. In addition to classical elements of autonomy, institutions now have the power to own their buildings and equipment, borrow funds, spend budgets to achieve their objectives, set academic structure and course contents, employ and dismiss academic staff, set salaries, decide the size of student enrollment, and decide the level of tuition fees. Thus, the weight of indicators that are used in measuring university autonomy has clearly shifted from classical ones such as the power to elect university heads toward indicators that measure financial and human resource management powers.

I have provided several cases from a number of countries that illustrate the changed view on university governance worldwide. These changes in governance structures have been summarized by OECD as follows (OECD 2003b, 71–72):

> Key common elements have been a transfer of power to the rector, vice-chancellor and other leading administrative figures, and a loss of authority and decision-making power on the part of traditional

participatory and collegial bodies. . . . Although election of university leaders still continues in a number of countries, the trend seems to be moving towards appointment, often by a board with a majority of external members.

More recently, OECD (2007, 13–14) has reiterated these views with the following somewhat stronger words:

> What is clear is that, for now at least, the demand for more and better education continues to rise, with still substantial payoffs in terms of earnings and productivity gains. And enrolments continue to grow in OECD countries, with more than 50 percent—in some countries more than seventy-five percent of high school graduates now entering university-level education. . . . For tertiary education, this means creating and maintaining a system of diverse, sustainable and high-quality institutions with the freedom to respond to demand and accountability for outcomes they produce. It means ensuring that the growth and development of tertiary educational systems are managed in ways that improve access and enhance quality. And it means that universities will have to evolve so that their leadership and management capacity matches that of modern enterprises. Much greater use needs to be made of appropriate strategic financial and human resource management techniques in order to ensure long-term financial sustainability and meet accountability requirements. Institutions must be governed by bodies that have the ability to think strategically and reflect a much wider range of stakeholder interests than only the academic community.

In the early 1990s, Clark Kerr made the following remarks concerning university autonomy:

> For the first time, a really international world of learning, highly competitive, is emerging. If you want to get into that orbit, you have to do so, on merit. You cannot rely on politics or anything else. You have to give a good deal of autonomy to institutions for them to be dynamic and to move fast in international competition. You have to develop entrepreneurial leadership to go along with institutional autonomy.[44]

It does appear that Kerr's prophecy has been fulfilled. The new paradigms of higher education are meritocracy and entrepreneurialism rather than democracy and egalitarianism. Many academics worldwide are highly critical of the new paradigms of higher education. Frank Newman, on the other hand, has offered the following view:

> The Futures Project does not advocate creating a market in higher education; rather the project's research has led to the conclusion that the market has arrived, and higher education institutions should acknowledge its existence and respond thoughtfully and effectively. (Newman et al. 2004, 104)

3.5. THE RISE OF MARKET FORCES IN RELATION TO INTERNATIONAL STUDENT MOBILITY

This chapter has been mainly concerned with the ways in which globalization and the worldwide shift to free-market economy has affected the governance and financing of traditional institutions of higher education. What has been paraphrased as "the rise of market forces" in the last decades of the previous century has manifested itself in higher education in the form of resource diversification and increasing reliance on tuition fees in public institutions, expanding share of private institutions in national higher education systems, and diffusion of practices from the world of business to the governance and administration of institutions of higher education, both public and private.

This transformation has come at a time of increasing demand for some form of postsecondary education worldwide, changing the view of the role and functions of the state and the resulting decrease in public subsidies. Institutions of higher education in many countries have been given freedom to generate resources, combine them with state subsidies, and use them as they see fit. In return, they are increasingly being held accountable by quantifiable output indicators, much like business enterprises in a free-market economy.

As far as families are concerned, the result has been an increase in their contribution to expenditures on institutions of higher education. Data presented in Table A.3 show that there are still large differences in annual costs of higher education in different countries and between public and private universities. For example, the average annual cost in a private institution in the United States, the leading host country for foreign students, is more than sixty times that in a public institution in China, the leading country of origin for foreign students. But that difference is only threefold between a private institution in the United States and a private institution in China—much smaller, but still significant. It appears that cost differential is just one of the factors affecting international student mobility.

On the other hand, the governance system in a given country seems to be a major factor influencing institutions' eagerness to recruit foreign students. Institutions in countries like the United States, the United Kingdom, Australia, and New Zealand that are closer to the market apex in Clark's triangle of coordination have the incentives and the means to act entrepreneurially in the global higher education market.

The next chapter deals with the impact of technology on higher education. New technologies have changed not only curricular contents, but also the methods by which higher education is provided and the ways in which institutions are structured. Chapter 4 is, in a way, a continuation of this chapter for three reasons. First, the impact of technology would not have been as strong in a more strictly regulated environment. Second, technology has made it possible for "new types of providers" to emerge, which have led to increased competition in the global higher education market. Third, ICT has affected traditional institutions, too, both pedagogically and organizationally.

FOUR

NEW PROVIDERS OF HIGHER EDUCATION

4.1. INTRODUCTION

The word *provider* is used as a generic term to include all types of higher education institutions as well as companies and networks that are increasingly involved in higher education and services related to it. Knight (2005a) uses the following four key factors to describe different categories of providers: (1) whether the provider is public, private, or religious; (2) whether it is nonprofit or for-profit; (3) whether it is recognized by a bona fide national licensing or accrediting body; and (4) whether it is part of the national "home" higher education system. On this basis, she identifies six categories. The first category comprises "traditional institutions," which can be public, private, or religious and are recognized as such by a bona fide domestic licensing or accrediting body as part of the home higher education system.[1]

"Nonrecognized" higher education institutions comprise the second group and are usually private and for-profit. Most are low quality and seek accreditation from bodies that sell a label. These are referred to as "rogue providers," which are different from "diploma mills" that only sell a degree without bothering to provide any education.

"Commercial company higher education institutions" are in general for-profit. Some of them are owned by traditional institutions, or they can be privately owned and publicly traded. They can be recognized institutions as part of the home national education system. They can be degree-awarding institutions or provide training that lead to certificates. They can be directly involved in the provision of education or are active in services related to education or both.

"Corporate higher education institutions" are part of major international conglomerates; they provide education and training for their employees. They are generally not a part of the national education system, but are increasingly regarded as such with increasing recognition of the importance of LLL. In general, they do not award degrees, although some of them are doing so in collaboration with traditional institutions or with new providers, which have degree-awarding powers.

"Networks" are partnerships that can be any combination of institutions, both traditional and newer type, and commercial enterprises.

"Virtual higher education institutions" deliver education by distance education methods, increasingly online, with, in some cases, face-to-face provision at designated centers. They may or may not be recognized as part of the home national education system.

New types of higher education providers have at least one of the following attributes: (1) they are for-profit; (2) they cater to nontraditional and/or foreign students in the international education market; and (3) they rely on technology for the provision of education and student services (CVCP-HEFCE 2000; Futures Project 2000c, 2002; Knight 2005a; Mendivil 2002; Morey 2004; Newman et al. 2004, 18–24; Persell and Wenglinsky 2004; Ryan and Stedman 2002; World Bank 2002, 32–41).

4.2. IMPACT OF TECHNOLOGY

Scientific and technological developments have been continuously changing curricula, syllabi, and research interests for centuries. Neither is the use of technology in the organization and delivery of education an entirely new phenomenon. Distance education, where the student and the instructor are in face-to-face contact during only part of the process, had started immediately after the establishment of postal delivery systems in the nineteenth century in England, France, and Germany. The first distance education program at the tertiary level began in Chicago University in 1897. By 1919, seventy American universities had launched correspondence courses, and were competing against three hundred private correspondence schools ("Brains Business," *The Economist*, September 8, 2005). Similar programs were started in Australia in 1911, in the USSR in 1926, and in South Africa in 1946 (Gürüz 2001, 143–8).

Open University in the United Kingdom provided the prototype for the first generation of distance education institutions; similar institutions were later established in many countries all over the world. The Labor Government of Prime Minister Harold Wilson founded Open University in 1969 as a low-cost alternative to meet the increasing demand for post-secondary education, especially for adults who had previously missed out on the opportunity of accessing tertiary-level education. Open University is the first of its kind, an independent institution with the power to award degrees. The first students were admitted in January 1971, and began work on their first units of the first foundation courses. By the end of the 1970s, enrollment had reached seventy thousand, and some six thousand were graduating each year (Open University 2005). Presently, Open University with a total home enrollment of 176,560 students in the 2006–2007 academic year, is by far the largest institution of higher education in the United Kingdom, and accounts for 7 percent of the national higher education enrollment.[2]

Faced with growing demand for higher education, many countries emulated the British model and founded distance education institutions. The names and the dates of foundation of some of these institutions Air and Correspondence University, Korea (f. 1972); *Universidad Nacional de Education Distancia*, Spain (*UNED*, f. 1972); Allama Iqbal Open University, Pakistan (f. 1974); *Ha'Universita Ha'Pethuo*, Israel (f. 1973); *Fern Universitat*, Germany (f. 1974); Athabasca University, Canada (1975); University of the Air, Japan, (f. 1975), *Universidad Estatal a Distancia*, Costa Rica (f. 1977); *Universidad Nacional Abierda*, Venezuela (f. 1977); Sukhotai Thammathirat Open University (STOU), Thailand (f. 1978); *Universita della terza Eta e del tempo disponibile*, Italy (f. 1978); Central Radio and TV University, China (f. 1960, renamed 1979); *Open Universiteit*, Netherlands (f. 1981); Institute of Distance Education, Sri Lanka (f. 1981); *Anadolu Üniversitesi Açıköğretim Fakültesi* (AÜAÖF), Turkey (f. 1982); *Universitas Terbuka*, Indonesia (f. 1984); Indira Gandhi National Open University (IGNOU), India (f. 1985); National Open University, Taiwan (f. 1986); Al-Quds Open University, Jordan (f. 1987); *Centre National d'Enseignment a Distance*, France (*CNED*, f. 1987, dates back to the 1940s); *Universidade Aberta*, Portugal (f. 1988); Open University of Hong Kong (f. 1989); University of the Philippines Open University (f. 1995); Open University of Malaysia (f. 2002); the Saudi-initiated Arab Open University (AOU) with branches in Bahrain, Egypt, Jordan, Kuwait and Saudi Arabia (f. 2002), SIM University, Singapore (UniSIM, f. 2005), and the Brazilian Open University founded as part of the reform package of 2006.

By the beginning of the 1990s, many countries had established institutions of distance education as components of their higher education systems. These were, in general, public agencies using a mix of technologies, both synchronous and asynchronous types, including correspondence by mail, radio and TV broadcasts, telephony, video cassettes, videoconferencing, and so forth, as well as face-to-face instruction.

The World Bank (2003, 51) reports values for the share of distance education in the higher education systems of various countries in the mid-1990s; these vary from 2 percent for France to 11 percent in India, 13 percent in Korea, 18 percent in Indonesia, 24 percent in China, 26 percent in Turkey,[3] and 37 percent in Thailand. Cost data reported by the World Bank show that unit costs in distance education programs in various countries varied from 13 to 73 percent of those in regular full-time programs, with 40 percent as a somewhat more representative value.

Some of these institutions actually predate the UK Open University that has served as the model for their present structures and missions, such as the University of South Africa, which traces its origins to the University of the Cape of Good Hope (f. 1873), the CNED in France, which started in the 1940s to provide education to children displaced by the war, and the China TV University (CTVU), founded in 1960, renamed in 1979. These universities come in various sizes and shapes. The CTVU is a four-layered national network of distance education comprising 44 provincial TV universities, 575 regional TV universities and 1,550 education centers. It is the largest learning system in the world, enrolling more than 3 million learners. IGNOU in India enrolls approximately 1.8 million students, AÜAÖF in Turkey has close to 900,000 students, and STOU in Thailand 500,000 students, 200,000 of whom are enrolled in degree programs. Because of their enrollment size, they are referred to as "mega universities." These institutions, in general, cater to nontraditional students that include adults who have missed out and those in LLL programs as well as to traditional students in degree programs (Daniel 1996; Murphy, Zhang, and Perris 2003). Currently, the *Handbook of Open Universities* lists fifty-nine such open universities in the world.[4] All of the institutions just listed are public institutions.

Then came the Internet and there is now general agreement worldwide that the advanced information and communication technologies may be the single greatest force for change in higher education worldwide (Green et al. 2002; Newman and Scurry 2001; Oblinger et al. 2001).

In 1994, only 35 percent of the U.S. public schools at the primary and the secondary levels had Internet access; by 1999, that ratio had grown to 95 percent. The percentage of instructional rooms with Internet access had increased from 3 to 63 percent in the same period (Newman and Scurry 2001). In 2000, 98 percent of the schools in the United States had Internet access, whereas 77 percent of the classrooms were connected, and virtually all full-time regular teachers in public schools had access to computers or the Internet somewhere in their schools. The rate of growth of Internet use in the United States is currently 2 million new users per month, more than half the nation is online, and about two thirds of the population use computers (NPEC 2004). As of June 2002, 15 percent of U.S. high schools were offering virtual courses, and twenty-six states had started virtual high schools, with enrollments as high as seven thousand in Florida and five thousand in Massachusetts (Futures Project 2002). By 2002, 50 percent of the U.S. households had Internet connection, compared to a world average of 3 percent in that year (van der Wende 2002). Worldwide, close to 2 billion people are using the Internet.

According to the surveys regularly carried out by the Institute of Education Sciences of the National Center for Education Statistics since the mid-1990s, in the 1997–1998 academic year, 34 percent of the accredited degree-granting postsecondary education institutions in the United States were offering online courses. In the 2000–2001 academic year, this ratio had increased to 56 percent, and was 66 percent in the 2006–2007 survey. Total student enrollments in the same academic years were 1,661,000, 3,077,000, and 12,200,000, respectively. In the 1997–1998 academic year, 1,230 degree and 340 certificate programs were offered completely online. The numbers in the subsequent two surveys were 2,810 degree and 1,330 certificate programs in 2000–2001, and 7,418 degree and 3,822 certificate programs in 2006–2007 (Lewis, Snow, and Farris 2000; Parsad and Lewis 2009; Walts and Lewis 2003). The growth observed in all three indicators in the past decade is staggering.

The World Bank (2002, 14–16) draws attention to the difference between the developed and the developing countries in terms of the availability of and the access to ICT, referred to as the "digital divide." Such differences exist not only among countries, but also within countries, such as between different ethnic groups, between the male and the female, and between the young and the old; the latter is referred to as the "generational divide, "and is quite distinct even in developed countries. Recent data, however, indicate that the ICT sector of the developing world, particularly Africa, is expanding at an explosive rate. The private sector is leading the growth (OBHE-BN, March 2005), and multimillion-dollar projects and investments are underway aimed at bolstering the ICT capabilities of diverse countries extending from Argentina and Mexico in Latin America (Garcia-Guadillo et al. 2002; OBHE-BN, December 2004) to Jordan in the Middle East (OBHE-BN, September 2004). Although in the past decade ICT has penetrated developing countries, the data shown in Table 1.3 clearly shows that the digital divide still exists.

The newly developed ICT revolutionized not only distance education, but also the ways in which institutions of higher education are organized and governed, as well as the methods and the techniques used in the provision of the education itself.

The new generation of students coming to institutions of higher education all over the world are growing up increasingly exposed to and using these technologies. They feel much more comfortable in front of the blue screen of a computer than facing a blackboard or reading a book; the cell phone is a part of their lives (Newman and Scurry 2001). Younger generations worldwide are generally much more "e-literate" compared with older ones—the generational divide, which I alluded to previously. According to research carried out in the United Kingdom, students prefer to access information on the Internet, rather than buying hard copies of course books (OBHE-BN, February 2002). High school students increasingly are coming to higher education institutions in the United States having already taken a number of freshman-level courses online and asking to be given credit for them (Newman and Couturier 2001). Even more striking is the new cohort born in the period between 1980 and 1994. Referred to as the "millenials," and equipped with an amazing arsenal of electronic devices, they expect to be able to choose what kind of education they buy, and what, where and how they learn (Carlson 2005; "Too much information," special report, *Newsweek* (intl. ed.), double issue, August 25–September 1, 2003).

Thus, between 1995 and 2000, a new industry emerged, called "e-learning," which uses advanced ICT for delivery, mainly the Internet and the World Wide Web. Many in the industry predicted that e-learning would be the next great Internet application, which would dwarf e-mail. Such forecasts were based on predictions that the physical campus would be diminished or it would disappear altogether. The demise of traditional campus universities and face-to-face interaction is not in sight, and the majority of the educators worldwide believe that nothing can be substituted for the human touch.

What did emerge, however, is a global market for education in general and postsecondary education and training in particular. Along with new types of providers, "distributed learning," "virtual arms," and "unbundling of services" emerged as new methods of delivery and organizational forms in traditional institutions in the increasingly competitive global higher education market.

4.3. IMPACT OF TECHNOLOGY ON TRADITIONAL INSTITUTIONS

4.3.1. Distributed Learning

The term *unbundling* of services refers to the separation of the teaching, research, and service functions of institutions of higher education. In particular, it implies the separation of teaching, which is potentially the most profitable of the three functions. The concept also implies outsourcing of the various services traditionally carried out by institutions, such as admission and library services, even course preparation, to vendors who use new ICT.

Recent surveys indicate that e-learning has changed higher education, not as a replacement for the physical campus, but as a supplement to the classroom. Hybrid environments are emerging in which the line between classroom and online instruction is blurred. Oblinger et al. (2001) refer to this type of learning environments as "distributed learning," which they define as a platform based on ICT where faculty and students interact for learning anywhere, on campus or off campus, and at any time. They also point out that distance learning is a subset of distributed learning, focusing on students who may be separated in time and space from their peers and the instructor. Thus, what is happening on campuses all over the world today is not an extension of the distance education in institutions of the type described here rather an augmenting of traditional provision of higher education by advanced ICT (Futures Project 2002; Newman and Couturier 2001; Ryan and Stedman 2002; Stella and Gnanam 2004).

The United States is the undisputed leader in e-learning. In the 1994–1995 academic year, there were an estimated 753,640 students enrolled in courses delivered online at accredited two- and four-year institutions in the United States (Newman and Couturier 2001; Newman and Scurry 2001). In the 1997–1998 academic year, enrollment in online courses had more than doubled to 1,661,000, with 1,343,580 of the students enrolled in such courses for credit (Lewis et al. 2000; NCES 2004; Newman and Couturier 2001). Student enrollment in online courses in the United States was predicted to rise to 2.2 million by 2002 (Futures Project 2002). Total course enrollments in 2000–2001, however, were 3,077,000, with growth particularly notable at public two-year institutions (NCES 2004; Walts and Lewis 2003). The total number of courses offered online in the 2001–2002 academic term was about 127,400 (NPEC 2004). In 2003, nearly 40 percent of instructional staff in U.S. institutions of higher education used e-learning technologies to supplement their teaching, up from 12 percent in 1999 and 30 percent in 2002 (Zastrocky et al. 2004). The figures reported by the National Center for Educational Statistics (NCES 2004; Walts and Lewis 2003) show that 56 percent of all postsecondary institutions in the United States offered online courses in 2000–2001, up from 34 percent three years earlier. Continued growth was expected with additional institutions planning to offer such courses. Indeed, the most recent statistics issued by NCES show that in 2006–2007, 66 percent of all accredited degree-granting postsecondary institutions in the United States were offering online courses to 12,153,000 students. In the 1997–1998 academic year, 1,230 degree and 340 certificate programs were offered completely online. The numbers in the subsequent two surveys were 2,810 degree and 1,330 certificate programs in 2000–2001, and 7,418 degree and 3,822 certificate programs in 2006–2007 (Lewis et al. 2000; Parsad and Lewis 2009; Walts and Lewis 2003). A survey sponsored by the Sloan Consortium showed that in 2005, 82 percent of all students in U.S. institutions had taken at least one course online during their studies (Allen and Seamann 2006, 5).

The growth observed in all three indicators in the past decade are staggering. The public sector is more likely than the private sector to offer courses online, with 97 percent of public two-year and 89 percent of public four-year institutions doing so in 2006–2007, versus 53 percent nonprofit four-year private institutions. Nonetheless, growth also is occurring in the private sector; the percentage of private four-year institutions offering online courses more than doubled between 1997–1998 and 2006–2007.

In the 2006–2007 survey, the most common factors cited as affecting distance education decisions to a major extent were meeting student demand for flexible schedules (68 percent of the institutions surveyed), providing access to college for students who would otherwise not have access (67 percent), making more courses available (46 percent), and seeking to increase student enrollment (45 percent). Asynchronous (not simultaneous or real time) Internet-based technologies were cited as the most widely used technology for the instructional delivery of distance education courses. Taken together, these two findings clearly show that the U.S. higher education institutions have indeed largely switched to a distributed teaching and learning environment. Furthermore, as almost all face-to-face courses now have some online component, such as message boards and chat rooms, the distinction between online courses and face-to-face courses is also becoming increasingly blurred.

All over the world, traditional institutions are delivering some of the courses in their curricula online, or are planning to do so. In the late 1990s and the early 2000s, more than half a million Canadians in the various adult education and training programs were doing part of their coursework through some form of distance learning (Green et al. 2002). In 2001, 57 percent of Canadian universities were offering some three thousand online courses (Stella and Gnanam 2004). By 2004, forty-four Canadian universities were offering courses online. In Australia, where 14 percent of university students studied online in 2003 (Stella and Gnanam 2004), the majority of courses offered online were at the graduate level, but more than 60 percent of the students enrolled in such courses were undergraduates (Olsen 2003). Surveys conducted in universities in twenty-six Commonwealth countries by Observatory on Borderless Higher Education (OBHE) in 2002, 2004, and 2006 show that some form of online provision is considerably up from what it was in 2002, and that online activity is significantly more intensive in English-speaking countries like Australia, United Kingdom, and Canada (Becker and Joikivirta 2007; OBHE-BfN, December 21, 2004).

In 2000, one in four Dutch universities were providing e-learning environments, and 90 percent were planning to do so. In Japan, as of 2001, 34 percent of the four-year institutions were using the Internet for online learning, 23 percent more were planning to do so, and 123 institutions had installed satellite communications systems for organizing seminars, lectures, and meetings. Furthermore, with more than one third of the Internet users worldwide in Asia, the open universities in Asia, which were mentioned previously, are increasingly switching to new technologies. In 2000, China started implementing the National Technology Plan. Sixty-seven universities, including leading institutions like Tsinghua and Beijing, were designated as "network-education colleges," and provided earmarked funding to develop and implement online learning. Beijing University had established its wireless campus in 2002 (OBHE-BfN 12, July 2003). In India, in addition to the IGNOU mentioned previously, there are ten other open universities and approximately sixty-two distance education directorates in traditional universities (Stella and Gnanam 2004). Most of the public universities in Mexico offer some form of online education (Mendivil 2002). The University of Kuopio in Finland established a virtual unit in 1999, and by 2004, had two hundred courses online. In 2004, Kuopio had 384 new courses in the pipeline, all based on WebCT technology (Bonk 2004).

National-level distance education institutions of the type discussed in the previous section increasingly are relying on advanced ICT, and new institutions referred to as "virtual universities," are emerging. A recently released policy paper by the Higher Education Funding Council for England (HEFCE), however, points to what may signal the beginning of a worldwide trend, that is, a shift from centralized initiatives such as national institutions for e-learning to supporting activities in individual campuses, with emphasis on developing new pedagogical methods that enable a fuller exploitation of the possibilities offered by technology (OBHE-BNA, March 24, 2005).[5]

It appears that a level of technology has been reached that present pedagogical methods are only partially able to use, much like the balance between the available hardware capabilities of the early 1990s and the then available software, which used only a small fraction of the former. The new approach by the HEFCE confirms the prediction by Oblinger et al. in 2001 that distributed learning rather than distance education will become the dominant paradigm for higher education. It was predicted that by the year 2009, more than half the courses offered in U.S. institutions of higher education will be a hybrid of face-to-face and online learning, with more than 80 percent of students using mobile/cell phone technology as a tool for learning (Zastrocky et al. 2004). No statistics were available at the time of writing of this book to prove or disprove this prediction. However, the previously mentioned NCES data on online course offerings in U.S. institutions in 2006-2007 indicate that this indeed is the case.

In other words, initial forecasts, which predicted that only two types of institutions, "brick universities" and "click universities" meaning purely traditional and purely virtual institutions, would survive, are proving to be untrue. Rather, what are emerging are "brick and click" universities, that is, hybrid institutions (van der Wende 2002).

4.3.2. Virtual Arms and Unbundling of Services in Traditional Institutions

Distributed learning is now an established feature of many of the traditional institutions in the developed countries. There are presently no technological barriers, but establishing the infrastructure may require significant invest-ment and may take years. Investments can exceed $1 million per course (Oblinger et al. 2001; Ryan and Stedman 2002). The support personnel involved in the preparation of online courses such as Web designers, data-base managers, graphic designers, and the like are in short supply, and need to be remunerated accordingly. Marketing of the product in an increasingly competitive environment, licensing of the course material and other prod-ucts developed along the way, student support services, and other activi-ties related to distributed learning and online delivery require governance structures that are very different from the traditional ones normally found in campuses. In any case, e-learning requires a cultural environment that is in many ways different from the cultural environment generally encountered in campuses; some go even as far as claiming that there is a contradiction between the core values of academia and the mindset required for successful e-learning ventures. For these reasons, traditional institutions have devel-oped three different types of structures to tackle the organizational aspects of distributed learning. Oblinger et al. (2001) have summarized these as follows:

1. Institutions like the University of Illinois, the University of Cal-ifornia–Berkeley, UCLA, the University of Texas, and SUNY have created separate units within their existing structures.

2. Monash University in Australia offers courses in a variety of modes, including off-campus learning. Sixteen percent of the students at Monash are enrolled in this type of program that requires little or no attendance at a teaching site.

3. Several universities have established nonprofit organizations that are separate from the institution. Michigan Virtual Uni-versity of Michigan University, World Campus of Pennsylvania State University, and the Learning Innovation Center of the University of Wisconsin are examples of this approach.

4. Many of the best-known universities in the United States, both public and nonprofit private, have established for-profit subsidiaries or joined with for-profit firms in joint educational enterprises. Some examples of the for-profit virtual arms of tra-ditional institutions are the following: iCarnegie (Carnegie Mel-lon), eCornell (Cornell University), NYUOnline (New York University), Duke Corporate Education Inc. (Duke University Fuqua School of Business), UMass Online (the University of Massachusetts), UMUC OnLine.com, Inc. (University of Mary-land), Virtual Temple (Temple University), Babson Interactive,

Inc. (Babson College) in the United States (Newman and Couturier 2001; OBHE-BN, June 2002), and MUP, the controversial private arm of Melbourne University (OBHE-BN, September 2003; OBHE-BN, August 2004). Such for-profit arms in China actually predate those in the United States. Some of the universities in the previously mentioned network-education colleges were permitted to establish private arms in order to market their online interests and research results as early as 1997, when Tsinghua Tongfang was listed in the Shanghai stock market.

The Massachusetts Institute of Technology (MIT), on the other hand, took an entirely different approach. Rather than going into business in learning, MIT made all its course material freely available online to any user anywhere in the world. MIT's OpenCourseWare (OCW) was launched in October 2002. OCW provides the content, but is not a substitute for an MIT education. It is simply a continuation of the tradition of open dissemination of educational materials in American public education in the age of the Internet and the World Wide Web (Futures Project 2002; OBHE-BN, October 2002; Ryan and Stedman 2002). Carnegie Mellon University followed in September 2003 by offering four introductory courses online free (OBHE-BN, September 2003).

For-profit virtual arms of traditional institutions have had mixed success. NYUOnline has closed as a separate division of NYU and has been absorbed into the School of Continuing and Professional Education. UMU-COnline was created in 1999 to market online courses and raise money to compete globally; however, its operations have recently been reorganized back into standard distance education programs (Newman and Couturier 2001). University of Maryland University College (UMUC) is now the Open University of Maryland, catering to the educational needs of nontraditional students. In 2009, it had an enrollment of more than 97,000, up from 15,673 in 1999. Forty-nine programs were offered that led to bachelor-, master- and doctoral-level degrees as well as a large number of certificate programs fully online. UMUC's overseas division offers on-site classes in twenty-three countries throughout the world, enrolling in excess of 70,000 students in undergraduate and graduate programs.[6] Temple University closed its virtual arm in 2001 because online programs could not pay for themselves, let alone make a profit (Ryan and Stedman 2002). The Michigan Virtual University (MVU) was founded in 1998 as the private, nonprofit virtual arm of Michigan University to widen access to online postsecondary education and training opportunities for the Michigan workforce. After six years in operation, faced with severe budget shortfalls and unclear mission at the postsecondary level, MVU shifted its focus from online university- and community college-level courses to expanding in the corporate sector and to the provision of K–12 courses (OBHE-BN, October 2004). Newman et al. (2004, 20) attribute the failure of the for-profit, virtual arms of some of the traditional institutions mostly to insufficient or poor planning.

In February 2005, four Australian universities, Monash, Deakin, New England, and Southern Queensland gained accreditation by the Distance Education and Training Council (DETC) to offer their online programs in the United States (OBHE-BN, February 2005). The so-called cyber universities project was initiated in Korea in 2000 with public funding, which aimed to make higher education more flexible and encourage LLL. Fourteen four-year universities and three two-year colleges were established as consortia of traditional institutions (Bonk 2004). The project, however, appears not to have produced the expected results. In the seventeen cyber-institutions across the country, only 46 percent of the projected twenty-four thousand places had been filled in 2003 (OBHE-BN, October 2003).

In 2003, National University of Singapore, a traditional, public university, entered into partnership with Fudan University, another traditional public university in China, to start a graduate school and a program for entrepreneurs (OBHE-BN, September 2003).

Some traditional institutions have partnered with noneducational commercial enterprises to provide e-learning for profit. The University of Maryland has partnered with ChinaCast Communications, a Chinese e-learning solutions provider, to offer online management courses in China (OBHE-BN, December 2004). BAE Systems, an international defense and aerospace company, has partnered with three UK universities to offer online programs in engineering (OBHE-BN, December 2004). Training Track, the IT and management training arm of Boston University, signed an agreement with PriceWaterhouseCoopers, an international auditing and management consultancy firm, to offer training in project management in Southeast Asia (OBHE-BN, March 2003).

The growing demand for some form of online provision of educational services has led to the emergence of a subsector, referred to as learning management systems (LMS) market, where ICT companies, called LMS vendors, provide services to institutions of higher education in the application of ICT to the provision of their educational and related services. These services include technical platforms, administrative or teaching systems, content provision, and consultancy services. Until recently, many services provided in-house in traditional institutions such as student information systems, library services (e-libraries or digital libraries), registration, bookstore management, and so on, now are being outsourced from vendors in addition to the services related to infrastructure building, course material preparation, content, and delivery related to e-learning. Such outsourcing is another example of unbundling of services in traditional institutions. Support companies that provide such e-learning services are collectively referred to as "service providers," regardless of whether they offer technical platforms, administrative or teaching systems, or consultancy services (Ryan and Stedman 2002).

Such service providers, also referred to as "vendors," are increasingly handling student enrollment, training of staff, and management of physical facilities. Outsourcing of IT services to commercial companies is particularly on the increase worldwide (CVCP-HEFCE 2000). Presently, WebCT, Blackboard,[7] eCollege, Learning Space, Intralearn, DigitalThink, KnowledgeNet, and many other vendors are active in the LMS market, with the first two companies in leading positions (OBHE-BN, September 2002; July 2002; March 2003; July 2004). In 2002, more than one hundred U.S. institutions outsourced student support to Smarthinking.com, one of a number of companies offering online student support services to institutions of higher education (OBHE-BN, May 2002). Qestia Media Inc., netLibrary Inc., XanEdu, and ebrary Inc. are examples of for-profit companies providing library and information services with direct and indirect access to information (Garrett 2002; Newman and Scurry 2001). Such companies are now active not only in the United States, but also in a large number of countries including China, Russia, Israel, Venezuela, and Algeria (Garrett 2003; OBHE-BN, September 2003, April 2004, June 2004, August 2004).

IDP Education Australia launched its portal that enables international students to enroll online at any Australian university (OBHE-BN, July 2002). In 2004, Chinese authorities signed deals with IDP, the Scottish Qualifications Authority and the Canadian International Management Institute to offer foundation programs in China that would potentially allow Chinese students access to higher education abroad (OBHE-BN, June 2004). Six public school boards in British Columbia have joined to establish for-profit branches abroad to provide programs that would facilitate the transfer of foreign students to universities in British Columbia (OBHE-BN, January, 2004).

The online component of the $735 billion U.S. education market in 2000 was 1.3 percent, corresponding to annual revenue of more than $9 billion, with estimates for 2003 exceeding $50 billion. The number of distance learning providers in the United States was 3,193 in 2002, compared with 167 in Australia, 450 in Canada, 324 in France, 324 in Germany, 25 in New Zealand, and 688 in the United Kingdom (van der Wende 2002). The global online market is clearly dominated by the United States and English as the language of instruction.

Distance education based on advanced technologies for delivery is projected to grow, and new technologies are emerging; Bonk (2004) identified thirty newly emerging technologies. The United States is expected to be the major driver of growth, and the major source for new technologies.

The failures of NYUOnline and Virtual Temple can possibly be likened to traditional institutions' failure to compete with for-profit entities in providing correspondence courses at the beginning of the twentieth century even when world-class institutions are involved. There may well be a lesson there for traditional institutions to stick to what they do best, such as incubating new knowledge-based companies such as Google, Yahoo!, Cisco, and Sun Microsystems, as did Stanford, and applying the newly developed educational technologies in hybrid environments for teaching and learning.

Guri-Rosenblit (2005) has identified the following eight paradoxes in e-learning, which possibly support the earlier argument:

1. Those higher education institutions that are well equipped to use the ICTs efficiently either need them less or are reluctant to use them on a wide basis in their teaching–learning processes. Those higher education institutions that can greatly benefit from the new technologies' potential are ill equipped to use their broad-spectrum possibilities.

2. The old distance education technologies were simple, and they replaced totally the learning–teaching processes in conventional classrooms. The new information and communication technologies are complex and offer a rich spectrum of uses, but they are used mostly for add-on functions. They do not replace most of the learning–teaching practices either in campus or in distance teaching universities.

3. The "old" distance teaching methods were used to overcome real problems, barriers, and obstacles. The problems and questions that the digital technologies assist in teaching–learning practices (mainly in campus universities) are blurred and not clearly defined.

4. The new technologies open up possibilities of widening access to higher education for new student clienteles. Second-chance and unprepared students are less qualified to use ICTs for their purposes (mainly at the undergraduate level and at distance education settings).

5. The Internet provides unlimited access to information and skill training. But information differs significantly from knowledge. Only expert teachers and professionals can guide novices to construct meaningful and relevant knowledge (particularly at the undergraduate level).

6. Distance education was largely justified for more than a century for its cost effectiveness and for providing economies of scale. Most evidence on the application of ICTs in higher education indicates that they cost more, not less, than face-to-face classroom interaction.

7. Developments of the new electronic technologies are very fast. The human capacity to adapt to new habits and new learning styles is very slow, and research in academia necessitates a perspective of time and reflection.

8. The costs of applying the new technologies, as well as their development, justifies strong cooperation between the academic and the corporate worlds.

However, the organizational cultures of these two worlds differ enormously, and this may result in failures of such collaborative ventures.

4.4. TYPES OF NEW PROVIDERS

4.4.1. Consortia and Networks

Other modalities of organization for providing e-learning by traditional non-profit institutions involve consortia, networks, and partnerships to share risk and leverage each other's expertise. Although the distinction between them is being increasingly blurred, the various modalities of cooperation, and the flurry of activity in the last decade, have been reviewed by Hans de Wit in a recent article for the OBHE (OBHE-BNA, January 25, 2006). Umbrella associations of and multilateral cooperation among higher education institutions date back to the Commonwealth Universities Association (f. 1913), the UNESCO-sponsored International Association of Universities (f. 1950), and the Standing Conference of European Rectors, Presidents and Vice-Chancellors (CRE; f. 1959).[8] With increasing internationalization of higher education, however, two new forms of collaboration emerged. de Wit identified these: *Consortia* refers to a grouping of institutions around a single purpose or contract. The term *institutional network*, on the other hand, generally is reserved for a group of institutions with a general framework objective that have come together for an indefinite period. It is common to use the two terms interchangeably. The perceived advantages in the increasingly complex international higher education market are (1) shared risks and costs that foster innovation, (2) strategic information sharing, (3) inroads into new markets, and (4) potential research projects of international significance. Most of the activities undertaken within such collaborative arrangements are traditional in scope, but require considerably more time and investment.

The Brussels-based Academic Cooperation Association recently issued a compilation of one hundred higher education associations from various continents as well as their global counterparts.[9]

An example of international consortia/network is Universitas 21, which is an international network of research-intensive universities. It was established in 1997 to facilitate collaboration and cooperation among its members and to create entrepreneurial opportunities for them on a scale that none would be able to achieve independently. It was the first international consortium to incorporate itself for commercial activities. Currently, it has twenty-one members in fifteen countries, four in the United Kingdom, three in Australia, two in China, and one each in Canada, Hong Kong, India, Ireland, Japan, Korea, Mexico, New Zealand, Singapore, Sweden, and the United States. Put together, member institutions of the consortium have a total enrollment of approximately 650,000 students (66,000 international), in excess of 2 million alumni, a staff of 130,000 and an annual budget turnover of $13 billion ($3 billion in research and consultancy grants and contracts). In 2001, the consortium entered into partnership with Thomson Learning, part of the Thomson Corporation (see Section 4.4.6), to found Universitas 21 Global (U21 Global) an online university to compete in the global marketplace. U21 Global opened for business in 2003 (OBHE-BN, June 2003). An organization to assure the quality of U21 Global's courses called U21 Pedagogica Ltd. also has been established. The U21 Global project received $25 million in startup funding from U21 members and $25 million from Thomson Learning. The formation of U21 Global was controversial, and currently, all but four (University of New South Wales, University of British Columbia, McGill University, and Lund University) of U21 members are partners in the U21 Global program. The organization's membership criteria state the following: "Member universities must be willing to embrace the mission and strategic objectives of Universitas 21, demonstrate a good fit with the profile and characteristics of existing members and be prepared to participate as a licensing partner in Universitas 21 Global" (OBHE-BNA, January 25, 2006). In 2007, Manipal Education, one of the largest education services providers in India, purchased the shares owned by Thomson Learning. The activities of U21 Global so far have been limited to offering a number of graduate-level programs online. Its headquarters are in Singapore, and it has offices in six other countries, currently enrolling approximately 5,000 students from 60 countries.[10]

EUROPACE is a trans-European network of twenty members comprising sixteen universities (five from Belgium, two each from Finland and Poland, and one each from France, Germany, Hungary, Italy, Slovakia, and

Spain) plus four educational enterprises, regional and professional organizations, and public authorities. Its mission is to foster networked e-learning and internationalization through R&D projects, seminars, and various other activities.[11]

The Worldwide Universities Network (WUN),[12] a group of eighteen universities (five each from the United States and the United Kingdom, two each from Australia, Canada and China, and one each from Netherlands and Norway), also is fostering e-learning collaboration among its members. Existing WUN e-learning collaborations include the University of York's master of administration in public policy and management, which brings together e-learning content developed by WUN member institutions with digital material provided by the program's corporate partner, the British Broadcasting Corporation. Unlike U21 Global, this program is not jointly branded by all WUN members, although the contribution of WUN to its development is clearly acknowledged on the University of York Web site. WUN members also are working together to create e-learning materials in subject areas as diverse as technical Chinese and medieval studies. The sharing of existing online programming and the collaborative development of new offerings allows participants to share expertise and the costs, and broadens the marketing reach and pool of available students for the finished product (OBHE-BNA, January 25, 2006).

Two recently formed consortia are the Online Consortium of Independent Colleges and Universities (OCICU) and the International Alliance of Research Universities (IARU). The OCICU currently has seventy-two members, and all are based in the United States, except for the National University of Ireland and the Ateneo de Manila University in the Philippines. Membership requirements include regional accreditation, independent nonprofit status, and a commitment to liberal arts education. The purpose is to provide opportunities to students in participating institutions to complete online courses from other members to count toward their degree or certificate requirements.[13] IARU, on the other hand, has only ten members, including Yale, California–Berkeley, Oxford, Cambridge, the National University of Singapore, Beijing University, ETH Zurich, Copenhagen University, Tokyo University, and Australian National University.[14] Student and staff exchange, collaborative research, and joint degree programs are among the envisioned activities of the alliance (OBHE-BNA, January 25, 2006).

Fathom was a very ambitious consortium. It was led by Columbia and comprised fourteen prestigious institutions in the United States and the United Kingdom, all counted among the leaders in their respective fields. These were American Film Institute, British Library, British Museum, Cambridge University Press, Columbia University, London School of Economics, Natural History Museum, New York Public Library, RAND Corporation,

Science Museum, University of Chicago, University of Michigan, Victoria and Albert Museum, and Woods Hole Oceanographic Institution. It closed in April 2003, and the material that was developed in a wide range of subjects is now freely available online (OBHE-BN, January 2003). According to Ryan and Stedman (2002), Fathom's strategy of attracting individual consumers to an online liberal education was flawed from the start, because so much material of a generalist nature is freely available online.[15]

There are many other types of groupings among traditional and non-traditional institutions and other commercial educational entities with a wide range of interests and objectives. Some examples of these are discussed in the following sections of this chapter.

4.4.2. For-Profit Higher Education

Clearly, globalization, revolutionary developments in ICT, and the increasing need for LLL are the major factors that have led to the growth of for-profit higher education in the United States. For-profit companies initially targeted vocational programs and support services, but as some of the examples cited previously indicate, they are increasingly involved in the development of course material.

For-profit higher education has a three-hundred-year-old history in the United States; Morey (2004) traces the origins of the for-profit providers to the proprietary schools, also known as career colleges, which provide entry-level skill training at the postsecondary level without awarding degrees. Of the 5,059 such schools that existed in the 2001–2002 academic year, 3,540 were for-profit, 1,018 were private nonprofit, and 501 were public (NCES 2004). Forty percent offer preparation in cosmetology; 24 percent offer preparation in business or marketing trades; and 36 percent offer programs in health, technology, transportation, industrial work, or other occupations. More than 77 percent of the for-profit providers in the United States are in the certificate and the associate degree-level market (Ryan and Stedman 2002). Such schools also exist in Australia, New Zealand, Germany, Japan, and some other countries (Persell and Wenglinsky 2004).

What emerged in the United States from the early 1990s on, however, are degree-granting for-profit institutions that are operating in the area that was considered the remit of nonprofit higher education. In the 1990s, the number of two-year for-profit degree-granting institutions grew by 78 percent, and the number of four-year institutions by 266 percent. In the 2008–2009 academic year, such institutions numbered 986 (533 two-year, and 453 four-year) in the United States, and enrolled more than 400,000 students, which correspond to approximately 2.5 percent of the national enrollment in degree-granting institutions. Moreover, roughly one third of the students enrolled in online courses are in for-profit institutions (Blumenstyk 2005a; *Chronicle of Higher Education* Almanac 2008–2009; Morey 2004).

As of 1998, half of the states in the United States awarded some money to students enrolled at private institutions, but the sums involved were small compared with the state funds given to students at nonprofit institutions. In 1998, however, the Congress treated for-profit institutions like traditional colleges in the legislation that reauthorized the Higher Education Act. In 2004, the bill to reauthorize the Higher Education Act, called the "College Access and Opportunities Act," removed the remaining distinctions between the nonprofit and for-profit sectors and between campus-based and distance learning for federal aid purposes, giving a big boost to for-profit institutions.

Qualification for federal student aid programs and employer-paid tuition for working adults have been major factors that have contributed to the growth of the for-profit sector, along with the increased demand for lifelong, flexible learning. For-profit higher education in the United States grew from a $3.5 billion a year business in 1998 to $15.4 billion in 2004, and was projected to grow to $23.1 billion in 2007 (Blumenstyk 2005a; Morey 2004). In 2004, investors poured in $161 million into private companies that run colleges for profit and into other businesses in the higher education industry, which was almost twice the amount invested in 2003 (Blumenstyk 2005b).

Presently, the annual revenues of the for-profit companies account for about 5 percent of the annual higher education business in the United States, which is valued at $395 billion.[16] According to the best-case scenario reported by Blumenstyk (2005c), the total volume of the higher education business in the United States will rise to $650 billion in 2015, and 7.5 percent of this amount will go to for-profit institutions, which will enroll 10 percent of the projected 20 million students in degree-granting institutions. Furthermore, traditional students and enrollment in online courses will account for most of the growth. In the worst-case scenario, the for-profit subsector faces stiff competition from traditional institutions in providing training to nontraditional students, and the slowdown observed in 2004 and 2005 persists. It appears that the economic downturn, which reached a global crisis proportions in 2008, is working in favor of the U.S. for-profit colleges. Increased unemployment nationwide is resulting in more unemployed adults seeking to acquire new skills, and increased tuition fees due to the budget cuts for the nonprofits are making for-profit colleges more attractive in terms of costs to students. According to Blumenstyk (2008a), in 2008, the for-profit higher education subsector had the highest profit margins since 2005.

According to the Chronicle Index of For-Profit Higher Education (Blumenstyk 2005d, 2007a, 2007b, 2007c, 2008c),[17] revenues of the eight major publicly traded companies in the United States are shown in Table

4.1, together with the sizes of their enrollment, the number of faculty they employ, and the number of programs they offer within the United States and abroad. They all offer programs at the associate, bachelor, and master levels, and Apollo, Capella, Career Education, DeVry, and Laureate also offer programs at the doctoral level. All rely on part-time faculty to a very large extent, and annual costs vary from $7,000 in Apollo to more than $19,000 in ITT for bachelor-level programs. The Apollo Group, with revenues of $2.7 billion and an enrollment of 313,700 students in 2007 is clearly a business giant and a mega education conglomerate.

Apollo Group Inc. was founded in 1973 in response to the anticipated demographic shift toward working, adult higher education students. Today, Apollo Group owns the University of Phoenix (UOP), the University of Phoenix Online, the Institute for Professional Development, the College for Financial Planning, and the Western International University (WIU).[18] UOP was founded in 1976.[19] It is the largest private university in the United States, offering undergraduate- and graduate-degree programs tailored to working adults in business, education, behavioral and social science, nursing and IT. The University of Phoenix Online offers degree programs at the undergraduate, master, and doctoral levels in Mexico, Canada, and twenty-one countries in Asia, Europe, and the Middle East (Morey 2004). More than half of the students of the UOP are adults, and eighty percent of them are employed full-time. The Apollo Group opened the first branch campus of an American university in India, in New Delhi, in 2002 (OBHE-BN, October 2002).

In October 2003, WIU signed an agreement with the Canadian Institute of Business and Technology (CIBT), a subsidiary of the Capital Alliance Group and a prominent player in the Chinese higher education market, to offer WIU programs through the three schools CIBT operates in Beijing (OBHE-BN, October 2003). The Apollo Group operates 200 campuses and learning centers in the United States, Canada, and other parts of the world. In order to expand its international operations, in 2007, the Apollo Group established Apollo Global in a joint venture with the Carlyle Group. In 2008, the new group acquired two new university campuses, University of Communication, Arts and Sciences in Chile and Universidad Latinoamericano (ULA) in Mexico, and also established Meritus University in Canada as its base for its online programs in that country. Expansion of the Apollo Group continued in 2008, and its enrollment reached 362,000. Currently, UOP together with its online arm accounts for close to 95 percent of the group's revenues. The Apollo Group also has an online high school subsidiary, the Insight Schools.[20]

Career Education Corporation has two operating groups: the Colleges, Schools, Universities group and the Online Group. It offers associ-

Table 4.1. Characteristics of the Largest Publicly Traded For-Profit Companies in the United States

Company	Revenue[a]		Enrollment[b] 2007	Number of Programs, 2007[c]					Academic Staff[d] 2007
	$	%		Associates	Bachelor's	Master's	Doctorate	Total	
Apollo Group	2.7 billion	9.9	313,700	9	31	42	6	88	1,263[e] (22,176)
Capella	226.2 million	25.8	96,200	0	2	6	5	13	130 (774)
Career Educaton	1.7 billion	-7.8	67,445	81	68	20	3	172	1,592 (3,969)
Corinthian	933.2 million	0.7	20,268	66	17	2	0	85	1,301 (2,971)
DeVry	933.5 million	11.2	57,538	5	9	7	2	23	885[f] (4,059)
ITT	869.5 million	14.7	53,675	10	13	1	0	24	600 (2,100)
Strayer	318.0 million	21.0	36,082	7	5	6	0	18	214 (1,200)
Laureate	nd	nd	nd	0	2	20	8	30[g]	13,000 (total)

[a]Blumenstyk (2008b).
[b]Blumenstyk (2007a).
[c]Blumenstyk (2007b).
[d]Blumenstyk (2007c).
[e]University of Phoenix only.
[f]DeVry University only.
[g]U.S. programs only.
%, percent change over the previous year; nd, no data available.

ate-, bachelor-, and master- and doctoral-level degree programs and diplomas in eighty-one global campuses located in the United States, Canada, the United Kingdom, France, and the United Arab Emirates in visual communication and design technologies, IT, business studies and culinary arts.[21] Its online programs are offered through its American InterContinental University Online and Colorado Technical University Online. Total enrollment in the corporation's programs stood at about 90,000 worldwide, with about one third of them in online programs.[22]

Corinthian Colleges Inc. was founded in 1995. The company presently comprises two groups of schools, Everest Colleges and Wyo Tech. The former comprises Everest College, Everest College of Business, Technology and Health Care (Canada), Everest Institute, Everest University, Everest University Online, a division of Everest University, and Everest College—Phoenix, offering on-site and online courses. WyoTech is dedicated to college-level, career-oriented education in the automotive, diesel, motorcycle, watercraft, HVAC, electrician, and plumbing fields. Corinthian Colleges Inc. has eighty-nine Everest campuses in twenty-four states and seventeen campuses in Canadian provinces, and six Wyo Tech campuses in the United States. Its total enrollment in 2008 stood at 76,000.[23]

DeVry Inc. has its roots in the Deforest Training School founded in Chicago in 1931 to prepare students for technical work in electronics, motion pictures, and radio and television, which then grew into DeVry Institutes in eight states and two Canadian provinces. In 1987, DeVry merged with Keller Graduate School of Management and in 2002 DeVry University was born, which now offers career-oriented undergraduate and graduate programs to forty-nine thousand students in technology, business, and management in seventy-two locations in North America and through DeVry University Online. DeVry Inc. also owns Ross University, which offers programs leading to a doctor of medicine degree and a doctor of veterinary medicine degree. Students complete their basic education in campuses in the Caribbean countries and complete their clinical rotations in teaching hospitals and veterinary schools in the United States. Becker Professional Review provides preparatory coursework for professional certification exams, including certified public accountant, certified management accountant, and chartered financial analyst, serving forty-three thousand students at three hundred locations around the world.[24] In 2008, DeVry acquired Apollo College with nine campuses, and Western College with eight campuses in the United States. In 2007, it entered the online secondary education market by acquiring Advanced Academics Inc., a leading provider in that subsector.[25]

Education Management Corporation dates back to 1962, and presently offers associate- and bachelor-level programs and nondegree programs in its thirty-one art institutes in the areas of design, media arts, culinary arts, and fashion. The company's Argosy Education Group operates Argosy University, with thirteen primary campuses and five extension sites in ten states; Western State University College of Law in Fullerton, California; and Argosy Professional Services, located in Ventura, California. Argosy Education Group provides graduate- and undergraduate-level education in clinical psychology, counseling, education, business, law, and health sciences. Brown Mackie College schools prepare students for entry-level qualifications in business, health sciences, legal studies, IT, and electronics leading to associate degrees, diplomas and certificates. South University has four campuses in the southeastern United States and offers undergraduate and graduate programs in business, legal studies, IT, and health sciences.[26] Altogether, Education Management Corporation operates eighty-nine primary campuses in the United States and Canada. Its total enrollment was 110,000 in 2008.[27] In June 2006, two private equity companies bought Education Management Corporation for $3.4 billion (Selingo 2006).

ITT Educational Services Inc. is a provider of technical postsecondary education at the associate and the bachelor levels and nondegree programs to students in a system comprising 105 technical institutes located in thirty-seven states in the United States in the areas of IT, drafting and design, business, and criminal justice. Its total enrollment in 2008 was 61,000.[28]

The university network previously known as Sylvan International Universities has been renamed and is now Laureate Education Inc. In 2003, the group abandoned its business in after-school tutoring at the K–12 level to expand in the postsecondary sector (OBHE-BN, March 2003). Laureate has been expanding in South America and Europe (OBHE-BN, June 2003). In November 2003, it bought Universidad Interamericana, a private university with campuses in Costa Rica and Panama (OBHE-BN, November 2003). In September 2004, it acquired 80 percent of the University of Applied Science in Lima, and 70 percent of an engineering school in Paris (OBHE-BN, October 2004).[29] In April 2004, the group bought the Dutch company KIT e-learning, and signed a long-term strategic agreement with the University of Liverpool to develop online degree programs (OBHE-BN, April, 2004). It closed its campus in India, South Asia International Institute, in 2004 (OBHE-BN, January 2004). The network now comprises forty-six campus-based institutions of higher education, thirteen in Europe (Cyprus, France, Germany, Spain, and Switzerland), ten in Central America (Costa Rica, Honduras, Mexico, and Panama), seventeen in South America (Brazil, Chile, Ecuador, and Peru), four in Asia (China and Malaysia), and two in Australia. The network caters to traditional full-time students as well as working professionals. Both campus-based and online undergraduate and graduate degree programs are offered in business, health sciences, engineering, IT, education, and other fields. The network also offers study abroad opportunities. Laureate Online Education owns the following subsidiaries. Walden University offers doctoral- and master-level degree programs in education, management, psychology, and health and human services, and bachelor completion programs in business. The National Technological University offers master-level programs, graduate-level certificates and professional development courses for engineers and IT professionals. Canter & Associates offers teacher training and education programs. Laureate Online Education, B. V. offers online graduate programs in partnership with the University of Liverpool. The total enrollment in Laureate Online Education network was more than twenty thousand students in 2005. They come from more than ninety-five countries in the world and fifty states in the United States.[30] In 2008, total enrollment in Laureate programs was 500,000 students worldwide.[31]

Strayer Education Inc. was established in 2000, but it traces its origins to Strayer's Business College of Baltimore founded in 1892. Its subsidiary, Strayer University, offers undergraduate and graduate degree programs to working adults in thirty campuses in the United States and worldwide through the Internet via Strayer Online in business administration, accounting, IT, education, and public administration. Total enrollment in its programs was 45,000 in 2008.[32] In addition to the major for-profit providers described here, there are hundreds of other similar commercial ventures in the United States.

For-profit providers of higher education are not restricted to the United States. The Singapore-based Raffles LaSalle, which was set up as a joint venture with the LaSalle College Group of Montreal established its first college in Singapore in 1990 with fifty students. It was renamed Raffles Education Corporation in 2004 (OBHE-BN, December 2004). After another reorganization, it is now Raffles Education Corp. Ltd. It is arguably Asia's leading creative design and management group. In 2008, it served a total student body of 68,000 in three universities and a network of colleges in Australia, China, Hong Kong, India, Indonesia, Malaysia, Mongolia, New Zealand, Singapore, Thailand, and Vietnam, offering diplomas as well as bachelor- and master-level degree programs in collaboration with Curtin University of Technology in Australia and the Middlesex University in the United Kingdom. The Raffles group acquired the Hartford Holdings Ltd., a Singapore-based provider of business and management programs at bachelor and master levels. The partners of Hartford are Newcastle University and Central Queensland University in Australia, Leicester University and Huddersfield University in the United Kingdom and California State University–East Bay in the United States. It also has subsidiaries in Hong Kong, Malaysia, Mongolia, and China.[33] In 2004, the group entered into partnership with Columbia Business School to open a branch campus in Jordan (OBHE-BN, December 2004).

Such franchise arrangements between a for-profit provider and a traditional nonprofit institution of higher education are quite common in the Asia-Pacific region. Another example is provided by the partnership between the Informatics Group, a company based in Singapore, and Heriot Watt University in Scotland (OBHE-BN, September 2002).

The Australia-based Institute of Business and Technology (IBT) Education Group owns eleven colleges in Australia, Kenya, Zambia, Sri Lanka, Indonesia, and the United Kingdom.[34] It operates at an interface between the secondary and the tertiary levels, specializing in preuniversity and freshman undergraduate provision to smooth admission to the Edith Cowan University, Curtin University, Griffith University, Macquarie University, and the University of South Australia in Australia and Brunel University in the United Kingdom. It is now expanding into India. The group went public in December 2004 on the Australian Stock Exchange, raising $39 million (OBHE-BN, December 2004).

Increasingly, companies with operations in other sectors have been eyeing the lucrative postsecondary education market in the Asia-Pacific region. In 2002, an Australian IT company, Amnet, bought a private university in Chongqing, Western China. NIIT, the Indian software development and IT education firm, announced an agreement with Indonesia's University of Atma Jaya to operate a computer education center at the university's campus (OBHE-BN, January 2003). Another example is the Tata Interactive Systems, part of India's giant Tata Group, which claims to operate the largest specialist e-learning development team in the world, who enlisted its first customer in summer 2003: the UOP (OBHE-BN, July 2003). Caparo Group, a UK firm with interests in steel, engineering, and hotels, announced a partnership with Carnegie-Mellon University, a private, nonprofit, traditional U.S. university, to establish a campus in India in summer 2003. This is another example of the growing number of noneducation firms trying to enter the lucrative international higher education market (OBHE-BN, July 2003).

Germany has one of the lowest shares of private enrollment, with about 1 percent of the total (see Section 3.3). It got its first for-profit university, the Hanseatic University (*Private Hanseuniversitat*), which was accredited/licensed by the Ministry of Education, Science and Culture of the Land of Mecklenburg-Vorpommern, where several German companies invested in the project (OBHE-BN, January 2006).[35]

4.4.3. Virtual Universities

Virtual universities are what may be termed second-generation distance education universities that have evolved out of the dot.com boom of the late 1990s. They are of two types: individual for-profit institutions, examples of which have been provided previously, or government-led initiatives aiming at expanding and improving flexible learning at regional, national, and sometimes international levels.

Thirty-three states in the United States have a statewide virtual university. Some of these just provide advisory services, referring students to providers, whereas others are full online service providers. Western Governors University (WGU) is a nonprofit online university founded by the governors of nineteen western states with a national advisory board comprising major ICT companies, corporations, and foundations. Launched in 1997, the mission of WGU is to expand access at the postsecondary level. Four regional commissions and the DETC have accredited the WGU. It offers bachelor's-and master's-level programs in education, business, and IT and health care. As of 2003, it had modest growth and appeared to fail in matching expectations (OBHE-BN, February 2003); later reports, however, indicated that it was making a comeback (OBHE-BN, January 2005). In 2008, it had a total student enrollment of 12,000.[36]

The OBHE has identified four main types of national virtual universities (OBHE-KI, September 2004): (1) export-based; (2) focused on widening access and participation; (3) research and development focused; and (4) industry focused in partnership with foreign providers.

The Open University (OU) of the United Kingdom, which served as a model for many countries for widening access at the national level, began offering courses overseas in 1982 (Open University Worldwide 2005). In 1997, Open University Worldwide Ltd. (OUW) was established as the international division of the OU. As of April 2009, OUW had in excess of forty-five thousand students in thirty-two countries where it works in partnership with local universities, colleges, and companies, and distributes more than twenty-five hundred learning resource products.[37] It, however, failed to enter the U.S. market via its for-profit subsidiary, the U.S. Open University, which closed in 2002.[38]

The Canadian Virtual University (CVU), founded in 2002, is an example of government-led initiatives that aim to increase access. CVU is a consortium of eleven Canadian universities, which is located in Athabasca, the seat of Canada's first distance education university, and is led by Athabasca's president. Quebec's *Tele-Universite*, the British Columbia Open University, the Royal Military College and traditional universities like the University of New Brunswick, the Memorial University of Newfoundland and the University of Manitoba are among its members. The CVU offers 2,300 courses and 280 degree programs, diplomas, and certificates completely online and through distance education.[39] Institutions similar to those described here have been founded in Sweden, Denmark, Norway, and Tunisia in the early 2000s.

The previously mentioned AOU, on the other hand, is a regional distance learning institution. It uses materials from the UK's Open University; it gained accreditation from the British Accreditation Council, a private UK-based postsecondary education accreditation organization (OBHE-BN, March 2004).

4.4.4. Corporate Universities

Meister (1998, 29; 2001) defines a corporate university as follows: "The strategic umbrella for developing and educating and training employees, customers, and suppliers in order to meet an organization's business strategies The corporation develops such programs through its own faculty or staff, or through external partners like higher institutions or commercial firms."

The origins of corporate universities can be traced back to the "corporate classrooms" of established within DuPont, General Electric, and Edison in the nineteenth century because of their dissatisfaction with the education system of the time. However, the term *corporate university* first appeared in management and business literature in the early 1980s to meet the rapidly changing training and development needs. Their number in the United States grew from fifteen in the 1980s to four hundred in the 1990s, and to more than two thousand in the early 2000s (Taylor and Paton 2006).

Estimates of the annual spending on corporate training vary from a low of $27 billion to a high of $66 billion (Ryan and Stedman 2002). The Motorola University, the best known of all, has an annual budget of $120 million, and manages ninety-nine sites in twenty-one countries. Other examples that operate through their own network of physical campuses are Disney and Toyota. IBM and Dow Chemical, on the other hand, are online, while Bell Atlantic and United Health Care provide training in partnership with traditional institutions (World Bank 2002, 34).

Ninety-two percent of corporations outsource their education and training programs, 60 percent outsource some aspect of course design, and 16 percent have partnerships with traditional universities and colleges as opposed to 37 percent of the contracts going to training vendors (Ryan and Stedman 2002). Corporations that now have their own universities include the U.S. Army, the IRS, the UK Health Service,[40] Banco Santander Central Hispanola SA, the health giant Kaiser Permanente, Coca Cola, Marlboro, Xerox, Wal-Mart, Eddie Bauer, Best Buy, Home Depot, Target, American Express, Ford, Apple, Microsoft, Sun, Oracle, British Aerospace, Daimler-Benz, and Lufthansa (Futures Project 2000; Newman and Couturier 2001; Newman and Scurry 2001; Mendivil 2002; Ryan and Stedman 2002; dos Santos 2002). One of the most recent additions to the list of corporate universities is the Interpol University founded in 2007 in Vienna, which began operating in 2009 with its first intake of 150 students. Its mission is to train high-level officials in the judiciary and the police services worldwide ("Interpol to establish its own university," *The Times Higher Education Supplement.* July 20, 2007.)

In 2000, there were sixteen hundred corporate universities, up from four hundred in 1988, including 85 percent of Fortune 500 companies, up from 40 percent a few years earlier in 1988. It was then believed that by 2005 their number would reach 2000. As part of the wider dot.com enthusiasm of the 1990s, it was forecast that e-learning would stimulate the need for corporate training to such a degree that by 2010, corporate universities would outnumber traditional institutions (Futures Project 2000a; Meister 2001). As previously mentioned, their number did indeed reach 2,000 by the mid-2000s. However, as it turned out, the majority of the corporate universities have remained exclusively focused on training in-house staff. In other words, they have remained as company training departments, which was what many of them were called before being re-branded as corporate universities. Most of them are not accredited. Thus, they cannot offer degree programs. Some of them, however, have formed partnerships with for-profit and nonprofit institutions so that their courses can carry credit toward degrees (Morey 2004; Ryan and Stedman 2002; World Bank 2002, 34). Even Motorola University, often cited as the epitome of successful corporate university, announced major losses in 2000. However, after restructuring it appears to pursue its goal of being a major for-profit training provider to outside customers by partnering with an increasing number of traditional institutions and vendors (OBHE-BN, October 2003; Ryan and Stedman 2002).

4.4.5. Certificate Programs

Until the 1990s, most ICT training took place in traditional tertiary institutions. The commercialization and the diffusion of the Internet and the World Wide Web all over the globe produced an explosion in the demand for ICT skills. With the method of delivery increasingly becoming a major part of the skill that the training aimed to impart in students, ICT companies, rather than going into partnership with traditional institutions to offer credit toward degrees, transformed their training units into profit centers, which offer training programs that lead to IT certificates. The first vocational certificate of this type, Certified Network Engineer (CNE), was awarded by Novell in 1998. By 2000, more than 2.5 million CNE certificates had been awarded to about 1.6 million people, about half of them American and the rest from all over the world. The biggest providers were Microsoft, which operates one hundred centers in the United States (more than 1 million) and Novell (more than 500,000; Mendivil 2002; Newman et al. 2004, 20).

Costs to the student can run in excess of $10,000. In a small number of the cases, it is possible to get credit for certificates that count toward degrees in two-year colleges.

Thus, a subsector of postsecondary education has emerged that operates in tandem with degree-awarding institutions. The main actors in this subsector, in addition to ICT companies, are the professional associations in the computer industry, which set the standards and act as accrediting agencies that authorize other entities, including traditional institutions, to operate "authorized training centers" or training partners. A number of secondary private companies have emerged, which are now competing with traditional, virtual, and for-profit institutions of higher education (Mendivil 2002).

Aptech Ltd. is an education and training company specializing in IT, with headquarters in Mumbai, India. It started in Bahrain in 1993, and now operates 235 international centers in fifty-two countries spread over five continents. It offers training leading to IT certificates in English, Spanish, Chinese, Russian, German, and Korean with Web-centric and face-to-face support. It boasts a global enrollment of more than 3.5 million students. According to information provided on its Web site, Aptech has trained in excess of 5 million trainees as of 2009. The company founded Aptech University in 2004, and thus entered degree-granting higher education activities in collaboration with universities in the United Kingdom, Australia, Canada, and the United States.[41]

A third layer in the IT certificate subsector comprises agencies and companies that administer the examinations that lead to certificates. The largest of these companies is Thomson-Prometric; it started out as an independent in 1990, Drake, which developed a computerized examination for Novell's CNE course. In 1997, Sylvan Group acquired Drake, and in 2000, Thomson Corporation bought the company.[42] The company provides testing and assessment services in twenty-five hundred centers in 140 countries. It is active not only in IT certification, but in a wide range of subjects, including GRE, GMAT, TOEFL (as a subcontractor to Educational Testing Services, ETS), medicine (the National Board of Medical Examiners), accountancy (the American Institute of Certified Public Accountants), and securities dealership (the National Securities Dealer's Association, Japanese Securities Dealers; Mendivil 2002). The parent company, Thomson Learning, was acquired by Apax Partners and became Cengage Learning in July 2007. In October 2007, Thomson Prometric was acquired by ETS. In October 2008, Thomson merged with Reuters, and became Thomson Reuters, which specializes in providing critical information in the financial, legal, tax and accounting, scientific, health care. and media markets by using innovative technologies and through one of the world's best known news organizations. Thus, Thomson is no longer active in higher education and training subsectors.[43]

Faced with the explosive growth in the volume and the complexity of the ICT certificate market, the industry established the Council of Computing Certification in May 2000 to define the norms of the entire process, from content and teaching to examinations and certificates (Mendivil 2002).[44]

4.4.6. Museums, Libraries, Publishers, and Media Enterprises

With a growing adult population that has time for leisure as well as a need for LLL, many museums, libraries, publishing companies, and media enterprises in developed countries, particularly in the United States and the United Kingdom, are providing education as well as services linked to course material design and preparation for online delivery services (World Bank 2002, 34). The most common form of this is as a partner in a consortium, and several examples are given in the previous sections. Thomson Scientific and Healthcare, now part of the Thomson Reuters, is a leading publisher that counts the ISI Web of Science and World Patents Index among its publications.

Pearson Education is another global group in integrated education publishing, which includes such names as Prentice Hall, Longman, Penguin Group, Financial Times Group, Scott Foresman, Allyn & Bacon, and Addison Wesley among its subsidiaries, that is active in the global education market beyond its activities as a publisher. The group also has nearly two thousand companion Web sites, the InformIT Web site for technology professionals, and the Family Education Network for parents, teachers, and children. Pearson's activities extend across the globe and reach an estimated 100 million people through its subsidiaries, seventy regional Web sites, and twenty-five publishing centers that offer a wide range of educational services and products for children, schools, universities, adults, and corporations. English-language training, assessment, and testing, including IT and professional certification, are among the activities of the group.[45]

One interesting example was the Barnes and Noble University, launched in 2000, which offered free courses and programs online leading to certificates as well as degrees at the associate-, bachelor-, master-, and doctoral-levels in a wide range of subjects, including liberal arts, business, education, health care, technology, and criminal justice.[46] Barnes and Noble University is no longer in existence.

4.4.7. Academic Brokers

Academic brokers can be of two types. The first category comprises virtual, often Web-based, entrepreneurs or consortia of traditional and new types of providers that specialize in bringing together suppliers and consumers of educational services in many different areas, ranging from students and degree programs to various types of suppliers and institutions and companies seeking to outsource services. Such brokers exist around the world. These can be portals supported by an administrative structure, like some of the statewide and national virtual institutions mentioned earlier and the various consortia to be described, or companies like Connect Education Inc. and the Electronic University Network that build, lease, and manage campuses; produce educational software; and provide guidance to serve corporate clients worldwide (World Bank 2002, 34). The Online University Consortium is a consortium of thirty nonprofit universities formed in 2003 to offer online programs under a common brand.[47] Among participating institutions are George Washington University, Syracuse University, various campuses of the University of Wisconsin, and Worcester Polytechnic Institute. It offers a large number of programs at all levels, including nine programs at the doctoral level in such diverse areas as clinical psychology, pharmacy, and education, and programs leading to certificates in areas extending from electrical engineering to personal financial planning (OBHE-BN, July 2004).

The University Alliance is arguably the largest online provider of higher education in the United States (OBHE-BN, July 2004). It is a consortium of ten nonprofit universities and schools, including Tulane University and Villanova University among its members. It offers programs at the bachelor and master levels as well as programs leading to certificates.[48] The OnlineUniversityGuide is a portal of eight for-profit online universities, including Phoenix, Jones, Kaplan, and Capella.[49]

UNext is a commercial company based in Illinois.[50] It was founded by a number of Nobel Prize-winning economists and professors from the University of Chicago to provide e-learning to Motorola University (Ryan and Stedman 2002). In 2000, the company founded Cardean University to offer an MBA program that blends Internet technology with the innovative ideas of the founders of the company.[51] Cardean then formed an academic consortium with the Columbia Business School, Stanford University, The University of Chicago Graduate School of Business, Carnegie-Mellon University and London School of Economics and Political Science to offer online programs in leadership and management, e-commerce, marketing, accounting, and business communications at the master level. In 2002, Thomson Enterprise Learning, a subsidiary of Thomson Corporation,[52] signed an exclusive deal with UNext to market courses offered by Cardean University (OBHE-BN, January 2002; OBHE-BN, March 2002). In 2003, UNext and New York Institute of Technology (NYIT) formed a strategic alliance to launch Ellis College of NYIT to serve working adults online; it now offers bachelor-level programs in twenty-two areas from communication arts and hospitality management to computer science and accounting, and an MBA program.[53] Ellis College received accreditation to operate inde-pendently in 2008 (Blumenstyk 2008b). Cardean is now Cardean Learn-ing Group, which provides administrative, technical, courseware, and other educational services. Of its original partners, only the University of Chicago still has relations with Cardean.[54]

Such consortia are not restricted to North America. The Australian OLA is an educational organization[55]; established in 1993. It offers all Aus-tralians regardless of age, location, or educational qualifications the opportu-nity to study university and vocational training subjects leading to degrees, diplomas, and other qualifications through specifically designed study pack-ages using all aspects of ICT. OLA students are eligible for financial assis-tance in the same schemes that apply to regular students. The OLA is owned by seven Australian universities, and its credits are eligible for transfer to these as well as other institutions. OLA was recently renamed Open Univer-sities Australia. As of 2007, it had 23,500 students, and since its inception in 1993, it had served more than 100,000 students.[56]

Other types of brokers even provide direct educational services, includ-ing preparatory training in the English language and for tests required for admission to U.S. and UK institutions of higher education. Such brokers commonly are found in many countries in the Asia-Pacific region, the Middle East, southeastern Europe and Latin America, major sources of stu-dents for institutions of higher education in the major English-speaking destination countries, the United States, the United Kingdom, Australia, New Zealand, and Canada. In the 1990s, a number of private prepara-tory colleges were opened in Australia offering programs in English and computing in "foundation programs,"[57] which prepare foreign students for entry to Australian universities. In addition to teaching, these schools help students with visas and employment while studying in Australia. By the end of the 1990s, enrollment in these schools had reached 158,000 (Gamage and Mininberg 2003).

4.4.8. Branch Campuses, Franchises, and Twinning Arrangements

In this subsection, I use terminology specific to international higher educa-tion. These pertain to new organizational relationships that have devel-oped over time, but especially in the last decades of the previous century, among traditional and new types of providers of higher education and related services. The following systematic descriptions provided by Knight (2008, 105–06) are useful in clearly understanding the new complex relationships in international higher education.

- "Branch Campus: Provider in country A establishes a satellite campus in country B to deliver courses and programs to to students in country B (may also include country A students taking a semester/courses abroad). The qualification awarded is from provider in country A.

- Franchise: An arrangement whereby a provider in source country A authorizes a provider in another country B to deliver its course/program/service in country B or other countries. The qualification is awarded by provider in country A.

- Twinning: A situation whereby a provider in source country A collaborates with a provider located in country B to develop an articulation system allowing students to take course credits in country B and/or source country A. Only one qualification is awarded by provider in source country A.

   — Double/Joint Degree: An arrangement whereby providers in different countries collaborate to offer a program for which a student receives a qualification from each provider or a joint award from the collaborating providers.

   — Articulation: Various types of articulation arrangements between providers in different countries permit students to gain credit for courses/programs offered/delivered by collaborating providers.

   — Validation: Validation arrangements between providers in different countries allow provider B in receiving country to award the qualification of provider A in source country."

According to Altbach (2004a, 2006), branch campuses date back to the institutions founded by the Roman Catholic universities in the Philippines and Latin America led by religious orders like the Jesuits. One group of historical antecedents include the institutions founded in the colonial period, when universities in the metropole set up branch institutions or sponsored new schools in the colonies, such as the British and French institutions in Africa and Asia, and Dutch institutions in today's Indonesia. Another group comprises the American type of liberal arts colleges founded by American Protestant missionaries in Turkey (Robert College, f. 1863), Lebanon (American University of Beirut, f. 1866), and Egypt (American University of Cairo, f. 1919).

American universities have long-standing branch campuses in various major European cities. These have traditionally been small international centers dedicated to short-stay study arrangements for expatriate Americans. Many of those in Europe date back to the post-World War II period, when they were opened to provide the military personnel stationed in Europe and their dependents access to U.S. institutions. Troy University, a public institution in Alabama is operating a network of eleven branch campuses that started fifty years ago to serve U.S. military personnel abroad. Others opened branch campuses later. Over time, with increasing revenues from transnational education, many different forms of branch campuses, satellite campuses, offshore, and "validation" arrangements have appeared worldwide (OECD 2004b, 120–4).

Franchise universities are institutions operating on behalf of the home institutions located generally in the MESDCs, but not necessarily restricted to these countries. These offer courses "validated" by the parent institutions, but in another country. Local providers operate franchises. Local instructors teach courses according to syllabi prepared and supervised by the parent institution, which, in effect, acts as a quality assurance agent. The cost of attending a franchise institution is 25 to 33 percent of what it would cost the student to attend the parent institution (Rizvi 2004; World Bank 2002, 33). Such franchises exist in the Asia-Pacific rim, mainly in the former British colonies but also increasingly in China, in the Middle East, eastern and southeastern Europe and Latin America, which are the major suppliers of foreign students in the international higher education market.

Branch campuses, on the other hand, are, in principle, operated directly by the parent institution with faculty traveling to teach the courses they have developed in short periods of one to two weeks. However, with increasing reliance on local instructors and local partners for facilities, the difference between the branch campuses and franchises is becoming less clear in many cases. In both cases, the main motive on the part of the parent institution is revenue generation. They are collectively referred to as "offshore" provision, in which case the student remains in his home country where the provider establishes a presence either physically (branch campus, collaborative agreement with a local institution, or franchise) or virtually (distance education). "Onshore" provision, on the other hand, refers to higher education services provided to students that are resident in the country of the provider (MinEduNZ 2005; Rizvi 2004; World Bank 2002).

In addition to the examples of both franchise arrangements and branch campuses given here, other examples follow, illustrating the wide range of arrangements that exist and the difficulty of classifying them into simple, well-defined groups.

American branch campuses in Japan, which had started during the booming 1980s and collapsed in the 1990s after reaching their peak number of around forty in 1985, provide just one of the group of examples of the hundreds of branch campuses that exist around the globe (Ohmori 2004a). These existed in various forms (consortia, independent and twinning) and prominent U.S. institutions like Stanford, Michigan, Minnesota, and Temple were involved (Mock 2005). Following the Japanese economic crisis of the 1990s, some thirty branch campuses pulled out of Japan, and by 2003, only a few of them were left in operation. In late 2004, Japan officially recognized branch campuses, allowing credits obtained there to be transferred to Japanese institutions. The condition for recognition is for the parent campus to be an accredited institution back in the United States. It was, however, too late for many (Brender 2004b; OBHE-BN, April 2004; Ohmori 2004a, 2004b).

Greece, Spain, and Italy are the three European countries that are major importers of higher education services from abroad, mainly from the United States and the United Kingdom. Although, as I have already mentioned, the Greek constitution does not allow private institutions, and the Greek government does not recognize their degrees for employment in the public sector, there are an estimated 130 foreign institutions/programs operating in the country (OBHE-BN, November 2004; see also Section 3.3).

With operations of U.S. institutions in various forms proliferating all over the world, higher education is becoming "America's hot new export" (Bollag 2006a). These vary from single graduate programs and various types of twinning arrangements to entire campuses. SUNY-Buffalo, after the success of its branch campus in Singapore (operated in partnership with SIM), is now moving into China, India, and the United Arab Emirates. Rochester Institute of Technology has a decade-old branch campus in Dubrovnik, specializing in hospitality management. Nearly all of the major for-profit companies have extensive operations abroad, enrolling tens of thousands of students. In 2005, Laureate Inc. enrolled 190,000 students in fourteen countries, and as mentioned in Section 4.4.2, Laureate's enrollment had risen to 500,000 students in 2008. Roger Williams University, a small, nonprofit liberal arts university with an enrollment of slightly less than four thousand, located in Bristol, Rhode Island, is the first foreign institution that has been given permission to open a branch campus in Vietnam; the new institution is called the American Pacific University (OBHE-BN, January 2005).

There is an increasing demand for American higher education in the Middle East ("Middle East still hungry to learn the American way," *The Financial Times*, February 11, 2004; OBHE-BN, April 2003; December 2004). American University in Sharjah, opened in 1997, is supported by American University in Washington D.C. Columbia University is in the process of opening a business school in Jordan, where Queen Rania is leading the campaign to attract American institutions.[58]

The Education City in Qatar is a government-backed initiative that houses branch campuses of American universities including Texas A&M University, Virginia Commonwealth University School of Arts, and Weill, Cornell Medical College; more U.S. institutions are expected to join.

Georgia Institute of Technology has degree programs in France, Singapore and China, and Carnegie-Mellon in Greece, Korea, Qatar, and Japan. Harvard is in the process of setting up its first branch campuses in modern times, one in Cyprus and the other in the United Arab Emirates (OBHE-BN, June 2004). American institutions put together have operations in forty-two countries, from Vietnam to Germany, the Czech Republic, France, the United Kingdom, Spain, and Italy (Bollag 2006a). In May 2006, Carnegie-Mellon opened first foreign-run branch campus in Adelaide, Australia. Full degree programs are being offered in entertainment technology, IT, and public policy, with tuition fees about four times those in Australian universities (Cohen 2006a).

According to an OBHE report (Verbik and Merkley 2006), as of 2006, there were eighty-four branch campuses in operation in thirty-eight countries. Forty-four of these belonged to U.S. institutions, followed by ten Australian, five Indian, and four each in UK and Irish institutions. The Knowledge Village in Dubai hosted fourteen of these, followed by eight in the Education City in Qatar, six in Singapore, and five each in China, Malaysia and Canada. Thirteen branch campuses were closed between 2002 and 2006. According to an Institute of International Education (IIE) survey, nineteen U.S. branch campuses, which represent about 40 percent of all U.S. campuses, reported a total enrollment of 9,357 students in 2007, with 52.5 percent of them international.[59]

Data on offshore provision are scant. Each of Australia's thirty-nine universities has an offshore provision of one form or another. The number of offshore programs offered by Australian institutions was sixteen hundred in 2003, up from only twenty-five in 1991. More than 85 percent of these programs are in China, Hong Kong, Singapore, and Malaysia with the remaining scattered around the world from India and Indonesia to Fiji, South Africa, and Canada. These programs, which started out as "twinning" arrangements with colleges and initially had an educational focus, now have many other commercial companies as partners and have a revenue-generating focus (Garrett and Verbik 2004b; MinEduNZ 2003; Rizvi 2004). Figure 4.1 shows that the number of students enrolled in Australian offshore programs grew from 8,431 in 1994 to 61,331 in 2007. Offshore provision in Australian satellite campuses is essentially restricted to specialized, vocationally oriented programs (Cohen 2004a).

By 1997, UK universities had established offshore programs in sixty-nine countries. By 2000, offshore enrollment had increased to 120,000, including those in Open University Worldwide. Total enrollment in offshore programs was about 190,000 in 2003, and forecasts run as high as 1,400,000 students enrolled in such programs by the year 2025 (British Council 2003; CVCP-HEFCE 2000; Garrett and Verbik 2004a). A more recent forecast puts the number projected for the year 2020 at 800,000 (Bohm et al. 2004). The first set of comprehensive data on offshore provision by UK institutions was recently released by Higher Education Statistics Agency (HESA).[60] There were 61,425 postgraduate and 135,215 undergraduate stu-

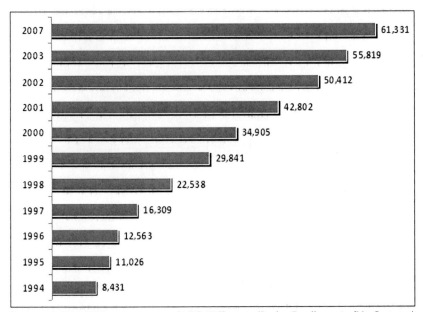

Sources: a) 1994–2001: www.aei.gov.au./AEI/MIP/Statistics/StudentEnrollmentAndVisaStatistics/; b) 2002–2003: www.universitiesaustralia.edu/; c) www.idp.com/research/fast_facts/higher_education. aspx

Fig. 4. 1 Growth of Enrollment in Australian Offshore Programs

dents enrolled in these programs in 2007–2008. The top fifteen countries with respect to enrollment in these programs were Hong Kong (21,280), Singapore (20,845), Malaysia (20,525), China (10,450), Greece (9,575), Russia (9,545), Ireland (8,980), Trinidad and Tobago (8,605), Oman (6,240), Germany (5,350), India (4,930), Spain (4,860), Israel (4,455), United Arab Emirates (4,180), and Egypt (3,500). Enrollment in British offshore delivery is currently about half of that in onshore programs, and the British Council has predicted that by 2010, demand for UK offshore provision will outstrip demand for student mobility to the United Kingdom (OBHE-BNA, April 21, 2006).

New Zealand, a relative newcomer to the international education market, has much more modest levels of offshore activity. In 2001, seventeen institutions of higher education in New Zealand offered sixty-three offshore programs, up from six in 1997, either alone or in cooperation with local partners. The total number of students in these programs was reported as 2,200, up from 380 in 1997, and programs were concentrated in Singapore and Hong Kong (MinEduNZ 2005; OBHE-BN Article, 15 April 2005). Programs were delivered either by campus-based teaching abroad (franchise or branch, 32 percent), or by distance education alone (42 percent) or a combination of the two modes (26 percent).

In 1999, Canadian universities were offering 268 academic and 87 training programs offshore, 155 of which were delivered by distance education, and 50 were developed and taught jointly by local partners. Total enrollment in the programs was thirty-six thousand. Only thirty-five of the training programs were completely taught by Canadian instructors (MinEduNZ 2003, 2004).

The United States, the United Kingdom, Australia, and Canada are by far the leading providers of offshore programs. However, such programs are increasingly being taught in languages other than English (Scarino et al. 2006).

Monash University claims to be Australia's most internationalized university. In addition to its online programs, it has campuses in South Africa, London, and Malaysia. Its campus in Malaysia was established in 1998 as a joint venture with the Sunway Group, a commercial company. Curtin University of Technology and Swinburne University of Technology are the other two Australian universities with branch campuses in Malaysia, which were opened in 1999 and 2004, respectively (Malaysia 2005). De Montfort and Nottingham are two British universities that have branch campuses in Malaysia. These were opened in 1999 and 2000, respectively.[61] Australia's Charles Stuart University has recently been given permission by the Ontario government to open the first degree-awarding branch of a foreign institution in the province, following the provincial legislation enacted in 2002 that allows branch campuses. (OBHE-BN, February 2005).

The University of Wollongong was the first foreign institution that was licensed in 1993 by the country's Commission for Academic Accreditation to open a branch campus in the United Arab Emirates, called the University of Wollongong Dubai (UOWD). The UOWD is now opening its second campus in the Knowledge Village Dubai in the United Arab Emirates (OBHE-BN, January 2005).

Launched in 2003, the "Knowledge Village" in Dubai is a unique site, where education and media interests are brought together to integrate the emirates into the global knowledge economy. Recently, the London School of Economics joined as a partner (OBHE-BN, June 2003, January 2005, March 2005). In what appears to be a move to make Dubai a major hub for transnational higher education, the Commission for Academic Accreditation of the United Arab Emirates waived its long-standing clause that no more than half of the provision may be delivered by distance education (OBHE-BN, July 2003). As of 2005, Knowledge Village was hosting thirteen foreign institutions from Australia, Canada, Ireland, Russia, the United Kingdom, India, Pakistan, Iran, and Belgium, and enrolled six thousand students; projections for the future include twenty-five to thirty foreign partners and thirty-six thousand students (Clark and Sedgwick 2005). The University of New Brunswick, University of Wollongong, University of Southern Queensland, Royal College of Surgeons, Middlesex University, Heriot Watt University, Saint Petersburg State University of Engineering and Economics, and Islamic Azad University of Iran are some of the universities that have branch campuses there.

After Qatar and Dubai, Bahrain is also poised to be another international education hub in the Gulf region with the announcement of the Higher Education City (OBHE-BNA January 16, 2007).

In 2004, South Korea allowed foreign institutions to open branch campuses in specially designated areas called Special Economic Zones. George Washington University was the first American institution to show interest in opening a branch in Korea under the new scheme (OBHE-BN, August 2004).

Private colleges in the Greek part of Cyprus have franchise agreements with UK and U.S. institutions, but they lack university status (OBHE-BN, April 2004).

Australian and UK universities have partnerships in Singapore that can be classified as both franchise arrangements and branch campuses. Eleven prestigious universities have branch campuses in Singapore. These are INSEAD (Institut Européen d'Administration des Affaires), the Graduate School of Business of the University of Chicago, the Wharton Business School, Johns Hopkins, MIT, Stanford, Technical University of Munich, Technical University of Eindhoven, and Shanghai Jiao Tong. The University of New South Wales of Australia[62] and the University of Warwick of the United Kingdom also accepted the offer of the Singaporean government to set up teaching and research-led branch campuses (Garrett 2005; OBHE-BN, April 2004). Local partners include both commercial enterprises like the Raffles Education Corporation mentioned earlier and colleges and private institutions like SIM (f. 1964), which do not have the power to award degrees themselves.[63]

In 2003, SIM offered sixty-two such programs, accounting for 12 percent of all registered offshore provision in Singapore. SIM's partners included George Washington University, Royal Melbourne Institute of Technology, Beijing University, SUNY-Buffalo, Sydney, Wollongong, London, Warwick, Melbourne, Manchester, and the Open University of the United Kingdom. As of 2005, altogether some 140 private tertiary providers offered such franchise programs and enrolled eighty-nine thousand students, fifty thousand of which were foreign (Clark and Sedgwick 2005).

In 2003, there were five branch campuses in Malaysia, two from the United Kingdom and three from Australia, with a German (OBHE-BN,

February 2003) and a Japanese university planning to join (OBHE-BN, March 2003).[64] Malaysia was already hosting more than forty-thousand foreign students. In order to make it more competitive compared to Thailand and Singapore as a hub in the international higher education market, the Malaysian government introduced stringent measures as well as incentives. These include the use of the various rankings of institutions in the country of the parent institution in its decision to grant permission for franchised provision in Malaysia (OBHE-BN, April 2004). New incentives are in place to attract more branch campuses of foreign universities (OBHE-BN, November 2004; OBHE-BNA, April 28, 2006).

The overwhelming desire on the part of Indian students, with their parents encouraging them, to acquire a foreign degree made India a big market for foreign for-profit providers, which started coming to India in the late 1980s and early 1990s. Russian universities offering medical courses were soon followed by universities in the Caribbean and Switzerland (Sharma 2001; Shivkumar 2001). Bushan (2006) identified three stages in the development of foreign educational activity in India. The unmet demand first attracted Canadian and UK institutions, which set up "study and examination centers" to offer their degree programs. These then developed into various forms of twinning arrangements, and later, into joint and collaborative degree programs between Indian and foreign universities. From the 2000s on, franchises started to be established in India, as well as direct provision by foreign providers. Foreign institutions and providers currently offer a large number of undergraduate and graduate courses in a wide variety of subjects in India, predominantly in management, engineering, and other vocational and professional areas. The number of providers is unknown, and they can only be tracked by monitoring their advertisements in Indian newspapers. Between July and December 2000, 144 such advertisements appeared, led by fifty-three institutions located in the United Kingdom, forty in Australia, twenty-four in the United States, and seven in Canada and New Zealand. Other institutions' advertising came from a diverse group of countries, which included Bulgaria, Cyprus, France, Hong Kong, Ireland, Mauritius, Nepal, Romania, Russia, and Switzerland. Although 117 of the advertisers were trying to recruit students to their home campuses, 27 were offering programs in India. Most of the Indian partners were not institutions of higher education, but commercial entities (Powar and Bhalla 2001). In 2001, two hundred foreign programs were being offered to thirty thousand students in India, which generated an annual income $1.2 billion for the foreign providers (Anandakrishnan 2001). In May 2003, India introduced new regulations on fees charged and profits repatriated by foreign providers and barred unapproved institutions (OBHE-BN, May 2003). According to data reported by Bushan (2006), as of 2004, sixty-six U.S., fifty-nine UK, two Canadian, and one each, Australian, Swiss, and French institutions and providers were operating in India, mostly in twinning arrangements with Indian partners. Annual tuition fees varied from $1,600 to $16,500, with the average around $4,500 in 2004.

Taiwan was an exception in the region; it was only in June 2003 that Taiwan allowed foreign institutions to operate in the country, with little interest from foreign providers so far (OBHE-BN, June 2003).

Thailand, along with Vietnam, Hong-Kong, and China, is emerging as a new hub in the international higher education market, under a government-led initiative, which has attracted institutions from the United States, Australia, China, and Egypt; the latter will be a branch campus of Al-Azhar to serve Thailand's Muslim minority (OBHE-BNA, March 12, 2004).

The first foreign joint venture in China was the joint MBA program by Tianjin University and Oklahoma City University in 1987. The number of such twinning arrangements in various forms had reached 712 by 1999, and climbed to 1,300 by 2006 (Feng and Gong 2003; OBHE-BfN 13, September 2003). U.S. institutions were the main source of such ventures by a wide margin, followed by Australia, Hong Kong, Canada, France, Netherlands, the United Kingdom, Belgium, and Singapore. Nottingham University opened the first branch campus in China in Ningbo (UNNC) in April 2006. This was the second Nottingham branch campus after the university's first branch campus in Malaysia in 2000—the latter was also the first branch campus of a UK university abroad. UNNC currently serves a student body of 4,000,[65] and charges $6,250 tuition per year (Feng and Gong 2006). Although UNNC is truly an outpost of Nottingham University, the Xian Jiatong-Liverpool University that opened in September 2006 is an independent institution with full-degree awarding powers. The project was completely financed by Laureate Education. It does appear that academic globalization and internationalization was what drove Nottingham, while the main driver of the Liverpool venture is financial. A recent report by the UK-based AGORA Forum provides an in-depth look at the various aspects of operating in China, and lists the difficulty of recruiting qualified academic staff both from abroad and within China, and the rather restrictive interpretation of the current legislation by the Chinese authorities at the top of the difficulties encountered (Fazackerley and Worthington 2007).

Since May 2000, the Royal Melbourne Institute of Technology (RMIT) has a branch campus in Vietnam, which it fully owns, RMIT Vietnam, and is in the process of building a second one (see also Section 3.3 for branch campuses and franchise arrangements in China and Vietnam). An international university is being built with foreign partners. Hue University is offering a bachelor-level joint program in tourism with the University of Hawaii (OBHE-BN, March 2002; January 2004; see also Section 3.3 for the Vietnamese policies of expanding private higher education). Mauritius launched its plans in 2003 to become a "cyber island," emulating successful city-states like Hong Kong and Singapore in attracting franchises and branch campuses to build higher education capacity (OBHE-BN, October 2003).

As pointed out previously, foreign activity in Latin America and the Caribbean started centuries ago as part of the colonization of the region by the Spanish and the Portuguese, and I return to this topic in the next chapter. In this subsection, I summarize recent foreign activity in the region, which, like in other parts of the world, started to intensify in the 1990s.[66] Since then, institutions and providers from many other countries have established branch campuses, virtual provision, mixed forms of provision and direct presence in the region, including Belgium, Canada, France, Germany, Italy, the United Kingdom, and the United States in addition to Spain and Portugal. Traditional institutions like Bologna University and Heidelberg University have branch campuses in the region, as well as for-profit providers like the Apollo Group's direct presence. Harvard provides distance learning in Costa Rica, Ecuador, and Mexico. Carnegie-Mellon, George Washington, Texas A&M, and Pittsburgh, University of Paris I, VII, and X offer graduate-level programs in various collaborative modes with institutions and providers in the region. Other than Laureate's learning centers in Brazil, Chile, Costa Rica, Ecuador, Honduras, Mexico, Panama, and Peru, and University of Phoenix Online' s virtual provision in Mexico, higher education provision by providers and institutions based in Anglo-Saxon countries is concentrated in the Anglophone Caribbean region. In contrast to other parts of the world, there is relatively limited market for higher education provided in English. Nevertheless, three UK institution, Heriot Watt, Leicester, and Manchester, are providing distance education across the whole region. Spanish institutions account for the largest share of foreign provision in the region. As of 2007, seven Spanish providers were active in the region, including two open universities, the national one (UNED) and the Catalunyan one (UOC), Autonomous University of Barcelona, University Complutense of Madrid, the Universities of Seville, Deusto and Coruna, the Polytechnic Universities of Madrid and Catalunya, and the Tertiary Institute for Postgraduate Studies, a consortium of the University of Alicante, Autonomous University of Barcelona, Carlos III University of Madrid, and Editorial Santillana. The Spain-based for-profit education group San Estanislao de Kostka has opened two university campuses in Chile and Ecuador. In addition to the presence of providers based outside of the region, there is significant cross-border provision within the region. Institutions and providers based in Argentina, Bolivia, Costa Rica, Cuba, Ecuador, and Mexico are providing higher education across the region in mixed modes, but mostly in the distance education mode. Annual tuition fees charged for transnational programs vary from $130 for a master's program in anthropology to $25,000 to $40,000 for graduate-level programs in business, and, on the average, are slightly higher than those charged by local private providers. Activity of Portuguese institutions is restricted to Brazil.

The Russian Ministry of Education also announced its plans in 2003 to export Russian higher education based on a strategy of establishing branch campuses of Russian institutions abroad. With improving economic and political stability, the country itself is increasingly becoming a target for foreign providers (OBHE-BN, October 2003, March 2006).

As part of the campaign to promote German higher education internationally, several German universities have been opened abroad in recent years. In addition to the German Institute of Science and Technology in Singapore operated by the Technical University of Munich, there is the German University in Cairo, which opened in 2003, and the Euro University in Bahrain, which the University of Hannover started establishing in 2004. German institutions abroad do not have a commercial agenda. Rather, they have small enrollments, and offer specialist programs more at the graduate level.

There were four officially registered branch campuses of Australian, Dutch, and UK institutions in South Africa. With the more strict review process that the South Africa Council for Higher Education has adopted, three of them have closed their operations in South Africa (OBHE-BN, February 2004, May 2004, June 2004). The Netherlands Business School also has a branch campus in Nigeria, called the *Universiteit Nyenrode*, which started in March 2004 (OBHE-BN, April 2004).

Institutions based in the United States, the United Kingdom, Australia, Canada, and New Zealand presently dominate the offshore higher education market. Indian institutions are emerging as key players in the ICT certificate subsector. It is likely that competition will intensify in the offshore market, with new entrants from different countries; Japanese and Indian institutions appear as the most likely new competitors, and the Asia-Pacific Rim is likely to remain as the main recipient of such programs. With increasing pressure to diversify their resources and act entrepreneurially as corporations, Japanese universities are increasing their efforts to recruit more foreign students and open branch campuses. Current activities seem to be focused on establishing partnerships with other Asian universities (OBHE-BNA, March 24, 2006).

According to Knight (2009a, 12), double- and joint-degree programs:

can lead to a deeper and more sustainable relationship than many internationalization strategies and create such academic benefits as innovation of curriculum, exchange of professors and researchers, and increased access to expertise and research networks. Students are attracted to double degrees for enhanced career opportunities, an international study and life experience, and the perception that "two degrees for one" means decreased workload and tuition fees. At the national and regional level, they are seen to contribute to increased status, competitiveness, and capacity building.

Such programs have long been in existence among European countries, and have recently been on the rise across the Atlantic, too. Definitions of such collaborative degree programs have been further refined in a recent report (Kuder and Obst, 2009, 10):

> A joint degree program: students study at (at least) two higher education institutions and receive upon completion of the study program a single degree certificate issued and signed by all the participating institutions jointly. . . . A dual or double degree program: students study at (at least) two higher education institutions and receive upon completion of the study program a separate degree certificate from each of the participating instutions.

According to the results of the survey reported by Kuder and Obst (2009), double degrees are much more common than joint degrees. The top five partners of European institutions for collaborative degree programs are the United States, France, Germany, Spain, and the United Kingdom, whereas those of U.S. institutions are China, France, Mexico, Korea, and Spain. U.S. institutions are more likely to offer collaborative degree programs at the undergraduate level, as opposed to European institutions, which are more likely to offer graduate-level programs. Business and management seem to be the most popular disciplines for collaborative degree programs. Tuition fees account for 26 percent of the funding for European institutions, and 58 percent of the funding for U.S. institutions. The EU is a major source of funding for collaborative degree programs between U.S. and European institutions as well as intra-European collaborative degree programs. On the other hand, the dual-diploma program between the SUNY system and a number of leading Turkish universities, which has been in existence since 2000, and currently enrolls 1,750 Turkish students is completely demand-driven and self-financing by tuition fees; as of March 2009, 262 students have graduated from the program. Knight (2009b) foresees an increase in collaborative-degree programs, but also draws attention to a number of significant challenges including compatibility of curricula, credit systems, academic calendars, and admission and graduation requirements and recognition of degrees and qualifications. She also cautions against double counting of credits, which, in effect, is another form of a "rogue provision."

As far as the students and the families are concerned, branch campuses, franchise, and other forms of locally provided higher education through various twinning arrangements offer a less expensive alternative close to home. The advantages perceived by the foreign provider institutions, other than being an additional revenue stream, are an international exposure for students and staff, access to high-quality students, and possible joint research projects for multinational companies.

4.5. THE GLOBAL HIGHER EDUCATION MARKET

Significantly increased demand for higher education, much more readily available and easily accessible information on higher education worldwide, improved and expanded means of travel, and development of advanced educational technologies based on ICT have interacted to create a global market for higher education in the last two decades. Newman and Couturier (2001, 6) described the higher education scene at the beginning of the new millennium as follows:

> The result of all these changes, taken together, is a market place for higher education that allows more choices among a wider array of alternatives; a growing interest in convenience and effectiveness (i.e., learner outcomes); and a readiness to attend multiple institutions on the way to a degree. The result of the new competition is likely to be an array of institutions that mix many of these approaches-virtual and face-to-face instruction, for-profit and non-profit, consortia and individual institutions, etc., along with a great deal of technology-each institution seeking to create a specific niche. The experience of the last half century, when institutions competed largely with their "own kind" and where each could count on a reasonably predictable cadre of applicants, is breaking down.

Such a market always existed in higher education; in fact, it may very well have been the existence of a market that led to the creation of the medieval European university, where, in many cases, students attended more than one institution on the way to their degrees. Until recently, the market involved the movement of students and teachers alone. The transnational or cross-border higher education market in today's global knowledge economy involves much more than that. The following are the three basic forms of transnational higher education in terms of what actually crosses the borders of nations (Knight 2003a, 2008, 97–107; OECD 2004b, 19–25): (1) "Movement of people" comprises "international student mobility" and "academic mobility." The former involves students who go abroad to study in an institution or trainees. Examples include full study abroad toward a degree, part of an academic partnership for a home degree (study abroad) or a joint degree, and students in exchange programs. Academic mobility involves professors and trainers who go abroad to teach and/or to do research for professional development, as an employee of a foreign institution, as part of an academic exchange program in a branch campus abroad. (2) "Movement of programs" involves educational programs delivered across borders in the form of academic partnerships or e-learning. Examples include programs or courses jointly offered by institutions in different countries, distance education, virtual universities and e-learning programs, and selling or franchising a course or a full-degree program to a foreign institution. (3) "Movement of institutions and providers" takes the form of branch campuses, foreign campuses, and foreign investments. Examples include opening a campus in a foreign country, buying all or part of a foreign educational institution and the creation of an educational provider abroad.

In addition to the provision of education itself, the global education market includes trade in the following services and products: (1) education-related publishing; (2) educational equipment and course material; (3) consultancy services provided to ministries and companies; (4) guidance, counseling, and placement services provided to students; (5) preparatory teaching, especially teaching of English as a foreign language; and (6) testing. The OBHE has developed the Global Education Index (GEI), and has been reporting it since 2003. The GEI is similar to the previously mentioned Chronicle Index of For-Profit. Whereas the latter only tracks the performance of the eight U.S.-based publicly traded for-profit higher education providers shown in Table 4.1, the GEI is based on the performance of fifty companies providing education and education-related services across the whole sector worldwide, including (Garrett 2005, 2):

- "firms that own for-profit universities and other higher education institutions (e.g., Apollo Group)

- firms that own for-profit college networks that typically have a collaborative relationship with non-local, nonprofit higher education for the purposes of offering degree programmes (e.g., Raffles Education)

- e-learning and related software vendors targeting either higher education, the corporate sector, or both (e.g., Blackboard/WebCT)

- administrative software vendors focused or part-focused on higher education (e.g., SAP, MXL)

- multinational publishers offering nonprofit higher education various support products and services; plus instances of direct course provision (e.g., Pearson, McGraw-Hill)

- firms that offer outsourcing services related to student support and/or course development (e.g., NIIT, IBT Education).

The 2005 GEI included twenty-three companies from the United States, four each from Canada, Malaysia, and the United Kingdom, three each from Australia, India, and Singapore, two each from India, Philippines, and South Africa, and one each from Germany and Ireland. It is clear that except for one German company, the international education market is dominated by companies based in English-speaking countries, and the U.S.-based companies are dominating the market by a wide margin.

According to Merrill Lynch, the international education sector is a $2.2 trillion business worldwide (Hezel Associates 2005). According to UNESCO (2007, 8), total government spending worldwide on education in 2004 was $2.46 trillion on the purchasing power basis and $1.97 trillion on the basis of current exchange rate, which correspond to 4.4 percent of the global GDP. Morey (2004) estimates higher education as a $231 billion enterprise in the United States; Oblinger et al. (2001) report the value of $740 billion a year for total U.S. spending on education at all levels, whereas Meister (2001) estimates that higher education alone takes in exactly that much every year. Another figure for total annual spending in the United States on higher education is obtained by multiplying the total enrollment figure in Table A.1 with the average annual expenditure per student given in Figure 3.2 and Table A.3. This gives the figure of approximately $400 billion per year (see note 15), which is in reasonable agreement with the $395 billion value reported by Blumenstyk (2005c).

There are differences between the estimates. These are caused by differences in the time of reporting, and what are included in the total. All, however, clearly show that global spending on higher education worldwide is on the order of hundreds of billions of dollars, probably well over $1 trillion, with the United States accounting for the major portion of the spending.

The amount of money involved in the international higher education market is even more difficult to estimate, and data are scant and relatively old. According to the OECD (2004b, 13), export revenue related to international student mobility alone amounted to an estimated minimum of $30 billion in 1998, or 3 percent of global service exports. Knight (2004) quotes the value of $35 billion for the total volume of international trade in postsecondary education in 1999. Hira (2003) quotes estimates that are projected to reach values as high as $50 billion by 2010. Hezel Associates (2005), on the other hand, describes e-learning as the fastest growing sub-sector of the global education market, and estimates that it will exceed $69 billion by 2015. If one adds up the annual revenues of the fifty companies included in the previously mentioned in the GEI in 2005, the figure is $56.4 billion (Garrett 2005).

One thing, however, is clear: International higher education is now a multibillion-dollar industry, which is demand-driven, characterized by intense competition among traditional institutions as well as new provid-ers. Chapter 1 of this book is, in essence, about the drivers of the increasing demand for higher education worldwide. Chapter 2 lays the background by analyzing the nature and the sources of the increasing demand. Chapter 3 deals with how governments' and traditional institutions' responses to these changes have evolved over time. These have transformed the role of the state from a regulatory to an evaluative one. The "entrepreneurial univer-sity" has emerged as an institutional model, blurring the demarcation line between public and nonprofit private institutions of the traditional type in terms of tuition fees, revenue diversification, spread of lay governance, and a redefinition of university autonomy.

This chapter is about new types of higher education providers, as well as traditional institutions' responses to demand outside of their home countries. The next chapter presents the globalization and the internation-alization of higher education in a historical context, and analyzes both the classical and the recently emerged rationales that are currently driving the international higher education scene at the national, the institutional and the family/student levels.

FIVE

GLOBALIZATION AND INTERNATIONALIZATION OF HIGHER EDUCATION

5.1. HISTORICAL ANTECEDENTS

5.1.1. International Academic Mobility in the Greco-Roman and the Muslim Worlds

A brief look at the intellectual journey mentioned in Section 1.1, which started on the Anatolian coast of the Aegean Sea and eventually found its way to the medieval European university, is interesting in itself, and sheds light on international mobility of students, scholars, and ideas in today's global knowledge economy.[1]

Legend has it that Pythagoras (c. 569–c. 475 BC) visited Miletus, where he received advice from Thales and attended lectures by Anaximander. Thus, Pythagoras is arguably the first example of the wandering international scholar. Welch (1997) cites the Sophists as the first examples of international academic mobility. The Sophists appeared around 445 BC; they were itinerant, professional teachers who traveled in the Greek-speaking world, teaching the children of the wealthy, for which they were paid.

Nakayama (1984) likens the shih in China to the Sophists in Greece. The shih were wandering scholars who sold their knowledge to warring rulers in China in the fifth century BC, the same period in which the Sophists appeared in Greece.[2]

The Hellenic world was united by a common language, Greek, and it was connected by trade routes that crisscrossed the Mediterranean Sea and the Black Sea basins. Students and scholars from all over the region traveled to Athens, the intellectual capital of the world at the time, and home to

Plato's (427–347 BC) Academy (f. 385 BC) and Aristotle's (384–322 BC) Lyceum (f. 335 BC). The academy and the lyceum survived in one form or another, at times serving as models for Roman schools, until AD 529, when the Roman Emperor Justinian closed them during his campaign to eradicate all vestiges of Greek paganism.

Alexandria ranked next to Athens, and then surpassed it as an intellectual center in the waning years of the Hellenic world. The Museum and the adjacent Library of Alexandria (f. 283 BC), generally considered to be the first state-sponsored research institution in the world, served as a center of study and research for centuries, attracting scholars from all over the Hellenic and the Roman world. Euclid (325–265 BC), Eratosthenes (276–196 BC), Archimedes (c. 287–212 BC), Strobe (c. 63 BC–AD 21), and possibly Ptolemy (second century) were among the resident scholars of the Museum; the latter two had left their birthplaces to study there.

In later years, Pergamum was the chief rival to Alexandria as an intellectual center. The most famous scholar from Pergamum, Galen (c. 130–c.200), considered second only to Hippocrates (460–377 BC) in the development of medicine, is believed to have based his medical writings partly on previous research done in Alexandria.

After Aristotle's death, his successors kept his works in the Peripatetic School in various parts of the Hellenic world. They reappeared in Athens, and the Romans took them to Rome, along with Plato's works, after they captured Athens in 86 BC.

The Romans were more interested than the Greeks were in practical matters such as law, governance, military and civilian technology, and engineering, and emphasized rhetoric, so that one could express oneself eloquently in business, law, and politics. Cicero (c. 106–43 BC), arguably the most famous orator of all times, was a Roman politician who studied Greek philosophy to gain an advantage in politics. In doing so, he developed Latin as a language of science and the arts, and helped transmit the Greek philosophical heritage to later generations.

Plotinus (204–270) is considered to be third in importance after Aristotle and Plato in the development of critical, rational thought. After studying in Alexandria, he came to Rome, where he founded neo-Platonism. His works were collected and edited by his most famous student Porphyry (c. 232–c. 305), who was born in Lebanon and later studied in Athens, before ending up in Rome. Through Plotinus, Plato's works reached Alexandria.

Following the adoption of Christianity as the official religion of the Roman Empire, Aristotle's works were completely ignored as quintessentially pagan, and the vast volume of Aristotelian philosophy remained unknown in the West until the twelfth century.

For centuries when Europe was living in the Dark Ages following the collapse of the Roman Empire, the Greco-Roman intellectual heritage was preserved and transmitted from generation to generation by Zoroastrians, pagans, Jews, Syrians, and Nestorian Christians in a region where the Sassanian and the Byzantine empires interfaced. Hospitals, temples, and meditation centers were established, which functioned as schools. In places like Edessa, Harran, Nisbis, and Jundi Shapur, they interacted with Muslims, and the Hellenistic intellectual heritage from the West and oriental knowledge from the East, mainly Chinese and Indian, permeated the Islamic intellectual life.

In the period 750–850, great Abbasid caliphs established and generously endowed translation centers, libraries, observatories, and hospitals, Muslim scholars were exposed to the works of Plato and Aristotle and learned methods such as dialectic, logic and rhetoric. Baghdad emerged as a cosmopolitan, intellectual center similar in importance to Athens and Alexandria, attracting scholars and students from places as far away as central Asia. The caliphs invited scholars and physicians to work in their courts regardless of their faith. A corps of scholar-translators emerged, who translated Greco-Roman texts both from Syriac into Arabic indirectly and from Greek and Latin into Arabic directly, and many of the earlier translations by Nestorians and Assyrians were revised.

In this vibrant intellectual atmosphere that prevailed in a vast region stretching as far as al-Andalus, Spain, a group of polymaths emerged. Starting with al-Kindi (the "Philosopher of Arabs," 801–873), al-Razi (Rhazes, 864–930), al-Farabi (Avennasar, 870–950), Ibn-Sina (Avicenna, 980–1037), al-Biruni (Alberuni 973–1048), and Ibn-Rushd (Averroes, 1126–1198), they preserved the Greco-Roman epistemic heritage, and improved on it by their commentaries and original contributions. Their interests covered a wide intellectual spectrum, which extended from philosophy, natural sciences and medicine to music, literature, and poetry.[3] The Muslims had acquired, preserved and further developed the philosophy of Plato and Aristotle, both moral and natural; Euclid's mathematics; Ptolemy's astronomy and optics; and Archimedes's mechanics and Hippocrates' and Galen's medical sciences. To these, they had added chemistry, algebra, and history (Rubenstein 2003, 6–22).

Similarities existed between the Hellenic world and the world of Islam. The latter, too, was united by a common language, Arabic, and was characterized by vigorous trading. A common language and the means to travel facilitated the mobility of ideas and made it possible for itinerant students and scholars to move over a vast region. In both worlds, anything beyond basic reading and writing was considered higher learning.

The premier institution of higher learning in the Muslim world was the *madrasa*, which was essentially a school of law (Makdisi 1981). The polymaths pursued their philosophical studies not in the *madrasas*, but in informal settings and in libraries, observatories, and hospitals.

Thus, itinerant polymaths, scholars, and students united by a common language and with the means to travel, the existence of informal structures for learning, and scholarly work such as museums, libraries, observatories, and learning centers in urban settings were common characteristics of both the Greco-Roman world, the West, and the world of Islam, the East.

Where these two worlds interfaced over a region stretching from the Middle East to Sicily, northern Africa and the shores of the Atlantic, the second flurry of translational activities took place, this time from Arabic to Latin, the lingua Franca of the emerging international scholarly world. Of particular importance are the translations made in Toledo and Sicily that attracted translators from all over Europe well into the thirteenth century.[4]

With increasing availability of the works of Plato, Aristotle, and others through translated Arabic texts, Greek philosophy, derisively referred to as Averroeism and strongly opposed by the church as destructive to religion, started permeating the Christian world through the new institution, the medieval university, which culminated in Thomas Aquinas' (1127–1274) *Summa Theologica* in 1273. Although left unfinished due to his death, Aquinas had reconciled Aristotle's logic and natural philosophy with Christian orthodoxy and authority based on the writings of early Christian fathers. He established scholasticism as a system of logic, philosophy, and theology that became the basis of all academic activity for centuries to come.

5.1.2. International Academic Mobility in Medieval Times

Out of these intellectual roots that followed a tortuous path over a vast geographical area, the university evolved as a uniquely western European institution, an autonomous, corporate body, sanctioned by a higher authority, initially spiritual and later temporal, to set its curricula, appoint teachers, admit students, and award degrees.[5] The fully structured medieval university consisted of the liberal arts faculty that offered a curriculum at the undergraduate level, which was preparatory to the three graduate schools: theology, law, and medicine.

The undergraduate curriculum consisted of the *trivium* (grammar, rhetoric, and logic) and the *quadrivium* (arithmetic, geometry, astronomy, and music). The works of Greek philosophers and Muslim scholars eventually became a major part of the curricula both in the lower faculty of arts and the graduate schools, transforming the medieval university into an international institution.[6] New universities were founded that were staffed by migrating scholars;[7] their number reached sixty-three in 1500, up from twenty-eight in 1378 (Verger 1992).

Students and teachers came to study and teach in these institutions from all over Europe. Those from particular regions were organized as "nations" (*nationes*), which played key roles in the governance of the institutions. The nation to which students belonged primarily depended on their mother tongue, and secondarily on their birthplace, cultural community, or shared history. A look at the nations in the two oldest universities, Bologna and Paris, clearly shows the international character of the medieval university and the degree of international mobility that existed centuries ago. There were four nations in the University of Paris, namely, the French (embracing all Latin races), the Normans from Normandy, the Picards (covering the Low Countries), and the English (including Germans and others from the north and east of Europe). The University of Bologna was even more complicated in organization as it in fact consisted of two guilds, the Citramontana and the Ultramontana. The former comprised students from the Italian peninsula and initially consisted of three nations: Romans, Tuscans, and Lombards. The Ultramontani, on the other hand, included students from north of the Alps and were subdivided into sixteen nations: Gaul, Portugal and Algarve, Provence, England, Burgundy, Savoy, Gascony and Auvergne, Berry, Touraine, Aragon, and Catalonia, Navarre, Germany, Hungary, Poland, Bohemia, and Flanders (Rashdall 1936, 182–183 and 318–320 in Vol. 1; Gieysztor 1992; Ridder-Symoens 1992b).

The universities in medieval Europe had a common teaching language, Latin, the Lingua Franca of European education and science at the time. They had a similar organizational structure, a common curriculum with common texts, and similar admission and graduation requirements, which were all supervised by a higher authority (Altbach 2004a, 2006; Altbach and Teichler 2001) All of these facilitated student and teacher mobility. Ridder-Symoens (1992b) refers to this as the European "academic pilgrimage" (*peregrinatio academica*). She lists the following as additional factors that supported academic mobility in medieval Europe:

1. Universities existed in only a few places, especially in the twelfth and thirteenth centuries. Students and teachers had to travel, particularly from Scandinavia, Ireland, Scotland, and eastern Europe.

2. A travel culture existed in Europe, which dated back to the previous tradition of traveling to monastic and Episcopal schools for ecclesiastical training, to Salerno for medical training, and to Toledo for translation.

3. The church provided support especially to students from the newly Christianized lands. So did the rulers to less wealthy students, in the form of direct financial assistance or in-kind assistance such as housing (colleges) and control of rents and food prices for students and teachers. In return, students were expected to work for the state or the church.

4. Different institutions were prestigious in different fields of study, such as law in Bologna, arts and theology in Paris and Oxford, and medicine in Bologna, Padua, Montpellier, and Paris.

5. A network of roads was built with the revival of international trade in the eleventh and the twelfth centuries.

6. Privileges were granted to traveling students and teachers, starting with the Authentica Habita (see Section 3.4.1), which exempted them from customs dues, tolls, and other taxes, levies, and exactions, and protected them from undue judicial and penal actions by local authorities.

Rulers provided "letters of safeguard" to foreign students that protected them and their property from reprisals. It was quite common to study and teach in more than one university in one's lifetime. A look at the lives of three prominent scientists gives further proof for the degree of international academic mobility in Europe. Nicholas Copernicus (1473–1543) studied liberal arts at the Jaegellonian University in Krakow (f. 1364), medicine in Padua and law in Ferrara (f. 1391); Galileo Galilei (1564–1642) taught at Pisa (f. 1343) and Padua; and Andreas Vesalius (1514–1564) taught at Louvain (f. 1425) and Padua.

No single person epitomizes international academic mobility more than Desiderius Erasmus (1466–1536), the itinerant scholar and the intellectual father of the Reformation. Born in Rotterdam and educated in a humanistic school, a monastic school, the University of Paris, and the University of Turin (f. 1404), but mostly self-taught, Erasmus spent time in many universities in France, England, Italy, Germany, Belgium, and Switzerland, spreading humanism across western Europe.

As universities spread all over Europe, with every state and political or ecclesiastical unit trying to establish an institution of its own, studying in a regional university or in the nearest university became the preferred option. Furthermore, rulers started to take protective measures forbidding students from studying abroad or requiring them to spend some time in the local institution before going abroad, so that they could keep an eye on the ideological training of their subjects, and to prevent the flight of capital abroad to the detriment of local traders and artisans. Consequently, from the fourteenth century on, international academic mobility started to wane, and European higher education became increasingly regionalized. This trend became more pronounced in the fifteenth century, when the composition of the student body started to change from mainly cleric to predominantly laymen, with an accompanying decrease in support for poor students to study abroad.

The universities became increasingly aristocratic institutions, and study abroad became a privilege only for the sons of the aristocrats and the emerging classes of urban intellectuals, wealthy merchants, and the landed gentry. Poorer students largely had to go to less expensive home or regional institutions. It is, however, possible to discern several rationales driving international academic mobility even then, such as economic, political, and cultural motives of the type referred to earlier, and the effect of the development of indigenous capacity on mobility. Furthermore, the effect that medieval international academic mobility had on spreading ideas and culture that eventually harmonized Europe was far more important than the numbers of students and teachers involved.

5.1.3. International Academic Mobility: 1500–1800

With the advent of humanism, both the total enrollment and the number of foreign students increased in European universities.[8] Ridder-Symoens (1996b) makes the following remarks concerning academic mobility in the sixteenth century:

1. Foreign travel in itself came to be considered as educational value in humanistic studies.

2. Students from the north of the Alps flocked to Italy to search for sources of knowledge as well as culture, spending time in a number of universities along an itinerary (*iter Italicum*) either directly or after spending time in French universities (*iter Gallicum*), increasing foreign enrollment in some Italian universities to values as high as 50 percent.

3. The desire to learn other languages, French, Spanish, Italian, and German, but especially Greek and Hebrew, as part of theological studies, literature, and history, the so-called Ciceronian sciences, increased.

4. There was a growing interest in the study of natural sciences as part of medical studies or in addition to law.[9]

Interest in the study of Greek and Hebrew was particularly stimulated by Erasmus and Melanchton as part of theological studies in Protestant Europe,[10] which made new institutions like the *Collegium Trilingue* in

Louvain and the University of Basle (f. 1459) important destinations for foreign students from the north. Preparatory study in the arts was usually done in the country of origin.

The so-called first transport revolution of the late fifteenth and the early sixteenth centuries made intercontinental sea voyages possible, and took the university to the newly discovered lands. Mendicant Catholic orders, especially Jesuits, Dominicans and Franciscans, were instrumental in spreading university in the new lands. The Dominicans founded the first university outside of Europe, Santo Domingo in today's Dominican Republic, and the first university in the Asia-Pacific, Santo Tomas in Manila, in 1538 and 1611, respectively. These were followed by others in Asia, Latin America, and the Middle East (Altbach 2006; Perkin 2006; Roberts et al. 1996).

It is relevant to note that in 1434, just before the first transport revolution, the Ming emperor effectively closed China to international trade, dismantling the world's largest and most advanced fleet of ocean vessels in order to allocate resources to fend off increasing nomadic incursions from the north. Until then, China had been the world's unrivaled technological superpower. It was only after China withdrew from the high seas that Europe was able to conquer Asia with the compass, gunpowder and the printing press, all Chinese inventions originally (Sachs 2005, 150).

On the other hand, the Reformation, the Counter-Reformation, and the ensuing religious wars seriously hampered international academic mobility in Europe. Following the Reformation, various Protestant sects, under Melanchton's influence, founded forty-two universities in northern Europe, whereas those founded by Catholics during the Counter-Reformation, mostly by Jesuits, numbered ninety-five in the period between 1500 and 1800 (Frijhoff, 1996). Thus, the nature of mobility had changed by the end of the sixteenth century, with Protestants attending Protestant universities, and the Catholics attending Catholic universities. The situation was compounded by the adoption of the principle that the subjects were to adopt the faith of their ruler (*cujus regio, eius et religio*), which led many rulers to forbid students to go abroad for fear of political and religious contamination.

A third group of universities, however, emerged, which Ridder-Symoens refers to as "tolerant universities." Such universities existed on both sides of the religious cleavage. Padua, Siena (f. 1246), Montpellier, and Orleans were the tolerant Catholic universities, and the Calvinist Dutch universities, particularly Leiden, were the tolerant Protestant universities.

Bologna and Paris started to lose their leading positions as intellectual capitals, and other universities emerged as new centers of excellence and destination for foreign students. German universities in Wittenberg (f. 1502), Leipzig (f. 1409), Jena (f. 1557), Rostock (f. 1419), Greifswald (f. 1456), and Königsberg (Kaliningrad, f. 1544) attracted Protestant students from all over Europe. Heidelberg (f. 1385), Geneva (f. 1559), Strasbourg (f. 1621), and Basle (f. 1459) were the main Calvinist universities. Foreign students accounted for up to 40 percent of the total enrollment in some universities. However, by the end of the sixteenth century, Dutch universities, particularly Leiden, which offered multidisciplinary studies, started to emerge as the main Protestant centers for advanced learning and scholarly work.

In general, Catholic universities were more resistant to curricular reform, with many of them turning into bastions of the Counter-Reformation. Furthermore, Italian universities in the Papal States required swearing fidelity to the Holy Roman Church, causing even Bologna to lose its foreign students. By the end of the seventeenth century, religious conflicts and wars had decimated the foreign student enrollment in French universities. Student mobility in the Iberian Peninsula was mainly localized, with Salamanca as a major destination for Portuguese students. In fact, Catholics who wished to study new subjects were seeking admission to Protestant universities. Jesuit institutions in Graz (f. 1585), Würzburg (f. 1402), and Dillingen (f. 1553), on the other hand, attracted Polish, Hungarian, and Czech students, but with the spread of Jesuit institutions in these countries, that is, development of indigenous capacities, foreign student numbers started to drop in these three universities. In comparison to Protestant universities, foreign enrollment was, in general, considerably lower in Catholic universities; foreign students came only from neighboring regions.

Padua attracted Protestant students by not requiring them to take the oath of fidelity, offering humanistic studies in its main campus, and offering a program in medicine in its affiliated medical school in Venice, which was considerably cheaper than the medical program in the main campus. Siena, on the other hand, offered dormitory space and food cooked according to the ways of the students' countries of origin.

There are estimates that international student mobility in Europe had reached 10 percent of the total enrollment in universities across the continent in the seventeenth century (Neave 2002; Ridder-Symoens 1996b). A major factor that led to an increase in foreign enrollment in European universities in the sixteenth and the seventeenth centuries was migration. Children of immigrants displaced by religious conflicts and wars attending institutions in the countries where they sought refuge were recorded mostly based on their countries of origin. Jesuits operated colleges for hosting immigrant Catholic students in many universities across continental Europe. French Huguenots sought refuge mainly in Dutch universities.

Oxford and Cambridge were able to attract only a relatively small number of students from the Continent, because of the obligation to take an oath of subscription to the Anglican Church. Even English dissenters, the Irish, and the Scots were rarely accepted as students or fellows in the colleges. Foreign student enrollment in Oxford and Cambridge did not exceed 1 percent before the eighteenth century, even counting the Irish and the Scots. Thus, England, presently the second largest destination for foreign students after the United States, was then only a minor actor in international student mobility.

In general, the Jews were not allowed to attend universities in medieval Europe. However, they were permitted to study medicine in Italian universities at the end of the fifteenth century. Montpellier also had a tolerant attitude, allowing Jews from Spain and Portugal to study medicine there. On the other hand, Dutch universities allowed Jews to study, when they sought refuge in Holland after Spain had expelled them. It was, however, not before the seventeenth century that German protestant universities opened their doors to them. Catholic universities followed a century later.

The social composition of students, too, began to change at the turn of the sixteenth century. Poor clerics were no longer the majority. Children of urban merchants, landed gentry, and aristocrats, who aspired to positions in the newly emerging state bureaucracies and diplomacy, started to attend universities in increasing numbers (Hammerstein 1983). In the seventeenth and the eighteenth centuries, it was fashionable among the children of the wealthy to attend multiple institutions during the so-called grand tour, in which some of them were accompanied by their private tutors; the latter were mostly high-achieving poor students trying to make a living while attending universities. During the tour, they would audit lectures in universities in Italy, Spain, France, Holland, and England; some would take examinations and receive degrees. Two itineraries, in Italy (*iter Italicum*) and in the Netherlands (*iter Hollandicum*), along which were reputable institutions like Bologna, Padua, and Leiden, were particularly favored. The grand tour was fraught with many problems, many of which are similar to those sometimes encountered in international student mobility in today's world. There were widespread allegations of rich people buying their degrees from what were then referred to as "graduation universities," which in today's terminology are called "diploma mills" or "rogue providers" (see Section 4.1). Even reputable universities that were trying to diversify their revenue sources were involved in such frauds. On the other hand, competition for students led to reduced fees. Total cost and the ease with which degrees were awarded were major factors in students' preferences for universities.

The numerical data reported by Ridder-Symoens (1996b) clearly shows that international student mobility in Europe was an important aspect of university life, with foreign student enrollment across the continent averaging about 10 percent of the total. Ridder-Symoens (1996b) and Perkin (2006) give the following as factors that affected students' choices of universities: (1) family tradition; (2) the reputation of the university or its location; (3) religious and/or political loyalties; (4) costs, distance, and ease of access; (5) facilities provided to students; and (6) fashion and opportunities for learning foreign languages.

International mobility started to wane again in the eighteenth century, by the middle of which the foreign nations in Italian universities had started to disappear for lack of students. Ridder-Symoens (1996b) and Perkin (2006) give the following factors that led to this decline in foreign student numbers:

1. The European wars of the late seventeenth century;

2. Increasing emphasis on the utility of education that came with the Enlightenment;

3. Restrictions imposed by home governments on holders of diplomas from foreign universities in entering civil service and licensing to practice the regulated professions.

There is a vast literature on the contributions of the university as an institution to the Scientific Revolution and the Enlightenment.[11] Research was not included among the functions of the university until the middle of the nineteenth century. For this reason, it is possible, and to some extent justified, to argue that the university as an institution did not contribute to the Scientific Revolution and the Enlightenment in a major way. It must, however, be pointed out that of the approximately three hundred scientists and scholars whose names are associated with the Scientific Revolution, the majority had attended universities and other higher education institutions—in today's sense—as students, and many held positions as teachers; a significant number of them studied and/or taught in multiple institutions in different countries.

5.1.4. The Birth of the Napoleonic University and the German Research University

By the beginning of the nineteenth century, the new sciences had started permeating curricula, new intellectual centers such as the Dutch and the Scottish universities had emerged, new types of higher education institutions providing technical and vocationally oriented education had appeared, and teaching in the vernacular languages had started.[12] There also were periods when international academic mobility had been severely disrupted, even stopped altogether. However, the basic international or supranational institutional character and the uniformity of structure and curricula inherited from the medieval European university were still intact. Ruegg (2004b, 4) describes the European university scene at the turn of the nineteenth century as follows:

Until the French revolution, European universities, although divided by their dependence on Catholic or protestant sovereigns, were organized in the same way and taught more or less the same branches of knowledge in four or five classical faculties. The structure and content of higher education converged to such a point that Rousseau complained in 1772: "Today, there are no longer any French, German, Spanish or even English in spite of what they say: there are only Europeans. They all have the same tastes, the same passions, the same morals, because none of them has received a national moulding from a particular institution."

However, all was to change with the French Revolution. The university was seen as an extension of the church and the ancient regime; all of the French universities then in existence were closed and all the colleges abolished. On May 10, 1806, Napoleon founded the *Université de France*, or the Imperial University. This was, in effect, a ministry of national education; in fact, it became one in 1828, when the country was divided into educational regions, called *academié*—not to be confused with academy of sciences.

The system comprised professional schools at the tertiary level and *lycées* at the secondary. The professional schools included the *grands écoles*, some of which were inherited from the previous regime, three medical schools, twelve law schools, and a faculty of arts (*lettres*) and a faculty of sciences in each *academié*. With the exception of Paris, the roles of the faculties of arts and sciences were restricted to holding examinations for the bachelor's degree and organizing public lectures. Research was concentrated in the *grands écoles*, the *Collége de France*, the *Institut de France*, and the learned societies, which had been spared by Napoleon. It was not until 1896 that sixteen of the French universities were restored.

In 1789, there were 143 universities in Europe. In 1815, only 83 were left; Napoleon had closed all universities in the regions he had conquered. In Germany, eighteen of the thirty-four universities had been closed by Napoleon. Spain had been left with only ten of the previous twenty-five institutions that had the semblance of academic activity. Only Leiden, Utrecht, and Groningen remained in the Netherlands, but Leiden was a ghost of its former academic self.

Following Napoleon's defeat, a heated debate took place in Prussia, the state that eventually unified Germany in 1871. There were those who advocated professional schools. However, it was the philologist and diplomat Wilhelm von Humboldt (1767–1835), the brother of the great naturalist Alexander, whose views were eventually adopted. As opposed and in reaction to the Napoleonic model, von Humboldt saw the university as an institution where one would learn how to create new scientific knowledge, rather than learn how to practice a profession. Thus, the university, according to von Humboldt, is an institution where teaching and research are carried out as parts of the whole, with the faculty of philosophy occupying a central position. The purpose of research is for its own sake. The role of the state is to provide the financial resources, and its authority is limited to the appointment of the professors.

Many of von Humboldt's views found their way into the statutes of Friedrich Wilhelms University (f. 1810; University of Berlin). However, as opposed to the role of the university as a provider of a general philosophical education, as extolled by von Humboldt, the University of Berlin was defined as an institution charged with providing a general as well as a specialist education.

Wilhelm von Humboldt's views on the structure of the university are collectively expressed as "the unity of teaching and research" (*Einheit von Forschung und Lehre*). His lasting legacy has been the introduction of research as the second function of the university in addition to teaching.

The Second Scientific Revolution and the epistemic bases for the science-based industries that followed had their roots in the German universities of the nineteenth century, where many intellectual giants studied, taught, carried out research, and trained researchers and other great minds.

The nineteenth century also witnessed the emergence of nation-states, systems of national education, and the absorption of institutions of higher education into the state bureaucracies emerging in continental Europe (Gerbod 2004; Ruegg 2004b). The process of secularization of higher education was essentially completed. Even church-affiliated private universities increasingly relied on the state for their finances, with only vestigial influences of religion left in their governance and curricula.

Across the channel in Britain, universities remained outside of direct government control. The "civic universities" were founded in the second half of the nineteenth century in the industrial regions. The newly emerging industrialists and merchants, who lived in these regions, supported and sponsored the new institutions.

Germany emerged as the academic center of the world in the second half of the century. It was in Germany that research became an integral function of universities, and the academic profession took shape through the introduction of the research-based doctoral degree, the various academic ranks, procedures, and requirements for progressing from one to the other, and rules and regulations for appointments. It also was Germany, where the various vocational and technical institutions of higher education that had earlier come into being outside the universities, were elevated to a status at par with the universities. *Technische Hochschule Aachen* (f. 1865 as a polytechnic) heralded the great German *technische hochschulen* that were to host so many great scientists and serve as a model for many countries.

5.1.5. International Academic Mobility in the Nineteenth and Early Twentieth Centuries

The nineteenth century thus witnessed the orientation of higher education toward utilitarian purposes.[13] The French and German institutions rather than the British pioneered this movement. It was a period when universities, higher education institutions, the various models described previously, and programs spread to eastern and southeastern Europe, the Middle East, Africa, the Far East, Latin America, and the Oceania (Perkin 2006).

China has one of the oldest traditions of vocational higher education. Competitive entrance examinations for public service began in 622, and these were given every three years. Tutoring to prepare candidates for these examinations is often cited as an earlier form of higher education (Nakayama 1984, 62–64). However, owing to the resistance from traditionalists to shed Confucian teaching structures, it was not before late in the nineteenth century that modern institutions of higher education entered China. The University of Beijing was established in 1898, and the imperial examination system was abolished in 1910. Many years passed, in which Chinese intellectuals heatedly debated the relative merits of the British, American, French, and German ideas and models. By 1936, China had seventy-eight institutions of higher education, half of which were private, founded by missionaries or wealthy individuals and some in collaboration with American institutions. The University of Hong Kong, founded in 1911, was modeled after the newly founded civic universities in Britain.

Foreigners, despite the Chinese themselves, introduced the university, a foreign institution, to China. Japan, on the other hand, willingly adopted it. Like China, Japan, too, had a long tradition of advanced education based on a Confucian curriculum that led to government service. Following the Meiji Restoration (1867–1912), a commission was sent to Europe to investigate the various educational systems and make recommendations to the government. Tokyo University was founded in 1877. It was later reorganized as the Imperial University of Japan in 1886. The Imperial University in Kyoto followed in 1897. The Japanese opened the first university in Korea in Seoul in 1924; they opened another in Taiwan in 1928.

Institutions of higher education, in particular the university, had spread to almost all parts of the world by the first quarter of the twentieth century. Governments viewed them as key instruments in indigenous capacity development, socioeconomic progress, nation building, and social cohesion. Many looked to the West where these institutions had been transplanted from both as a source of teachers for the new institutions as well as for training the future teachers and other key personnel required by modern state bureaucracies and modern economies.[14]

Indian students started going abroad from 1870, most to England, and some to Germany. M. K. Gandhi was trained as a barrister at the Inns of Court, and India's first prime minister, J. Nehru, was an undergraduate at Cambridge (Shils and Roberts 2004, 205). Between 1850 and 1870, many Russian young men were sent to study in German and Swiss universities (Luyendhijk-Elshout 2004).

Thus, although institutions of higher education were no longer the international institution that the medieval university was, international academic mobility continued until World War I. An "invisible university" appears to have evolved in this period, which rested on the international mobility of professors and students. Altbach and Teichler (2001) attribute the growth of internationalism in this period to the establishment of the scientific disciplines and the emergence of the German research university as an international model. The increase in students' choices for places of study, and scholarly interchanges through conferences, scientific organizations, and publications were starting to overcome the inherently restrictive policies of the nation-states in Europe (Charle 2004). Foreign student enrollment in Swiss universities was 57 percent in 1910, and many foreign faculty members were employed (Gerbod 2004).

Other factors also contributed to international student mobility. Many student radicals were studying abroad (Gevers and Vos 2004). Another factor was the discrimination against Jews and women. Many Hungarian Jews left the country to study abroad (Charle 2004). Many Russian Jews and women,[15] whose access to higher education was restricted in Tsarist Russia, went abroad to study, especially to Paris, Berlin, and the Swiss universities (Charle 2004; Luyendhijk-Elshout 2004).

By the end of the nineteenth century, Britain, France, and Germany had emerged as the leading academic centers of the world. Institutions of higher education founded in other countries were based on one of these models or a combination of them. Consequently, British, French, and German teachers were recruited to teach abroad, and students were sent to these countries to be trained as future faculty members for institutions back home. The outward mobility of teachers from Europe and the inflow of students to Europe increased during the era of European colonization, when European institutions were implanted in the colonies (Altbach and Teichler 2001).

Data on international academic mobility in the late nineteenth century and the early twentieth century are scant. Because the British universities did not report to a higher authority such as a ministry or an intermediate body at the time, there are no data available on foreign student enrollment in the country as a whole. Ringer (2004) gives the values of 6 and 12 percent for the share of foreign students at Oxford in the years around 1900 and 1930, respectively.

On the other hand, data exist on foreign student enrollments in France and Germany. Throughout the nineteenth century, Paris was the destination of choice for students of mathematics; many of the faculty members of Russian universities had studied in Paris (Bockstaele 2004). Table 5.1 shows the number of foreign students enrolled in French institutions of higher education. It is interesting to note that foreign enrollment in French institutions had peaked at close to fifteen thousand and made up more than 20 percent of the total tertiary enrollment in the country in 1927–1928. This was just before the Great Depression of 1929, from when on, with the onset of the global economic crisis and the looming global conflict, it started to decline noticeably. It also is interesting to note that in 1927–1928, female students accounted for 22 percent of the foreign enrollment in France, which was very close to the female participation rate among French students in the same year. The values reported by Klineberg (1976) are in reasonably good agreement with those of Ringer (2004), who gives the share of foreign enrollment in France as 6 percent for c. 1900, 13 percent for c. 1920, and 22 percent for c. 1930.

Table 5.1 shows foreign student enrollment in German institutions in the same period (Klineberg 1976, 113–14). By 1911–1912, foreign student enrollment in Germany had reached its peak value of 7,088 for the period in question when it accounted for 10.7 percent of the total tertiary enrollment in the country. In that year, European students made up 92.3 percent of the foreign enrollment in Germany, followed by Americans 4.6 percent, and Asians only 2.6 percent. Ringer (2004) reports the ratio of foreign enrollment to total enrollment in Germany as 6 percent for c.1900 and 4 percent for c.1930. By 1936, the share of European students had dropped to 71.3 percent, and those of the Americans and Asians had increased to 11.5 percent and 10 percent, respectively. From the data shown in Table 5.1, it appears that foreign students in Germany picked up soon after World War I. World War II obviously had a devastating effect on international student mobility worldwide. By 1939–1940, the number of foreign students in Germany had dropped to less than two thousand; however, it started increasing again as Germany started to recover from the debacle of the war.

5.1.6. The Emergence of the Modern American University

Of the international academic mobility that took place in the nineteenth and the early twentieth centuries, none had more far-reaching consequences than that which involved American students who went to study in German

Table 5.1. Foreign Students in France and Germany in the Late Nineteenth and Early Twentieth Centuries

	France[a]			Germany[b]	
Year	Number of Students	Share of Enrollment, %	Year	Number of Students	Share of Enrollment, %
1899	1,635	5.7	1860–1861	753	6.1
1916	1,945	15.4	1880–1881	1,129	5.2
1924–1925	8,789	16.5	1900–1901	1,751	7.6
1927–1928	14,368	22.3	1911–1912	7,088	10.7
1935–1936	9,061	12.2	1930–1931	7,422	5.7
			1933–1934	4,853	4.5
			1939–1940	1,927	4.3

[a]Klineberg (1976, 76); [b]Kleineberg (1976, 113–4).

universities. Benjamin Franklin (1706–1790) was the first American to visit a German university, Göttingen in 1766. Between 1815 and 1914, there was an extraordinary migration of about 10,000 American students to Germany. Students from Harvard, Yale, and other universities on the East Coast started to go to Germany in increasing numbers. Göttingen, Berlin, and Heidelberg were favorite destinations. In 1890, American students accounted for 21.9 percent of the enrollment at Göttingen (Jarausch 1995). Thus, from about the middle of the nineteenth century, the German research university model permeated American higher education, effectively diminishing British influences (Perkin 2006; Shils and Roberts 2004).

Until the turn of the nineteenth century, American universities were teaching institutions—small liberal arts colleges. As students returned from Germany and took up positions in universities, this all began to change. The idea of the unity of teaching and research became central to the new universities like MIT (f. 1860), Johns Hopkins (f. 1867), Cornell (f. 1868), Clark (f. 1887) in the east, Chicago (f. 1890) in the midwest, Texas A&M in the west (f. 1867), and Berkeley (f. 1868) and Stanford (f.1895) on the West Coast.

Daniel Coit Gilman (1813–1908) was the first president of Johns Hopkins. Before becoming president, he toured German universities to recruit staff and learn about their organization. The first graduate school was established at Cornell in 1868. William Rainey Harper (1856–1906), the first president of the University of Chicago, designed the new institution with an English-style undergraduate college and a German-style research institute. Granville Stanley Hall (1844–1924), the first president of Clark University, had studied psychology in Germany. He set up the first psychology laboratory at Johns Hopkins before he moved on to Clark where he pioneered the quarter system and introduced extension programs. Charles William Eliot (1834–1926) served as the president of Harvard between 1869 and 1909. He had studied chemistry in Germany for two years, beginning in 1863. During his term as Harvard's president, he initiated the elective system, founded the graduate school, and instituted strict requirements for admission and graduation.

In 1862, the Morril Land Grant Act was enacted; it provided public land and federal funds for educational institutions that offered programs in liberal, agricultural and mechanical arts. The Hatch Act of 1887 provided funds to the experimental research stations in these institutions and set forth requirements for granting them university status. In this manner, the public state universities were born.

Thus, by the beginning of the twentieth century, American universities had transferred and adapted the German research university model to build what would grow into the largest (until recently overtaken by China) and, by any measure, the best higher education system in the world today. The innovations made in this process were the following:

1. The graduate school was established.

2. Departments were established as the basic academic unit rather than chairs under the direction of one professor, which could at times be autocratic.

3. The PhD degree was introduced, which included research and coursework, as well as a qualifying examination, and the rank of assistant professor was introduced, which made it possible for young faculty members to carry out research independently.

4. Community service became the third function of the university, which covered a wide spectrum ranging from applied contract research and consultancy to continuing education of adults— now referred to as LLL.

5. Student services, admission offices,[16] and other professional administrative units were established within the central administration, and undergraduate and graduate admission procedures were standardized.

6. Universities built their own libraries and museums, and academic librarianship became an academic discipline in itself.

7. Degree programs in a wide variety of professional, vocational, and technical fields were established that led to degrees at both the graduate and the undergraduate level.

Abraham Flexner (1866–1959) led the second wave of the "Germanization" of American higher education. He was educated at Johns Hopkins and the University of Berlin. He traveled extensively in Europe a number of times, compared higher education institutions, and wrote reports, which were very critical of American universities and full of praise for German universities (Flexner 1932).

The number of doctoral students increased by a factor of three; many of them continued to do research and advanced studies in Germany with post-doctoral fellowships from philanthropic organizations, which were founded in this period to provide support for scholarly work and higher education. They came back to join American institutions as young faculty members. The U.S. institutions soon became centers of excellence and attracted scientists and scholars from all over the world. Academic emigration from Germany to the United States increased after the Nazis came to power.

Twelve of the many German scholars who immigrated to the United States in this period were Nobel Prize winners, and Enrico Fermi (1901–1954) was an Italian, who had studied in Germany.

The German contribution to American higher education was very broad and deep. It involved the transplantation of an organizational model and its underlying philosophy, and the scholars who emigrated from Germany covered nearly all branches of the natural sciences, engineering, medicine, humanities, and social sciences.

Altbach (2004a, 4) summarizes the formative international influences on the American university as follows:

> The structure of the American university itself, so influential worldwide, constitutes an amalgam on international influences. The original colonial model, imported from England, was combined with the German research university idea of the 19th century, and the American conception of service to society, to produce the modern American university.

The early years of the twentieth century also witnessed the emergence of a new and quintessentially American institution of higher education, the junior college, which was initially intended to be preparatory for higher education.

World War II shaped American higher education in many ways. The G.I. Bill of Rights was enacted in 1944 to provide financial aid to veterans returning from the war. Following the war, greater emphasis began to be placed on mid-level vocational and technical education, which resulted in the establishment of a second type of nonuniversity institution, the community college, which, together with the junior college played a central role in the "massification" and the "universalization" of American higher education.

The U.S. Office of Scientific Research and Development was established to channel the scientific research potential of the country in support of the war effort. The experience acquired in scientific and technological R&D led to the establishment of the National Science Foundation, the Atomic Energy Commission, and the National Institute of Health (Bush 1980). This was a major step in the transformation of the United States from an industrial to a knowledge-based economy, and a major factor in the United States assuming an undisputed leadership role in the world.

The supremacy of the United States is based on a number of comparative advantages, among which the country's strengths in higher education and R&D figure prominently. This was a major reason why the English language became the global language of communication in science and the newly emerging *Lingua Franca* of higher education in the increasingly internationalized higher education in the global knowledge economy, with the United States as its main hub.

5.2 GLOBALIZATION AND INTERNATIONALIZATION OF HIGHER EDUCATION SINCE 1950

The foregoing discussion clearly shows that international academic mobility in the past has comprised not only the movement of people, but also the movement of institutions and programs across borders. Throughout history, it has been driven not only by academic considerations, but also by cultural, political, and economic rationales. The situation is not much different in today's global knowledge economy.

Alliance Française was founded as early as 1883 to spread French culture and language. Today it has nearly one thousand schools in 129 countries. French teachers are sent abroad under the *Services de la Coopération Culturelle et Technique* program of the Ministry of Foreign Affairs to serve in educational institutions in the French-speaking countries (Klineberg 1976, 50–59). However, it was at the beginning of the twentieth century that international academic mobility started to be viewed as an instrument of foreign policy, when governments started to establish institutional structures to support and promote it. The IIE was established in the aftermath of World War I, the precursor to today's *Deutscher Akademischer Austausch Dienst* (DAAD: the German Academic Exchange Service), *Akademischer Austauschdienst e. V.* (Academic Exchange Service) was founded in Heidelberg in 1925, and the forerunner of the British Council, the British Committee for Relations with Other Countries, in 1934.[17]

The use of academic exchanges as foreign policy instruments accelerated after World War II. New programs were started and many scholarships were established, both by international organizations, such as NATO and the European Economic Community, now the EU, and by governments. The United Kingdom and France had special scholarship programs for their former colonies. Many other academic exchange and technical aid programs were established by member countries of both NATO and the Soviet Bloc (Klineberg 1976, 50–60).

Barblan (2002) has summarized the postwar context in Europe with respect to academic cooperation and mobility. The rectors, vice chancellors, and presidents of European universities met for the first time in Cambridge in 1955 to reaffirm the potential of international cooperation among their institutions, which led to the institutionalization of the CRE in 1959. From 1955 to 1975, academic cooperation in Europe developed mainly at the institutional level. The transformation of academic exchange to academic mobility started to take shape with the initiation of joint study programs by the Institute of Education of the European Cultural foundation in Paris. These programs eventually led to the establishment of the European Community Action Scheme for the Mobility of University Students (ERASMUS) program in 1987 (see Appendix E).

The Fulbright program was created in 1946. Its first participants went overseas in 1948. War reparations and foreign loan repayments to the United States funded the program. By 1968, thirty-two thousand awards had been made. That number today is more than 250,000, with operations in 144 countries. More Fulbright alumni have won Nobel Prizes than those of any other academic program.

The Fulbright program is just one of the many programs administered by IIE. Throughout its history, the IIE has played a key role in making the United States the world leader in international academic mobility, both directly through the various programs it administers, as well as indirectly through the structures and organizations it helped to establish and the meetings it organized. In the 1940s, it organized conferences for foreign student advisors. These eventually led to the foundation of today's National Association of Foreign Student Advisors (NAFSA; f. 1948) and the Association of International Education Administrators (f. 1982) to support international academic mobility. Every year, eighteen thousand men and women from 175 nations participate in programs administered by IIE.[18] It has one office in Mexico and Egypt each, three in eastern Europe, and seven in Southeast Asia. The teaching of the English language, administration of the various language tests and tests related to admission to U.S. institutions of higher education, and the promotion of American higher education are among its traditional activities.

The DAAD and the British Council administer similar scholarship and exchange programs as well as programs to promote their national cultures aimed at promoting national interests. The DAAD has fourteen regional offices and forty-six information centers throughout the world. The British Council operates in 220 cities in 110 countries; the teaching of the English language, administration of the various English language tests, and the promotion of British higher education are among its traditional activities.

Foreign student enrollment in Australian and New Zealand universities dates back to the Colombo Plan, which was initiated in 1950 for international cooperation and economic development in south and southeast Asia. IDP Education Australia dates back to 1969 with its roots in the Colombo Plan of 1950.[19] Its structure and focus was changed in 1994 to reflect the new policies of the government. It is now an unlisted, nonprofit company owned by Australian universities, and rather than providing educational aid, it focuses on the business of recruiting students to Australian institutions through such activities as education counseling, publications, exhibitions, and English-language testing. Presently, IDP has a wide spectrum of activities in fifty-six countries. It provides application, counseling and enrollment services through its ninety student offices in thirty-five countries and worldwide through its Global Apply Online system. It has seventy-five English-language test centers in twenty-seven countries, and it manages development and fellowship projects in thirty-seven countries. It also provides marketing, research, and consultancy services in all aspects of education, international education, health, and governance.

Similar organizations were established in Soviet Bloc countries, too, to organize and administer aid programs to developing countries. The Patrice Lumumba Peoples' Friendship University was established in 1960 in Moscow. Its primary goal was to spread Russian-style Communism in Africa, Latin America, and Asia by providing scholarships to poor students from these regions to get a university education that prepared them as "native specialists." Following the collapse of the Soviet regime, its name was changed to the Peoples' Friendship University of Russia. It is now an institution catering primarily to Russian students.

Until the 1980s, internationalization meant exchange of students and scholars, the teaching of foreign languages, and the inclusion in the curricula of courses on different countries and cultures, and programs in international relations and area studies. By this time, curricula in natural sciences, engineering, and medicine had essentially been internationalized. English was the language of natural sciences and technology, and most of the material covered in the courses was based on the new knowledge originating mainly from English-speaking countries as well as the majority of the textbooks used. The same description could be used to describe the teaching of and research in economics in the noncommunist world. The MBA degree, which was an American innovation, was spreading in the non-Communist countries.

In the second half of the twentieth century, international organizations like the OECD, UNESCO, and the EU and, at a later stage, the World Bank started to take an interest in education. Thus, whereas the nineteenth century witnessed the "nationalization" of higher education with the emergence of the nation-state, the second half of the twentieth century saw the interaction of governmental policies with the views espoused by international organizations. Collection and analysis of comparative educational data increased, which allowed international comparisons to be made and conclusions to be drawn thereof. Higher education started to be viewed from an international perspective when formulating and implementing national policies (Enders 2004; OECD 2004b, 89–90).

With the advent of globalization, higher education worldwide started to "internationalize," in both the content and the scope of its activities. To analyze the impact of these developments on higher education, Scott (1998, 2000) starts from the premise that internationalization reflects a world order based on nation-states, while globalization involves both competition and collaboration among nations. He also points out that the contemporary university is the creature of the nation-state, and is therefore a national institution. From these starting points, he argues that the forces of globalization challenge the university in the following three areas: (1) promotion of national cultures in an increasingly global environment; (2) the impact of ICT on the content and the methodology of teaching and research; and (3) revenue diversification.

Since the mid-1990s, globalization has been recognized as "perhaps the most fundamental challenge faced by the University in its long history" (Scott 2000). As a result, the terms *globalization* and *internationalization* have acquired new contents in the context of higher education, which require additional terminology with definitions specific to this particular sector.

In van der Wende's (2001a) view, internationalization of higher education is a response to globalization. It no longer can be considered as a secondary function of institutions focusing primarily on the international mobility of students and teachers in the classical sense; rather, internationalization should be taken up as an important element of higher education policy at both the institutional and the national level in order to address the challenges posed by globalization.

5.3. DEFINITION OF TERMS

5.3.1. Globalization and Internationalization

The sophistication that seems to have permeated definitions of internationalization and globalization as they relate to higher education in the last decade indicates both a growing confusion as well as a move toward clarification (Altbach 2004a, 2006; Marginson and Rhoades 2002; Teichler 2004; Vaira 2004). Jane Knight provided clear operational definitions of the terms related to globalization and the internationalization of higher education. She thus established a framework for the systematic analysis of the phenomena involved (Knight 1994, 1999, 2003a, 2003b, 2004, 2005a, 2006b, 2008). The following are the definitions that she provided. *International* is a term that emphasizes the notion of nation, and refers to the relationship between and among different nations, cultures, or countries. *Intercultural* refers to the diversity of cultures that exist within countries, communities and institutions; it is used to address the aspects of internationalization at home. *Transnational* is used in the sense of across nations. It does not specifically address the notion of relationships. It is used interchangeably with the term *cross-border*.

In order to make it generic enough so that it applies to many different cultures, countries and education systems, Knight (2004, 2008, 1–17) proposed the following definition for the internationalization of higher education at the national/sector/institutional levels: "the process of integrating an international, intercultural or global dimension into the purpose, functions or delivery of postsecondary education."

The term *process* is deliberately included to underscore the continuous and ongoing nature of internationalization. The verb *integrating* is used to ensure that internationalization is central, not marginal to higher education in today's world. Finally, the term *purpose* is used to refer to the overall role and objectives that higher education has for a country or a region where individual institutions have specific mandates and missions.

The definition provided by Knight recognizes that internationalization of higher education can take place at the national, sectoral, and institutional levels, either independently as the case is in some countries or in an integrated manner as in other countries.

National policies on foreign relations, development assistance, trade, industry and commerce, immigration, employment, science and technology, culture and heritage, education, social development, and others have a direct bearing on the internationalization of higher education at the sectoral and institutional levels. The various academic exchange and educational programs I have discussed, which were devised and implemented as instruments of foreign policy, are some examples.

Such programs can also be devised, implemented, and funded by a group of countries as in the EU and in the Bologna Process (see Section 5.4), NGOs, charitable foundations, international organizations and funding agencies, and multinational companies, each with different objectives, but all affecting policies, strategies, programs, and activities at the sector and the institutional levels.

At the sectoral, or system level, all policies that are concerned with the purpose, licensing, accreditation, funding (including national, regional, and international sources), curriculum, teaching, research, and regulation of postsecondary education bear directly on the internationalization of higher education.

Whether a country allows foreign providers, either nonprofit or for-profit, to operate within its territory or across its borders by using advanced distance education technologies is a case in point, where all sorts of policy considerations interact both at the national and the sectoral level.

Individual institutions, in general, respond to policies and programs implemented at the national and the sectoral levels. Until the recent past, individual institutions responded to such national and sectoral policies and the programs implemented under them by taking up international activities. Since the past two decades, however, it is increasingly recognized that to address the challenges posed and benefit from the opportunities provided by globalization, individual institutions should develop internationalization strategies of their own. Knight (2004, 2008) uses the term *internationalization strategies* to underscore this point, which is a notion that includes more planning, an integrated approach and strategic thinking. At the institutional level, Knight lists the following as programs that institutions can devise and implement within their internationalization strategies. Academic programs focused on teaching include student exchange programs, foreign-language study, internationalized curricula, area or thematic studies, work/study abroad, international students, teaching–learning process, joint-degree programs, double-degree programs, cross-cultural training, faculty and staff mobility, visiting lecturers and scholars, and establishing links between academic programs and other strategies. Research and scholarly collaboration include area and theme centers, joint research projects, international conferences and seminars, published articles and papers, international research agreements, and research exchange programs. International academic programs based on external relations include international development assistance projects, cross-border delivery of education programs, both commercial and noncommercial, international linkages, partnerships and networks, contract-based training and research programs and services, and alumni-abroad programs. International programs of extracurricular nature include student clubs and associations, international and intercultural campus events, and liaison with community-based cultural and ethnic groups.

Knight (2004, 2008) also lists the organizational strategies at the institutional level that are required for the implementation of programs of the type described here. These include strategies that are related to governance, operations, services, and human resources. It is probably more realistic to describe what Knight refers to as organizational strategies as prerequisites for the successful implementation of international programs at the institutional level. Foremost among these are the following:

1. Unequivocal commitment by senior leaders, involvement of faculty, staff, and students; articulated rationales and goals for internationalization; and the recognition of the international dimension in institutional mission statements, planning and policy documents;

2. Appropriate organizational structures, monitoring processes, adequate financial support, and integration of services such as support for foreign students, orientation programs, counseling, cross-cultural training, and visa advice;

3. Rewards for international expertise and contributions to internationalization, support for international assignments and sabbaticals, and faculty and staff development.

5.3.2. Rationales for Internationalization of Higher Education

Knight (1999, 2004, 2008) described the classical rationales that have driven internationalization of higher education throughout the history in the following four main groups: sociocultural, political, economic, and academic.[20]

With the advent of the global knowledge economy, however, new rationales have emerged, or the classical ones have assumed new dimensions and contents. The reasons why nations want to host foreign students and scholars or send their youth abroad are referred to as the "rationales at the national level." The factors that motivate, or force, institutions to internationalize their programs and campuses and provide services offshore are the "rationales at the institutional level." The thinking behind families' spending large sums of money to send their children to study abroad forms the basis for the "rationales at the family and the student level" (Knight 2004; OECD 2004b, 23–32).

International relations of all kinds—confrontational, collaboration, political, cultural, and commercial—require people on all sides who know about each other's history, culture, social fabric, strengths, and weaknesses. Being in contact with each other, living in other countries and exposure to other cultures generally create goodwill and understanding, and contribute to global peace and security. Hosting foreign students is intended to spread the host country's cultural and political values as well as nurturing friends in other countries. The various national and international scholarships and exchange programs are driven by this rationale and national policies based on it are referred to as the "mutual understanding approach" to the internationalization of higher education.

Higher education has always played a key role in the development of national cultural identity and nation-building. The importance of an educated citizenry to nation-building and a well-trained workforce to economic development has become even more crucial in the global knowledge economy. Thus, countries that do not have developed higher education systems have resorted to importing higher education services from countries with advanced higher education systems, either by sending students, or by allowing foreign providers to operate in their countries. Ability to work in international environments has become a key requisite for employment in the global labor market, and hence the importance of the development of intercultural skills in students and staff in institutions of higher education worldwide. This is referred to as the "capacity-building approach" to policy formulation at the national and the institutional levels. It can be extended to include the desire of students themselves to acquire a good education, as well as developing intercultural skills that will make them employable in the global labor market.

"Know-how and technology transfer" should be considered as a variant or subset of capacity building. As part of their industrialization strategies, many developing countries had programs in which scholarships were provided for personnel to be trained, especially in technical fields, in return for compulsory public service at home; some countries still have programs of this kind. This was human resource development in the industrial economy, and represented know-how rather than technology transfer, because technology was then transferred in packaged form, such as turnkey plants. In the global knowledge economy, on the other hand, the development and transfer of technology is not as straightforward as it was in the industrial economy; technology and know-how is increasingly being transferred in electronic media, Petri dishes, and most importantly, in human brains. Thus, technology and know-how transfer now is a major rationale for internationalizing higher education systems, especially for increasing student mobility in both directions, for developing as well as developed countries.

Human population is predicted to peak at about 9 billion in the year 2070 and then start to contract. However, long before then, many nations will shrink in absolute size, and the average age of the world's citizens will shoot up dramatically (Longman 2004; see also Table 1.1). This will occur especially in developed countries, a number of which are already feeling some of the adverse effects of this demographic trend. Furthermore, well-trained young minds are already the most sought-after asset as key factors of production in the global knowledge economy. A number of countries with advanced higher education systems are now recruiting foreign students and providing incentives for them to join the workforce of the host country (Docquier and Marfouk 2006; Hira 2003). Thus, the possibility to immigrate to a developed country is a rationale for students to seek opportunities to study abroad. Knight (2004, 2008) refers to this rationale on the part of host countries as "human resources development through 'brain-power.' " The OECD (2004b, 27) refers to national policies driven by this rationale as "skilled migration approach" to international higher education, which, in fact, may be viewed as a "developed-nation version" of the capacity-building approach.

Of the rationales that have emerged with the advent of the global knowledge economy, several others deserve special attention. The first one is "strategic alliances." The importance of this rationale is embedded in the previously given definition of globalization by Nye (see Section 1.3) and the basic characteristics of the global knowledge economy. At the national level, with the collapse of Communism, there has been a definite shift from alliances for political and cultural purposes to alliances for economic purposes. Countries are increasingly viewing the internationalization of post-secondary education as a foreign policy tool to establish strategic alliances bilaterally, regionally, and multilaterally to gain both a political advantage and to increase their competitiveness in global markets.

At the institutional level, research and teaching networks have emerged. At the company level, neither R&D nor manufacturing are done at a single site anymore; rather, these activities are done in "networks" that include multiple subcontractors in a number of countries. Families send their children abroad primarily for a better education that will lead to better job prospects, but also with the expectation that the friendships they will develop with fellow students from other countries will lead to future business networks. Thus, "networking" is a variant or a subset of strategic alliances, and is an increasingly important driver of internationalization at all three levels.

The cost to the families of international education, either abroad or at home through a foreign provider, is still a consideration, but no more an exclusive one, especially for students in countries where higher education is not subsidized to the same degree as in others.[21] Students and families are now looking beyond the borders of their countries for educational opportunities. They are willing to pay top dollar for what they perceive to be high-quality education.

Getting a share of the multibillion dollar global higher education market and expanding that segment has become a priority for a number of countries. The OECD (2004b, 26) refers to this rationale as the "revenue-generating approach." The national policies of a number of countries driven by this rationale are discussed in the next chapter. In those countries where national policies based on this approach are being implemented, incentives are provided to and conditions are being imposed on institutions to compete in the global higher education market to diversify their revenue sources and supplement their income. Table 5.2 (OECD 2004b, 32) shows the growth in annual revenues from foreign students in the five MESDCs for foreign students: Australia, Canada, New Zealand, the United Kingdom and the United States. These figures, which reach billions of dollars, clearly underscore the increasing economic importance of international education as a revenue-generating subsector of the service economy. Tables 5.3 and 5.4 show more recent data that allow direct comparisons of the revenues of the MESDCs from foreign students in higher education and the expenditures of major countries of origin for higher education students abroad. Sum of the revenue values for the MESDCs confirm the previously given figure of at least $ 30 billion for the annual foreign student market in higher education

Table 5.2. Export Earnings from Foreign Students, in Million $ and as Percentage of Service Exports

Country	1989 $	1989 %	1997 $	1997 %	2001 $	2001 %
Australia	584	6.6	2,190	11.8	2,145	13.1
Canada	530	3.0	595	1.9	727	2.0
New Zealand	nd	nd	280	6.6	353	8.1
UK	2,214	4.5	4,080	4.3	11,141	nd
U.S.	4,575	4.4	8,346	3.5	11,490	4.2

Source: OECD (2004a, 32).

Note: Data for Australia and New Zealand include all foreign students at all levels, while data for other countries include only foreign students at the tertiary level.

nd, no data

(see Section 4.5). It also should be noted that annual expenditures for students studying abroad are comparable to the domestic public expenditures for higher education except for Japan, and in the case of Indonesia, they exceed the total domestic public expenditures.

The revenue-generating approach is not specific to policy formulation at the government level; it applies equally at the institutional level. International recognition of an institution of higher education for the quality of its teaching, research, and services has always been an aspiration. Such pursuit of international recognition based on the achievement of international standards is even more crucial in today's competitive global environment for not only funds and foreign students, but also increasingly for the recruitment of high-quality academic staff and bright students. Knight (2004, 2008, 2009b) refers to this new institutional rationale as "international branding," or "status building."

The largest and the most intensely competitive segment of the transnational higher education market is international student mobility. The policies of individual countries and the rationales on which they are predicated are discussed individually for major host countries and for major countries of origin of foreign students in Chapter 6. The next two sections in this chapter are concerned with the responses by two groups of developed countries, the EU (the Bologna Process) and the Anglo-Saxon countries (the General Agreement on Trade in Services [GATS]). The last section in this chapter, on the other hand, is concerned with quality assurance in transnational education. Many regard this as the multinational agencies' response to the opportunities and the challenges that exist in the cross-border education.

Table 5.3. Export of Education Services (Foreign Students) by Main Exporting Countries, 1999–2005 (US$ Million)

Country	1999	2000	2001	2002	2003	2004	2005	% Inc.
Australia	2,038	2,259	2,528	2,892	3,925	4,827	5,863	173
New Zealand	273	257	343	632	925	998	1,000	265
Canada	568	615	699	784	1,014	1,268	1,573	177
UK	4,101	3,766	3,921	3,891	4,709	5,627	6,064	48
U.S.	9,620	10,357	11,480	12,630	13,310	13,640	14,120	47
Total	16,600	17,247	18,971	20,834	23,883	26,405	28,320	71

Source: Bashir (2007).

% Inc., Percent increase in revenues in 1999–2005

Table 5.4. Estimated Imports of Higher Education from Five Main Exporters by Selected Developing Countries, 2004

Country	Estimated Value of Higher Education Imports, US$ Million	Higher Education Imports as % of GDP	Public Expenditure for Higher Education as % of GDP
China	5,080	0.26	0.44
India	3,151	0.46	0.59
Malaysia	850	0.12	2.96
Hong Kong	805	0.49	1.50
Singapore	460	0.43	0.85
Indonesia	515	0.20	0.17
Turkey	455	0.13	1.04
Korea	1,855	0.27	0.69
Japan	1,506	0.03	0.52

Source: Bashir (2007).

GDP, gross domestic product.

5.4 THE EUROPEAN RESPONSE: THE BOLOGNA PROCESS

5.4.1 Chronological Background

The Bologna Process is the commitment by ministers responsible for higher education from European countries, which as of March 2009 numbered forty-six, to reform their higher education systems in order to create convergence at the European level. The ultimate aim of the process is to establish the European Higher Education Area (EHEA) by 2010.

On May 25, 1998, the ministers in charge of higher education of France, Italy, the United Kingdom, and Germany met in Paris at the invitation of then-French Minister of National Education Claude Allégre, to commemorate the eighth centennial anniversary of the University of Paris, the second oldest university in the world. They signed the Sorbonne Declaration, which invited governments and institutions to "*harmonize*" academic services and university provision and to redefine the "architecture of the European higher education system."

On June 19, 1999, the ministers, which at that time numbered twenty-nine, met in Bologna, the site of the oldest university in the world, and signed the Bologna Declaration. The Bologna Declaration has a clearly defined common goal, which is the creation of a coherent EHEA by 2010. Specified objectives in the Bologna Declaration include the following: [22]

1. Adoption of a system of easily readable and comparable degrees;

2. Adoption of a system essentially based on two main cycles, one at the undergraduate level with a minimum duration of three years, and the other at the graduate level with automatic qualification for the second cycle on the completion of the first;

3. Establishment of a system of credits, such as in the European Credit Transfer and Accumulation System (ECTS, see Appendix C) as a proper means for promoting and expanding student mobility;

4. Promotion of mobility for students, teachers, researchers, and administrative staff, recognition and valorization of periods spent in a European context researching, teaching and training without prejudicing their statutory rights;

5. Promotion of European cooperation in quality assurance, introduction of standards of accreditation and peer assessment;

6. Promotion of the necessary European dimensions in higher education, including joint degrees.

Two years after signing the Bologna Declaration, the ministers met on May 19, 2001 in Prague to follow up the Bologna Process and to set directions and priorities for the coming years. LLL and promoting the competitiveness of the EHEA in transnational higher education and its attractiveness to students and scholars in other parts of the world were incorporated into the Bologna Process. Representative bodies of the institutions of higher education—the EUA (the successor to the CRE) and students, International Union of Students in Europe—were invited to join the process formally. Significantly, the constructive assistance of the European Commission (EC) was noted, which was effectively tantamount to making the process a policy instrument of the EU. This manifested itself in the designation of a follow-up group responsible for the continuing development of the process and a preparatory group responsible for the planning of the next ministerial conference. The Bologna Follow-Up Group (BFUG) was composed of representatives of all participant countries and the EU and chaired by the rotating EU presidency.

It also is interesting to note that the phrase "competitiveness in transnational higher education" entered the Bologna Process lexicon two years later.

When ministers met again in Berlin in September 2003, they defined three intermediate priorities for the next two years: quality assurance, the two-cycle degree system based on bachelor- and master-level studies, and recognition of degrees and periods of studies. In the Berlin Communique of September 19, 2003, the following specific goals were set for each of these action lines:

1. Under quality assurance, the need to develop mutually shared criteria and methodologies in quality assurance was underlined. It was agreed that by 2005 national quality assurance systems should include a definition of the responsibilities of the bodies and institutions involved; evaluation of programs or institutions, including internal assessment, external review, participation of students and the publication of results; a system of accreditation, certification, or comparable procedures; and international participation, cooperation, and networking.

2. Under the two-cycle system for degrees, the development of an overarching framework of qualifications for the EHEA was required, where degrees should have different defined outcomes with different orientations and various profiles for the first- and the second-cycle degrees in order to accommodate a diversity of individual, academic and labor market needs. A call was also made to all signatory countries to ratify the Lisbon Recognition Convention (see Appendix D), and to issue a "Diploma Supplement" (see Appendix C) to every student graduating from 2005 on, automatically and free of charge.

3. The focus on two main cycles of higher education was extended to include the doctoral level as the third cycle in the Bologna Process in order to promote closer links between EHEA and the European Research Area to form the "Europe of Knowledge." In this manner the Bologna Process became linked to the Lisbon Agenda.[23]

In the ministerial meeting in Bergen on May 19–20, 2005, the European Qualifications Framework for Higher Education was adopted, and a commitment was made to establish National Qualifications Frameworks. These are intended to provide commonly understood reference levels on how to describe learning, from basic skills up to the doctorate, with an ECTS-like credit range attached to each level. "The Standards and Guidelines for Quality Assurance in the European Higher Education Area," which was prepared and proposed by ENQA, was adopted. The principle of a European register of quality assurance agencies based on national review was confirmed.[24]

The next ministerial meeting was held in London on May 17–18, 2007. The ministers adopted the communiqué entitled "Towards the European Higher Education Area: Responding to Challenges in a Globalized World," and agreed to establish a European Register of Quality Assurance

Agencies managed by representatives of the key stake holders: EUA, ENQA, the European Association of Institutions in Higher Education and the European Student Union, the so-called E4 Group. The register is intended to be an important tool for building trust in EHEA globally. The ministers also underlined the need for strong autonomous universities, and made employability of graduates and the social dimension of higher education key priorities.[25] The European Quality Assurance Register for Higher Education (EQAR) was founded in March 2008 as an independent association in charge of establishing and managing a register of quality assurance agencies. EQAR manages a register of quality assurance agencies operating in Europe that substantially comply with the European Standards and Guidelines for Quality Assurance, adopted in the Bergen ministerial meeting.[26]

At the time of writing, the last ministerial meeting was held in Louvain, Belgium on April 28–29, 2009. The new three priorities set by the ministers for the coming decade are:

1. Further articulation of the **social dimension**: Participating countries will set national measurable targets to widen overall participation in higher education, in particular for the under-represented groups.

2. Making LLL an integral part of education systems: implementation of LLL policies through partnerships with all the relevant stakeholders and by developing national qualifications frameworks. It is intended to have the latter self-certified against the overarching Qualifications Framework for European Higher Education Area by 2012.

3. Fostering **employability**: The ministers' aim is to raise initial qualifications and maintain and renew a skilled workforce, and encourage work placements to be embedded in study programs.[27]

The trademark of the EHEA in the coming decade, however, will be student mobility. In 2020, at least 20 percent of those graduating in the EHEA countries should have been mobile, either for study or for training purposes. A number of measures that could help reach this target are enumerated, and the BFUG has been given the task of defining the indicators used for measuring and monitoring mobility and identifying the means by which balanced mobility can be achieved inside the EHEA.

5.4.2. An Evaluation of the Bologna Process

The Bologna Process is an ambitious undertaking that aims to bring transparency and a measure of uniformity to the maze of higher education practices, as well as increasing mobility in Europe. It is neither an international agreement nor an EU project or program. However, it is supported by the various programs funded by the EC, which are outlined in Appendix E. It is thus obvious that the EU bureaucracy in the Commission in Brussels is taking an increasingly active role in European higher education.

It is interesting to note that institutions of higher education did not initiate the Bologna Process. Rather, it was a subtle imposition on them by politicians. In fact, Corbett (2005, 203) refers to it as "policy making in higher education through partnership with state actors and with non-state actors based on cooperation rather than legislation." In other words, the Bologna Process seems to have replaced the European practice in the 1970s of enforcing practice by legislation (see Section 3.4.2).

Neave (2002) summarized the core objectives of the Bologna Process that reflect particular ideological commitment on which it is predicated as *mobility, employability, competitiveness,* and *attractiveness.* Such terminology de-emphasizes, or, in the thinking of some, even "desecrates" the concept of university, is anathema to many, especially in continental Europe.[28] For example, van der Wende (2001a) describes the Bologna Process as a "cooperative European approach to counter the aggressive Anglo-Saxon approach to internationalization of higher education."

Indeed, many of the intended outcomes of the process are strikingly similar to the distinguishing features of the Anglo-Saxon, if not the American, higher education system. Claude Allégre, arguably the intellectual leader of the pre-Bologna Process and a distinguished scholar himself, was openly critical of European higher education and an admirer of the American research university. In an interview in 1997, soon after taking office as the Socialist government's education minister, and just a few months before the Sorbonne Declaration, he stated that "it was a pity that France had never succeeded in creating a Massachusetts Institute of Technology (MIT) or a Caltech." ("Knowledge factory," *The Economist,* October 4, 1997, p. 5.) That the ultimate aim of the Bologna Process is to incorporate some of the basic features of the American system is shared by many. The following words by Corbett (2005, 195–6) are an example:

> The not-so-hidden agenda for the original signatories was that the great university systems of Europe should develop the features widely seen as making the American system a world-beater. They needed to counter the brain-drain to the United States, and to do more to attract bright students to the EU.

The British, on the other hand, "believed that Bologna would not have any impact on UK structures, but would open the way to Europe-wide competition for students and resources, at which the British would do well."

The two-cycle degree structure and the credit system are perhaps the most controversial issues in Europe. The main idea behind their introduction is to make European degrees comparable to the Anglo-Saxon undergraduate and postgraduate degree system, in particular the bachelor- and master-level degrees in the United States, which are globally in demand in the transnational higher education market. The proposal at the time was for the first cycle at the bachelor-level to be relevant to the labor market and cover three years of study with 180 ECTS credits (minimum), and the second cycle at the master-level to be two years in length with 120 ECTS credits (minimum) and comprise further studies and research training. The ECTS credit unit is based on the amount of effort that the student needs to spend outside the class, while the American credit unit is based on contact hours alone.

Many in Europe are skeptical about the new degree structure. The first degree is considered too short to prepare students for employment. Many view the combined 3+2 structure as a first degree in disguise, rather than being the two separate degrees intended. It was eventually agreed to allow a choice between a 3+2 or a 4+1 degree structure. Despite the skepticism, however, the two-cycle degree structure is spreading in Europe at a pace much faster than thought possible; more than one thousand bachelor's programs were being offered in German universities in 2004 (Hochstettler 2004). According to a recent EUA survey of more than nine hundred universities, 82 percent now have Bologna-compliant degree cycles in place, compared with 53 percent in 2003 (Labi 2007). On the other hand, anecdotal evidence indicates that professional bodies in a number of areas are showing reluctance to admit holders of first-stage degrees as members with the result that the second stage is becoming more professionally oriented.

A major problem area is the American response to the outcomes of the Bologna Process. Although the ECTS and the Diploma Supplement are welcome by American institutions, the new three-year bachelor's degree is being viewed with increasing skepticism across the Atlantic (Bollag 2004a; Spinelli 2005). Europeans argue that the final year in a European high school is equivalent to the American freshman year. Yet, the majority of the American graduate schools remain unconvinced that the new three-year European bachelor-level degree designed as an outcome of the Bologna Process is sufficient for admission to graduate-level programs in the United States. The British three-year bachelor-level degree is an exception, which has been in existence and recognized by American institutions long before. If the issue is not resolved, it can potentially harm student flows from Europe to the United States. Furthermore, the American bachelor's degree, even in regulated professional areas, includes a significant amount of liberal arts content and electives in related areas, which provide a basis for lifelong learning, while European degrees emphasize more profession-specific content. It would be interesting to see how European degrees would be evaluated by

U.S. accrediting bodies, such as the Accreditation Board for Engineering and Technology (ABET), for example. The previously mentioned new register of European quality assurance agencies, EQAR, is hoped to help allay fears in the United States about the qualifications of European graduates applying to U.S. programs (Labi 2007). The responses of the U.S. graduate schools to Bologna-compliant degrees were recently surveyed by the IIE (Three-year Bologna-compliant degrees: Responses from U.S. graduate schools. An IIE Briefing Paper, April 2009). The results of the survey show that there is a clear understanding of what the Bologna Process entails, and that half the respondents have an official policy in place for evaluating applicants with the new degrees. However, only a third of those held the three-year Bologna degree as equivalent to the American four-year bachelor-degree, and another third decided equivalency on a case-by-case basis.

The strains between governments and academia resulting from linking the Bologna Process and the Lisbon Agenda surfaced. In April 2005, just before the Bergen Ministerial Meeting, the EC announced its views on what was required to enable universities to make their full contribution to the Lisbon Agenda.[29] In particular, it was noted that tertiary education in Europe was, "uniform and egalitarian, insular, overregulated and underfunded." To "mobilize the brainpower of Europe," the commission recommended a new compact between the state and academia, which is based on a balance between autonomy, responsibility and self-governance on one hand, and strategic guidance from governments on the other. In the commission's view, real accountability to society and a stable and medium-term funding framework that includes a creative mix of public and private funding are the underlying principles of the new compact. The commission also underlined the importance of the reforms called for in the Bologna Process for achieving the Lisbon objectives.

However, in the words of Barroso, the commission president, "Excellence needs flagships." To that end, the commission revealed its plans for a European Institute of Technology (EIT) on February 22, 2006. The EIT would be a two-level organization consisting of a central governing body, a system of "knowledge communities," and other partnering organizations. The governing board, composed of "top personalities" from the science and business sectors, would decide on the strategy and the budget of the EIT, and would select and evaluate the knowledge communities. The knowledge communities would bring together departments of universities, companies, and research institutes to perform research, education, and innovation activities in interdisciplinary strategic areas. These departments and their personnel would be seconded to the EIT and thus cease to be part of their home organizations for a certain period. The EIT would have its own legal personality and be independent of national regulation. Strategic research areas would include at least nanotechnology and ICT. Whether the proposed EIT will be the institution that Allégre was longing for almost a decade ago remains to be seen.

As of 2007, progress in five key areas of the Bologna Process was summarized as follows:[30]

1. Three-cycle Structure

   • Virtually in place in all signatory countries, but transitional phase often necessary

   • Certain study fields remain organized in long cycles

   • Not introduced in three countries or regions

2. Doctorates

   • Notional length: often three or four years

   • Research training included in doctoral programs in virtually all signatory countries

3. ECTS

   • Introduction made obligatory in most signatory countries

   • Implemented in the vast majority of countries

   • Generally used at bachelor/master levels

4. Diploma Supplement:

   • Mandatory introduction in more than half of signatory countries

   • Not introduced in six countries or regions

   • Generally issued automatically and free of charge in English or in the language of instruction and in English

5. National Bodies for Quality Assurance

   Status

   • One independent body in the majority of countries

   • One nonindependent body in nine countries

   • No quality assurance body in six countries or regions

   Participation

   • Student representation in the governing body of half of signatory countries.

The sixth key area of the Bologna Process is student mobility, where the process is supported by the EU-funded Erasmus Program and a number of other initiatives funded by the EU (see Appendix E). Figure 5.1 shows the number of students participating in the program. Whereas 107,666 students had participated in the program in 2000, that number increased to 159,317 in 2007. The top countries of origin of participating students in 2007 (student numbers in 2000 shown in parentheses) were Germany 23,884 students (15,715), France 22,981 students (16,824), Italy 17,195 (12,421), Spain (22,322), and Poland 11,219 (2,813). The top five host countries in 2007 were: Spain 27,463, France 20,663, Germany 17,881, the United Kingdom 16,507, and Italy 14,784 students. It is interesting to note that only 7,235 UK students participated in the program in 2007, whereas the United Kingdom hosted more than twice that number in the same year.[31] In the first phase of the Erasmus Mundus Program, 140 students from fifty-two countries and 28 scholars from sixteen countries had participated in the program in its first year. In the final year of the program, 2008–2009, the number of participating students and scholars was 1,957 from 186 countries. The second phase of the program, 2009–2013, was launched with budget of nearly 500 million euros.[32]

It is now obvious that what began as a multinational collaborative effort to face the challenges of globalization has become a subtle way of accomplishing change in European higher education, which could not have

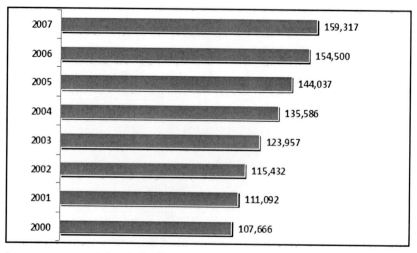

Source: www.wissenschaft-weltoffen.de

Fig. 5.1. Students Taking Part in the ERASMUS Program

been achieved by legislation alone. The Bologna Process has indeed provided an unprecedented environment conducive to change and reform in continental European higher education, which until the late 1970s consisted of essentially closed national systems funded by the state.

5.5. GATS: A "COMMERCIAL/ANGLO-SAXON RESPONSE"

Two issues are pertinent to internationalization and globalization of higher education. The first is concerned with the regulation of the commercial aspects of transnational education, and is intertwined with both the quality concern and the reconciliation of national and global concerns in a sector hitherto considered to be in the national domain. This topic is discussed in this section. A brief summary of the history, the content, and the present state of the ongoing negotiations on the GATS is presented.[33] The second issue is concerned with quality and recognition at the international level. It is intricately linked to the integration of the labor market in a truly globalized world. That topic is discussed in the next section.

The origins of GATS date back to efforts by major Western powers to liberalize trade immediately after World War II, which resulted in the General Agreement on Trade and Tariffs (GATT), an ongoing and expanding negotiation process that focused on international trade in industrial goods. In 1995, the World Trade Organization (WTO) replaced GATT and a decision was made to include trade in services under the auspices of the WTO. Within five years, the multilateral negotiating process on international trade in services started, which now covers 149 members of the WTO. The GATS is a voluntary agreement, which aims to expand the opportunities for global trade in services by removing barriers. The structure of the GATS that pertains to education is given in Appendix G.

Once a nation becomes a member, it is subject to the general obligations of GATS, and makes specific commitments regarding the opening of its markets to service providers from other members in twelve service sectors comprising 163 subsectors, and education is one of the sectors. There are five education subsectors: primary education, secondary education, higher education (including postsecondary technical and vocational education services), adult education (e.g., education for adults outside the regular education system), and other education (e.g., testing and certification). Governments can respond to "requests" from other members by making "offers," which may include commitments for one area, several sectors, all sectors, or none of them.

The GATS, in general, is pushed by the United States, the EU (through its executive arm, the EC), and Japan. The United States tabled the first so-called "negotiating proposal" for education on December 18,

2000, immediately after the start of the negotiations. New Zealand (June 27, 2001), Australia (October 1, 2001), and Japan (March 15, 2002) followed. Currently, these are the only proposals for negotiation.

At the present time, 149 nations are participating in GATS, but as of January 2006, only forty-five countries (counting the EU as one country) agreed to include at least one subsector of education, and only thirty-six of these made commitments to liberalize their higher education subsectors.

Education overall is one of the least committed sectors. This stems from Article 1.3 of GATS, which excludes from the agreement:

> services supplied in the exercise of governmental authority, namely, services that are not supplied on a commercial basis or in competition with other suppliers, such as social security and, in many countries, other public services, such as health or education that are provided under non-market conditions; and air transport services, which are measures affecting air traffic rights and services related to those rights.

According to the decision made in the Doha Round, countries that were the subject of offers were to present their commitments by March 31, 2003. The EU was one of the last to respond, and made public the full text of its offer on April 29, 2003. The general tone of the document was proliberalization. It claimed that the GATS particularly benefited businesses and individuals in developing countries, and offered deregulation in sectors such as banking, telecommunications, and environmental services. Nevertheless, it made a clear distinction between "commercial" and "public" services by making "no offer" in "European public services and in particular European health and social services, education and audio-visual services to ensure that public services within the EU are fully safeguarded, and to retain the right to set the rules that service providers will have to respect."

This clearly sets the EU apart from the Anglo-Saxon world in their approach to the provision of educational services. The title of this section was chosen to underscore this difference. The sharp distinction becomes much clearer by the U.S. requests, which call for full commitments to market access for higher education and training services (see Appendix G). However, the OBHE questioned the validity and the usefulness of the blanket EU exclusion of education from the GATS (OBHE-BNA, May 3, 2003). The following was their view: "Given the industry-related and international activities of many European universities, not least in the UK, the growth of ever less regulated student fee systems, and the decline of public money as a proportion of university income, is it reasonable to position European higher education as exempt?"

Transnational education accounts for only a small fraction of the annual volume of total global trade in services, between 2 and 3 percent. The inclusion of education in a comprehensive international agreement on trade led to strong opposition worldwide for mainly two reasons. First, despite the historical international roots of higher education, and the expansion of transnational education in the last two decades, many regard higher education, and especially education at the lower levels, as a matter of national policy. Second, although private institutions have always been components of national education systems at all levels, and despite the recent expansion of private education, including for-profit education, education is widely regarded as a semipublic service even by many of the advocates of free markets and liberal trade. Those who consider higher education to be an entirely private service, which is tradable and must be paid for in full by those who benefit from that service, are a distinct minority. However, the difference between the Anglo-Saxon and the European approaches concerning education as a tradable commodity should not be interpreted to mean that the American academic community as a whole shares the values implicit in the GATS; in fact, quite the opposite is true. Green (2004) and Altbach (2004a) summarized the concerns of the academic community regarding GATS as follows:

1. The GATS is an international treaty, and as such supersedes decision making at the national, sectoral, and institutional levels. It has the potential of directly interfering with academic autonomy, which may lead to unintended consequences.

2. It is underpinned by an entirely different set of values than those that have historically shaped higher education worldwide. Higher education is considered a public good that cannot and should not be traded. The terminology used in the GATS, the "trade-creep," is anathema to most of the academic community (Knight 2002b).

3. A small, but very powerful segment of the education and trade community is pushing the GATS. The interests of the for-profit education sector, the testing industry, and the English-language schools are quite different from those of the academic community (Altbach 2006, 126).

4. The ongoing negotiation process is inherently opaque, in which the academic community is not involved.

5. The ambiguity of the clause that excludes services supplied "in the exercise of governmental authority," "on a noncommercial

basis," and "those not in competition with other suppliers," has led to confusion as to how the agreement would work in national higher education systems comprising public, nonprofit private, and for-profit private institutions.

NGOs in education worldwide unanimously opposed the inclusion of education in the GATS (OECD 2004b, 258–9). The following quote from the joint declaration of the leading organizations in higher education summarizes the thinking of the majority of the academic community:

> Some governments seek to manage cross-border higher education through multilateral and regional trade regimes designed to facilitate the flow of private goods and services. There are three main limitations to this approach. First, trade frameworks are not designed to deal with the academic, research, or broader social and cultural purposes of cross-border higher education. Second, trade policy and national education policy may conflict with each other and jeopardize higher education's capacity to carry out its social and cultural mission. Third, applying trade rules to complex national higher education systems designed to serve the public interest may have unintended consequences that can be harmful to this mission. (Joint statement by the IAU, the AUCC, the ACE, and the CHEA; see International Higher Education, spring 2005).[34]

The GATS negotiations were supposed to conclude by the end of 2005. However, no agreement could be reached at the end of the so-called Doha Round of negotiations, which included negotiations not only on international trade in services, but also in goods. Strong disagreements on issues related to agriculture led to the collapse of the Doha Round. Nevertheless, following the meeting of trade ministers of member countries in December 2005, an agreement was reached to resume the negotiations and conclude them by the end of 2006. More important, however, is the new procedure adopted for negotiations on trade in services, and it has severe implications for higher education worldwide (Knight 2006a, 2008, 149–86; Robinson 2006).[35]

The negotiation procedure adopted in the first so-called Uruguay Round of negotiations was based mainly on the "request-offer" method, and liberalization could be advanced through bilateral approaches. This method obviously included built-in mechanisms, the most important of which allowed countries to make offers in response to requests to liberalize their markets at their own pace. This made it possible for developing countries to harmonize the pace of liberalization of their markets with the countries' developmental objectives. It was, in fact, a method that convinced many of the developing countries to participate in a process that many of them, rightly or wrongly, believed would produce results to their disadvantage.

During the first two rounds, the Uruguay and Doha rounds, the requests from developed countries were concentrated in the "cross-border (Mode 1)" and the "commercial presence (Mode 3)" modes of service provision (see Appendix G). It is important to point out that 80 percent of the international trade in services is dominated by multinational corporations from the developed countries, and service provision by Mode 1 is, in general, more likely to be knowledge- and technology-intensive. Developing countries are on the receiving end of these types of service provision, where they feel disadvantaged. On the other hand, service provision by "the movement of natural persons (Mode 4)" is intrinsically related to free movement of labor across borders, and it is in this mode that developing countries feel they may have a comparative advantage, despite the inherent "brain-drain" danger involved. At the end of the Doha Round, the general feeling of the developing countries was that they had made too many concessions in Mode 1 and Mode 3, and received no concession in return that would be of any meaningful commercial value to them. The reason for this was that market access under Mode 4 was linked to commercial presence and limited to professionals.

However, the United States and the EU were dissatisfied by the pace of progress in the first two rounds of the negotiations. Together with India, they proposed "a new flexible GATS architecture" as a new method of negotiation (Knight 2006a; Robinson 2006).[36] According to the proposed procedure, it will be possible for members to enter into "plurilateral request-offer" negotiations instead of the earlier one-on-one bilateral one. In Knight's (2006a) view, developing countries are now faced with the daunting task of confronting, what she refers to as "groups of powerful countries that represent the most aggressive 'demandeurs' in a particular sector."[37] Second, the new architecture gives wider oversight powers to the WTO to challenge domestic restrictions, even if they are consistent with the nondiscrimination and market-access prohibitions of the GATS, such as qualification requirements and procedures. This obviously can have far-reaching implications for procedures in place in many countries for accreditation of foreign providers and for recognizing degrees and qualifications obtained abroad and transnationally. Third, in what is referred to as "Quantitative Targets," developed members are being obliged to make new or improved commitments in at least 139 subsectors, and developing countries in 93. This new requirement further weakens the previous bilateral negotiation procedure by essentially introducing a multilateral one. Furthermore, it obviously intends to speed up the overall negotiation process. Finally, under "Quantitative Targets" it is suggested to remove specific types of barriers for all commitments to a particular mode of service provision. Both Knight (2006a) and Robinson (2006) point out that this new procedure, if approved, will strengthen the hands of countries like the United States, Australia, and New Zealand in the provision of transnational higher education, while many countries will be put under pressure to make new commitments or modify any commitment already made to further open up their national higher education systems to foreign providers.

There are numerous gains to be made from competition for all sides involved. Many of those who have critical views on the GATS certainly are not opposed to internationalization of higher education and international student mobility. Furthermore, as long as international trade exists in education, it needs to be regulated. The issue that needs to be addressed, therefore, is not whether there should be an international regulatory framework, but what its underpinning principles should be, in particular, how a quality assurance system should be built in, and how unfair competition can be prevented against public and nonprofit private institutions, which are driven by motives other than financial.

The eventual outcome of the GATS can indeed be an international higher education market that is more regulated than the present one. This, however, depends largely on whether structures and enforceable mechanisms can be put in place at the international level for quality assurance and mutual recognition of degrees and qualifications. This is the topic of the next section.

At present, however, all seem to be in vain, because the negotiations being carried out in Geneva to keep the Doha Round alive ended in disagreement, again on agricultural issues. Renewed efforts to restart the GATS negotiations had borne no fruit as of the end of May 2009.

5.6. QUALITY ASSURANCE IN TRANSNATIONAL HIGHER EDUCATION: "MULTINATIONAL ORGANIZATIONAL RESPONSES"

Many countries now have a national body with varying degrees of statutory powers in quality assurance (see Section 3.4.3). On the other hand, presently no such body with statutory powers exists for quality assurance at the international level, despite the growing volume of transnational education and the increasing diversity of the types of providers. Countries like the United States,[38] the United Kingdom, and Australia, which are major exporters of higher education services, and in which many of the providers involved in transnational education are parts of the national systems, issued codes of practice for transnational education in the late 1990s. These codes include recommendations to the providers that aim to ensure the quality of the education provided and the standards of the degrees awarded.

Quality assurance is a major concern in transnational provision of higher education, but the problem is compounded in the case of online provision (Billing 2004; OBHE-BfN, February 22, 2005, March 23, 2005; OECD 2004c; Stella and Gnanam 2004; van Damme 2001). Many countries started to take measures. In December 2003, Malaysia announced new regulations for foreign distance education providers, which must seek approval from the national approval and accreditation authority (*LAN*) (OBHE-BN, December 2003; see Section 3.4.3). In 2004, South Africa adopted "A Code of Conduct for Cross-Border/Transnational Delivery of Higher Education Programs," which aims to regulate foreign-sourced distance learning (OBHE-BN, February 2004).

In 2004, the United Kingdom's QAA issued its code of practice for transnational delivery of higher education. Generally recognized as the first of its kind in emphasizing academic infrastructure as a means of safeguarding academic quality, the code provides means for institutions, both in the United Kingdom and elsewhere, to demonstrate the quality and standards of the programs they provide overseas, both face-to-face and online (OBHE-BN, September 2004).

UNESCO recognized the International Council for Open and Distance Education (ICDE) as the global NGO responsible for quality assurance in transnational distance education.[39] ICDE, with its headquarters located in Oslo, Norway, was founded in 1983 to organize worldwide and regional conferences on issues of global concern related to distance education. ICDE has now founded its ICDE Standards Agency (ISA) to carry out audits concerned with the quality and standards of services to students at the point of delivery, and an institution's responsibility for what is done in its name. The ISA does not involve an audit of the quality of courses and academic standards for qualifications and curriculum. Because there are no international standards for these, the ISA assumes that institutions operate within the overall national and state legislation and guidelines (OBHE-BN, May 2003, March 2004).

The Global Alliance for Transnational Education (GATE) is a global quality assurance body. GATE was established in 1995 by Glenn R. Jones, the founder of Jones International University, as a forum for governments, academics, accrediting agencies, students, and businesses to discuss and implement quality assurance related to transnational education. It was transferred to the U.S. Distance Learning Association in summer 2003 (OBHE-BN, September 2003). The GATE certification is a voluntary quality assurance process for transnational education programs. According to OBHE, however, the GATE initiative is not an effective one in the complex environment of the global higher education market (OBHE-BN, March 2004).

The International Network for Quality Assurance Agencies in Higher Education (INQAAHE), founded with only eight members in 1991 in Australia, is now recognized by UNESCO, and currently has more than two hundred members. Promotion of good practices, better-informed international recognition of qualifications, and alerting members to dubious accrediting practices are among the aims of the organization.[40]

There presently is no binding international mechanism or institutional structure with the power to enforce standards for quality assurance in transnational higher education (World Bank 2002, 35). The OECD (2004c, 10) described the state of affairs as of the beginning of the new century in the area of quality assurance, accreditation, and recognition of qualifications as follows:

> The lack of comprehensive frameworks for coordinating various initiatives at the international level, together with the diversity and unevenness of the quality assurance and accreditation systems at the national level, create gaps in the quality of higher education delivered across borders. It makes students and other stakeholders more vulnerable to low-quality provision of cross-border higher education.

Following the resolution adopted by the General Conference of UNESCO in 2003, OECD and UNESCO started to work on drafting guidelines on the quality of transnational higher education as an educational response to growing commercialization. The OECD (2004c) publication was the first comprehensive review of where the world stood on this important issue. Joint Guidelines for quality provision in cross-border higher education, based on UN and UNESCO principles and instruments, were issued after the thirty-third session of the UNESCO General Conference in October 2005 (OECD-UNESCO 2005). The guidelines are neither a normative nor a standard-setting document. The objectives of the guidelines are to propose tools and a synthesis of best practices that can assist member states in assessing the quality and relevance of higher education provided across borders and to protect students and other stakeholders in higher education from low-quality higher education provision. The guidelines address six stakeholders in higher education (governments, higher education institutions/providers including academic staff, student bodies, quality assurance and accreditation bodies, academic recognition bodies, and professional bodies), provide a set of orientations to practitioners, and seek to promote mutual trust and international cooperation between providers and receivers of cross-border higher education. The guidelines address key higher education issues in a more globalized society and are equally relevant for developed and developing countries. As such, they aim to support and encourage international cooperation and enhance the understanding of the importance of quality provision in cross-border higher education. The purposes of the guidelines are to protect students and other stakeholders from low-quality provision and disreputable providers, as well as to encourage the development of quality cross-border higher education that meets human, social, economic, and cultural needs. The guidelines are based on the principle of mutual trust and respect among countries and on the recognition of the importance of international collaboration in higher education. They also recognize the importance of national authority and the diversity of higher education systems, and the importance countries attach to national sovereignty over higher education. As they are not in any way binding on national states, the effectiveness of the guidelines largely depends on the possibility of strengthening the capacity of national systems to assure the quality of higher education.

Despite this shortcoming, the OECD-UNESCO guidelines represent a big first step forward. According to Judith S. Eaton, president of the CHEA (Eaton 2005, 4): "The Multinational organizational response through the OECD/UNESCO project is conceived, at least in part, as a reaction to WTO/GATS and may ultimately emerge as a defining feature of the international higher education space."

However, it should be kept in mind that the OECD-UNESCO guideline is a secretariat document rather than a UNESCO convention, and as such is nonbinding. This was demanded by the United States. Furthermore, the GATS does not include provisions for quality assurance (see Appendix G). Thus, if in the future the international free trade envisioned in the GATS is ever established, it is not difficult to envision many diploma mills and rogue providers pervading countries where there are demand–supply imbalances in higher education (Robinson 2005).

It is interesting to compare the roles of WTO and UNESCO in international higher education. The former is pushing for international trade liberalization for profit. On the other hand, UNESCO has long recognized the need for mechanisms for international recognition of qualifications and quality assurance in transnational education as a means of promoting international academic mobility. The various UNESCO conventions on recognition of academic and professional qualifications are provided in Appendix D. There is, in general, limited awareness of these conventions, except for the Lisbon Convention for Europe. UNESCO and the Council of Europe established a "Code of Good Practice for Trans-national Education," and made it a part of the Lisbon Convention in 2001. More than one hundred member countries have ratified the UNESCO conventions, and as such, they are the only legally binding instruments currently available dealing with transnational education. Knight (2002a) makes a distinction between "non-profit internationalization of education," and "for-profit internationalization of education. The general perception is that while UNESCO is associated with the former type of internationalization of education, WTO/GATS is associated with the latter. This is why the UNESCO-OECD guidelines are viewed as a multinational response to globalization/internationalization of education, as opposed to the perceived commercial Anglo-Saxon response embodied in the GATS.[41]

The vacuum caused by nonbinding mechanisms in the area of quality assurance and recognition in transnational higher education is recently being filled by individual institutions' desire for "international branding." Bona fide national and international accreditation agencies are now operating in fifty countries. The U.S. national, regional, and professional/program accrediting bodies such as ABET are selling services in more than sixty-five countries (Knight 2005b). Institutions all over the world are lining up to build an international reputation by a "U.S. brand." Demand for a U.S. institutional brand apparently is increasing just like the demand by students and families for an American type of higher education. The lack of an internationally recognized body for accrediting the accreditors, however, remains an elusive target. The European ENQA and the Australia-based INQAAHE stand out as possible models at least to start with, and UNESCO, OECD, and, if the GATS is ever realized, the WTO certainly have roles to play in this crucial area.[42]

5.7. THE GLOBAL HIGHER EDUCATION AGENDA AND INTERNATIONAL STUDENT MOBILITY

This chapter completes the discussion on the global higher education agenda, and ties it to the transformations that have led to the emergence of the global knowledge economy. The findings of the global higher education scene in the preceding chapters can be summarized as follows:

1. Most jobs in the global knowledge economy require educational qualifications at the tertiary level. Jobs are disappearing, skills needed to perform existing jobs are changing, and new jobs are appearing, which require entirely new skills. These have led to an increasing demand by the tertiary age cohort for higher education worldwide, and a change in the student profile, which now includes increasing numbers of nontraditional students.

2. The increasing demand for higher education has coincided with a changing view of the role of the state in the global knowledge economy and in the provision of what were until recently regarded as purely public services. The result has been the "rise of market forces" in higher education, which has manifested itself in the form of (a) resource diversification and tuition fees; (b) increasing share of private institutions in national higher education systems worldwide; and (c) spread of lay governance, increased lay governance, and strengthened institutional leadership. In summary, the role of the state has changed from prescriptive (regulatory) to transformative (evaluative), public institutions have moved from the traditional state–academia axis to the market society apex, becoming entrepreneurial to varying degrees in different countries such that the demarcation between public and private has become increasingly blurred.

3. The changing socioeconomic outlook, coupled with dizzying developments in ICT, has led to the emergence of new types of "providers," most of which are for-profit. In many countries, this has replaced the traditional public–private divide with the new nonprofit–for-profit divide.

4. Internationalization has intensified in response to globalization. Internationalization is no longer confined to the study of foreign languages and cultures. It is now an end in itself. Intercultural skills are one of the most desirable attributes in the emerging "global workforce."

5. The interdependent and convergent nature of the global higher education agenda items have resulted in the formation of a *"global higher education market."* This market is characterized by intense competition for students, scholars and resources. Moreover, competition is no longer just among traditional institutions, but increasingly involves the new types of providers, too, and competition is no longer circumscribed by national boundaries; it is now global in scale.

6. Countries, institutions, students and their families have an array of rationales driving their efforts at internationalization and seeking what they perceive to be a good education. In addition to classical social/cultural and economic rationales, new rationales have emerged. Chief among them are the competition for creative young minds as key factors of production, and networking in the global knowledge economy.

The last section of this chapter has been concerned with the responses of various groups of countries and multinational organizations to the new global higher education agenda, in particular to the global higher education market. The biggest and, in many other ways, potentially the most rewarding segment of this market involves international student mobility, that is, students studying abroad. The next chapter is concerned with the global picture of international student mobility, as well as the positions of the major host countries and the major countries of origin of foreign students, and the analysis of drivers/rationales from different national perspectives.

SIX

INTERNATIONAL STUDENT MOBILITY

6.1. THE GLOBAL PICTURE TODAY

According to the UNESCO definition (UNESCO 1971, 9): "A foreign student is a person enrolled at an institution of higher education in a country or territory of which he is not a permanent resident."

Many countries comply with this definition when reporting statistics on international student mobility, but there still are variations among countries in the way a foreign student is defined. Appendix F gives the definitions adopted by a number of OECD countries. The OECD is currently working with member countries to improve the scope and quality of internationally available data on mobility of students, academics, educational programs, and institutions (OECD 2004b, 309). The Atlas of Student Mobility (Davis 2003) is a major contribution to the reporting of statistical data on foreign student enrollment and its breakdown into countries of origin and host countries. This is an ongoing project, in which the British Council, the Australian Education International (AEI), IIE, DAAD, EduFrance (recently renamed Agence Campus France), and similar organizations from a number of other countries are participating. The publication of the Atlas was followed by the first Project Atlas conference in France, which focused on several aspects of data collection and the definitions used (Gallup-Black 2004, 2005).

The Global Education Digest 2006 by UNESCO has an expanded section on international student mobility, where three criteria are cited to define foreign, or, in UNESCO's terminology, "internationally mobile students." The criteria are citizenship, permanent residency, and prior education. In the Global Education Digest, UNESCO defines internationally mobile students as those who are not permanent residents of the host country and excludes those who are on exchange programs of one year or less (UNESCO 2006, 33–34).

Eurodata was a one-year project to develop a method of reporting data on student mobility into thirty-two European countries in order to measure progress toward the mobility-related objectives of the Bologna Process and the Lisbon Agenda. In their report of the results of the project, Kelo, Teichler, and Wachter (2006), too, elaborate on issues and difficulties related to the collection and reporting of data on international student mobility. They distinguish between statistics on foreign students and data on internationally mobile students, and conclude that student mobility data should include, in addition to statistics on foreign students, information about prior or permanent places of residence and prior education of students. Their second recommendation is to distinguish between students staying for short periods such as study abroad students and those studying toward a degree. To complete the data set, they recommend reporting separately on students in bachelor-, master- and doctoral-level programs.

The OBHE, however, rightfully points out that, despite the earlier statement by UNESCO, the data are reported by the individual countries according to their own definitions of foreign students (OBHE-BNA, June 7, 2006). A further difficulty involved is which students should be included in reporting student mobility data. Here, too, there is no standard, and each country has a different way of reporting data. In what follows, wherever available, I have provided data on the types of students included for each country.

UNESCO and OECD are currently working on a more strict definition by including prior education as a criterion. Thus, more consistent and more reliable data on foreign student mobility is forthcoming.

With these caveats, Figure 6.1 shows the global number of foreign students in higher education since 1950, and projections to the year 2025. In the second half of the twentieth century, the number of foreign students increased by a factor of nearly twenty from 110,000 in 1950 to 2.10 million in 2002. This increase also may be regarded as a quantitative measure of the degree of the progress of globalization in that period in history. The period from 1999 to 2006 witnessed a 57 percent jump in internationally mobile students, from 1.75 to 2.75 million, possibly the biggest surge in the number of foreign students in history. Projections for the first quarter of the twenty-first century vary from 5 to 8 million foreign students in higher education worldwide. According to a more recent projection by IDP Education Australia, global demand for international higher education will grow to 3.720 million students in 2025. This is growth of 71 percent over twenty years, or compound growth of 2.7 percent per year (IDP 2007).

Table A.6 shows the number of foreign students hosted by and the number of students abroad for a large number of countries in 2002, 2004,

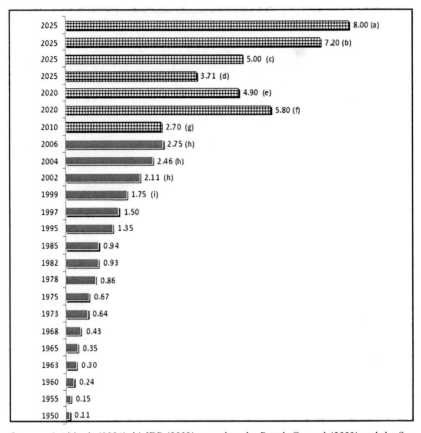

Year	Value
2025	8.00 (a)
2025	7.20 (b)
2025	5.00 (c)
2025	3.71 (d)
2020	4.90 (e)
2020	5.80 (f)
2010	2.70 (g)
2006	2.75 (h)
2004	2.46 (h)
2002	2.11 (h)
1999	1.75 (i)
1997	1.50
1995	1.35
1985	0.94
1982	0.93
1978	0.86
1975	0.67
1973	0.64
1968	0.43
1965	0.35
1963	0.30
1960	0.24
1955	0.15
1950	0.11

Sources: a) Altbach (2004); b) IDP (2002) quoted in the British Council (2003) and the Sussex Centre (2204); c) The Ministry of Education New Zealand (2003); d) Blight (1995, 43) quoted in McBurnie (2001); e) Bohm et al. (2004); f) CVCP-HEFCE (2000); g) Table A.6.; UNESCO (2004); h) Table A.4; UNESCO (2004); OECD (2004); i) Bohm et al; j) UNESCO (2006); 1950-1997: UNESCO (1971)-UNESCO (1998)

Fig. 6.1. Growth of Global Foreign Student Enrollment, Millions

and 2006.[1] Figures 6.2, and 6.4 to 6.6 are based on the data shown in Table A.6 for 2006. Figure 6.2 shows the top twenty-five host countries, led by the United States, which hosted 564,766 students in 2006.[2] The United Kingdom was a distant second with 330,075 students. In 2006, Australia climbed to the third place with 279,989 students, France overtook Germany with 265,039 students, and Germany came in fifth with 248,357 students.

A very important feature of the international student mobility becomes evident in Figure 6.2. The combined foreign student enrollment in the United States, the United Kingdom, Australia, Canada, and New Zealand, the MESDCs, was 1,348,751 in 2006, which accounted for nearly half the global enrollment, up from 1,096,000 in 2005 (Bohm et al. 2004). This is a clear indication of the nature of the global demand, that is, Anglo-Saxon type of higher education in the English language, in particular, American type of higher education, which presently accounts for almost 25 percent of the foreign student enrollment worldwide.

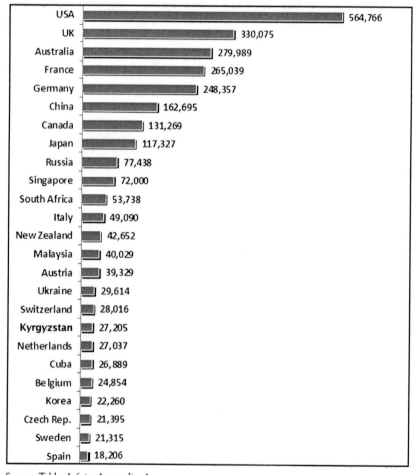

USA — 564,766
UK — 330,075
Australia — 279,989
France — 265,039
Germany — 248,357
China — 162,695
Canada — 131,269
Japan — 117,327
Russia — 77,438
Singapore — 72,000
South Africa — 53,738
Italy — 49,090
New Zealand — 42,652
Malaysia — 40,029
Austria — 39,329
Ukraine — 29,614
Switzerland — 28,016
Kyrgyzstan — 27,205
Netherlands — 27,037
Cuba — 26,889
Belgium — 24,854
Korea — 22,260
Czech Rep. — 21,395
Sweden — 21,315
Spain — 18,206

Source: Table A.6 in Appendix A.

Fig. 6.2. International Student Mobility: Number of Students Hosted; Top Twenty-Five Host Countries in 2006

Altbach (2004a, 2006) refers to English as the Latin of the twenty-first century. English is the most widely studied language, the language of commerce and banking, the language at the pinnacle of scientific communications, and the language of instruction not only in Anglo-Saxon countries, but also in an increasing number of non-Anglophone countries, from Kyrgyzstan and Ethiopia to Mexico and France. In terms of enrollment in the programs offered and courses taught in English, Turkey has the second largest English-medium higher education system in Europe. Many of the newly established bachelor's programs in Germany and the Netherlands, and even in France are taught in English.[3]

Figure 6.3 shows the projected demand for a place in higher education in the MESDCs reaching 2,614,000 by 2020, and maintaining the combined share of these five countries of over half the global enrollment. It is important to point out that institutions of higher education in all of the MESDCs, both public and private, are the closest in the world to the "market–society" apex in Clark's triangle of coordination, shown in Figure 3.5, with governance structures that include incentives to act entrepreneurially as global conditions require. It also should be added that universities in the MESDCs are consistently at the top of both the ARWU by Shanghai Jiao Tong University and the THES rankings (see Tables 3.1 and 3.2).

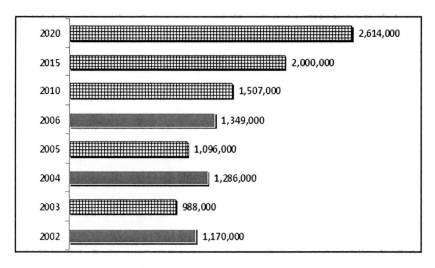

Year	Value
2020	2,614,000
2015	2,000,000
2010	1,507,000
2006	1,349,000
2005	1,096,000
2004	1,286,000
2003	988,000
2002	1,170,000

Source: Shaded bars are projections by Bohm et al. (2004); solid bars are actual enrollment figures from Table A.6 in Appendix A.

Fig. 6.3. Forecast of Global Demand for International Student Places in MESCDCs

China, Canada, and Singapore are now international hubs, attracting students from all over the world. It also is worth noting in Figure 6.2 that South Africa has emerged as a major host country with a foreign student enrollment of 53,738 (up from 15,494 in 2002), corresponding to 7.3 percent of the higher education enrollment in the country. Other emerging regional hubs are Cuba with 26,889 students (up from 10,700 in 2002), and Czech Republic with 21,395 students (up from 9,753 in 2002).[4]

When foreign student enrollment is expressed as a percentage of the total enrollment in the host country, a different picture emerges. Figure 6.4

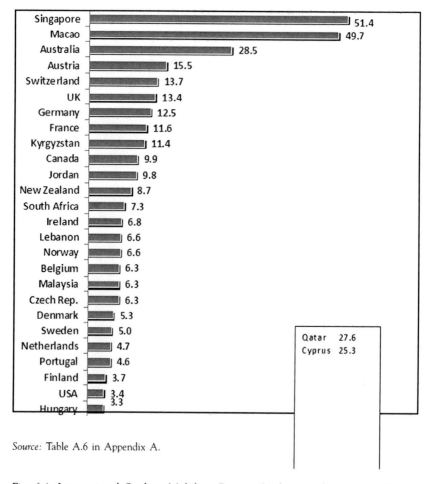

Source: Table A.6 in Appendix A.

Fig. 6.4. International Student Mobility: Foreign Students as Percentage of Host Country Enrollment: Top Twenty-Five Countries in 2006

shows that in that case, among countries that host more than ten thousand students, Singapore is the world leader with 51.4 percent, followed by Macao with 49.7 percent, Australia with 28.5 percent, Austria with 15.5 percent, Switzerland with 13.7 percent, and Germany with 12.5 percent; the United States is way back with 3.4 percent. When all countries are included, Qatar with 27.6 percent and Cyprus with 25.3 percent, take second and the third places. With the recently established Education City, Qatar is acquiring a regional hub status in the Middle East. Cyprus owes its position to the influx of students from Greece rather than being a regional hub.[5]

Figure 6.5 shows the global picture of international student mobility viewed from the opposite angle, that is, number of students abroad from

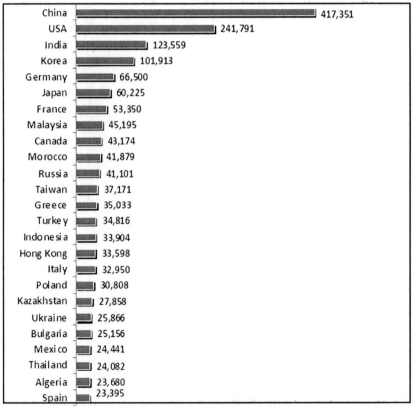

China	417,351
USA	241,791
India	123,559
Korea	101,913
Germany	66,500
Japan	60,225
France	53,350
Malaysia	45,195
Canada	43,174
Morocco	41,879
Russia	41,101
Taiwan	37,171
Greece	35,033
Turkey	34,816
Indonesia	33,904
Hong Kong	33,598
Italy	32,950
Poland	30,808
Kazakhstan	27,858
Ukraine	25,866
Bulgaria	25,156
Mexico	24,441
Thailand	24,082
Algeria	23,680
Spain	23,395

Source: Table A.6 in Appendix A.

Fig. 6.5. International Student Mobility: Top Twenty-Five Countries of Origin in 2006

various countries. Shown in this figure are the major countries of origin, led by China with 417,351 students studying in institutions of higher education in other countries, a huge increase from 184,664 in 2002. The United States with 241,791 students is a distant second to China, and is followed by India (123,559, up from 87,978 in 2002), Korea (101,913, up from 84,001 in 2002), and Germany (66,500, up from 58,100 in 2002). There is, however, a major difference between American and German students and students from the other three countries in the sense that the majority of American students abroad are there for short periods, at most one year in study-abroad programs, and nearly half of the German students are in Erasmus program (see Figure 5.1) also on short stays, whereas most of those from China, India, and Korea go abroad for full-degree programs.

It is interesting to note that students from the Asia-Pacific Rim countries—China, India, Korea, Japan, Malaysia, Indonesia, Taiwan, Hong Kong, Singapore, and Thailand—account for about one third of the foreign student enrollment worldwide. Except for Japan, the higher education systems of these countries are characterized by demand exceeding supply, especially for places in the more prestigious universities, little public subsidy and relatively high levels of tuition fees, and large shares of private institutions. In Japan, too, there is fierce competition for places in the prestigious institutions. In other words, there exist traditions of families paying for the education of their children in these countries (see Figure 3.3 for the share of households in expenditures on institutions of higher education in different countries).

Figure 6.6 shows the ratio of students abroad to students enrolled in the home institutions of the countries of origin. Luxembourg (234.7 percent), Cyprus (90.8 percent), Congo (36.6 percent), Albania (32.8 percent), and Zimbabwe (29.9 percent) top the list. Major countries of origin in terms of student numbers like Hong Kong (21.3 percent), Greece (5.4 percent), Morocco (11.3 percent), Malaysia (7.1 percent), and Singapore (14.5 percent down from 17.8 percent in 2002) are in the second tier. Clearly, these countries have policies of encouraging their students to study abroad, which are based on the capacity-building approach. This is especially the case for many of the African countries. On the other hand, countries like Singapore and Malaysia are rapidly developing indigenous capacity, which explains the drop in the case of Singapore and the slowdown in the case of Malaysia. Both Malaysia and Singapore are now aspiring to become regional hubs of international education. Capacity-building is diminishing as a rationale driving outward student mobility from these two countries. Bulgaria, on the other hand, is emerging as a major country of origin with 25,156 students abroad (up from 17,738 in 2002), corresponding to 10.4 percent of the home enrollment. This is due to the new policies in Germany based on skilled migration approach, rather than capacity building approach on the part of

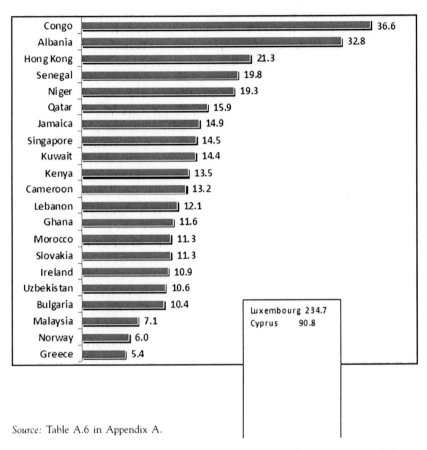

Congo	36.6
Albania	32.8
Hong Kong	21.3
Senegal	19.8
Niger	19.3
Qatar	15.9
Jamaica	14.9
Singapore	14.5
Kuwait	14.4
Kenya	13.5
Cameroon	13.2
Lebanon	12.1
Ghana	11.6
Morocco	11.3
Slovakia	11.3
Ireland	10.9
Uzbekistan	10.6
Bulgaria	10.4
Malaysia	7.1
Norway	6.0
Greece	5.4

Luxembourg 234.7
Cyprus 90.8

Source: Table A.6 in Appendix A.

Fig. 6.6. International Student Mobility: Students Abroad as Percentage of Home Enrollment, Top Twenty-Five Countries of Origin in 2006

Bulgaria (see Section 6.2.3). China, the United States, India, Korea, and Japan, which are at the top of Figure 6.5, are way behind, with students abroad to students at home institutions ratios between 1.1 and 3.2 percent.

Table 6.1 shows the top ten host countries in 1968, 1980, 1985, 2002, 2004, and 2006. The United States has been the clear choice of destination for foreign students throughout the second half of the twentieth century. Several trends are discernible in this table. The USSR was among the major players until the 1980s, obviously pursuing policies driven by a political rationale. With the collapse of Communism, it disappeared from the scene in the 1980s, and its successor, the Russian Federation, is now making a

Table 6.1. Top Ten Host Countries in Different Years

1968	1980	1985	2002	2004	2006
U.S.	U.S.	U.S.	U.S.	U.S.	U.S.
France	France	France	UK	UK	UK
Germany	USSR	Germany	Germany	Germany	Australia
Lebanon	Germany	UK	Australia	France	France
Canada	UK	Italy	France	Australia	Germany
UK	Lebanon	Canada	Japan	Japan	China
USSR	Canada	Lebanon	China	China	Canada
Egypt	Italy	Belgium	Russia	Russia	Japan
Argentina	Egypt	Saudi Arabia	Canada	Canada	Russia
Italy	Romania	Australia	Spain	South Africa	Singapore

Sources: 1968–1985: Cummings (1991); 2002–2006: Table A.6

comeback, this time driven by an economic rationale, that is, income from tuition fees (revenue-generation approach).

Lebanon and Egypt have always been major destinations for Arab students, but the appearance of Saudi Arabia in the 1980s was probably financed by the Saudi regime, and driven by the rationale to spread its version of Islam. An in-depth study of the role of those who studied in Egypt, Lebanon, and Saudi Arabia, and the role of Saudi-financed Egyptian and Pakistani teachers teaching in institutions throughout the region can possibly shed light on Islamic fundamentalism in today's world.

In the cases of France (see Section 6.2.5), Belgium, and Spain, the colonial connections are obvious. Internationalization policies of these countries and Italy traditionally have been driven by political and cultural rationales. Germany, especially since the rise of the German research university, always has been a major destination attracting students and scholars from across the globe (see Section 6.2.3).

Foreign student enrollment in European countries has increased significantly since the 1980s owing to the implementation of EU programs aimed at increasing mobility (see Appendix E and Section 5.4 on the Bologna Process, and Figure 5.1 for the growth of student numbers in the ERASMUS program), and the increasing number of the children of resident immigrants availing themselves of the opportunities for essentially free higher education in continental Europe.

The United Kingdom, too, has always been a major destination for foreign students based on colonial connections, the reputation of her institutions, and policies driven by political and cultural rationales. In the post-Thatcher period, however, the economic rationale (revenue-generation approach) became the main driver, and British universities, supported by the

British Council, started an active campaign for recruiting foreign students, elevating the United Kingdom to the second position in the early 2000s (see Section 6.2.2).

The Australian policies, much like those in the United Kingdom, also are driven by the economic rationale. Australian institutions, supported by IDP Education Australia, started to implement active recruitment practices in the late 1980s, making Australia now a major player in the global higher education market (see Section 6.2.4). These policies have paid off, and Australia has risen to the third position in 2006.

Throughout the second half of the twentieth century, Canada has been one of the major destinations for foreign students, based on the reputation of her institutions as high-quality providers of Anglo-Saxon type of higher education at considerably lower costs compared with private U.S. institutions.

As host countries, China and Japan are newcomers to the global higher education market, together with New Zealand. China and Japan traditionally were major countries of origin. Recently, however, they also have entered the league of major host countries. The rationales driving the policies pursued by these countries are discussed in the sections to come. In 2006, Singapore replaced South Africa in the top ten host countries. This has been the result of Singapore's policy-based drive to acquire a global education hub status through the Education Excellence Framework put into effect in 2004 (see Section 3.4.3).

Table 6.2 shows the change in the top ten countries of origin of foreign students over time. What is shown as China, the leader of the world in terms of students abroad in 1968 is today's Taiwan, which then represented China in the international organizations before mainland China joined the UN in 1971. Several points observed in this table are worth noting. First,

Table 6.2. Top Ten Countries of Origin in Different Years

1968	1980	1985	2002	2004	2006
China	Iran	China	China	China	China
U.S.	Malaysia	Malaysia	U.S.	U.S.	U.S.
Canada	Greece	Iran	India	India	India
Syria	China	Greece	Korea	Korea	Korea
UK	Nigeria	Morocco	Japan	Germany	Germany
Germany	Morocco	Korea	Germany	Japan	Japan
Greece	U.S.	Jordan	Morocco	France	France
Korea	Hong Kong	Hong Kong	Greece	Turkey	Malaysia
Italy	Germany	Germany	France	Morocco	Canada
Malaysia	Jordan	U.S.	Turkey	Greece	Russia

Sources: 1968–1985: Cummings (1991); 2002–2006: Table A.6

Iran rose to the top in 1980, immediately following the regime change that led to a widespread Iranian diaspora. Second, Greece and Morocco have always figured prominently among the major source countries. Third, from the 1980s on, with the advent of globalization, countries in the Asia-Pacific Rim, led by China, Korea, Japan, and India have emerged as the major countries of origin of foreign students, driving international student mobility worldwide. Fourth, a growing interest seems evident in the United States for study-abroad programs. Fifth, the rise of Germany as a major country of origin is due first to the perceived decrease in the quality of education provided in home universities by a section of the German students themselves, and second due to increased mobility supported by the EU programs. On the other hand, the increasing number of French students abroad is possibly due mostly to EU programs. Finally, sixth, Malaysia, Canada, and Russia have replaced Turkey, Morocco, and Greece in the top ten countries of origin in 2006.

6.2. MAJOR HOST COUNTRIES

6.2.1. The United States[6]

6.2.1.1. Enrollment Statistics

The first foreign student in the United States was Fransisco de Miranda of Venezuela, who came to study at Yale in 1784. For many years, the United States was not the favorite destination of foreign students.[7] Figure 6.7 shows the growth of foreign student enrollment in the United States. The sharp drop in foreign student enrollment from 9,961 in 1931 to 5,641 in 1936 can be attributed to the looming World War II. With the end of the war, foreign student enrollment in the United States steadily increased, reaching its maximum value of 586,323 in 2003. In 2004, however, for the first time since the end of the war, a drop occurred to 572,509. This was the effect of the heinous crime committed on September 11, 2001 not only against the United States and the American people, but also against the civilized world and humanity as a whole. Nevertheless, the decrease continued with foreign student enrollment dropping to 565,039 in 2005, and 564,766 in 2006. However, policies put into effect and measures implemented since then seem to have reversed the tide; foreign student enrollment increased to the historic high figure of 623,805 in 2008.

The breakdown of the primary sources of funds for foreign students, expressed as a percentage of the total enrollment, were as follows in 2008: self-financing students 62.3 percent; students supported by U.S. institutions, private sponsors, and government 27.4 percent; students supported by for-

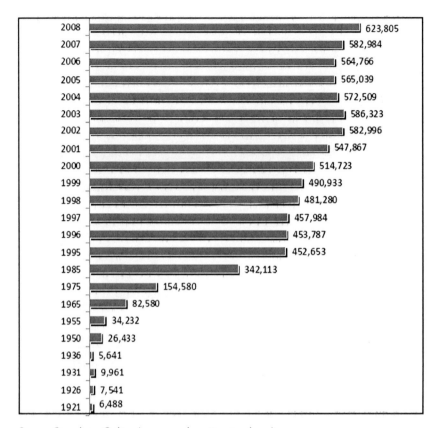

Year	Enrollment
2008	623,805
2007	582,984
2006	564,766
2005	565,039
2004	572,509
2003	586,323
2002	582,996
2001	547,867
2000	514,723
1999	490,933
1998	481,280
1997	457,984
1996	453,787
1995	452,653
1985	342,113
1975	154,580
1965	82,580
1955	34,232
1950	26,433
1936	5,641
1931	9,961
1926	7,541
1921	6,488

Source: Opendoors Online (www.opendoors.iienetwork.org).

Fig. 6.7. Growth of Foreign Student Enrollment in the United States

eign sponsors 4.6 percent; and those supported by current employment and other sources 5.7 percent. It is worth noting that self-supporting students accounted for only 30 percent of the foreign enrollment in the United States in 1962 (Weidner 1962, 4–5). Since then, the share of students who pay their own way has more than doubled. More than 80 percent of the undergraduate students are currently self-financing; this ratio drops to slightly more than 50 percent for graduate students. These figures indicate that the revenue-generation approach is more at work at the undergraduate level, whereas the skilled migration approach is the major driver at the graduate level.

As seen in Table 5.2, in the period between 1989 and 2001, revenues from foreign students in the United States grew from $4.575 billion to

$11.046 billion. Until 1980, financial sections of the *Open Doors* reports focused on financial assistance to and sources of support for foreign students. In the 1980–1981 report, a new section was included on "expenditures for living costs by foreign students." Terms and phrases such as "the economics of exchange," "economic contribution that foreign students make to the U.S. domestic economy," and "economic impact" entered the *Open Doors* parlance from the 1994–1995 report on. A section entitled "Economic Impact on States from International Students" now is regularly included in the *Open Doors* reports, reflecting the increasing importance of the revenue-generation approach in U.S. internationalization policies.

In 1996–1997, the economic impact of foreign students was estimated as $6.930 billion. The net contribution of foreign students to the U.S. economy in 2003 was $12.851 billion, and this rose to $13.491 billion in 2006, $14.499 billion in 2007, and $15.543 billion in 2008, of which $10.639 billion came from tuition fees paid by foreign students. According to an article entitled "Report Suggests 9/11 Hasn't Derailed Overseas Study programs" (*USA Today*, November 18, 2002), the U.S. Department of Commerce ranks higher education as the fifth largest service-sector export in the United States.

Table 6.3 shows the breakdown of foreign student enrollment by academic level and program type in the years 1949 to 2008. Until the mid-1990s, undergraduate students accounted for more than 50 percent of the foreign student enrollment, reaching 60 percent in some years. This trend started to change beginning in 1995, and in 2002, the number of graduate students passed that of undergraduates; this trend has continued since then. In 2008, 39 percent of the foreign students were enrolled in undergraduate programs, 44 percent in graduate programs, and 17 percent in optional practical training and other nondegree programs, including intensive English-language programs (IELP). The number of foreign students enrolled in institutions offering associate-level programs was 70,616 in 2000. This number increased to 82,923 in 2002, and fell to 65,378 in 2008, corresponding to 11.5 percent of the total foreign enrollment. It is more realistic to assume that a small fraction of the students are enrolled in these programs for a terminal degree; most aim to transfer to bachelor-level programs.

The distribution of foreign students according to fields of study in 2008 was as follows: business and management 19.6 percent; engineering 17 percent; physical and life sciences 9.3 percent; social sciences 8.7 percent; mathematics and computer sciences 8.2 percent; fine and applied arts 5.6 percent; health professions 5.1 percent; IELP 4.6 percent; humanities 3.1 percent; education 3.1 percent; agriculture 1.6 percent; and other 14.2 percent. This distribution allows a generalization to be made concerning student rationales for studying abroad. Enrollment in business and management,

Table 6.3. Foreign Student Enrollment in the United States[a]

Year	Undergraduate[b]	Graduate[c]	Nondegree[d]	Opt[e]	Total
2008	243,360 (39)	276,842 (44.4)	46,837	56,766	623,805
2007	238,050 (40.8)	264,288	38,986	41,660	582,984
2006	236,342 (41.8)	259,717	30,611	38,096	564,766
2005	239,212 (42.3)	264,410	28,418	32,999	565,039
2004	248,200 (43.4)	274,310	20,659	29,340	572,509
2003	260,103 (44.4)	267,876	30,551	27,793	586,323
2002	261,079 (44.8)	264,749	34,423	22,745	582,996
2001	254,429 (46.4)	238,497	33,833	21,108	547,867
1995	228,184 (50.4)	195,166	29,284	*	452,635
1990	184,590 (47.7)	169,820	32,440	*	386,850
1985	202,760 (59.3)	122,590	21,880	*	342,110
1980	172,520 (60.3)	94,130	19,690	*	286,340
1965	39,382 (48)	34,459	8,204	*	82,045
1955	19,124 (55.9)	12,110	2,998	*	34,232
1949	13,451 (52.8)	8,941	3,072	*	25,464

Source: Open Doors online www.opendoors.iienetwork.org.

Note: Numbers in parentheses show percentages of the total enrollment.

[a]Breakdown by academic level.

[b]Undergraduate includes associate- and bachelor-level programs.

[c]Graduate includes master- and doctoral-level programs.

[d]Non-degree includes intensive English-language programs and others.

[e]Opt includes optional training programs.

*Non-degree and Opt are shown together under non-degree.

engineering, computer sciences, and health professions programs accounts for more than half the total, indicating that the quest for a better education that will lead to better employment opportunities is the dominant rationale for students worldwide.

In 2008, 153 institutions of higher education in the United States hosted more than one thousand foreign students. The top ten leading host institutions for foreign students in 2008 were the University of Southern California (7,189 students), New York University, Columbia University, the University of Illinois at Urbana–Champaign, the University of Texas–Austin, Purdue University, the University of Michigan–Ann Arbor, the University of California–Los Angeles, the University of Texas–Austin, Harvard, and Boston University (4,789 students). New York, Los Angeles, Boston, Washington, D.C., and Chicago are the top five metropolitan centers hosting foreign students. California, New York, Texas, Massachusetts, and Florida are the top five host states, each with a foreign student population in excess of twenty-five thousand.

The top twenty-five countries of origin of foreign students in the United States in 2008 are shown in Figure 6.8. These were India 94,563, China 81,127, Korea 69,124, Japan 33,974, Canada 29,051, Taiwan 29,001, Mexico 14,837, Turkey 12,030, Saudi Arabia 9,873, Thailand 9,004, Nepal 8,936, Germany 8,907, Vietnam 8,769, the United Kingdom 8,367, Hong Kong 8,286, Indonesia 7,692, Brazil 7,578, France 7,050, Colombia 6,662, Nigeria 6,222, Kenya 5,838, Malaysia 5,428, Pakistan 5,345, Russia 4,906, and Venezuela 4,446.

Table 6.4 shows the change over time in the top ten countries of origin. India and China have always figured prominently among the top countries of origin.[8] In 1986, China, as Peoples Republic of China, made it into the top ten, and in 1989, she rose to the first place, until Japan took over in 1995, and remained there for four years in a row. China was again in the first place in 1999, 2000, and 2001, until overtaken by India in 2002. India has remained at the top of the list since then.

Table 6.5 shows the growth over time in the number of students from the top twenty-five countries in 2008. It is possible to identify in this table nearly all of the political, economical, and social developments since the end of World War II. In particular, the strong link between the growth in the number of students and the increasing diversity of the countries from which they come and the pace of globalization can be observed. One can take the argument one step further and conjecture that a correlation exists between the number of students from China, India, Korea, Japan, Taiwan, Mexico, Turkey, and Malaysia and the socioeconomic development of these countries.

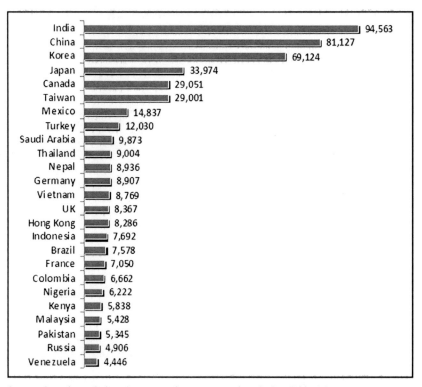

India	94,563
China	81,127
Korea	69,124
Japan	33,974
Canada	29,051
Taiwan	29,001
Mexico	14,837
Turkey	12,030
Saudi Arabia	9,873
Thailand	9,004
Nepal	8,936
Germany	8,907
Vietnam	8,769
UK	8,367
Hong Kong	8,286
Indonesia	7,692
Brazil	7,578
France	7,050
Colombia	6,662
Nigeria	6,222
Kenya	5,838
Malaysia	5,428
Pakistan	5,345
Russia	4,906
Venezuela	4,446

Source: Opendoors Online (www.opendoors.iienetwork.org). See Table 6.5.

Fig. 6.8. Top Twenty-five Countries of Origin of Foreign Students in the United States in 2008

The case of Iran is interesting as it embodies a number of the salient aspects of international student mobility. In 1955, there were 997 Iranian students in the United States. This number steadily increased, reaching an all-time high of 51,310 in 1980, and has been steadily decreasing since then. Between 1955 and 1985, Iran was always in the top ten countries of origin, and was the first for five consecutive years between 1975 and 1980.[9] Following the regime change, Iranian enrollment started to drop dramatically. In 2005, it had dwindled to 2,251 students, but seems to have picked up since then, reaching 3,060 in 2008.

For more than two decades, the top six countries of origin have not changed, that is, India, China, Korea, Japan, Canada, and Taiwan. In 2005, Canada passed Taiwan to make it to the first five countries. Figures 6.9 to

Table 6.4. Top Ten Countries of origin of Foreign Students in the United States Over Time

1949	1955	1965	1975	1980	1986	1989	1995	2000	2002	2005	2008
Canada	Canada	Canada	Iran	Iran	Taiwan	China	Japan	China	India	India	India
China	Taiwan	India	H. Kong	Taiwan	Malaysia	Taiwan	China	Japan	China	China	China
India	India	Taiwan	Taiwan	Nigeria	Korea	Japan	Taiwan	India	Korea	Korea	Korea
Mexico	Japan	Iran	India	Canada	India	India	India	Korea	Japan	Japan	Japan
Cuba	Philippines	Korea	Canada	Japan	Canada	Korea	Korea	Taiwan	Taiwan	Canada	Canada
Philippines	Colombia	Japan	Nigeria	Hong Kong	Iran	Malaysia	Canada	Canada	Canada	Taiwan	Taiwan
Turkey	Mexico	Philippines	Thailand	Venezuela	China	Canada	Hong Kong	Indonesia	Mexico	Mexico	Mexico
Norway	Korea	Mexico	Japan	S. Arabia	Nigeria	Hong Kong	Malaysia	Mexico	Turkey	Turkey	Turkey
Colombia	Iran	Venezuela	Mexico	India	Japan	Iran	Indonesia	Thailand	Indonesia	Germany	S. Arabia
Iran	Venezuela	Greece	Korea	Thiland	Hong Kong	Indonesia	Thailand	Turkey	Thailand	Thailand	Thailand

Source: Open Doors Reports 1948–2008.

Table 6.5. Major Countries of Origin of Foreign Students in the United States

Country	1949	1955	1965	1975	1980	1985	1990	1995	2000	2002	2004	2005	2006	2007	2008
India	1,493	1,673	6,813	9,660	8,760	14,620	26,240	33,540	42,337	66,836	79,736	80,466	76,503	83,833	94,563
China	3,914	2,553	2,160	22	1,000	10,100	33,390	39,400	54,466	63,211	61,765	62,523	62,582	67,723	81,127
Korea	203	1,192	2,604	3,390	4,890	16,430	21,710	33,600	41,191	49,046	52,484	53,358	59,022	62,392	69,124
Japan	75	1,572	3,386	5,930	12,260	13,160	29,840	45,280	46,872	46,810	40,835	42,215	38,712	35,282	33,974
Canada	4,197	4,655	9,253	8,430	15,130	15,370	17,870	22,750	23,544	26,514	27,017	28,140	28,202	28,280	29,051
Taiwan	2	nd	4,620	10,250	17,560	22,590	30,960	36,407	29,234	28,930	26,178	28,140	27,876	29,094	29,001
Mexico	1,344	1,247	1,370	4,000	5,650	5,750	6,540	9,000	10,607	12,518	13,329	13,063	13,931	13,826	14,837
Turkey	555	396	1,070	1,410	2,210	2,640	3,400	6,716	10,100	12,091	11,398	12,474	11,622	11,506	12,030
Saudi Arabia	9	40	552	1,540	9,540	7,760	4,110	4,075	5,156	5,579	3,521	3,035	3,448	7,886	9,873
Thailand	93	586	1,630	6,250	6,500	7,220	6,630	10,890	10,983	11,606	8,937	8,637	8,765	8,886	9,004
Nepal	2	4	84	58	180	1,480	610	1,264	2,411	3,019	4,384	4,861	6,061	7,754	8,936
Germany	293	759	1,504	1,610	3,000	4,190	6,750	8,592	9,800	9,613	8,745	8,640	8,829	8,656	8,907
Vietnam	6	101	399	2,060	5,050	3,220	1,850	794	2,266	2,531	3,165	3,670	4,597	6,036	8,769
UK	471	710	1,959	2,770	4,280	6,030	7,100	7,780	7,990	8,414	8,439	8,637	8,765	8,438	8,367
Hong Kong	nd	nd	3,279	11,060	9,900	10,130	11,230	12,940	7,545	7,757	7,353	7,180	7,849	7,722	8,286
Indonesia	1	133	766	1,080	2,440	7,190	9,390	11,870	11,300	11,614	8,880	7,760	7,575	7,338	7,692
Brazil	457	507	691	1,970	2,910	2,790	3,730	5,017	8,600	8,972	7,799	7,244	7,009	7,126	7,578
France	454	472	833	1,610	2,250	3,390	5,340	5,843	6,877	7,401	6,818	6,555	6,640	6,704	7,050
Colombia	537	1,301	1,196	2,380	3,200	4,060	3,320	3,208	6,277	8,068	7,533	7,334	6,835	6,750	6,662
Nigeria	117	268	1,382	7,210	16,360	18,370	4,480	2,147	3,602	4,499	6,140	6,335	6,192	5,943	6,222
Kenya	2	19	774	870	1,850	1,890	2,200	2,603	5,684	7,097	7,381	6,728	6,559	6,349	5,838
Malaysia	80	189	536	1,580	3,660	21,720	14,110	13,620	9,074	7,395	6,483	6,142	5,515	5,281	5,428
Pakistan	88	255	nd	3,140	2,660	4,750	7,070	7,299	6,107	8,644	7,325	6,296	5,759	5,401	5,345
Russia	18	nd	35	35	600	230	510	4,832	7,025	6,643	5,532	5,073	4,801	4,751	4,906
Venezuela	356	882	1,173	2,680	9,860	10,290	2,740	4,092	5,125	5,627	5,575	4,792	5,279	4,523	4,446

Sources: 1949–2004: *Open Doors* CD-ROM; 2005–2008: *Open Doors Online* www.opendoors.iienetwork.org.

6.14 show the change in the number of students from these countries over time.

The number of Indian students (Figure 6.9) was 34,796 in 1994, fell to 30,641 in 1997, from which year on it steadily increased to 94,563 in 2008. The number of Chinese students in the United States (Figure 6.10), which was 39,403 in 1995, increased to its peak value of 64,757 in 2003, fell to 61,765 in 2004, and then increased to 81,127 in 2008. The number of Korean students (Figure 6.11) steadily increased from 31,076 in 1994 to 69,124 in 2008, whereas the number of Japanese students (Figure 6.12) fell from its peak value of 47,073 in 1998 to 40,835 in 2004, picked up again to 42,215 in 2005, and again fell to 33,974 in 2008. The number of Taiwanese students (Figure 6.13) almost steadily fell from 37,581 in 1994 to 25,914 in 2005, and then increased to more than 29,000 in 2007 and 2008. The number of Canadian students (Figure 6.14) increased from 22,660 to 20,051 in the same period.

India (72.0 percent) and China (65.4 percent) are unique among the major countries of origin in that graduate students account for about 70 percent of the students from these two countries. Thailand (56 percent), Taiwan (55.4 percent), and Turkey (54.8 percent) are in the next group, with more than 50 percent of their students at the graduate level. The

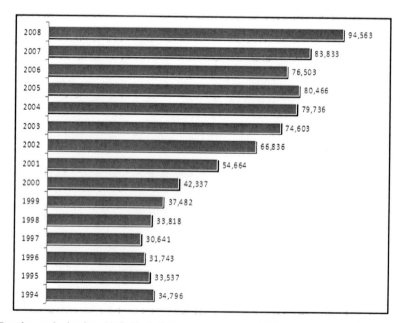

Distribution by level in 2007–2008: 72.2 percent graduate; 14.4 percent undergraduate; 13.6 percent other.
Source: Opendoors Online (www.opendoors.iienetwork.org)

Fig. 6.9 Indian Students in the United States

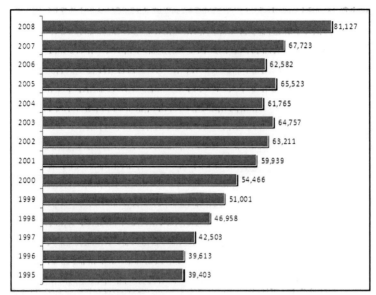

Distribution by level in 2007–2008: 65.4 percent graduate; 20.3 percent undergraduate; 14.7 percent other.

Source: Opendoors Online (www.opendoors.iienetwork.org)

Fig. 6.10. Chinese Students in the United States

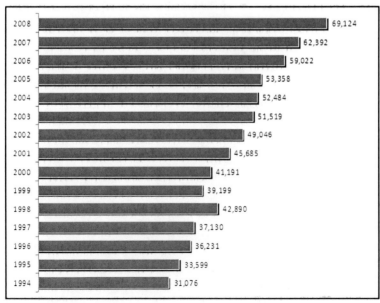

Distribution by level in 2007–2008: 35.7 percent graduate; 47.6 percent undergraduate; 16.7 percent other.

Source: Opendoors Online (www.opendoors.iienetwork.org)

Fig. 6.11. Korean Students in the United States

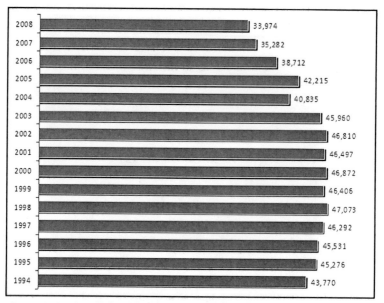

Distribution by level in 2007–2008: 20.2 percent graduate; 61.3 percent undergraduate; 18.5 percent other.

Source: Opendoors Online (www.opendoors.iienetwork.org)

Fig. 6.12. Japanese Students in the United States

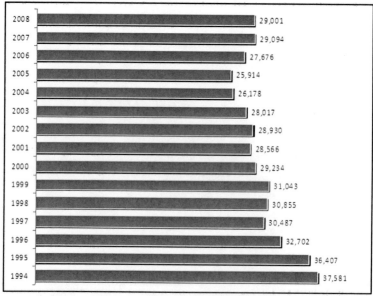

Distribution by level in 2007–2008: 55.4 percent graduate; 26.0 percent undergraduate; 18.6 percent other.

Source: Opendoors Online (www.opendoors.iienetwork.org)

Fig. 6.13. Taiwanese Students in the United States

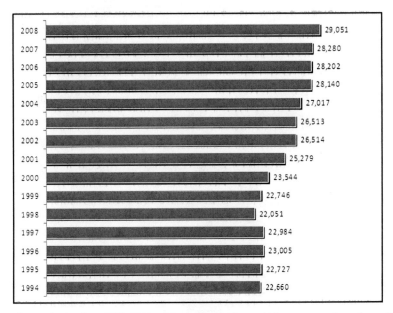

Distribution by level in 2007–2008: 46.9 percent graduate; 44.9 percent undergraduate; 8.2 percent other.
Source: Opendoors Online (www.opendoors.iienetwork.org)

Fig. 6.14. Canadian Students in the United States

corresponding ratios for some other countries in 2008 are as follows: Canada 46.9 percent, Russia, 45.6 percent, Colombia 41.8 percent, Germany 41.2 percent, Pakistan 40.5 percent, France 39.8 percent, Brazil 37 percent, Korea 35.7 percent, Nigeria 31.6 percent, Mexico 30.6 percent, United Kingdom 30.5 percent, Kenya 28.8 percent, Nepal 28.7 percent, Malaysia 25.2 percent, Indonesia 23.9 percent, Saudi Arabia 23.4 percent, Japan 20.2 percent, Vietnam 18.8 percent, and Hong Kong 18.1 percent.

In 2008, Turkey was the only European country in the top ten; Germany, the United Kingdom, France, and Russia were the only other European countries in the top twenty-five, each with considerably lower student numbers compared with Turkey. In 1949, 555 Turkish students were studying in the United States, and Turkey was the seventh among the major countries of origin (see Tables 6.4 and 6.5). Turkey reentered the top ten countries in 2000, and has remained there since then. The number of Turkish students in the United States (Figure 6.15) was 6,716 in 1995, reached 12,091 in 2002, fell to 11,398 in 2004, and then increased again to 12,030 in 2008. The 9.4 percent increase from 2004 to 2005 was very significant in a period when most major countries of origin either recorded much lower levels of increase or significant drops in student numbers.

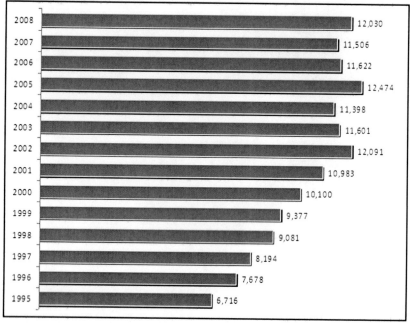

Distribution by level in 2007–2008: 54.8 percent graduate; 30.6 percent undergraduate; 14.6 percent other.
Source: Opendoors Online (www.opendoors.iienetwork.org)

Fig. 6.15. Turkish Students in the United States

It is interesting to compare the case of Turkey with those of Hong Kong (Figure 6.16), Indonesia (Figure 6.17), Thailand (Figure 6.18), and Malaysia (Figure 6.19). In 1994, there were 13,752 students from Hong Kong in the United States, and the number fell to 7,180 in 2005, and increased to 8,286 in 2008. The number of students from Indonesia steadily fell from its peak of 13,282 in 1998 to 7,760 in 2005, and has essentially remained steady since then—7,692 students in 2008. The number of students from Thailand was 12,165 in 1996, and fell to 8,637 in 2005, and increased to 9,001 in 2008. The drop in the number of Malaysian students was from 9,074 in 2000 to 6,142 in 2005, and the downward trend has continued since then, dropping to 5,281 in 2007, with a very modest increase to 5,428 in 2008. There was a major economic crisis in Asia in 1997, in which Malaysia, Korea, Indonesia, and Thailand were the most adversely affected countries. Turkey underwent even more serious economic crises, not just one, but two, at the beginning of the new millennium. However, the economic crises seem to have affected the outflow of students from Turkey and southeastern Asian countries in different ways. While except for Korea students from Asian countries to the United States decreased considerably, the number of Turkish students increased in the aftermath of economic

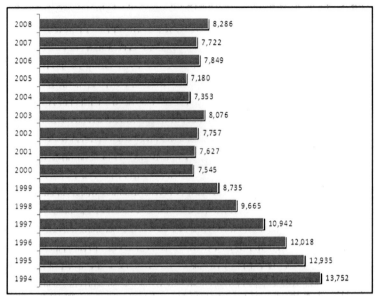

Distribution by level in 2007–2008: 18.1 percent graduate; 69.7 percent undergraduate; 11.2 percent other.

Source: Opendoors Online (www.opendoors.iienetwork.org)

Fig. 6.16. Students from Hong Kong in the United States

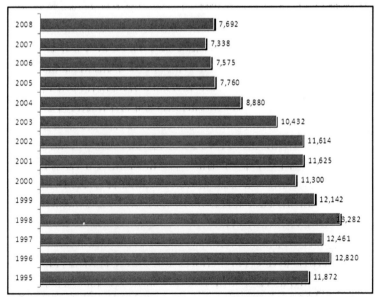

Distribution by level in 2007–2008: 23.9 percent graduate; 63.6 percent undergraduate; 12.5 percent other.

Source: Opendoors Online (www.opendoors.iienetwork.org)

Fig. 6.17. Indonesian Students in the United States

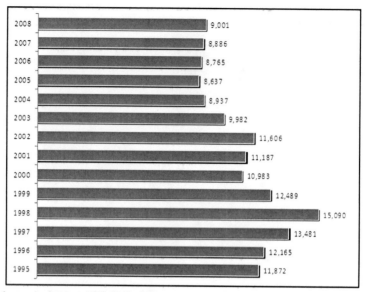

2008	9,001
2007	8,886
2006	8,765
2005	8,637
2004	8,937
2003	9,982
2002	11,606
2001	11,187
2000	10,983
1999	12,489
1998	15,090
1997	13,481
1996	12,165
1995	11,872

Distribution by level in 2007–2008: 56.0 percent graduate; 28.4 percent undergraduate; 15.6 percent other.

Source: Opendoors Online (www.opendoors.iienetwork.org)

Fig. 6.18. Thai Students in the United States

2008	5,428
2007	5,281
2006	5,515
2005	6,142
2004	6,483
2003	6,595
2002	7,395
2001	7,795
2000	9,074

Distribution by level in 2007–2008: 25.2 percent graduate; 61.9 percent undergraduate; 12.9 percent other.

Source: Opendoors Online (www.opendoors.iienetwork.org)

Fig. 6.19. Malaysian Students in the United States

crises. Obviously, more than one factor is at work in this phenomenon. The United States is facing growing competition from other MESDCs for foreign students. National capacities are increasing. In the case of Japan, there is the declining population of the higher education age cohort. In the cases of Korea and Turkey, the strategic alliance and networking rationales seem to have played a stronger role on the part of the students and their families after economic crises. The United States is perceived as the capital of the global world, both politically and economically, and is regarded by many to be a safe haven in times of uncertainty.

Several countries are emerging as significant new sources for U.S.-bound foreign students. In 1989, there were 1,587 Vietnamese students (Figure 6.20) in the United States, and the number more than doubled to 3,670 in 2005; the upward trend has continued, reaching 8,769 students in 2008, with 67.8 percent of the students at the undergraduate level. The increase in the number of Russian students (Figure 6.21) has been even more dramatic in the period immediately after the collapse of the communist regime, from 1,582 in 1994 to 7,025 in 2000, but falling to 5,073 in 2005, possibly owing to the economic crisis that the country underwent, right after the Asian crisis. The number of Russian students in the United States seems to have leveled off at about 5,000. On the other hand, the

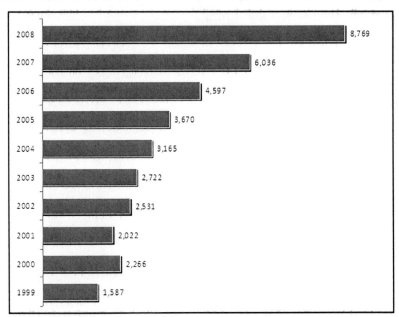

Distribution by level in 2007–2008: 18.8 percent graduate; 67.8 percent undergraduate; 13.4 percent other.
Source: Opendoors Online (www.opendoors.iienetwork.org)

Fig. 6.20. Vietnamese Students in the United States

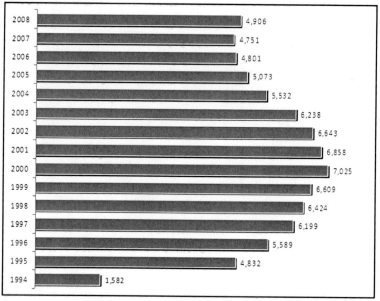

Distribution by level in 2007–2008: 45.6 percent graduate; 39.7 percent undergraduate; 14.7 percent other.
Source: Opendoors Online (www.opendoors.iienetwork.org)

Fig. 6.21. Russian Students in the United States

number of Nigerian students (Figure 6.22) has steadily increased from 2,184 to 6,335 in the period from 1997 to 2005. The downward trend observed in 2006 and 2007 seems to have abated in 2008, with the number of Nigerian students leveling off at about 6,000.

The case of Mexico (Figure 6.23) is interesting in that one would expect more students from this country with a population of nearly 100 million, relatively high purchasing power, and the next-door neighbor to the most advanced higher education system in the world, especially after the signing of the North American Free Trade Agreement (NAFTA). Yet the number of Mexican students in the United States has increased from 9,003 in 1995 to only 13,329 in 2004, falling to 13,063 in 2005, followed by another period of increase to 14,837 in 2008—an increase of 65 percent in nearly fifteen years. Brazil (Figure 6.24) is another country with the number of students in the United States less than what one would expect from a country of her size and wealth. The number of Brazilian students in the United States peaked at 8,972 in 2002, and then fell to 7,244 in 2005.The number in 2008 was 7,578, pointing to a period of leveling off. The number of students from Colombia (Figure 6.25), on the other hand,

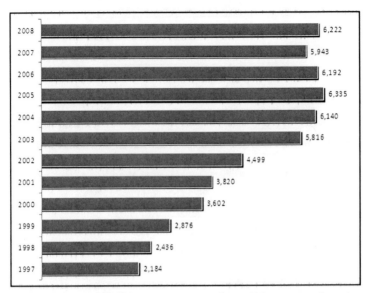

Distribuiton by level in 2007–2008: 31.6 percent graduate; 60.2 percent undergraduate; 8.2 percent other.

Source: Opendoors Online (www.opendoors.iienetwork.org)

Fig. 6.22. Nigerian Students in the United States

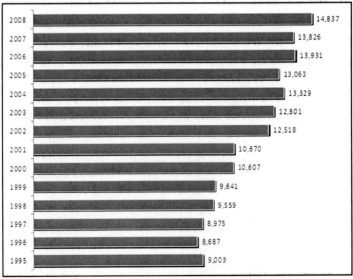

Distribution by level in 2007–2008: 30.6 percent graduate; 58.8 percent undergraduate; 11.6 percent other.

Source: Opendoors Online (www.opendoors.iienetwork.org)

Fig. 6.23. Mexican Students in the United States

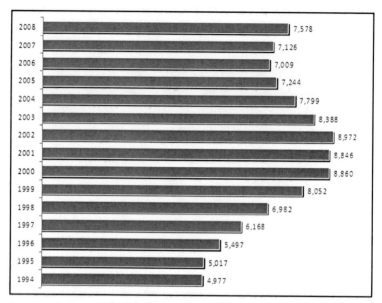

Distribution by level in 2007–2008: 37.0 percent graduate; 49.0 percent undergraduate; 14.0 percent other.

Source: Opendoors Online (www.opendoors.iienetwork.org)

Fig. 6.24. Brazilian Students in the United States

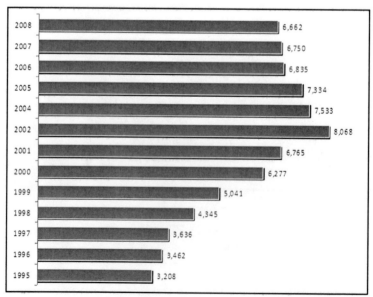

Distribution by level in 2007–2008: 41.8 percent graduate; 42.5 percent undergraduate; 15.7 percent other.

Source: Opendoors Online (www.opendoors.iienetwork.org)

Fig. 6.25. Colombian Students in the United States

increased from 3,208 in 1995 to 8,068 in 2002, but then started to drop, falling to 6,662 in 2008.

Figures 6.26 and 6.27 show the numbers of Saudi Arabian and Nepalese students in the United States. Following the oil bonanza of the 1970s, Saudi Arabia has figured prominently among major countries of origin, making it into the top ten in the early 1980s. The upward trend continued until 2001, and the numbers fell significantly from then on, dropping to 3,448 in 2006. In 2007, however, the Saudi government started another program of sending students and trainees to the United States, and the number nearly tripled to 9,873 in 2008. Nepal, as seen in Figure 6.27, is another interesting case, where the number of Nepalese students in the United States has increased by a factor of more than seven in less than fifteen years, from 1,264 in 1995 to 8,936 in 2008.

The United States traditionally has been a major host for international scholars. In 1955, the United States hosted only 635 foreign scholars, but the number started to climb up rapidly, reaching 2,539 in 1960, close to

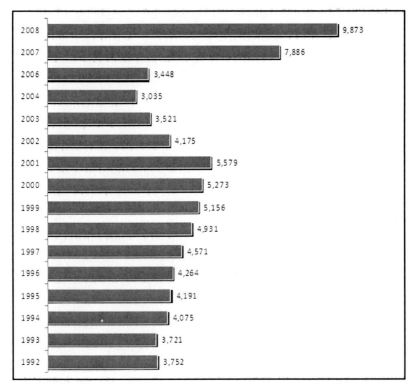

Distribution by level in 2007–2008: 23.4 percent graduate; 58.5 percent undergraduate; 18.1 percent other.

Source: Opendoors Online (www.opendoors.iienetwork.org)

Fig. 6.26. Saudi Arabian Students in the United States

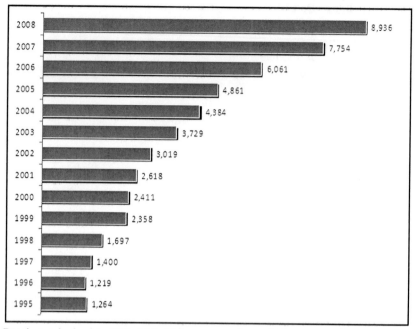

Distribution by level in 2007–2008: 28.7 percent graduate; 64.0 percent undergraduate; 7.3 percent other.
Source: Opendoors Online (www.opendoors.iienetwork.org)

Fig. 6.27. Nepalese Students in the United States

9,000 in 1965, and 46,779 in 1990. Figure 6.28 shows the number of visiting scholars in the United States, which was 59,981 in 1994, steadily increased to 86,015 in 2002, and then fell sharply to 82,905 in 2004, but significantly increased to 89,634 in 2005, and 106,123 in 2008. As seen in Table 6.6, top ten countries of origin of visiting scholars in the United States in 2008 were China (23,779), India (9,959) Korea (9,888), Japan (5,692), Germany (5,269), Canada (4,758), France (3,802), Italy (3,273), United Kingdom (2,823), and Spain (2,320), with China recording a very impressive annual increase of 18 percent over 20,149 scholars in 2007, and India overtaking Korea for the second place.

Visiting scholars in life, biological, and health sciences accounted for 39.5 percent of the total, physical sciences, engineering, computer sciences, mathematics and engineering 30.5 percent, with business and economics a distant third with only 3.9 percent of the visiting scholars. Leading host institutions were the University of California (all campuses), Harvard, Stanford, Columbia, Yale, Michigan–Ann Arbor, University of Washington, University of Florida, MIT, and University of Southern California.

Table 6.6. Major Countries of Origin of Foreign Scholars in the United States, 2001–2008

Country	2001	2002	2003	2004	2005	2006	2007	2008
China	14,772	15,624	29,690	29,382	17,035	19,017	20,149	23,779
India	5,456	6,249	6,565	6,809	7,755	8,836	9,138	9,959
Korea	5,830	7,143	7,286	7,290	8,301	8,907	9,291	9,888
Japan	5,905	5,736	5,706	5,627	5,623	5,600	5,557	5,692
Germany	5,221	5,028	4,648	4,737	4,846	5,117	5,039	5,269
Canada	3,735	3,905	4,222	4,125	4,262	4,496	4,398	4,758
France	3,154	2,985	2,789	2,842	3,078	3,380	3,588	3,802
Italy	2,226	2,257	2,242	2,317	2,565	2,983	3,148	3,273
UK	3,352	3,314	3,113	3,117	3,185	3,334	2,877	2,823
Spain	1,706	1,822	1,717	1,893	2,402	2,185	2,193	2,320
Taiwan	1,196	1,294	1,241	1,347	1,543	1,737	1,813	2,185
Brazil	1,315	1,493	1,458	1,341	1,499	1,711	1,862	2,071
Israel	1,205	1,270	1,290	1,409	1,500	1,618	1,591	1,698
Turkey	918	1,141	1,171	1,215	1,427	1,355	1,362	1,539
Mexico	898	1,068	1,185	1,032	1,158	1,250	1,218	1,396
Australia	1,212	1,316	1,183	1,197	1,183	1,265	1,175	1,163
Netherlands	1,037	1,001	955	975	946	996	959	1,108
Poland	862	960	827	927	925	983	877	840
Argentina	638	837	922	822	825	864	834	781

Source: http://www.opendoors.iienetwork.org.

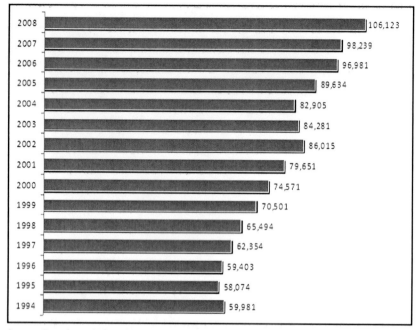

Source: Opendoors Online (www.opendoors.iienetwork.org)

Fig. 6.28. International Scholars in the United States

The total number of foreign students in the IELP at all levels was 54,487 in 2007, significantly down from 78,521 in 2001, but up from 44,565 in 2004. This particular sub-sector of international student mobility is witnessing increasingly fierce competition among the MESDCs. It is interesting to note that the top five countries in terms of students in IELP in 2007 were Korea (12,568), Japan (7,917), Saudi Arabia (6,117), Taiwan (5,926), and China (3,134).

In 1954, there were 18,092 American students abroad. This number had dropped to 13,651 in 1959, and reporting of data on students abroad was discontinued in 1973 due to lack of interest. When it was resumed in 1978–1979, the number was just 24,886. The number of American students in study-abroad programs is shown in Figure 6.29. The number of Americans studying abroad was 76,302 in 1994, and this number steadily increased to 241,791 in 2007, an increase of more than 200 percent in just over a decade. The leading destination countries were the United Kingdom (32,705), Italy (27,831), Spain (24,005), France (17,253), China (11,064), Australia (10,747), Mexico (9,461), Germany (7,355), and Ireland (5,785);

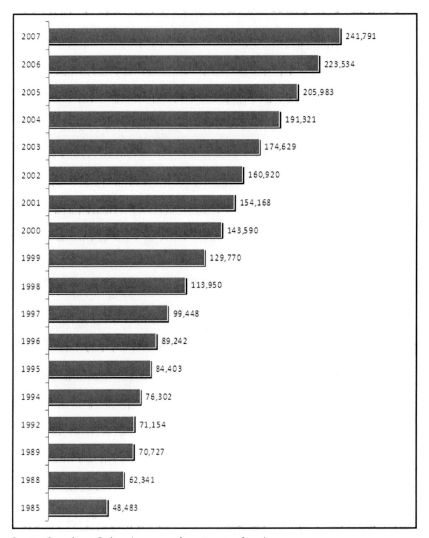

Source: Opendoors Online (www.opendoors.iienetwork.org)

Fig. 6.29. American Students Abroad

with 57.4 percent of the students opting for Europe, and Latin America a distant second with 15.0 percent. The share of Asia as a destination had decreased from 6.8 percent in 2002 to 5.65 percent in 2003 due to the severe acute respiratory syndrome (SARS) epidemic, but was back to 6.9 percent in 2004, and increased sharply to 10.3 percent in 2007. In particular, in the period from 2002 to 2006, the number of American students going to China almost doubled every year, from 2,493 in 2003 to 4,737 in 2004, and to 8,830 in 2006, indicating the growing interest in China.

The leading fields of study of American students abroad in 2007 were social sciences and humanities (34.6 percent), business and management (19.1 percent), fine or applied arts (7.7 percent), physical or life sciences (7.3), and foreign languages (7.2 percent), a distribution that is asymmetric to the fields of study of foreign students in the United States, with 11.9 percent in engineering, physical sciences, mathematics, and computer sciences combined, and only 4.1 percent in health sciences.

Another asymmetry exists in the lengths of stay. Although the majority of foreign students in the United States stay for the duration of degree programs, American students go abroad for relatively shorter periods rather than for a full degree. In 2007, the breakdown according to period of stay was as follows: short-term (eight weeks or less) 55.4 percent; mid-length (one semester) 40.2 percent; and long-term (academic or calendar year) 4.4 percent. Major sending institutions by long-term duration of study in 2007 were University of Notre Dame (335), New York University (230), University of California–Santa Barbara (185), University of Wisconsin–Madison (185), University of Arizona–Tucson (184), and Pepperdine University (183). Leading institutions by short-term duration of study in 2007 were Michigan State University (2,239), University of Georgia (1,759), University of Texas–Austin (1,504), University of Delaware (1,377), and University of Florida (1,363).

6.2.1.2. An Evaluation of Internationalization Policies of the United States

In the second half of the twentieth century, the United States emerged as by far the biggest host country for foreign students, and despite increasing competition from other countries, it is likely to remain so for the conceivable near future. The reasons for this are the country's uncontested leadership position in the world economically, politically, scientifically, technologically, militarily, and culturally, but as important, the excellent U.S. higher education system, which can offer a wide array of choices to students both in terms of content and the student support services unmatched anywhere else in the world (see Tables 3.1 and 3.2). It is, however, interesting to note that, until recently, of the five major host countries, the United States was the only one that had never had a coordinated policy of internationalizing higher education, in particular in recruiting students, at the federal or the state levels. Yet, the United States has emerged as arguably the most successful country in the world in internationalizing higher education. It was the institutions of higher education themselves, driven by various combinations, depending on individual institutional objectives, of all of the rationales and motives summarized in Section 5.3.2 that made it possible.

The first junior year abroad program was established at the University of Delaware in 1923, followed by Smith (1925) and Mount Holyoke (1926). But it was after World War II that internationalization of the American higher education really took off, with the United States striving to widen its area of influence, and the growing American interest in understanding different cultures (see Section 5.2). In 1960–1961, 53,107 foreign students from 143 countries and political areas were enrolled at 1,166 institutions of higher learning in the United States. More than 15,300 American students were attending foreign universities. More than 3,600 members of foreign faculties were affiliated with 304 American colleges and universities, and more than 2,200 members of American faculties were teaching abroad. U.S. universities and colleges played key roles in technical assistance programs abroad, and in making recommendations to the government, foundations, and institutions regarding all aspects of international relations, political, economic, cultural (Weidner 1962, 4–5, 56).

The National Association of State Universities and Land-Grant Colleges (NASULGC; 2004) lists the benefits of internationalization to the United States as follows:

1. Internationalization helps students develop the global critical thinking skills essential to contributing as citizens of the world and competing in the international marketplace.

2. Internationalization links communities to the world, expanding opportunities for university service and engagement while also enhancing their global competitiveness.

3. Internationalization contributes to national security and a vital economy, and prepares world leaders who know and value American democracy.

4. Internationalization enlivens faculty scholarship and teaching, expands research opportunities, and provides a pathway to national and international distinction.

Many of these benefits are included either explicitly or implicitly in the rationales driving internationalization worldwide. But they also include some aspects that are particular to the United States as the world leader, such as linking communities to the world, national security, competitiveness, and preparing the world's leaders.

In many ways, U.S. institutions of higher education are unique in the world in terms of the intimately close relations they have with their local communities; in no other country in the world is there such a mutually rewarding "town-and-gown" relationship. Foreign students on U.S. campuses do indeed provide links to the world at large.

It is in the area of science and technology that internationalization of U.S. higher education, particularly the influx of foreign students and scholars, pays dividends. The United States has a wide lead in both the number of published scientific papers and the number of citations to papers, as well as in prize winners. Nearly 30 percent of all PhDs currently engaged in R&D were born abroad.[10] Of the sixty-five Nobel Prizes in medicine and physiology awarded to Americans since 1949, 40 percent have gone to foreign-born scientists; eighteen of the forty-four Nobel Prize winners in physics were foreign-born, as were thirteen of the thirty-seven winners in chemistry (NASULGC 2004). Foreign-born scientists account for 19.8 percent of the U.S. workforce in engineering, 11.7 percent in life sciences, 17.1 percent in computer and mathematical sciences, 15.8 percent in physical sciences, and 7.5 percent in social sciences. At the PhD level, foreign-born scientists make up 51.5 percent of the workforce in civil engineering, 49.2 percent in mechanical engineering, 47.2 percent in electrical engineering, and 40.8 percent in chemical engineering (OECD 2004b, 280).[11]

It was innovation and technological entrepreneurship based on scientific research originating from universities in the second half of the last century that ensured the economic prosperity and military supremacy of the United States (Paarlberg 2004; Segal 2004). Schramm (2004) counts universities along with the government, mature firms, and high-impact entrepreneurs among the four pillars of the American entrepreneurial economy. Of the PhDs in science and engineering awarded to foreign students in the United States from 1985 to 2000, more than half went to students from China, India, Korea, and Taiwan. Without foreign students employed as research and teaching assistants, most of the graduate-level programs in U.S. institutions of higher education, but especially those in natural sciences and engineering, would be very difficult to run (Dassin 2005; Segal 2004; see also note 11).

Chellaraj et al. (2006) have studied the impact of foreign students and skilled immigrants on innovative activity in the United States. Their findings show that a 10 percent increase in the number of foreign graduate students raises patent applications by 4.7 percent, university patent grants by 5.3 percent, and nonuniversity patent grants by 6.7 percent. Clearly, any reduction in the inflow of foreign graduate students is likely to have significantly negative effects on innovative activity in the United States.

The United States benefits from a "brain gain" that derives directly from the foreign students who come to study in the United States, and the magnitude of the gain has increased since the early 1990s. This has been

referred to as "neo-colonialism of the mind," citing as an example the estimated $30 billion net worth of the graduates of IITs who have stayed in
the United States rather than going back to India ("Brains Business," *The
Economist*, September 8, 2005). The average rate of stay of foreign doctoral
recipients in science and engineering fields four to five years after graduation
increased from 41 to 56 percent between 1992 and 2001. The increase was
from 65 to 96 percent for Chinese doctorate holders, and from 72 to 86
percent for Indian doctorate holders (OECD 2004b, 279).

Abdullah bin al-Hussein, king of Jordan, Vicente Fox, president of
Mexico, Gloria Macapagal-Arroyo, president of the Philippines, Jacques
Chirac, president of France, Kofi Annan, secretary general of the UN, Martin Torrijos Espino, president of Panama, and Lee Hsien Loong, prime minister of Singapore are among the alumni of U.S. institutions (NASULGC
2004). The positive impact of the U.S. Fulbrighters, who numbered 170 in
the period from 1979 to 1989 in China, on China's integration into the
global economy is inestimable (Guangqui 1999). In the early 1990s, Poland's
minister of finance, Leszek Balcerowicz, studied in the United States for two
years and received a master's degree, while no one among the Russian leaders
of the time had such experience; according to Sachs (2005, 134), this gave
a nearly decade-long lead to Poland in integrating into the global economy.
In an article in *The New York Times* (November 29, 2004), Joseph Nye
underscored the key role played by the some fifty thousand Soviet academics, journalists, officials, and artists who visited the United States between
1958 and 1988 in the erosion of the Soviet system upon their return home.
In the words of the former Secretary of State Colin Powell: "I can think of
no more valuable asset to our country than the friendship of future world
leaders who have been educated here."

In Nye's (2004) view, the West won the Cold War through a combination of soft and hard power.[12] The U.S. higher education system has been,
is, and will be the most effective global asset in the soft-power arsenal of
the United States.

It was the intellectual level and the farsightedness of the Founding
Fathers, together with immigration, that makes the United States what it
is today—an "international nation" and a world leader. The skilled migration aspect of international student mobility into the United States has
indeed been very rewarding for the country, and it is now having a "multiplier effect." An astounding 60 percent of the top science students in the
United States and 65 percent of the top math students are the children
of immigrants. Additionally, foreign-born high school students make up 50
percent of the U.S. math Olympiad's top scorers, 38 percent of the U.S.
Physics Team, and 25 percent of the Intel Science Talent Search finalists
(Anderson 2004).

Foreign student enrollment in the United States had always grown from one year to the next since the mid-1950s (see Table 6.3 and Figure 6.7). In 2000–2001 and 2001–2002, 6.4 percent annual growth rates had been achieved consecutively. These were the biggest year-to-year increases since 1979–1980, and despite the slowdown, the number of foreign students in the United States had peaked at 586,323 in 2002–2003. Then, in 2003–2004 for the first time, the foreign student enrollment in the United States fell to 572,509. The consternation that this decrease caused in the United States was much greater than that caused by declining U.S. lead in patents and publications (Bollag 2004b, 2004c; Paarlberg 2004; Sarotto 2004). Segal (2004) underscored the point that declining foreign applications to U.S. science and engineering graduate programs could potentially lead to a critical weakness for the United States, which is so dependent on foreign talent.

The increasing security concerns that followed in the post-9/11 era are understandable; as Nye pointed out in an article entitled "You Can't Get Here from There" in *The New York Times* (November 29, 2004): "Balancing security risks against the political and economic benefits of admitting foreign students has always been a problem." Visa procedures were tightened, and many blamed the downturn in foreign student numbers on these tightened procedures and on the alleged less-than-welcome treatment that new applicants were accorded in the U.S. consular offices.[13] It is now recognized that the issues arising from tightened visa procedures are only part of the problem in attracting foreign students to the United States. Economic conditions are improving and educational opportunities are expanding all over the world, particularly in the major countries of origin. Increased competition from the United Kingdom, Australia, New Zealand, and Canada is providing alternatives, and recent policy changes in Germany and France are providing even more attractive alternatives in terms of cost and future employment opportunities. Technology now has made it possible to receive high-quality education in some fields online. Branch campuses, franchises, and the various offshore arrangements provide access to high-quality higher education without leaving one's country (see Chapter 4).

Concerns about the changing international setting, the effects this would have on international higher education in the United States, and the need to address issues that would be faced by U.S. institutions in a more coordinated way is not new to international educators in the United States (AIEA 1988, 1995). The need to articulate, in the post-9/11 era, new policies and develop a strategic plan involving the Department of State, the Department of Commerce, and the Department of Education was proposed by many, for example by NAFSA (2003a, 2003b), which set in motion a process that is leading to a much more concerted and coordinated effort in the United States for the first time at the federal level. This new approach at the federal level in the United States, which recognizes the increasingly fierce competition in international student mobility and all of the rationales driving it, appears to be bearing fruit; U.S. embassies are collaborating with IIE in organizing exhibitions and fairs promoting U.S. higher education, and closely monitoring visa applications from major source countries.

The policy initiatives at the federal level took a significant turn on November 4, 2005, when the U.S. Senate unanimously approved a bipartisan amendment authored by Sen. Norm Coleman and Jeff Bingaman to the fiscal year 2006 Labor, Health and Human Services, and Education Appropriations bill to help America regain lost ground in attracting the world's best and brightest students. This amendment contains a key provision of the Coleman-Bingaman American Competitiveness through International Openness Now bill by requiring the development of a strategic marketing plan to encourage international students to consider American schools through international ad campaigns and innovative Web-based resources. This amendment will also require clearly defined responsibilities and better cooperation among the Departments of Education, State, Homeland Security, Commerce, and Energy in facilitating international student access (see IIE Interactive, November 4, 2005).

The further decrease observed in foreign student numbers from 2004 to 2005 intensified efforts at the federal level to counter the perception, which now appears to be worldwide, that the United States no longer welcomes foreign students. In an unprecedented move, the State Department invited 120 college leaders for a two-day U.S. University Presidents Summit in Washington, D.C. in January 2006, cohosted by the secretary of state and the secretary of education. In the meeting, several new scholarship programs were announced and a pledge was made to further relaxing the visa restrictions imposed after 9/11, but more importantly, then-Secretary of State Condoleezza Rice underlined the importance of international academic mobility to the security of the United States. Furthermore, improved cooperation between the departments of State and Commerce in promoting U.S. higher education worldwide to counter competition from the United Kingdom, Australia, and Canada also is a new dimension in U.S. foreign policy, which, for the first time, openly identifies international student mobility as an area of intense competition worldwide, and a potential threat to U.S. interests, both commercial and political. As a follow-up to the summit, several higher education associations wrote a joint letter to the secretaries of state and education calling for strengthened international higher education "as a means to operate effectively and securely in the global environment of the twenty-first century," and in a separate letter, NAFSA stressed the "importance of international education to remaining competitive in a global society."[14] Data for 2006 (McCormack 2006) showed that applications to graduate schools were up by 11 percent compared with 2005, but still down 23 percent compared with 2003, which indicated that relaxing of the visa procedures seemed to be working, especially for India (up 23 percent over 2005) and China (up 21 percent), the two key countries of origin for graduate students in the United States. Data released by IIE for 2005–2006 showed that students enrolling for the first time in fall 2005 had increased 8 percent over the previous year, but the total number of foreign students in the United States had fallen for the third year in a row to 564.766; the decrease compared with the previous year, however, was only 0.05 percent. Since then, further visa incentives have been put in place, which make it easier for students enrolled in science, engineering, technology, and mathematics to obtain a green card after graduation (Bollag 2006b). In a statement dated March 31, 2009, NAFSA has called on the Congress to enact a comprehensive immigration reform that should include the adjustment or removal of unrealistic caps on temporary and permanent employment-based visa categories with a view to facilitating the employment of skilled foreign graduates.

Enrollment data shown in Table 6.3 and Figure 6.7 indicate that the new policies and measures implemented at the federal level for the first time in U.S. history seem to be affecting foreign student enrollment in the United States; the 7 percent increase in enrollment from 2007 to 2008 is a historic high.

It is now quite clear that internationalization of higher education will play an increasingly important role in U.S. foreign policy. The fact that the Government Accountability Office (GAO) has issued a report that compares the policies followed by a number of major host countries and the EU in itself is a clear testimony to the initiatives at the federal level (GAO 2009). Many U.S. agencies are now involved in promoting American higher education to international students. The Bureau of Education and Cultural Affairs of the State Department now provides an online guide for international students on higher education called *EducationUSA*, and supports a network of more than 450 advising centers around the world. In addition to the vast amount of practical information useful to potential students, the Web site provides information on the benefits of a U.S. education, such as the accreditation system that helps ensure higher education institutions maintain quality standards for their faculty, curriculum, administration, and student services (GAO 2009).

6.2.2. The United Kingdom

The United Kingdom historically has been a major destination for foreign students, based on colonial connections, the reputation of UK institutions and the British policies driven by the political and cultural rationales. Figure 6.30 shows the growth in foreign student enrollment in the United Kingdom. Table 6.7 shows the breakdown of the enrollment in recent years

Table 6.7. Foreign Student Enrollment in the United Kingdom[a]

Year	Undergraduate[b]	Postgraduate[c]	Total, Higher Education	Further Education[d]
1996	113,922	82,424	196,346	nd
1997	120,335	77,729	198,064	nd
1998	131,332	81,932	213,264	nd
1999	130,507	88,778	219,285	nd
2000	129,180	95,480	224,660	nd
2001	119,505	111,365	230,870	nd
2002	122,330	120,425	242,755	nd
2003	135,100	140,165	275,265	82,465
2004	143,500	156,550	300,050 (281,500)	83,620
2005	152,600	165,795	318,395 (297,120)	87,845
2006	158,495	171,580	330,075 (307,015)	87,175
2007	167,225	184,245	351,470 (325,985)	84,340
2008[e]	174,310	167,485	341,795	nya

Source: www.hesa.ac.uk

Note: Enrollment values recalculated accordingly for the years 2004–2007 are shown in parentheses. See www.hesa.ac.uk/index.php/content/view/1356/161.

[a]Breakdown by academic level.
[b]Undergraduate includes all programs below bachelor-level, and excludes students in the further education sector.
[c]Postgraduate includes all programs leading to higher degrees, diplomas, and certificates, including professional degrees and postgraduate certificate of education.
[d]Further education data supplied by the British Council office in Turkey.
[e]From 2008 on, "writing-up" and "sabbatical students" will be excluded from enrollments. Values given for the year 2008 are provisional values calculated according to the new method.
nd, no data available; nya, not yet available.

by academic level, as well as the total foreign student enrollment in the further education subsector. The enrollment figures shown in Figure 6.30 include only the students in institutions of higher education comprising universities, various nonuniversity tertiary-level institutions and that part of the further education subsector carried out at the tertiary level. They do not include students residing outside the United Kingdom, who are enrolled in the programs of OUW and the various offshore programs (see Section 4.4.8 for offshore enrollment).

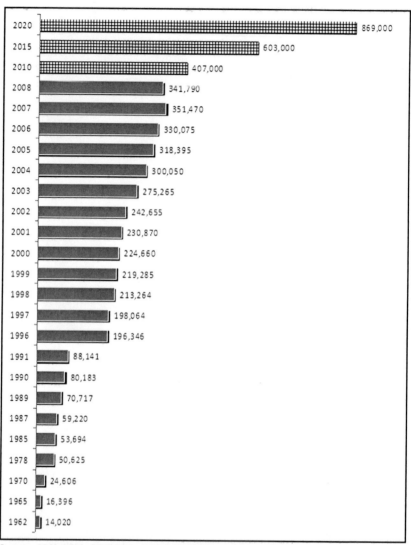

Year	Enrollment
2020	869,000
2015	603,000
2010	407,000
2008	341,790
2007	351,470
2006	330,075
2005	318,395
2004	300,050
2003	275,265
2002	242,655
2001	230,870
2000	224,660
1999	219,285
1998	213,264
1997	198,064
1996	196,346
1991	88,141
1990	80,183
1989	70,717
1987	59,220
1985	53,694
1978	50,625
1970	24,606
1965	16,396
1962	14,020

Sources: 1962–1991: UNESCO (1963)–UNESCO (1994); 1996–2008: www.hesa.ac.uk; and 2010–2020. See Table 6.7. Projections: Bohm et al. (2004); Optimistic Scenario.

Fig. 6.30. Growth of Foreign Student Enrollment in the United Kingdom

British universities were radically restructured during the Thatcher years, especially in the second half of the 1980s, known as the "Post-Jarrat Period," when they had to act entrepreneurially to diversify their revenue sources (see Section 3.1). This is reflected in the nearly fourfold increase in foreign student enrollment in the late 1980s and the first half of the 1990s, from 53,694 in 1985 to 196,346 in 1996.

The 275,265 foreign students enrolled in UK institutions of higher education in 2002–2003 generated more than £1.8 billion in fee revenue, and together with their spending while studying in the United Kingdom contributed in excess of £4 billion to the UK economy. Total contribution to the economy including offshore provision and other income related to higher education was 5,075 billion pounds in 2002–2003, and 5,804 billon pounds in 2003–2004 (Lenton 2007).

In addition to the foreign students enrolled in institutions of higher education onshore and offshore, the international education economic sector in the United Kingdom currently includes the following:

1. More than 80,000 foreign students in further education colleges in the United Kingdom;

2. More than 500,000 students in private colleges, schools, and English-language training institutions;

3. Foreign scholars on short visits and research attachments;

4. An estimated 3 million students who take UK examinations overseas, including English language, music, professional, and technical studies;

5. Foreign-contracted R&D projects carried out in UK institutions; and

6. Export of other education-related goods and services, which include education-related publishing, education equipment, and consultancy services.

Combined revenues from these represented an annual gross contribution to the UK economy of 25.910 billion pounds in 2002–2003, and 27.772 billion pounds in 2003–2004 (Lenton 2007). Thus, the economic rationale has been the main driver of UK policies in international higher education since the mid-1980s (Bohm et al. 2004).

Subsequent Labor governments have pursued the policies of Thatcher governments even more vigorously. On June 18, 1999, Prime Minister Tony Blair announced the start of a worldwide campaign, now referred to as the first phase of Prime Minister's Initiative (PMI). The British Council led the campaign, and its aim was to promote British universities and colleges internationally and attract more foreign students to the United Kingdom. The following was a part of the statement Blair made: "Our universities and colleges are second to none. Their world-class reputation means that they are among the most popular for international students. I am determined to build on this strength with a long-term strategy to attract many more. The institutions, their students and our economy will reap considerable rewards."

The target for 2005 was set as one fourth of the foreign students in the MESDCs to be hosted in the United Kingdom, which corresponded to 271,000 students. However, as seen in Figure 6.30, this target was surpassed in 2003, when 275,265 students were enrolled in UK institutions, and total enrollment reached 351,470 in 2007.

Initial projections into the future are based on two scenarios: a low-growth one with an annual growth rate of 5 percent, and a high growth one with 8 to 9 percent annual growth. These two scenarios predict a foreign student enrollment between 511,000 and 971,000 students in 2020, and between 644,000 and 1,330,000 students in 2025, respectively (British Council 2003). Another study also commissioned by the British Council made projections based on three scenarios for worldwide demand for international education, which took into account a diverse set of factors, including relative performance of the major host countries, growth in the capacity of major source countries, population growth, and so forth. According to the "base scenario," the number of foreign students in the United Kingdom will be 325,000 in 2010 and 511,000 in 2020. The "pessimistic scenario," on the other hand, forecasts a drop in foreign student enrollment to 158,000 in 2010 followed by an increase to 254,000 in 2020, whereas the "optimistic scenario" shown as shaded bars in Figure 6.30 forecasts a total foreign student enrollment of 407,000 and 869,000 for the said years, respectively (Bohm et al. 2004).

The figures available for the United Kingdom from HESA for 2004 and 2005 indicated that foreign student enrollment in the United Kingdom was rising, but at a slower rate than in the past—6.1 percent from 2004 to 2005, and 3.7 percent from 2005 to 2006. Many institutions were reporting significant downturns, with half the institutions missing their recruitment targets. Vice-chancellors were citing the introduction of big increases in student visa charges among the reasons, and were particularly worried about the fall in applications from China in 2005 (MacLeod 2005; see Table 6.8). However, enrollment figures for 2006 and 2007 shown in Figure 6.30 indicate that the annual growth rate rose to 6.5 percent from 2006 to 2007. The growth rate from 2007 to 2008, based on enrollment figures calculated according to the new method shown in Table 6.7 was 5.1 percent from 2007 to 2008.

Table 6.8 shows the student numbers from major countries of origin in the period 1997–2008. The top fifteen countries of origin of foreign students in the United Kingdom in 2008 were China 45,355, India 25,905, Ireland 15,260, United States 13,905, Germany 13,625, France 12,685, Nigeria

Table 6.8. Major Countries of Origin of Foreign Students in the United Kingdom, 1997–2008

Country	1997	1998	1999	2000	2001	2002	2003	2004	2005	2006	2007	2008
China	2,660	2,883	4,017	6,310	12,095	20,710	35,155	47,740	52,675	50,755	49,595	45,355
India	2,302	2,965	3,498	3,760	4,875	7,750	12,465	14,625	16,885	19,205	23,835	25,905
Ireland	15,575	15,894	15,144	13,930	13,510	13,235	13,460	14,715	16,345	16,790	16,255	15,260
U.S.	9,448	10,117	10,981	11,470	9,425	9,985	11,630	13,380	14,385	14,755	15,955	13,905
Germany	12,582	13,037	13,568	13,750	11,370	10,960	11,785	12,095	12,555	13,265	14,010	13,625
France	12,101	12,844	13,254	12,910	9,950	9,940	10,560	11,295	11,685	12,455	13,070	12,685
Greece	21,737	25,602	28,605	29,580	31,150	28,585	26,005	22,825	19,685	17,675	16,050	12,625
Nigeria	1,834	1,920	1,902	2,120	2,650	3,340	4,585	5,940	8,145	9,605	11,135	11,785
Malaysia	18,015	17,380	12,632	10,140	10,005	10,680	11,780	11,805	11,475	11,450	11,810	11,730
Hong Kong	7,767	7,977	8,829	8,380	8,335	8,870	10,105	10,575	10,780	9,455	9,640	9,700
Italy	4,990	5,254	5,748	6,080	5,415	5,170	5,440	5,215	5,315	5,460	5,990	5,605
Japan	4,665	5,332	5,686	6,150	6,470	6,355	6,300	6,395	6,180	6,200	5,705	4,465
Singapore	5,646	6,081	6,016	5,460	4,410	4,175	4,250	3,905	3,630	3,275	nd	nd
Spain	6,945	7,220	7,660	7,780	5,860	5,705	6,095	6,105	6,000	6,225	6,350	5,740
EU Total	88,124	96,424	101,995	102,510	94,575	90,135	90,580	89,545	100,005	106,225	112,260	118,150

Sources:1997–2006: Verbik and Lasanowski (2007, Table 2); 2007: HESA Press Release No. 120, March 19, 2008; and 2008: HESA Press Release No. 133, April 16, 2009. Figures for EU are from HESA statistics www.hesa.ac.uk.

EU, European Union; nd, no data.

11,785, Malaysia 11,730, Cyprus 9,795, Hong Kong 9,700, Nigeria 8,145, Pakistan 9,305, Poland 8,578, Spain 5,740, and Taiwan 5,215.[15]

China, now the largest country of origin, was a distant third with 12,095 students, when Greece was at the top with 31,150 students in 2001. In 2003, China was at the top with 35,155 students, followed by Greece with 26,005 students and India was fourth with 12,465 students. Despite the significant decrease in the number of Greek students from 2001 on, Greece was still the largest European source of foreign students in the United Kingdom until 2006. The reasons for this are the insufficient supply of university places in Greece and the "equal-treatment principle" in the EU. The latter is based on several decisions of the European Court of Justice, which imply that in all member states students from other EU countries are treated as domestic students and pay the same tuition fees as national students, but that they are not entitled to the support provided by national governments toward living costs of home students (OECD 2004b, 105).

Also shown in Table 6.8 is the number of students from EU countries. From 2000 to 2004 there was a significant decrease in EU students. With the enlargement of EU, this started to change in recent years; there was still a decrease in the number of students from the first fifteen members of the EU, but this was more than offset by the students from the accession countries led mainly by Cyprus and Poland (MacLeod 2005). Cypriot and Polish students are now taking advantage of the equal-treatment principle. There were 4,325 Polish students in 2006, 6,770 in 2007 and 8,578 in 2008.[16] In 2005, Norway with 3,345 students was the major source of non-EU European students, followed by Russia (2,025), Turkey (1,915), Switzerland (1,500), and Ukraine (525).[17] Singapore, once a major supplier of students, dropped out of the top ten countries in 2005, and out of the top fifteen in 2007.[18]

Enrollment figures given in Table 6.7 show that the number of foreign students in postgraduate programs significantly increased from 1996 to 2008. In 2007 and 2008, postgraduate students accounted for nearly half the total foreign enrollment in the United Kingdom.

In 2008, students in business and administrative studies constituted the largest group, followed by engineering and technology, social studies, computer science, and languages. At the graduate level, MBA programs were by far the most popular.[19]

In 2008, top ten host institutions in the United Kingdom were University of Manchester (8,380), University of Nottingham (7,485), University College London (6,840), University of Warwick (6,800), University of Oxford (6,425), London Metropolitan University (6,370), London School of Economics and Political Science (6,170), University of Central Lancashire (5,860), University of Westminster (5,445), and Imperial College of Science, Technology and Medicine (5,365).[20]

Data for 2007 show that top ten countries in terms of enrollment in the further education subsector were Poland (16,455), India (4,735), Ireland (4,580), China (3,985), Spain (3,970), Italy (3,335), France (3,050), Germany (2,380), Czech Republic (2,100), and Pakistan (1,920).[21]

On April 18, 2006, Blair announced the launching of the second phase of PMI, which, this time, aims to attract an additional one hundred thousand students to the United Kingdom from outside of the EU (OBHE-BNA, April 21, 2006). In announcing the new initiative, the prime minister stated that Britain could not afford to be complacent in the face of increased competition and expanding higher education systems in countries that are traditionally sources of foreign students in the United Kingdom, such as Hong Kong, Singapore, and Malaysia. However, the new initiative is broader in scope, more ambitious in its aims and is supported by secure funding and a number of bilateral programs. The UK–China Partnership (Labi 2006b) and the India–UK Research Initiative (Labi 2006c) involve joint research projects, various twinning arrangements, and academic exchanges as well as providing support to fee-paying students. Although the first PMI was entirely driven by the revenue-generation approach, it does appear that the new PMI is driven as much by international branding approach to support growing offshore delivery by UK institutions, the skilled migration rationale to attract the best and the brightest to the United Kingdom and networking to expand trade as it is by revenue-generation approach. Furthermore, visa restrictions have been relaxed, and, effective as of May 2006, any international student who obtains a postgraduate degree, and undergraduates in sectors with key labor market gaps, are authorized to work in England for up to twelve months upon graduation (the International Graduate Scheme). In a foreword to the new strategy, UK home secretary Charles Clarke emphasized the need for a "world-class migration system to attract the brightest and the best from across the world," which clearly shows the increased importance of the skilled migration approach as a driver of the UK internationalization policies (OBHE-BNA, May 4, 2006).

6.2.3. Germany[22]

Germany is where research formally became a function of the university in addition to teaching. Germany today is a major producer of scientific knowledge; in terms of Nobel Prizes won, Germany ranks second to the United States, and is just ahead of the United Kingdom. Beginning around the middle of the nineteenth century, Germany emerged as a major destination for foreign students. Figure 6.31 shows the growth of foreign student enrollment in Germany over time. Germany does not distinguish between resident (*Bildungsinlaender*) and nonresident (*Bildungsauslaender*) foreign stu-

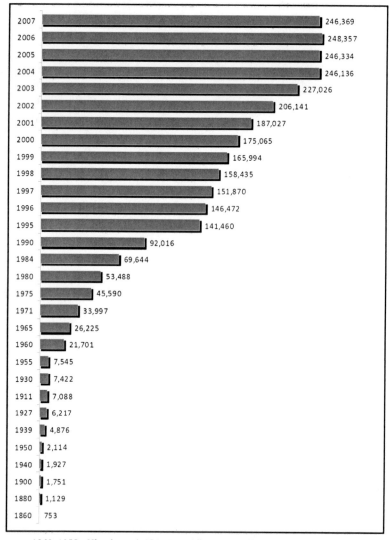

Sources: 1860–1955: Klineberg (1976, 93–126); 1960–1976: UNESCO (1963)–UNESCO (1986); and 1975–2007: www.wissenschaft-weltoffen.de. See Table 6.9.

Fig. 6.31. Growth of Foreign Student Enrollment in Germany

dents.[23] For this reason, foreign enrollment in Germany shot up from 21,701 in 1960, when labor migration started, to 92,016 in 1990, and 141,460 in 1995, when children of the *gastarbeiter* started to avail themselves of the free higher education opportunity in increasing numbers, and total foreign enrollment in German institutions steadily rose to 246,369 in 2007.

Table 6.9 shows the breakdown of foreign student enrollment in Germany in recent years according to residency and institution type. The number of resident foreign students rapidly increased to 51,387 in 1997, reached its peak value of 65,830 in 2004, and fell to 57,933 in 2007, when resident foreign workers started to take advantage of the new naturalization and immigration laws to become German citizens. Nonresident foreign enrollment, on the other hand, steadily increased from 100,033 in 1997 to 125,714 in 2001, from which year on it accelerated to 208,089 in 2007.

The breakdown of the foreign student enrollment in 2007 according to the type of institution and immigration status of students was as follows: (1) universities: 143,843 nonresident, 35,671 resident; (2) art schools (*Kunsthochschulen*): 5,858 nonresident, 2,606 resident; and (3) *Fachhochschulen*: 38,735 nonresident, 19,656 resident. It also should be noted that, although foreign student enrollment in universities and art schools have stagnated in recent years, that in *Fachhochschulen* has been steadily increasing, reaching 58,301 in 2007.

Table 6.10 shows the change over time in the numbers of foreign students from major countries of origin. The dramatic effects of political events and the accompanying increased pace of globalization as well as the change in the policies of the host country and the countries of origin are strikingly evident in this table. There were only 66 Chinese students in Germany in 1976, and that number increased by a factor of 411 to 27,129 in 2005, and has remained steady until 2007. Chinese policy for outward student mobility has been driven by the capacity-building and know-how transfer rationales; so was the Korean policy, but the increase in student numbers was a much more modest sixfold. That ratio was 108-fold in the case of Cameroon, and 56-fold for Morocco.

The corresponding ratios for Poland, Bulgaria, Russia, and Ukraine were 89-, 152-, 478-, and 336-fold, respectively, which brought the numbers of students from these countries from a handful in 1976 to thousands in 2005. The increase in student numbers from former communist countries should be attributed to a number of factors. These include the collapse of the communist regime, success of host country policies, which are increasingly driven by the skilled migration approach, and the economic rationale (better job prospects and a better life) on the part of the students rather than the capacity-building approach followed by countries of origin.

The case of Turkey also is interesting. The vast majority of the Turkish students in Germany are the children and the relatives of the *Gastarbeiter*—67 percent in 2007. Their number increased from 4,208 in 1976, reached its peak of 24,448 in 2004, and started to decline in 2005, when

Table 6.9. Foreign Student Enrollment in Germany[a]

Year	Universities			Colleges of Art (Kunsthochschulen)			University of Applied Science (Fachhochschulen)			Country Total
	Resident[b]	Nonresident[c]	Total	Resident[b]	Nonresident[c]	Total	Resident[b]	Nonresident[c]	Total	
2007	35,671	143,843	179,514	2,606	5,858	8,464	19,656	38,735	58,391	246,369
2006	36,826	146,612	183,438	2,872	5,509	8,381	19,209	37,329	56,538	248,357
2005	37,612	146,183	183,795	2,951	5,316	8,267	19,151	35,171	54,322	246,334
2004	42,626	142,377	185,003	3,258	4,900	8,158	19,946	33,029	52,975	246,136
2003	41,367	130,671	172,038	2,965	4,821	7,786	19,481	27,721	47,202	227,026
2002	42,244	114,744	156,988	2,787	4,402	7,189	18,324	23,640	41,964	206,141
2001	41,665	101,565	143,230	2,540	4,109	6,649	17,108	20,040	37,148	187,027
2000	42,112	92,154	134,266	2,428	3,836	6,264	17,642	16,893	34,535	175,065

Source: www.wissenschaft-weltoffen.de.
[a]Breakdown by type of institution and country of residence.
[b]Resident: Graduate of a secondary school in Germany (Bildungsinlaender).
[c]Nonresident: Graduate of a secondary school outside of Germany (Bildungsauslaender).

Table 6.10. Major Countries of Origin of Foreign Students in Germany, 1997–2007

Country	1997	1998[a]	1999[a]	2000	2001	2002	2003	2004	2005	2006	2007
China	4,980	4,773	5,054	6,256	9,109	14,070	20,141	25,284	27,129	27,390	27,117
Turkey	21,856	6,414	6,306	23,762	23,640	24,041	24,114	24,448	22,553	22,914	22,090
Poland	5,271	5,020	5,805	8,181	9,328	10,936	12,601	14,350	14,896	15,183	14,493
Bulgaria	1,434	1,541	2,022	3,307	5,015	7,321	9,897	12,048	12,848	12,794	12,170
Russia	3,622	3,761	42,80	5,946	6,987	8,383	9,601	10,814	11,479	11,953	12,197
Ukraine	1,145	1,407	1,841	2,836	3,688	4,917	6,071	7,238	8,066	8,671	8,839
Morocco	4,606	4,109	4,376	5,699	6,204	6,765	7,421	8,097	8,019	8,213	7,931
Italy	5,784	3,203	3,376	6,547	6,771	6,879	7,074	7,183	6,810	6,710	6,614
Austria	6,187	3,377	3,557	6,106	6,127	6,422	6,389	6,373	5,770	5,930	6,153
France	5,894	5,410	5,449	6,204	6,246	6,356	6,245	6,431	6,290	6,074	5,982
Greece	7,945	4,125	3,870	7,708	7,516	7,451	7,254	7,043	6,115	5,850	5,643
Cameroon	1,900	2,164	2,851	3,638	4,141	4,464	4,896	5,332	5,393	5,521	5,503

Sources: www.wissenschaft-weltoffen.de; see also Verbik and Lasanowski (2007, Table 4).

[a]Figures include the number of *bildungsinlaender* foreign students only.

the Turks in Germany started to take advantage of the new immigration and naturalization laws to become citizens—another consequence of new German policies on inward student mobility based on the skilled migration approach. It is also interesting to note that the number of Indian students, though comparatively smaller at the present, is also increasing rapidly, from 1,412 in 2001 to 4,249 in 2005, and then fell to 3,780 in 2007.

In marked contrast, the increase in the numbers of students from the EU countries has been much more modest despite the considerable support provided through the ERASMUS program. Students from Italy and France numbered 6,614 and 5,982, respectively, in 2007, and represented increases of only about threefold compared with 1976.

The top ten host universities in 2007 were Technical University of Berlin (3,494), München (3,287), Heidelberg (3,237), Frankfurt (2,968), Köln (2,860), Stuttgart (2,731), Aachen (2,600), Duisburg-Essen (2,483), and Mainz (2,419). Foreign student enrollment in two *Fachhochschulen*, Köln (2,642) and Frankfurt (2,127), also was more than 2,000.

Figure 6.32 shows the number of German students abroad. The positive effects of the EU programs clearly are seen in this figure. Whereas only 9,709 Germans were studying abroad in 1962, and the number in 1985 just before the start of the ERASMUS program was 24,900, 75,800 Germans were studying abroad in 2005. The most popular destinations for German students were the United Kingdom, Austria, the United States, Netherlands, and Switzerland, France, and Austria (UNESCO 2008). The drop in German students abroad from 10,077 in 1968 to 7,278 in 1974 in the aftermath of the widescale campus unrest and student riots in Europe in 1968 is noteworthy.

The change in the numbers and the composition of foreign students in Germany is dramatic, reflecting the skilled migration approach to internationalization of higher education in Germany. *DAAD* has been charged with several new functions, in addition to its traditional role in academic exchange. These include (1) scholarships for foreigners to study in Germany; (2) scholarships for Germans to study abroad; (3) support for internationalization of the institutions of higher education in Germany; (4) promoting German studies and German language abroad; and (5) educational cooperation with developing countries.[24] This new initiative led by *DAAD* is similar to the recently launched British initiative in that they both aim to develop an international brand for their higher education systems.

Table 6.11 shows the number of graduate students and senior researchers in Germany. The number nearly doubled from 1999 to 2006, but the increase in the number of graduate students funded from German sources is even more dramatic, from 1,130 to 12,140, reflecting the German internationalization policies driven by the skilled migration approach.

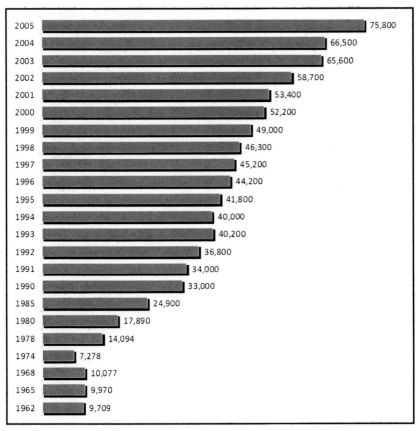

Year	Value
2005	75,800
2004	66,500
2003	65,600
2002	58,700
2001	53,400
2000	52,200
1999	49,000
1998	46,300
1997	45,200
1996	44,200
1995	41,800
1994	40,000
1993	40,200
1992	36,800
1991	34,000
1990	33,000
1985	24,900
1980	17,890
1978	14,094
1974	7,278
1968	10,077
1965	9,970
1962	9,709

Sources: 1962–1978: UNESCO (1963)–UNESCO (1982); and 1980–2005: www.wissenschaft-weltoffen.de.

Fig. 6.32. German Students Abroad

6.2.4. France

Figure 6.33 shows the number of foreign students enrolled in French higher education institutions in the period 1899–2006. Foreign student enrollment in France steadily increased after World War II, reaching its highest value of 139,563 in 1994, which is when it started to decrease, but then started picking up once again, and reached 265,039 in 2006, when France overtook Germany to be the fourth largest host country in the world.

Table 6.11. Foreign Scholars[a] in Germany, 1999–2006

	1999	2000	2001	2002	2003	2004	2005	2006
Graduate students[b]	1,130	2,337	9,081	9,909	10,272	11,380	11,808	12,140
Postdoctoral fellows[b]	2,706	2,886	3,141	4,486	3,355	2,661	3,214	3,561
Academics[b]	1,227	2,018	5,866	5,121	6,210	4,941	4,846	5,371
Other[c]	7,385	7,888	859	177	244	1,908	1,999	1,951
Total	12,448	15,129	18,947	19,693	20,081	20,890	21,867	23,023

Source: http://www.wissenschaft-weltoffen.de.

[a]Foreign scholars in Germany include graduate students, postdoctoral fellows, and senior academics.
[b]Funded from German sources.
[c]No information available on funding source and classification.

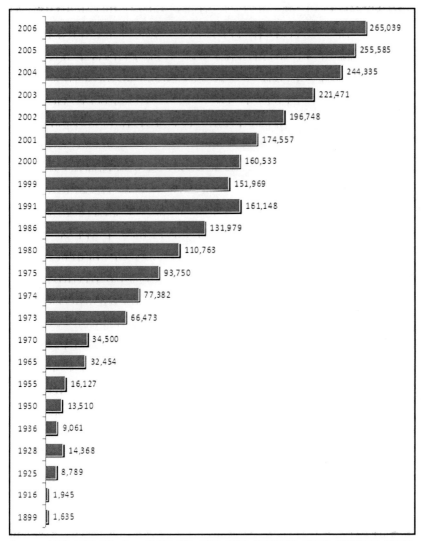

Year	Value
2006	265,039
2005	255,585
2004	244,335
2003	221,471
2002	196,748
2001	174,557
2000	160,533
1999	151,969
1991	161,148
1986	131,979
1980	110,763
1975	93,750
1974	77,382
1973	66,473
1970	34,500
1965	32,454
1955	16,127
1950	13,510
1936	9,061
1928	14,368
1925	8,789
1916	1,945
1899	1,635

Sources: 1899–1936: Klineberg (1976, 76); 1950–1986: UNESCO (1963)–UNESCO (1995); and 1991–2006: http://media.education.gouv.fr/file/42/6/2426.pdf. See Table 6.12.

Fig. 6.33. Growth of Foreign Student Enrollment in France

Table 6.12 shows the distribution of foreign students in France accord-ing to institution type. In 2006, 77.6 percent of the foreign students were enrolled in universities, 3.1 percent in STS (*Section de Technicien Supérieur*), and 2.8 percent in IUT (*Institut Universitaire de Technologie*) and IUFM (*Institut Universitaire de Formation des Maitres*), 1.1 percent in CPGE (*Clas-se Préparatoire aux Grandes Ecoles*), and 15.4 percent in other institutions, including the prestigious *grandes écoles*. The distribution of foreign students in French universities in 2004 according to levels of study was as follows: first cycle (undergraduate) 34 percent; second cycle (bachelor and master levels) 35 percent; and third cycle (master and doctoral levels) 31 percent. The distribution according to fields of study was as follows: social sciences, economics and administration 20.7 percent; medicine 14.4 percent; litera-ture and humanities 13.7 percent; science 13.2 percent, law 12.8 percent; other fields 13.7 percent.[25]

Table 6.13 shows the breakdown of the foreign student enrollment in France according to countries of origin from 1999 to 2006. Top ten countries of origin in 2006 were: Morocco 29,699; Algeria 21,241; China 17,132; Tunisia 10,386; Senegal 9,399; Germany 6,565; Cameroon 5,587; Lebanon 5,038; and Italy 4,658.

The colonial connections and the political/cultural approach in the French policies are clearly evident, with Morocco and Algeria at the top of the major countries of origin in both 1999 and 2006. The growth in the number of Chinese students is again a staggering 886 percent, from 1,934 in 1999 to 17,132 in 2006.

The student numbers shown in Figure 6.33 also point to a lack of a coherent policy in France with respect to attracting foreign students in the period from the mid-1980s to the beginning of the new century, when foreign enrollment in fact decreased. However, the recent growth in foreign student numbers, which corresponds to an impressive 26 percent increase in a matter of five years, as well as the emergence of China and other new major countries of origin from eastern Europe, clearly reflects the shift in the French approach to internationalization from the cultural/political to the skilled migration. Nevertheless, foreign student enrollment in France still appears to be driven mainly by the cultural/political approach and colonial connections.

The drive to attract more foreign students to France is led by *Agence EduFrance* (recently renamed *Agence CampusFrance*) a public agency found-ed in 1998 and supervised by the ministries of foreign affairs and national education, higher education and research. This new agency represents 192 institutions of higher education in France and currently has more than one hundred offices in seventy-five countries. Its mission is to (1) enhance the

Table 6.12. Foreign Student Enrollment in France[a]

Type of Institution	1991	1999	2000	2001	2002	2003	2004	2005	2006
Universities	129,333	115,148	122,070	133,541	150,176	170,202	189,744	198,925	205,912
IUT	3,058	4,095	4,554	5,219	6,027	6,444	5,926	5,466	6,590
IUFM	—	—	—	477	408	408	510	712	752
STS	5,969	8,172	8,352	8,280	8,760	9,693	9,625	8,746	8,136
CPGE	1,310	1,670	1,868	2,166	2,587	2,955	2,806	2,822	2,961
Other[b]	21,478	22,884	23,689	24,964	28,790	31,769	35,724	38,914	40,688
Total	161,148	151,969	160,533	174,557	196,748	221,471	244,335	255,585	265,039

Source: http://media.education.gouv.fr/file/42/6/2426.pdf.

[a]Breakdown by type of institution.

[b]Other includes grandes écoles and higher education establishments.

[c]CPGE, Classes préparatoires aux grandes écoles; IUFM, Institut universitaire de formation des maitres; IUT, Institut universitaire de technologie; STS, Section de technicien supérieur.

Table 6.13. Major Countries of Origin of Foreign Students in France

Country	1999	2000	2001	2002	2003	2004	2005	2006
Morocco	18,849	21,048	24,284	29,504	34,826	32,802	29,859	29,299
Algeria	14,559	13,539	12,572	14,056	18,432	22,250	22,228	21,641
China	1,934	2,111	3,068	5,477	10,665	11,514	14,316	17,132
Tunisia	5,582	6,268	6,921	7,843	9,409	9,749	9,750	10,386
Senegal	13,545	4,079	5,114	6,123	7,978	8,329	8,768	9,399
Germany	5,162	5,436	5,287	5,276	6,908	6,698	5,887	6,565
Cameroon	3,249	3,279	3,325	3,563	4,612	4,963	5,043	5,387
Lebanon	2,457	2,500	2,796	3,219	4,420	4,671	4,695	5,083
Vietnam	1,146	1,226	1,445	1,548	2,404	2,960	3,735	4,658
Italy	3,777	3,950	3,722	3,813	4,740	4,686	4,021	4,455

Source: Les etudiants internationaux:chiffres cles. http://editons.campusfrance.org/chiffres_cles/brochure_campusfrance_chiffres_cles08.pdf.

attractiveness of French higher education and to promote it throughout the world, in the manner of the *DAAD* in Germany and the British Council in France; and (2) provide information, counseling, and enrollment service for international students considering higher education in France.

It is interesting to note that *Agence EduFrance* published the first catalogue of degree programs taught in English as part of the new drive to attract more foreign students to France, entitled "Enhancing the Appeal of France" in 2005. That catalogue listed three hundred programs taught in English. The most recent catalogue entitled "Programs Taught in English," published by *Agence CampusFrance* in January 2009, lists thousands of programs taught in English.[26]

Figure 6.34 shows the number of French students abroad in the period 1962–2006, when a tenfold increase occurred from 5,677 to 54,046 students in forty years. The United Kingdom, Belgium, the United States,

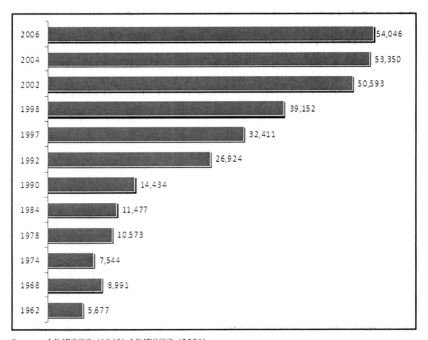

Sources: UNESCO (1963)–UNESCO (2008).

Fig. 6.34. French Students Abroad

Canada, and Germany were the major destinations for French students in 2006 (UNESCO 2008).

The drop in the number of French students abroad from 8,991 in 1968 to 7,544 in 1974, although smaller compared with the drop in German students in the same period, is again noteworthy. A plausible explanation for the drop observed for both countries is the feeling of insecurity by students and their families after the student riots of the late 1960s. This is a conjecture, but it may indicate how sensitive international student mobility is to political and social stability in the world.

A further point is concerned with international student mobility within Europe. Comparison of the major source countries of foreign students in the United Kingdom, Germany, and France indicates that mobility of western European students within western Europe has increased, owing possibly to the EU programs like ERASMUS and the distance covered in the Bologna Process. However, compared with the increase in student numbers from China and eastern European countries, the observed increase is quite small. This indicates that the major global drivers of change also are the major drivers of international student mobility, such as an economic approach, strategic alliances, technology, know-how transfer, and the quest for a better education that will lead to better job prospects anywhere in the world.

6.2.5. Australia

Figure 6.35 shows the growth in foreign student enrollment in Australia. In 1950, there were only 339 foreign students in Australia, and until the mid-1980s, foreign students comprised mostly those under international aid programs such as the Colombo Program (see Section 5.2). In 1986, the Australian government replaced the subsidized overseas student places with fee-paying student places (Gamage and Mininberg 2003). From the mid-1980s on, in tandem with the changing domestic policies on higher education (see Sections 3.1, 3.2, and 3.4), Australia adopted a combination of the revenue-generating approach with the international branding of institutions for the internationalization of higher education, and started an active recruitment campaign for foreign students led by IDP Education Australia (see Section 5.2). The Education Services for Overseas Students (ESOS) Act, which was enacted in 1991, was amended in 1997, and replaced by a new act in 2000 to build confidence in the Australian system. Measures that apply to all Australian institutions providing international educational services include the following: (1) codes of ethical practice, (2) official registration of institutions and course;, (3) tuition assurance schemes, (4) ESOS Assurance Fund, and (5) government-endorsed qualification system (Nuna 2001).

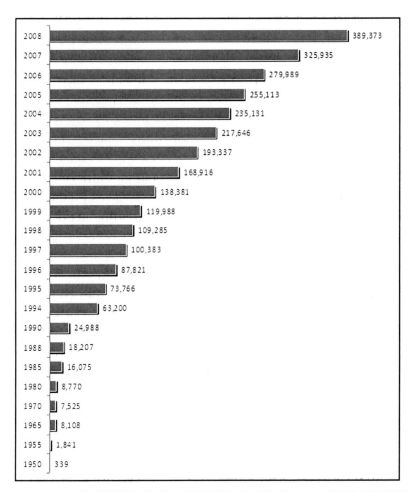

2008	389,373
2007	325,935
2006	279,989
2005	255,113
2004	235,131
2003	217,646
2002	193,337
2001	168,916
2000	138,381
1999	119,988
1998	109,285
1997	100,383
1996	87,821
1995	73,766
1994	63,200
1990	24,988
1988	18,207
1985	16,075
1980	8,770
1970	7,525
1965	8,108
1955	1,841
1950	339

Sources: 1950–1983: UNESCO (1963)–UNESCO (1994); 1985: Cummings (1991); 1988–1990: www.avcc.edu.au; 1994–2008: http://aei.gov.au/AEI/Statistics/StudentEnrolmentAndVisaStatistics, www.universitiesaustralia.edu, and www.idp.com/research/fast_facts/higher_education.aspx. *Note:* Enrollment data shown include students in higher education institutions, students in vocational and technical education (VET), and other programs; see Table 6.14.

Fig. 6.35. Growth of Foreign Student Enrollment in Australia

The Migration Act of 1958 also was amended accordingly to facilitate visa procedures for students and immigration of those with Australian qualifications. The result of all these policies and measures has been the more than tenfold increase in foreign student enrollment in Australian institutions of higher education, from 16,075 in 1985 to 163,930 students in 2005.

International education in Australia today is a full-fledged component of the service sector of the national economy comprising, in addition to students in higher education, those in English-language Intensive Courses for Overseas Students, vocational and technical education, school education (Schools), and others. Since the late 1990s, many private schools have been established, which offer courses in English and computing to prepare students for admission to Australian universities, and help students with entry visas and employment opportunities, together with schools at the primary and the secondary levels, they comprise the schools subsector in Australia. In 2008, total foreign student enrollment in all sectors was 543,898.

Foreign student enrollments in each of these so-called sectors over the years are shown in Table 6.14. Total foreign student enrollment at the tertiary level in 2008 was 389,873 students, up from 235,131 in 2004 and 279,989 in 2006. Although foreign student enrollment data for 2007 and 2008 are not yet available for France and Germany, it is obvious that Australia has risen to the third place among the major host countries for foreign students in 2008, and competing with the United Kingdom for the second place.

Table 5.2 shows that annual revenues from foreign students at all levels in Australia rose from $584 million in 1989 to $2.145 billion in 2001. The latter figure accounted for 13.1 percent of total service exports in that year, which made education the eighth largest item among Australian exports in 1999 (McBurnie 2001). The figures for 2006 to 2008 were as follows: 2006: AUD 10.075 billion; 2007: AUD 11.479 billion; and 2008: 14.638 billon, including AUD 438 million from offshore students. From 1998 to 2008, education export income grew at an average annual rate of 16 percent, rising to first place among service exports ahead of tourism (AUD 12 billion) in 2008.[27]

Major countries of origin of foreign students in Australia are shown in Table 6.15 for the period 1997–2008. The phenomenal growth in the numbers of students from China and India manifests itself in the case of Australia, too. At the tertiary level, the numbers of Chinese and Indian students hosted by Australia are now approximately equal to those hosted by the United States. On the other hand, the number of students from Singapore is decreasing, and the growth in the enrollment of students from Malaysia, Indonesia, Thailand, Japan, Korea, and Hong Kong clearly are slowing down.

The growth in revenues from education as an export industry also has driven the cost of education in Australia. A study by IDP Education Australia compared the annual costs in U.S. dollars to foreign students in a number of countries in 2004.[28] It is interesting to note that Australia with an annual cost of $9,519 provides the second most expensive higher education in the world after the United Kingdom ($11,152), and the most expensive in the Asia-Pacific region. Yet, it is one of the major destinations not only

Table 6.14. Foreign Student Enrollment in Australia[a]

	Higher Education			VET	Other[b]	Total Tertiary	ELICOS[c]
Year	Onshore	Offshore	Total				
1994	35,290	8,431	43,721	19,479	*	63,200	26,173
1995	39,285	11,026	50,711	23,055	*	73,766	34,209
1996	46,773	22,563	59,338	28,483	*	87,821	43,307
1997	52,897	16,309	69,206	31,177	*	100,383	37,348
1998	56,810	22,538	79,348	29,937	*	109,285	27,356
1999	60,914	29,481	90,395	29,593	*	119,988	29,226
2000	72,717	34,905	107,622	30,759	*	138,381	36,767
2001	n/a	28,266[c]	nd	nd	nd	168,916[f]	nd
2002[d]	n/a	53,419[c]	115,893	53,923	23,321	193,137	58,456
2003	n/a	58,513[c]	135,392	56,924	25,330	217,646	63,310
2004	n/a	nd	151,479	58,379	25,273	235,131	62,906
2005	n/a	nd	163,695	66,042	25,376	255,113	65,724
2006	n/a	nd	171,246	83,405	25,338	279,989	77,885
2007	n/a	61,331[g]	177,760	121,422	26,753	325,935	101,824
2008	n/a	nd	182,770	175,461	31,142	389,373	125,727

Sources: http://aei.gov.au/AEI/MIP/StudentEnrolmentAndVisaStatistics; www.universitiesaustralia.edu (Formerly, Australian Vice-Chancellors Committee, AVCC); www.idp.com/research/fast_facts/higher_education.aspx.

[a]Breakdown by sector.

[b]Other: Includes students in enabling, foundation, and nonaward programs.

[c]ELICOSnot included in the tertiary-level enrollment values.

[d]AEI enrollment data from 2002 do not include students enrolled in offshore programs. AEI enrollment data from 2002 on are not strictly comparable with previous data. Total higher education enrollments shown from 2002 on include onshore students only. Offshore data in 1994–2000 are from AEI; other sources are as indicated above. Offshore enrollments are shown to illustrate the developments in this subsector of higher education.

[e]AVCC data

[f]Total tertiary-level enrollment for the year 2001 is from Verbik and Lasanowski (2007, Appendix B, 37).

[g]IDP data, 11,622 students studying online, and 49,709 students in offshore campuses.

*Not reported separately

ELICOS, English-Language Intensive Courses for Overseas Students; n/a, not applicable; nd, no data available; VET, vocational education and training.

Table 6.15. Major Countries of Origin of Foreign Students in Australia, 1997–2008

Country	1997	1998	1999	2000	2001	2002	2003	2004	2005	2006	2007	2008
China	3,828	5,273	4,633	6,191	11,640	23,332	31,255	41,562	54,274	63,543	70,598	82,144
India	5,690	8,073	9,420	10,399	10,316	11,271	13,920	19,587	26,303	36,078	53,701	80,895
Malaysia	16,257	16,485	15,767	18,868	19,385	16,431	18,554	18,519	18,262	18,074	18,754	19,851
Korea	18,312	11,184	4,287	4,534	6,719	8,904	8,889	9,138	10,506	12,352	14,438	16,889
Hong Kong	1,236	18,161	16,205	17,888	21,753	16,131	18,159	18,175	17,196	16,558	11,377	14,951
Indonesia	18,384	17,715	12,650	13,484	15,822	17,632	17,092	15,405	13,830	13,025	12,925	13,603
Thailand	7,395	6,299	3,756	4,228	5,793	11,602	10,279	10,289	10,408	10,934	11,778	13,140
U.S.	1,660	2,087	2,533	3,319	4,629	10,864	11,985	12,463	12,277	11,901	11,634	11,511
Singapore	14,308	16,509	18,742	20,405	22,725	11,639	11,384	10,368	9,460	8,906	8,573	8,620
Japan	11,817	10,739	3,984	4,169	5,438	7,509	8,495	9,131	9,352	9,110	8,196	7,186
Brazil	1,023	1,073	280	458	1,027	1,704	1,793	2,097	2,869	4,081	5,030	6,161
Taiwan	7,492	6,403	2,985	3,235	3,967	5,698	6,051	5,996	5,683	5,614	5,502	5,387

Sources: 1997–2006: Verbik and Lasanowski (2007, Table 3); 2007–2008: http://aei.gov.au/Statistics/StudentEnrolmentAndVisaStatitistics

for students from Hong Kong, where the annual cost is $7,081, but also for students from China ($5,219), Malaysia ($3,785), Thailand ($2,918), and even India ($1,515), where the cost is almost one sixth of that in Australia. This supports the argument previously presented that cost is just one of the factors that affects the choice of destination by foreign students.

Australia is a country of immigrants (Ziguras and Law 2006). She needs highly skilled workers to sustain economic growth and development. Measures introduced in July 2001 (Holroyd 2006), which include less-cumbersome visa procedures, relaxed requirements for work permits, and elimination of the requirement to leave the country after graduation in order to apply for permanent residency, indicate that Australia is increasingly relying on foreign student recruitment to expand the country's pool of highly trained workers. All of these added together indicate that Australian policies of internationalization of higher education are increasingly being predicated on the skilled migration approach as well as revenue generation.

According to figures reported in an article in *Chronicle of Higher Education* (Cohen 2006b), there was a slowdown in the growth of foreign enrollment in Australian institutions of tertiary education from 2005 to 2006, with more declines in the numbers of students from Hong Kong, Malaysia, and Singapore, and this is reflected in Figure 6.35 and Table 6.15. An increase in students from China and India appears to have prevented a drop in total enrollment. The increase in enrollments in Australian offshore programs, which now number about fifteen hundred, could be one of the reasons for the slowdown in those years. However, data for 2007 and 2008 clearly show that foreign student enrollment is once again significantly on the rise in Australia. Key findings of a more recent report by IDP (2007) are as follows. Demand for Australian international higher education will grow from 163,695 in 2005 to 290,848 in 2025. Demand for international higher education places in Australia will grow 4.25 percent per year to 2010, then slow to 3 percent per year to 2015, then slow further, The Australian university system has the capacity to provide 268,156 international student places, onshore in Australia, by 2025. Demand will exceed supply in 2020, and by 2025 there will be a shortfall of 22,692 international places on projected demand of 290,848.

6.2.6. Other Major and Emerging Host Countries: Japan, Russian Federation, Canada, and New Zealand

6.2.6.1. Japan

The Japanese word for internationalization is *kokusaika*, which also implies change under international influences. As part of the internationalization drive, the Ministry of Education, Science and Culture, abbreviated as MONBUSHO at the time, now MONBUKAGAKUSHO, announced a plan in 1983 to have 100,000 foreign students in Japanese institutions of higher education by the year 2000 as part of its internationalization strategy (Horie 2002, Umakoshi 1997;). Figure 6.36 shows the growth of foreign student enrollment in Japanese institutions of higher education. There were only 2,149 foreign students in Japan in 1950, and the number had increased to 15,009 in 1985, but by 2000 foreign enrollment in Japan comprised only 64,011 students, far below the ambitious target of 100,000 set in 1983. In 2000, visa procedures were simplified, and it was made easier for foreign students to obtain part-time employment. The result was increased enrollment as seen in Figure 6.36; the target was passed in 2003, and foreign student enrollment in Japan reached 117,302 in 2004 and 123,829 in 2008. There were an additional 9,756 short-term students in 2008, up from 8,636 in 2007.

In 1983, 20 percent of the foreign students in Japan were on Japanese government scholarships, 74 percent were self-financing, and 6 percent were supported by their own governments. One of the elements of the policies announced in 1983 was to increase funding for students from poorer countries to offset the high costs of living and tuition in Japan. By 1999, the number of foreign students on Japanese government scholarships had quadrupled, but accounted for 16 percent of the total enrollment, with 82 percent of the students paying their own way, and 2 percent supported by scholarships from their own governments (Horie 2002). In 2008, 90 percent of the students were self-financing, 8 percent were on Japanese government scholarships, and 2 percent were supported by their own governments.

Of the 123,892 foreign students in Japan in 2008, 73.3 percent were enrolled in private institutions, 24.6 percent in national institutions, and 2.1 percent in local institutions. As seen in Table 6.16, breakdown of the 2008 foreign student enrollment according to level of study was as follows: university undergraduate 48.9 percent; graduate schools 26.4 percent; special training college 20.8 percent; junior college 1.7 percent; university preparatory college 1.9 percent and college of technology 0.4 percent. Humanities and social sciences with 62.5 percent of the foreign student enrollment was by far the most popular subject area of study, with engineering (15.8 percent) a distant second.

Major countries of origin of foreign students in Japan are shown in Table 6.17. Students from Asia account for more than 90 percent of the foreign students in Japan, with Chinese students making up 59 percent of the total. The only non-Asian major country of origin is the United States.

The number of Japanese students abroad is shown in Figure 6.37. The number was only 3,553 in 1962, increased to 14,117 in 1978, and then shot up to 64,284 in 1998, making Japan a major country of origin in interna-

Table 6.16. Foreign Student Enrollment in Japan[a]

Year	1996	1997	1998	1999	2000	2001	2002	2003	2004	2005	2006	2007	2008
Undergraduate[b]	25,504	25,052	25,159	26,160	30,612	39,502	50,321	57,911	62,311	64,774	63,437	62,159	63,176
Graduate	19,779	19,856	20,488	22,679	23,585	25,146	26,229	28,542	29,524	30,278	30,910	31,592	32,665
College of Technology	7,638	6,139	5,656	6,916	8,815	12,324	17,173	21,233	23,838	25,197	21,562	22,399	25,753
Preparatory courses[c]	—	—	—	—	999	1,840	1,827	1,842	1,842	1,563	2,018	2,348	2,235
Total	52,921	51,047	51,298	55,755	64,011	78,812	95,550	109,508	117,302	121,812	117,927	118,498	123,829
Privately funded	43,573	41,273	41,390	45,439	53,640	68,270	85,024	98,135	105,592	110,018	106,102	106,297	111,225

Source: International students in Japan 2008. Japan Student Services Organization (JASSO) www.jasso.go.jp/statistics/intl_students/data08_e.html#2.

[a]Breakdown by type of institution.
[b]Undergraduate includes students in bachelor-level programs in universities and associate-level programs in junior colleges and colleges of technology.
[c]Preparatory courses are for foreign students with less than twelve years of schooling in their countries.

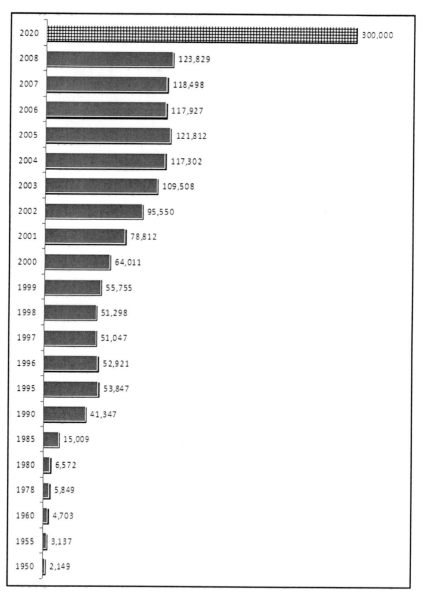

Year	Enrollment
2020	300,000
2008	123,829
2007	118,498
2006	117,927
2005	121,812
2004	117,302
2003	109,508
2002	95,550
2001	78,812
2000	64,011
1999	55,755
1998	51,298
1997	51,047
1996	52,921
1995	53,847
1990	41,347
1985	15,009
1980	6,572
1978	5,849
1960	4,703
1955	3,137
1950	2,149

Sources: See Table 6.16; 1950–1980: www.mext.go.jp/english/; 1985–2008: International Students in Japan 2006, 2007, and 2008, Japan Student Services Organization (JASSO), www.jasso.go.jp/statistics/intl_students; and 2020 projection, "Japan aims to more than double number of students to 300,000 by 2020." Quoted in http://atlas.iienetwork.org/page/127953.

Fig. 6.36. Growth of Foreign Student Enrollment in Japan

Table 6.17. Major Countries of Origin of Foreign Students in Japan, 1997–2007

Country	1997	1998	1999	2000	2001	2002	2003	2004	2005	2006	2007	2008
China	22,323	22,810	25,907	32,297	44,014	58,533	70,814	77,713	80,592	74,292	71,277	72,766
Korea	11,785	11,467	11,897	12,851	14,725	15,846	15,871	15,533	15,606	15,974	17,274	18,862
Taiwan	4,323	4,033	4,085	4,189	4,252	4,266	4,235	4,096	4,134	4,211	4,686	5,082
Vietnam	nd	nd	nd	717	938	1,115	1,336	¿570	1,745	2,119	2,582	2,873
Thailand	992	949	1,073	1,245	1,411	1,504	1,641	1,665	1,734	1,734	2,090	2,203
U.S.	999	949	1,073	1,044	1,141	1,217	1,310	1,456	1,646	1,790	1,805	2,024
Malaysia	2,128	2,040	2,005	1,856	1,803	1,885	2,002	2,010	2,114	2,156	2,146	2,271
Indonesia	1,070	1,140	1,220	1,348	1,388	1,441	1,479	1,451	1,488	1,553	1,596	1,791
Bangladesh	732	750	806	800	805	823	974	1,126	1,331	1,456	1,508	1,686
Mongolia	nd	nd	nd	nd	nd	544	714	806	924	1,006	1,110	1,145
Sri Lanka	nd	nd	nd	nd	nd	nd	608	764	907	1,143	1,181	1,097
Philippines	447	434	497	477	490	483	508	525	544	542	538	527

Sources: 1997–2006: Verbik and Lasanowski (2007, Table 6); 2007–2008: International students in Japan 2008. Japan Student Services Organization (JASSO) www.jasso.go.jp/statistics/intl_students/data08_e.html#2.

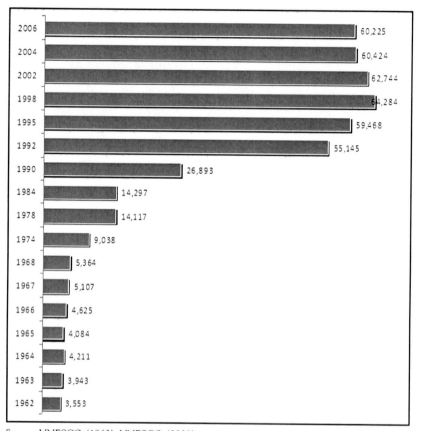

Source: UNESCO (1963)–UNESCO (2008).

Fig. 6.37. Japanese Students Abroad

tional student mobility. The continuous drop from 64,284 students in 1998 to 60,225 students in 2006, although small, mainly is due to the shrinking population of the Japanese university-age cohort. It also possibly underscores the sensitivity of international student mobility to economic difficulties at home such as the Asian economic crisis of 1998. Leading countries of destination in 2006 were the United States, the United Kingdom, Australia, France, and Germany (UNESCO 2008).

The number of foreign scholars in Japan was a meager 1,168 in 1983, and had increased to only 3,858 in 1995, far below what one would expect from the second largest economy in the world. Furthermore, 60 percent of the foreign scholars in Japan in 1995 were employed by private institutions of higher education, which meant that the majority of them were in Japan for teaching, not research (Umakoshi 1997).

In Umakoshi's (1997) view, until recently, the Japanese system was ill prepared to accept foreign students. Horie (2002) implies that this state of "ill-preparedness" to receive foreign students and scholars sowed the seeds of change in reform of the system that came much later (see Sections 3.2.2 and 3.4.4). However, the Japanese higher education institutions' attitude to foreign students is changing rapidly. Following the radical restructuring of the system in 2004, public subsidies to both the state and the private institutions were severely cut, but this was accompanied by increased financial and administrative flexibility. Both private and public institutions are now looking overseas and expanding their international contacts to recruit more foreign students to fill higher education places left vacant from a dwindling population, and to make up for lost revenues from severely reduced state subsidies (OBHE-BNA, March 23, 2006). This new attitude is on the part of the institutions and is driven by the revenue generation rationale, rather than by a concerted effort at the government level to attract skilled immigrants to Japan to make up for the aging Japanese population. The Japanese society does not appear to be favorably disposed to receiving waves of immigrants, and this may adversely affect the higher education institutions' initiatives to recruit more foreign students.

6.2.6.2. Russia

In the period following World War II, the former USSR was a major destination for students from countries under Soviet influence. Figure 6.38 shows the change in foreign student enrollment in the USSR and its main successor, today's Russia. The USSR had a clear policy of recruiting foreign students, which was driven entirely by a political rationale. Thus, foreign student in the USSR, which was only 14,400 in 1962, had reached 115,300 in 1988. This figure should be compared with the 356,187 foreign students enrolled in U.S. institutions of higher education in the same year. With the collapse of communism, part of the Soviet higher education system remained in the newly formed countries, and Russia inherited only a part of that. This is one of the reasons for the drop of foreign student enrollment to 66,809 in 1990. Since then, foreign enrollment in the Russian federation seems to be increasing; in 2002, it stood at 70,172, and further increased to 75,786 in 2004 and 77,438 in 2006.

However, the rationale driving the foreign student enrollment policy of Russia is completely different from that of her predecessor. Obviously, the revenue-generating approach is now the main driver of foreign student recruitment by Russian institutions of higher education. The state does not

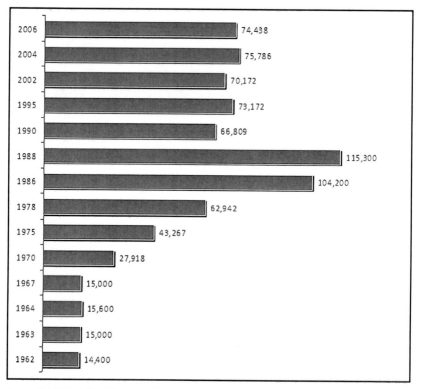

Source: UNESCO (1963)–UNESCO (2008).

Fig. 6.38. Foreign Student Enrollment in the Former USSR and Russia

seem to be caring for the quality of the education provided in a significant number of the institutions. In 2006, there were 41,101 Russian students studying abroad (UNESCO 2008), up from 34,473 in 2004 (UNESCO 2006), 25,671 in 2002 (OECD 2004a; UNESCO 2004;), and 20,161 in 2001 (Davis 2003). The leading countries of destination in 2006 were Germany, the United States, Ukraine, France, and the United Kingdom (UNESCO 2008).

The upward trend in the number of Russian students going abroad to study is noteworthy. This is partly stemming from the Russian population that remained in countries that were part of the USSR. Nevertheless, it is mainly being driven by the Russian youth's aspirations to a better life through a better education that can now be financed by the increasing prosperity of a part of the population. There also is no doubt that Russia, with its advanced secondary education system inherited from the USSR, also is benefiting from new internationalization policies in countries like Germany and France, which are increasingly being predicated on the skilled migration approach. With improving economic and political stability, the country itself is increasingly becoming a target for foreign providers. The Russian Ministry of Education announced its plans in 2003 to export Russian higher education based on a strategy of establishing branch campuses of Russian institutions abroad (OBHE-BN, October 2003). In a 2006 speech, Russian President Vladimir Putin called for further internationalization of Russia's education sector by reducing restrictions on foreign students, attracting more students from and opening branch campuses in neighboring countries. The tone of Putin's speech indicates that Russia has not met the objectives set forth in 2003 (OBHE-BN, March 2006).

Russia is yet to make the recently founded National Accreditation Agency of the Russian Federation (*NICA*, see Section 3.4.3) operational, and establish a functioning quality assurance mechanism in her domestic higher education system. Thus, it is reasonable to assume that any transnational Russian activity in the conceivably near future will be restricted essentially to Commonwealth of Independent States countries. On the other hand, with a per-capita income nearly twice that of China and more than three times that of India, and a comparable population, more outward mobility of Russian students should be expected, despite the fact that Russia has no unmet demand problem in higher education.

6.2.6.3. Canada

The Canadian international education sector comprises, in addition to universities, nonuniversity institutions offering vocational and technical education and training, collectively referred to as "trade-level," other postsecondary institutions offering language and other preparatory courses, and primary and secondary schools.

In Canada, education is within the jurisdiction of the provinces, and there is no central coordinating body at the federal level. For this reason, data on Canadian education in the form of a coherent time series has been lacking, and comprehensive data on foreign student enrollment is just emerging. Table 6.18 shows the growth in foreign student enrollment at different levels in Canada from 1996 to 2007. According to Citizenship and Immigration Canada,[29] the number of foreign students in Canada at all levels was only 37,000 in 1980, and rose to 57,000 in 1990. Total foreign student enrollment at all levels stood at 176,116 in 2007, representing a nearly sixfold increase in less than three decades. In 2004, foreign students contributed an estimated C\$4 billion to the country's economy annually (Holroyd 2006).

Table 6.18. Foreign Student Enrollment in Canada[a]

Year	Trade	University	Other Postsecondary	Total Tertiary	Total All Levels
1996	10,660	30,844	4,544	46,048	71,054
1997	11,322	32,578	4,853	48,763	75,970
1998	10,652	39,547	5,695	55,894	85,803
1999	12,763	45,712	7,399	65,847	97,341
2000	16,504	53,168	9,092	78,764	114,093
2001	20,127	63,613	12,785	96,525	136,716
2002	22,857	72,970	14,485	110,312	150,552
2003	24,717	81,117	15,801	121,635	159,727
2004	25,179	88,647	13,910	127,736	164,855
2005	24,079	91,727	14,506	130,312	167,188
2006	22,581	92,865	15,823	131,269	170,194
2007	21,553	94,621	19,375	135,549	176,116

Sources: 1996–1997: Third-quarter data. *The Monitor.* www.cig.gc.ca; 1998–2007: Citizenship and Immigration Canada. Facts and figures 2007–Immigration overview: Permanent and temporary residents. Retrieved on March 9, 2009 from www.cig.gc.ca.

[a] Breakdown by type of provider.

Figure 6.39 shows the growth of foreign student enrollment in Canadian higher education, including students in universities, vocational education at trade-level, and other postsecondary institutions. Total enrollment, which was only 8,518 in 1962, had increased to 78,764 in 2000. With increasing demand for the Anglo-Saxon type of higher education in the English language, Canada has recently become one of the MESDCs, and foreign student enrollment in Canadian universities reached an estimated 135,549 students in 2007, of which 94,621 were in universities.

Time-series data on major countries of origin exist for total foreign student enrollment at all levels. Table 6.19 shows that China and Korea are by far the leading countries of origin, with China having overtaken Korea for the first place in 2002. Savage and Kane (2005) provide data on major countries of origin of students enrolled at different levels for 2000 to 2002, and similar data exist for 2003 and 2004 from AEI.[30] Although limited in its time span, those data indicate the following:

- The top five countries of origin of students enrolled in trade-level programs in 2002 were Korea, China, Japan, Mexico, and Taiwan.

- The breakdown of the university enrollment in 2002 by level was 69 percent in undergraduate- and 31 percent in graduate-level

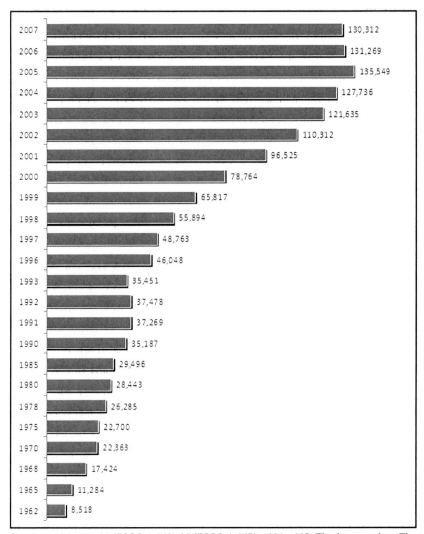

Year	Enrollment
2007	130,312
2006	131,269
2005	135,549
2004	127,736
2003	121,635
2002	110,312
2001	96,525
2000	78,764
1999	65,817
1998	55,894
1997	48,763
1996	46,048
1993	35,451
1992	37,478
1991	37,269
1990	35,187
1985	29,496
1980	28,443
1978	26,285
1975	22,700
1970	22,363
1968	17,424
1965	11,284
1962	8,518

Sources: 1962–1993: UNESCO (1963)–UNESCO (1967); 1996–1997: Third quarter data. The Monitor. www.cic.gc.ca; and 1998–2007: Citizenship and Immigration Canada, www.cic.gc.ca. *Note:* Enrollment figures for 1962–1999 do not include trade-level institutions; see Table 6.18.

Fig. 6.39. Growth of Foreign Student Enrollment in Canada

programs. The top five countries of origin of foreign students enrolled in universities in 2004 were China, the United States, France, India, and Korea.

Table 6.19. Major Countries of Origin of Foreign Students in Canada, 1998–2007

Country	1998	1999	2000	2001	2002	2003	2004	2005	2006	2007
China	3,505	6,468	11,059	20,417	29,811	36,615	39,396	39,598	39,845	41,082
Korea	9,169	11,038	15,715	20,745	24,138	25,564	26,721	27,254	29,030	30,075
U.S.	9,828	10,768	11,837	12,683	12,763	12,632	12,566	12,624	12,266	11,853
France	4,855	5,733	6,286	6,742	6,324	6,482	6,591	6,737	7,774	8,353
Japan	10,303	10,278	10,277	11,145	10,608	9,722	9,447	9,370	8,512	7,793
India	1,042	1,335	1,753	2,448	3,835	5,365	5,761	6,293	6,690	6,337
Taiwan	5,628	5,610	5,988	5,872	5,934	5,390	5,288	4,962	4,907	4,747
Hong Kong	6,832	6,458	6,403	6,381	6,355	5,974	5,671	5,172	4,765	4,484
Mexico	2,558	3,030	3,856	4,559	3,689	3,234	3,390	3,597	3,789	3,830
Germany	1,856	1,970	2,233	2,333	2,291	2,250	2,329	2,457	2,615	2,941
UK	2,055	2,325	2,386	2,673	2,532	2,385	2,392	2,453	2,628	2,765

Source: Facts and Figures 2007, Citizenship and Immigration Canadawww.cic.gc.ca/english/pdf/pub/facts2007.pdf p. 99.

Note: Enrollment figures shown are "student stocks" on December 1 of every year, and includes students at levels below the tertiary, too. Total foreign student enrollments at all levels are shown separately in table 6.18 to allow comparison with tertiary enrollments. Data shown by Verbik and Lasanowsky (2007, table 7) are "initial entry" numbers, i.e., first time registrants at all levels.

- The growth in the number of Chinese students was a remarkable 390 percent from 2000 to 2004. China overtook the United States in 2002 to become the leading country of origin of foreign university students in Canada.

- In 2000, there were only 860 Indian students in Canadian universities; since then, India has overtaken Korea, Hong Kong, Japan, and the United Kingdom as a country of origin.

- More than half of the foreign students are in Toronto, Vancouver, or Montreal, and almost all of the students from France are in Quebec.

Canada is a country that is demographically dependent on immigration, much like the United States and Australia. It is, however, only recently that the Canadian authorities began to take note of immigration and education in the same context. One difficulty encountered in formulating policies at the federal level stems from education being totally a matter of provincial competence; Canada is the only OECD member without a national department of education. The federal government has shied away from taking an active role, citing lack of constitutional authority. In 1995, the federal government provided initial funding for setting up the Canadian Education Centres Network, which now entirely relies on membership fees; there now are seventeen centers around the world. Thus, it only is recently that Canada started implementing internationalization policies in education, which are driven by a combination of skilled migration and revenue-generating approaches, and international branding. These, however, are the results of initiatives by the provinces and individual institutions. A noteworthy development was the founding of the Canadian Education Trade Alliance in 2004 by representatives of private-sector companies and institutions of education to promote the Canadian education export sector and improve its international competitiveness by implementing bold new strategies in diverse areas related to education.

The recently enacted Immigration and Refugee Protection Act includes specific provisions aimed at attracting foreign students to Canada, such as giving extra points to periods of study in Canada for immigration purposes. Beginning in 2006, students are allowed to work off campus during the summer and part time during the school year after completing their first year. Foreign graduates with the desired skills will not have to leave Canada in order to apply for permanent residency (Birchard, 2006; Holroyd 2006).

6.2.6.4. New Zealand

The international education sector in New Zealand comprises primary and secondary schools, English-language schools, private training establishments (PTEs), and higher education institutions. The latter include universities, polytechnics, and colleges of education, all of which are public. English-language schools and PTEs, on the other hand, are private.

Table 6.20 shows the breakdown of foreign student enrollment in New Zealand at the tertiary level according to the type of provider and academic level in the period 1997–2007. In 2006, students enrolled in subbachelor-level programs (certificates and diplomas) accounted for 43 percent, bachelor-level programs 45 percent, and postgraduate-level programs 12 percent of the foreign student enrollment. In 2006, private providers accounted for 17 percent of the enrollment.

Figure 6.40 shows the growth of foreign student enrollment at the tertiary level in New Zealand. In 1955 there were only 211 foreign students in New Zealand, and until the late 1980s, the country was a backwater in international education. The 1989 Education Act empowered tertiary-level institutions to set tuition fees, and New Zealand embarked on an active policy of recruiting foreign students at all levels, driven almost entirely by the revenue-generating rationale (MinEduNZ 2003). This policy is supported by an immigration policy, based on legislation enacted in 1999, which, much like the Canadian legislation mentioned earlier, gives extra credit to a New Zealand degree for those seeking to become permanent residents in New Zealand (Pickering 2001).

As seen in Figure 6.40, the growth in foreign student enrollment at the tertiary level has been phenomenal since then, steadily increasing from 3,229 students in 1990 to 50,442 students in 2004. The breakdown of the enrollment in 2004 in the public subsector by institution type was as follows: universities 72.8 percent, polytechnics 25.8 percent, and colleges of education 1.4 percent. Sixty-three percent of the students were in undergraduate programs, 30 percent in programs leading to certificates and diplomas, and only 7 percent in graduate-level programs. Overall, management and commercial studies was the preferred area (52.2 percent), followed by engineering, computer sciences and physical sciences (20.2 percent).

As seen in Figure 6.40, foreign student enrollment at the tertiary level peaked in 2004, and then steadily decreased to 39,942 students in 2007.

Table 6.21 shows the major countries of origin of foreign students in New Zealand at the tertiary level. In 2006, China was by far the leading country of origin with 21,036 students, the United States was a distant second, with India (2,143) and Korea (2,137) coming next.

Table 6.20. Foreign Student Enrollment in New Zealand[a]

Academic Level/Year	2001	2002	2003	2004	2005	2006	2007	% in 2007
Certificate	12,618	19,326	15,330	12,541	9,183	8,190	8,858	21
Diploma	5,119	9,356	14,425	15,539	13,704	10,736	9,344	22
Undergraduate	8,726	13,342	18,972	23,525	24,324	22,139	19,138	45
Postgraduate[b]	1,940	2,480	3,631	4,368	4,242	4,437	5,154	12
Total	26,403	44,504	52,358	55,973	51,483	45,502	42,494	100
Corrected total[c]	26,236	40,825	47,116	50,442	47,366	42,652	39,942	100
Public institutions	20,026	29,763	37,732	41,572	39,344	35,457	nd	nd
Private providers	6,210	11,062	9,384	8,872	8,022	7,195	nd	nd
Total	26,236	40,825	47,116	50,442	47,366	42,652	39,942	100

Sources: "International Student Enrolments in New Zealand 2001–2007." Ministry of Education. 16 April 2008. www.educationcounts.govt.nz

[a]Breakdown by academic level and type of provider.

[b]Postgraduate totals include honors degrees and postgraduate diplomas, masters, and doctorates.

[c]Students who were enrolled at more than one qualification level have been counted in each level. Consequently, the sum of students is less than the sum of course enrollments. Values shown are actual student numbers, not "equivalent full-time students."

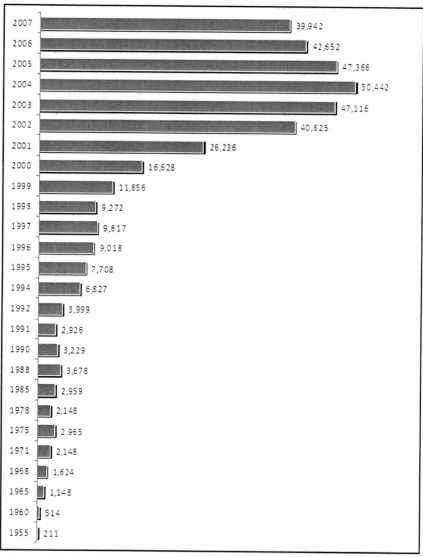

Sources: 1955–1992: UNESCO (1963)–UNESCO (1995); and 1994–2007: www.education-counts.govt.nz

Note: Enrollment figures from 1994 on include students in publicly funded tertiary education institutions, and PTEs. Students in English language schools are not included; see Table 6.20.

Fig. 6.40. Growth of Foreign Student Enrollment in New Zealand

Table 6.21. Major Countries of Origin of Foreign Students in New Zealand, 1997–2007

Country	1997	1998	1999	2000	2001	2002	2003	2004	2005	2006
China	88	139	888	3735	9,513	18,831	27,212	29,881	26,543	21,036
U.S.	nd	459	595	778	1,013	1,354	1,801	2,302	2,480	2,429
India	36	71	764	1,256	2,014	2,434	2,169	2,035	2,095	2,143
Korea	585	389	123	332	820	1,589	2,037	1,940	1,889	2,137
Japan	1,240	1,207	1,541	1,850	2,385	2,560	2,142	2,104	2,041	1,978
Malaysia	2,769	2,302	1,942	1,656	1,517	1,216	1,129	1,258	1,329	1,519
Germany	nd	nd	245	321	510	698	835	934	1,178	1,277
Fiji	291	464	462	500	650	803	698	695	643	723
UK	nd	nd	213	253	324	448	528	678	752	697
Vietnam	nd	nd	113	146	281	398	553	584	630	670
Thailand	504	481	606	681	800	867	748	688	656	653
Taiwan	423	462	578	738	828	816	594	564	573	538
Canada	nd	nd	122	146	207	252	391	483	514	523
Hong Kong	408	437	491	504	612	612	566	554	520	450
Indonesia	342	312	496	522	543	525	498	463	417	375
Singapore	203	213	271	254	253	254	318	314	321	309

Sources: 1997–1998: Verbik and Lasanowski (2007, Table 8); 1999–2006: http://www.educationcounts.govt.nz.

nd, no data available for the year shown.

The international higher education subsector in New Zealand clearly caters to students from countries in the Asia-Pacific Rim, which in 2006 accounted for 81 percent of the enrollment. Enrollment figures shown in Table 6.21 also indicate that New Zealand has become a favored destination for study-abroad students from the United States and Canada. Until 1999, Malaysian and Japanese students accounted for more than 50 percent of the foreign enrollment; their share was only 8 percent in 2006. The downturn in Malaysian enrollment, which was due to a number of factors, including the economic crisis of 1997 and increasing indigenous capacity, thus has been more than made up for by the increase in enrollments from other Asian countries, in particular China. In 1997, there were only eighty-eight Chinese students in higher education institutions; the number in 2004 was 29,881, which corresponds to an astounding 340-fold increase in less than a decade. There were only thirty-six Indian students in 1997, and the number was 2,434 at its peak in 2002.

Foreign enrollment in the PTEs had peaked at 11,062 students in 2002, up from 1,282 in 1997. Chinese students again accounted for more than half the enrollment. They also were the largest group of foreign students in the English-language schools.

International education is big business in New Zealand. In 1999, there were a total of 28,340 foreign fee-paying students in the international education sector. Total foreign enrollment peaked at 120,142 students in 2003, and then fell to 102,154 in 2004 after years of phenomenal growth. The setback in student numbers was due to adverse publicity over language school practices. In fact, the drop from 2003 to 2004 was due mainly to the sharply decreased enrollment in English-language schools, and partly to the relatively small drop in school enrollment. On the other hand, as seen in Table 6.20, enrollment at the tertiary level kept increasing until it peaked at 50,442 students in 2004. It was the increase in tertiary-level enrollment, where fees are significantly higher, that kept the annual revenues from international education almost constant, NZ$2.19 billion in 2003 and NZ$2.21 billion in 2004 (MineduNZ 2005). In 2004, international education was the third largest export industry of the country after tourism and dairy products, and had created twenty thousand jobs (OBHE-BNA, November 15, 2005). Export income from international education kept decreasing; it was NZ$ 2.034 billion in 2005, NZ$ 1,880 billion in 2006, and NZ$ 1.826 billion in 2007. This time, tertiary-level enrollment, too, was falling due to decreased enrollments as shown in Figure 6.40 and Table 6.20. Export income from public institutions in billions of NZ$ were 1.194, 1.174, 1.060, and 0.955 in 2004–2007; the corresponding values for the PTEs subsector were 0.187, 0.204, 0.161, and 0.153. International education has thus fallen from the third to the fifth place among New Zealand exports (MinEduNZ 2008).

The government in New Zealand has an active role in promoting the country's education sector in the international market with policies predicated on the revenue-generation approach. Since 2003, there is a "foreign student levy" paid by all types of providers, 0.45 percent of the tuition fee income, which is channeled back to finance various initiatives to develop an international brand in education, improve international competitiveness, and recruit more foreign students. For example, to restore confidence in New Zealand education and win back market share, the government enacted the International Education Framework in 2004, which put in place mechanisms for quality assurance and student protection from malpractice in the sector (MinEduNZ 2005; OBHE-BN, April 2005). These measures do not seem to have produced the desired results so far.

The New Zealand brand of international education is promoted in the international market by Education New Zealand, a nonprofit charitable trust founded in 1988 that is governed by the New Zealand export education industry, and is committed to an "NZ Inc" approach to the export of New Zealand's education services offshore.

Although presently not included among the MESDCs, Ireland, too, is emerging as a major destination for foreign students, driven by the increasing demand for the Anglo-Saxon type of higher education in the English language. According to UNESCO statistics, the number of foreign students in Ireland in 2002, 2004, and 2006 were 9,206, 10,201, and 12,740, respectively (see Table A.6). According to figures compiled by Education Ireland, the number of foreign students enrolled in Ireland's thirty-six institutions of higher education was 18,608 in 2004, up 19 percent from the previous year. Students from non-EU countries numbered fifteen thousand, with Americans leading by 16 percent, closely followed by Chinese students (15 percent). The increase in the number of Chinese students was 235 percent since 2002. The revenue generated by foreign students in Ireland has been estimated at $347 million in 2004.[31]

6.3. MAJOR COUNTRIES OF ORIGIN OF FOREIGN STUDENTS

6.3.1. China: A Major Source Country and an Emerging Major Host Country

Figure 6.41 shows the phenomenal growth in Chinese students studying abroad.[32] According to UNESCO data, there were only 119 Chinese students abroad in 1960, and the number was 190 in 1968. In 1971, China became a member of the UN, replacing Taiwan. In 1973, Deng Xiaoping became the vice premier of China, and began opening China to the West. The number of Chinese students abroad was 13,997 in 1974. Deng stepped down in 1976. Following Mao's death in 1976, he was reinstated in 1977, this time as the chairman of the Central Committee of the People's Liberation Army. He emphasized the importance of acquiring know-how and technology from the West, and in 1978, started reforms, which were predicated on opening to the West. Thus, Chinese policies of reform and internationalization of higher education (see Sections 3.2.2 and 3.2.4) were driven by the capacity-building, technology, and know-how transfer rationales even in the early 1970s. By the late 1970s, Chinese leaders had realized that to modernize in science and technology, industry, agriculture, and defense, China had to open its educational system to developments in the outside world even more (Guangqui 1999).

F. Huang (2003) identifies two phases in the internationalization of Chinese higher education. In the first phase, from 1978 to 1992, the emphasis was on sending students and scholars abroad, inviting visiting scholars from abroad, and learning English. The emphasis in the second phase, 1993 to the present, has been on encouraging those who were sent abroad and the expatriate Chinese scholars to come back,[33] attract more foreign students, and internationalize curricula.

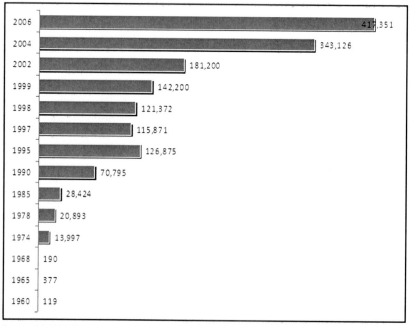

Source: UNESCO (1963)–UNESCO (2008).

Fig. 6.41. Chinese Students Abroad

The student numbers in Figure 6.41 show that Chinese enrollment in institutions of higher education abroad have increased more than tenfold, from 13,997 in 1974 to 181,200 in 2002, and a staggering 417,351 in 2006, putting China at the top of the major countries of origin by a wide margin. In 1993, Chinese students started to return home in large numbers. By 2000, more than 100,000 Chinese students who had studied abroad since 1978 had returned home, and started to contribute to the economic growth.[34]

The United States, Japan, the United Kingdom, Australia, and Germany are the first five destination countries for Chinese students abroad; Australia overtook Germany for the fourth place in 2004 (Davis 2003, 79; UNESCO 2006, 2008).[35]

Present Chinese policies aim to increase indigenous capacity by creating world-class universities, and allowing foreign-sourced provision in various modalities within China. This is believed to be a more cost-effective alternative to sending students abroad as well as stemming brain-drain (Garrett 2004). It is estimated that 680,000 students have gone abroad in the past twenty-five years. About one third of these are expected to return eventually. However, recent numbers on returnees indicate that more may do so. Almost half the current presidents and provosts of Chinese universities have spent some time abroad. The links and the networks they have established are having a major impact on Chinese economic growth in and the quality of higher education (Ross 2004).

Figure 6.42 shows the growth in foreign student enrollment in China. There were only 3 foreign students in China in 1950 and 119 in 1960. By 1999, foreign student enrollment in Chinese institutions had reached 44,711, a nearly twofold increase over the 22,617 students in 1993 (F. Huang 2003). On December 11, 2001, China joined the WTO, and foreign student enrollment in Chinese institutions started to take off. The number of foreign students attending higher education institutions in China was 85,829 in 2002, which corresponds to a more than fortyfold increase in the preceding two decades. China had a target of attracting 120,000 foreign students by 2007 (Mooney 2004). Enrollment figures for the year 2004 showed that China would have no difficulty in reaching the target, with 110,844 foreign students from 178 countries enrolled in 420 Chinese institutions. This corresponds to a 43 percent increase over the previous year's enrollment. Moreover, 104,129 (94 percent) of these students were self-financing. Korean students were the largest group. However, the largest increase was in the number of American students, which, according to *Open Doors 2005* rose by 90 percent from 2,493 in 2003 to 4,737 in 2004.

More and more countries are reaching mutual recognition agreements with China, and this is expected to increase foreign student enrollment even more (*IIE Networker*, May 23–27, 2005). In fact, as seen in Figure 6.42,

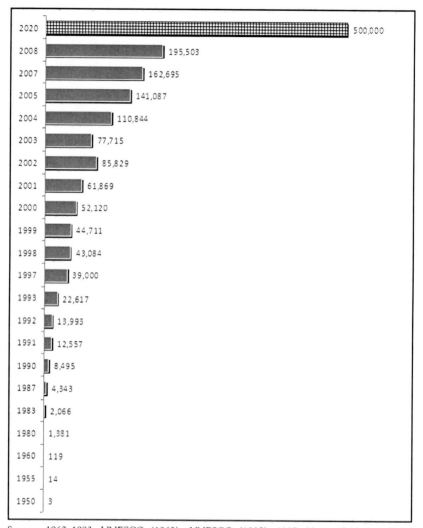

Sources: 1960–1993: UNESCO (1963)—UNESCO (1995); 1997: Hvistendahl; M. China moves up to fifth as importer of students. www.chronicle.com/weekly/v55/issue; 1998–2003: Ross (2004); 2004–2008: Atlas of Student Mobility, http://atlas.iienetwork.org/?p=53467; and 2020 Projection: "Foreign student quota to expand." China Daily. Quoted in: http://atlas. iienetwork.org/page/128207.

Fig. 6.42. Growth of Foreign Student Enrollment in China

foreign student enrollment figures were 141,087 in 2005, 162,695 in 2007, and 195,503 in 2008, which mean that the target set for 2007 was too low. In fact, as shown in Figure 6.42, the new target set by Chinese authorities is 500, 000 students in 2020.

Breakdown of the foreign student enrollment according to major countries of origin in 2008 was as follows: Korea 33 percent, Japan 9.5 percent, United States 7.5 percent, Vietnam 5 percent, Thailand 3.7 percent, Russia 3.7 percent, India 3.7 percent, Indonesia 3.4 percent, France 2.4 percent, and Pakistan 2.3 percent.[36]

According to an article in *The New York Times* (December 9, 2005), twenty years ago, students went to China to study Chinese literature and history; China is now a job market. Enrollment in Chinese-language courses was 86,679 in 2005, accounting for 60 percent of the foreign students in 2005. However, economics, law, and medicine also are becoming popular.[37] In the face of growing domestic and international demand for higher education; China has invested significant resources to enhance the institutional and human resource capacities of its higher education institutions in the last ten years. As pointed out previously, the steps taken to increase institutional capacity include encouraging private funding for China's higher education and modernization of schools' facilities and equipment. Additionally, China has consolidated specialized schools, such as engineering and art schools, and added additional academic programs to create institutions with more of a comprehensive breadth of curricula, making them more adaptable to employment needs and improving the schools' resources through economies of scale. Furthermore, China is encouraging teaching in English and providing leadership training to its senior management staff through international exchange programs with various Western countries to enhance the human capacity of China's higher education institutions (GAO 2009).

It is clear that the student rationales driving the growth in foreign enrollment in China are now better job prospects, and forming strategic alliances and networking in a country with a growing economy and an increasing international influence.

6.3.2. India

Educational exchanges in contemporary India started in 1950, soon after the country gained independence. Large numbers of Indian students and scholars went to the United States, the United Kingdom, and Germany (Klineberg 1976, 127–46). Additionally, an educational exchange link was soon established between India and the USSR, which solely was driven by the political rationale (Shivkumar 2001).

The overwhelming desire on the part of Indian students, with their parents encouraging them, to acquire a foreign degree led to large numbers of Indian students going abroad, as well as making India a big market for foreign providers (see Section 4.3.7). Figure 6.43 shows the growth in the number of Indian students studying abroad. In 1955, the number was 3,190, and remained almost constant throughout the 1960s, at a level between

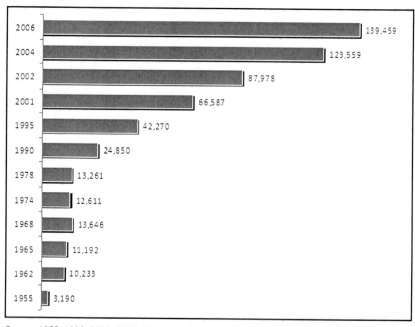

Source: 1955–1995, 2002–2006: UNESCO (1963)—UNESCO (2008); and 2001: Davis (2003, 90).

Fig. 6.43. Indian Students Abroad

10,000 and 13,000, but took off in the 1990s, reaching 42,270 in 1995 and 139,459 in 2006. It should be noted that the period in which the number of Indian students abroad took off coincides with the opening up of the Indian economy in 1991. The similarity between India and China in this respect is striking.

The United States is by far the top choice of Indian students, Australia is a distant second, but in front of the United Kingdom, which has traditional colonial ties with India, followed by Germany, and New Zealand and Canada competing for the fifth place (Davis 2003, 90; UNESCO 2008).[38]

It is clear that colonial ties no longer play a role in Indian students' choice of a country of destination. Rather, it is the quest for a better education and, more recently, employability in the global labor market, and the desire to establish strategic personal links and networking, that are now the main drivers of the international mobility of Indian students. Indian students are now a major source of high-level, skilled workforce for the United States. The average stay rate in the United States of Indian doctoral degree holders in science and engineering fields of four to five years after graduation increased from 72 percent in 1992 to 86 percent in 2001 (OECD 2004b, 279).

A 7 percent average annual economic growth, English as one of the official languages, the unmet demand in the world's second most populous country, and the Indian culture that values education is attracting an increasing number of providers to India. More than thirty U.S. institutions signed collaborative agreements with Indian institutions in 2005 and 2006, and the National University of Singapore has signed an agreement with the prestigious Indian Institute of Science to open a campus there. The government is currently introducing more stringent legislation for regulating foreign providers (OBHE-BNA, February 6, 2006).

India is currently the third largest higher education system in the world, with many institutions with impeccable credentials such as the Indian Institute of Science in Bangalore, and the various IITs and Indian Institutes of Management (IIMs) throughout the country. English is the main language of teaching. Yet, India has never figured prominently as a destination of choice for foreign students. Klineberg (1976, 144) reports that the number of foreign students in India was 3,510 in 1959, had peaked at 8,994 in 1969, and dropped to 7,217 in 1971. Sharma (2001) gives the following enrollment figures for foreign students in India: 6,022, 5,455, and 2.908 in 1995, 1996, and 1997, respectively. Recently available figures for 2002, 2004, and 2006 are 7,791, 7,738 and 7,589 (UNESCO 2004, 2006, 2008).[39] It seems rather unlikely that India will become a major destination for foreign students in the near future. On the other hand, Indian for-profit providers such as Aptech (see Section 4.4.5), which are already active in the certificate market, are expected to play a growing role in that particular subsector of the transnational education market. Prestigious institutions like the IIM in Bangalore seem to have won the battle against the government to set up branch campuses abroad. The government first rejected the proposal to open a branch campus in Singapore, citing unmet domestic demand, but recently gave in (Neelekantan 2006a, 2006b). India itself may not be a destination of choice for foreign students in the conceivably near future. On the other hand, offshore provision by prestigious Indian institutions may soon take off, given the Indian entrepreneurial spirit and vast human resource.

6.3.3. Other Major Countries of Origin

Figures 6.44 to 6.52 show the numbers of students abroad from Korea, Morocco, Greece, Turkey, Malaysia, Indonesia, Hong Kong, Singapore, and Mexico, respectively. Figure 6.44 shows that the number of Korean students attending institutions of higher education abroad, which was only 5,304 in

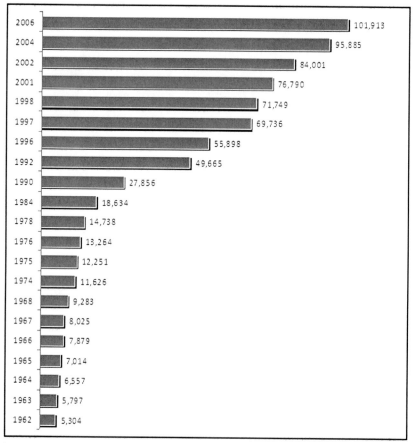

Sources: 1962–1998, 2002–2006: UNESCO (1963)—UNESCO (2008); and 2001: Davis (2003, 58).

Fig. 6.44. Korean Students Abroad

1962, but steadily increased to 101,903 in 2006. Major destination countries in 2006 were United States, followed by a distance by Japan, Germany, Australia, and the United Kingdom, Australia having overtaken the United Kingdom since 2001 (Davis 2003, 58; UNESCO 2008).[40]

    Korea, together with Indonesia, Malaysia, and Thailand, was one of the most adversely affected countries during the Asian economic crisis of 1997. Yet, this does not seem to have had an effect on the number of Korean students going abroad.

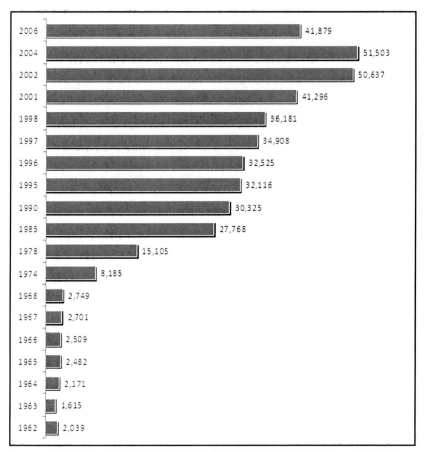

Sources: 1962–1998:, 2002–2006: UNESCO (1963)—UNESCO (2008); and 2001: Davis (2003, 58).

Fig. 6.45. Moroccan Students Abroad

Figure 6.45 shows the growth in the number of Moroccan students studying abroad, which numbered between two thousand and three thousand throughout the 1960s. The number of Moroccan students abroad made three big jumps, the first one in the 1970s and 1980s when the numbers shot above 20,000, the second one in the 1990s when the number approached 40,000, and the third one at the beginning of the new century, when the number reached 51,503 in 2004. However, the number has dropped to 41,879 in 2006. The first choice of destination in 2001 was France due to the colonial

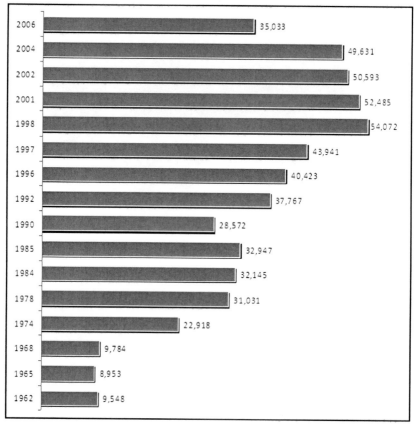

Sources: 1962–1998, 2002–2006: UNESCO (1963)—UNESCO (2008); and 2001: Davis (2003, 59).

Fig. 6.46. Greek Students Abroad

connection, followed at a significant distance by Germany, Belgium, and Spain (Davis 2003, 80). In 2006, France maintained its commanding position at the top, again followed by Germany, but this time Spain was the third, the United States was the fourth and Canada was the fifth (UNESCO 2008).

Figure 6.46 shows the number of Greek students studying abroad, which was 9,548 in 1962, reached its maximum value of 54,072 in 1998, and was down to 49,631 in 2004, and to 35,033 in 2006. There is no explanation for the drop from 1998 to 2006 other than a demographic saturation of the demand. Greece has always been a major country of origin for foreign students. The Greek higher education system is one of the most strictly

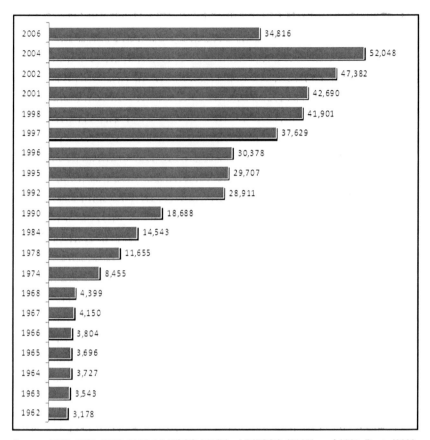

Year	Value
2006	34,816
2004	52,048
2002	47,382
2001	42,690
1998	41,901
1997	37,629
1996	30,378
1995	29,707
1992	28,911
1990	18,688
1984	14,543
1978	11,655
1974	8,455
1968	4,399
1967	4,150
1966	3,804
1965	3,696
1964	3,727
1963	3,543
1962	3,178

Sources: 1962–1998, 2002–2006: UNESCO (1963)—UNESCO (2008); and 2001: Davis (2003, 79).

Fig. 6.47. Turkish Students Abroad

regulated in the world, and is characterized by a demand–supply imbalance. The big jump in Greek students abroad came in the 1990s, after Greece joined the EU. In 2001, the United Kingdom was by far the major choice of destination of Greek students, followed at a significant distance by Italy, Germany, the United States, and France (Davis 2003, 59). In 2004, France overtook the United States for the fourth place (UNESCO 2006). In 2006, leading destinations were the United Kingdom, Italy, Germany, the United States, and France (UNESCO 2008).

Figure 6.47 shows the number of Turkish students studying abroad. As mentioned previously, in the early years of the republic, when Turkey

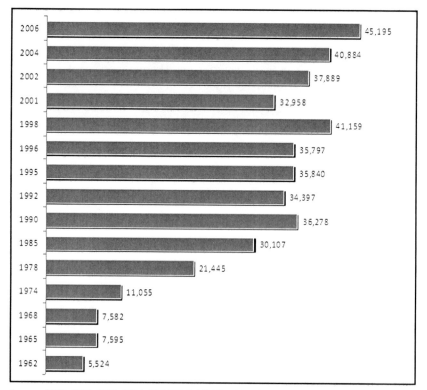

Sources: 1962–1998, 2002–2006: UNESCO (1963)—UNESCO (2008); and 2001: Davis (2003, 72).

Fig. 6.48. Malaysian Students Abroad

had not yet developed its national education system, Law No. 1416 was passed, which covered the government scholarships to be provided to students who would be selected to be sent abroad in return for compulsory service in the public sector upon completion of their studies. Thus, Turkey had a policy that was predicated on the capacity-building approach. Until the 1970s, many of the Turkish students abroad were on such government scholarships. As the country prospered, the expansion in the higher education system could not catch up with the increase in population, which was approximately sixfold over a period of eight decades. In the face of such a huge unmet demand, many families began sending their children abroad. Furthermore, beginning in the 1960s, many Turks went to Europe to work, and by the 1990s, second- and third-generation Turks in Europe,

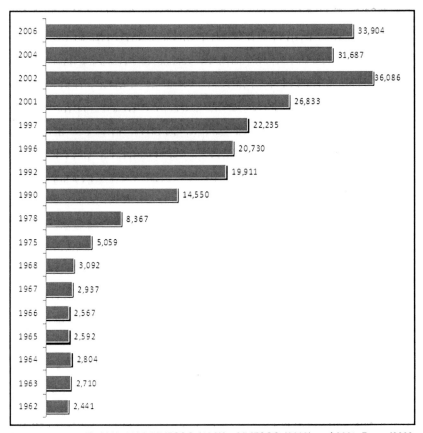

Year	Value
2006	33,904
2004	31,687
2002	36,086
2001	26,833
1997	22,235
1996	20,730
1992	19,911
1990	14,550
1978	8,367
1975	5,059
1968	3,092
1967	2,937
1966	2,567
1965	2,592
1964	2,804
1963	2,710
1962	2,441

Sources: 1962–1997, 2002–2006: UNESCO (1963)—UNESCO (2008); and 2001: Davis (2003, 91).

Fig. 6.49. Indonesian Students Abroad

in particular the children of the *gastarbeiter* in Germany, started attending higher education institutions. The result of these two factors combined led to the increase in the number of Turkish students abroad in the 1990s, seen in Figure 6.47. The number of Turkish students abroad was 52,048 in 2004, but, according to UNESCO (2008) statistics, enrollment abroad dropped to 34,816. Figures on Turkish students abroad do not include the Turkish students in the Turkish side of Cyprus, which now stands over thirty thousand.[41] Furthermore, UNESCO gives the figure of 7,101 for the number of Turkish students in Germany in 2006. Cross-check with DAAD data, however, shows that the total number of Turkish students in Germany in

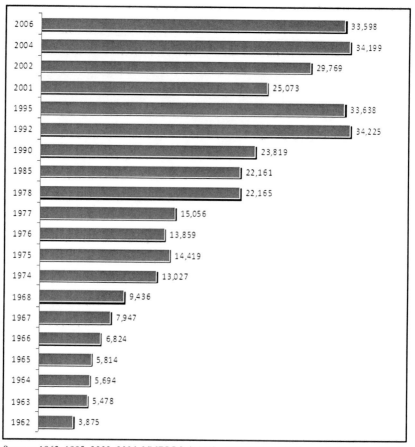

Sources: 1962–1995, 2002–2006: UNESCO (1963)—UNESCO (2008); and 2001: Davis (2003, 63).

Fig. 6.50. Students from Hong Kong Abroad

2006 was 22,419, of which 7,077 were *Bildungsauslaender* (nonresident), and the rest were *Bildungsinlaender* (resident).[42] Thus, to be consistent with past years' data, the actual number of Turkish students abroad in 2006 should have been reported as 50,158. This is typical of the difficulties encountered in comparative mobility studies.

In both 2001 and 2004, Germany was by far the largest host country for Turkish students, followed by the United States, France, the United Kingdom, and Austria. The order of major destinations in 2006 was Ger-

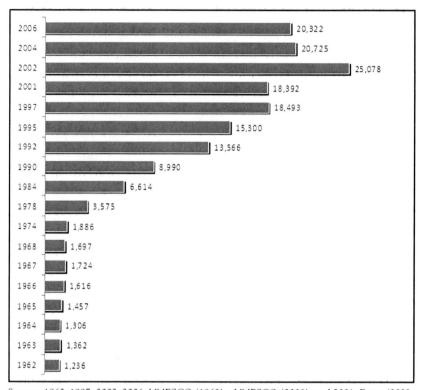

Year	Number
2006	20,322
2004	20,725
2002	25,078
2001	18,392
1997	18,493
1995	15,300
1992	13,566
1990	8,990
1984	6,614
1978	3,575
1974	1,886
1968	1,697
1967	1,724
1966	1,616
1965	1,457
1964	1,306
1963	1,362
1962	1,236

Sources: 1962–1997, 2002–2006: UNESCO (1963)—UNESCO (2008); and 2001: Davis (2003, 64).

Fig. 6.51. Singaporean Students Abroad

many (after the correction above), the United States, Azerbaijan, France, and the United Kingdom (UNESCO 2008). It should, however, be pointed out once again that the majority of the Turkish students in Germany, France, and Austria are either the children or the relatives of the resident workers in those countries, while most of those in the United States, Azerbaijan, and the United Kingdom are nonresident.

Figure 6.48 shows the number of Malaysian students abroad. The number of Malaysian students abroad was 5,524 in 1962, passed 20,000 in the late 1970s, reached its peak value of 41,159 in 1998 and fell to 32,958 in 2001, from which year on it started increasing again, reaching 40,884 in 2004, and 45,195 in 2006. It appears that until the 1980s, Malaysia had a policy of sending students abroad, which was predicated on the capacity-building approach and the technology and know-how transfer rationales.

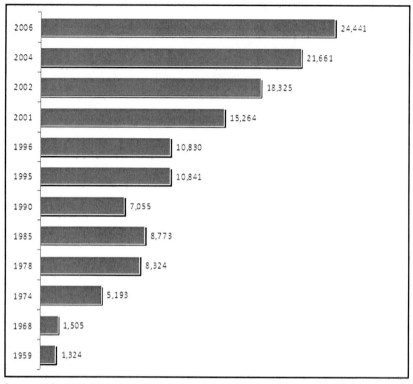

Sources: 1959–1996, 2002–2006: UNESCO (1963)—UNESCO (2008); and 2001: Davis (2003, 73).

Fig. 6.52. Mexican Students Abroad

The country did not have sufficient places in her institutions of higher education to meet the demand. The families, on the other hand, sent their children abroad so that they could get a better education in English.

Obviously, the Asian economic crisis of 1997 adversely affected the number of Malaysian students abroad. During 1997 to 2001, the number of Malaysian students declined sharply especially in the United Kingdom (down 41 percent) and the United States (down 50 percent), and the slump is continuing in both countries, although much less in the latter with only a 3 percent fall from 2004 to 2005 (OBHE-BNA, 28 April 2006). This is due to changes in Malaysian policies. Malaysia now has a developed public higher education system, and a sizable private sector comprising eleven universities, an equal number of colleges, five foreign university branch campuses, many twinning arrangements with prestigious foreign institutions, and more than five hundred nonuniversity institutions. The government is now trying to curb student outflow as well as trying to compete in the global higher education market as a major hub for transnational education, offering a spectrum of choices, including franchises, branch campuses, and offshore programs (see Sections 3.2 and 4.4.8). As part of the Knowledge-Based Economy Master Plan, the Malaysian government recently launched a $4.8 billion new higher education strategy that aims to curb the outward mobility of Malaysian students as well as increasing the number of foreign students in the country to 100,000 by 2010. Among the new measures are a new quality assurance agency, *LAN* (see Section 3.4.3), an online admission systems, and the relaxation of the requirement of teaching in the Malay language, encouraging teaching in English, Chinese, Tamil, and Arabic (OBHE-BNA, April 28, 2006). Malaysia has the potential to attract Muslim students from countries in the region as well as in the Middle East, who are increasingly feeling unwelcome in the West. In recent years, Malaysia also has opened a number of education bureaus in countries including China, Indonesia, Vietnam, the United Arab Emirates, and South Africa to promote Malaysian higher education abroad.

Initiatives put in place to curb outward mobility of Malaysian students also include government support for private higher education institutions, strategic import of foreign transnational higher education, both in the area of collaborative provision and through branch campus establishment.

The new initiatives plus stable government, cultural diversity, improving economic conditions, strategic location, relatively low costs and growing English-language competence, indicates that Malaysia will remain a very attractive market for overseas institutions, and an increasingly attractive option for both domestic and foreign students (OBHE-BNA, April 28, 2006). This is seen in the number of foreign students in Malaysia shown in Table A.6, which were 16,480 in 2002, 27,731 in 2004, and 40,029 in 2006, corresponding to 6.3 percent of the country's total enrollment in higher education.

The major destinations of choice by Malaysian students in 2001 were Australia, the United Kingdom, the United States, almost in equal numbers, followed by Japan and Jordan (Davis 2003, 72); in 2004, New Zealand replaced Jordan (UNESCO 2006). Leading destinations in 2006 were Australia, the United Kingdom, the United States, Japan, and Ukraine (UNESCO 2008). The colonial connection to the United Kingdom is self-evident. On the other hand, the choice of Jordan as a destination by more than one thousand students from Malaysia possibly indicates a difference in the choices of Muslim students of Malay origin and students of Chinese origin.

It appears that Australia is not affected by the downturn in the outflow of Malaysian students, whose enrollment increased from 16,431 students in 2002 to 19,851 in 2008 (see Table 6.15).

Figure 6.49 shows the growth in the number of Indonesian students abroad, which had essentially remained constant between twenty-five hundred and three thousand until the 1970s, started taking off in the 1970s, and shot up in the 1990s. It is interesting to note that although the number of Indonesian students in the United States decreased after the economic crisis in 1997, the total number of Indonesian students abroad increased from 22,235 in 1997 to 36,086 in 2002. According to the figures reported by Davis (2003, 91), there were 26,833 Indonesian students abroad in 2001, with 11,625 of them in the United States, 9,283 in Australia, 2,128 in Germany, 1,143 in Japan, and 1,049 in the United Kingdom. This number increased to 36,086 in 2002, and than sharply dropped to 31,687 in 2004. The major destination countries, too, changed, and Australia came to the top, followed by the United States, Malaysia, Germany, and Japan. The latest figure available from UNESCO (2008) is 33,904 Indonesian students abroad in 2006, with Australia, the United States, Malaysia, Germany, and Japan as the major destinations.

Indonesia is the country with the largest Muslim population in the world. The drop in the number of Indonesian students can be explained by the conditions that are prevailing in the post-9/11 period. It is, however, an interesting message to the United States that students in the global higher education market now have a wide array of choices in terms of host countries. The fact that Malaysia became the third country of destination for Indonesian students possibly supports this argument, as well as giving credence to the Malaysian strategy of attracting Muslim students. It is also interesting to note that no colonial connection appears to exist between Indonesia and the Netherlands.

Hong Kong is a country that has adopted the capacity-building approach by educating large numbers of students abroad for many years, as seen in Figure 6.50. The number of students from Hong Kong attending institutions abroad reached its peak value of 34,225 in 1992, and then fell to 25,073 in 2001, but from then on, increased to 34,199 in 2004, and once again fell to 33,598 in 2006. It seems that being taken over by China has not affected the outflow of students from Hong Kong.

The United Kingdom, the United States, Australia, in almost equal numbers and in that order, with Canada a distant fourth, were the destinations of choice for students from Hong Kong in 2001 (Davis 2003, 63). However, the order of major destination countries changed in 2004 to Australia, the United Kingdom, the United States, Canada, and Macao (UNESCO 2006), and, in 2006, to Australia, the United Kingdom, the

United States, Canada, and New Zealand (UNESCO 2008). The Commonwealth connection is self-evident in the case of the United Kingdom, Canada, Australia, and New Zealand. However, more than that, Australia appears to have drawn a large number of Hong Kong students away from the United States, beginning in the 1990s. The drop in the number of students from Hong Kong in the United States from 13,752 in 1994 to 7,353 in 2004 seems to have been balanced by an almost equal number currently in Australia, or attending Australian and British offshore programs, branch campuses, or franchises.

The higher education system in Hong Kong has significantly expanded in the last quarter of the previous century. With English as the medium of teaching and high-quality international academic staff, higher education institutions in Hong Kong are poised to play a key role in making Hong Kong not only another major hub of transnational education in the region, but also another academic bridge between China and the world (Postiglione 2005); the number of students from mainland China in the University of Hong Kong has increased from 64 in 1993 to 265 in 2001, many of them fee-paying.

Figure 6.51 shows the number of Singaporean students abroad, which has steadily increased from 1,236 in 1962 to 3,575 in 1978, 15,300 in 1995 and 25,078 in 2002, from which year on it has dropped sharply to 20,725 in 2004 and to 20,322 in 2006.

In 2001 Australia was by far the major destination of Singaporean students, followed by the United Kingdom and the United States in almost equal numbers (Davis 2003, 64); in 2004, the United States overtook the United Kingdom, and became the second major country of destination for Singaporean students. Leading destinations in 2006 were Australia, the United States, the United Kingdom, Canada, and Malaysia. The commonwealth connection is again self-evident for the United Kingdom, but Australia, emerged as a major host much later, in the 1990s, and Canada and Malaysia only recently.

For many years, Singapore, like Hong Kong, adopted a capacity-building approach, educating students abroad while at the same time developing her own higher education system. In 2002, Singapore Economic Development Board (EDB, supported by the Ministry of Education, Singapore Tourism Board, SPRING Singapore, and International Enterprise Singapore, launched the Global Schoolhouse vision. This is a coordinated, three-pronged strategic plan to attract leading foreign institutions and international students to Singapore, and enhancing the regulation of private providers. Today, Singapore has a developed system, offering a wide array of choices to students in the English language. In 2007, the education sector contributed S$ 3.8 billion in value-added, corresponding to 2 percent of the

GDP; the target for 2015 is 5 percent of the GDP. Singapore, like Malaysia, now aspires to a major regional hub status. The current target is 150,000 students in 2015. The higher education system comprises three universities, including the new Singapore Management University established as a "publicly funded private university" in 2000, five polytechnics, and more than three hundred other nonuniversity institutions, all of which are private and offer a wide array of programs at all levels. The National University of Singapore (NUS; f. 1905), the oldest institution in the country, already has four branch campuses in the United States, China, and Sweden. It is currently in the process of opening another one in Bangalore. The Bangalore campus will provide opportunities to NUS students to work in Indian high-tech companies.[43] INSEAD, the prestigious French business school, the University of Chicago Business School, Georgia Institute of Technology, Johns Hopkins, MIT, Shanghai Jiao Tong University, Stanford, the Wharton School, *Technische Universiteit Eindhoven*, and *Technische Universität München*, all have branch campuses and twinning arrangements with local partners in Singapore. U21 Global has its headquarters there, and Singapore is the e-learning hub of the Asia-Pacific region. Recently, the CASE trust of education was launched by the Consumer Association of Singapore to act as a quality assurance agency for the corporate postsecondary education subsector in Singapore (see Sections 3.4.3 and 4.4.8).

Singapore has an aging population, which means that it will have excess higher education capacity in the future. Thus, Singapore, too, much like Hong Kong and Malaysia, is quite likely to emerge as another major hub of transnational education, rather than being a major country of origin for foreign students (Garrett 2005). The latest figure available for foreign student enrollment in Singapore is 72,000 students in 2006, corresponding to 51.4 percent of the total enrollment in her higher education system (see Table A.6).

Figure 6.52 shows the number of Mexican students abroad, which grew from 1,324 in 1959 to more than 10,000 in the mid-1990s, and in the aftermath of the coming into force of NAFTA in 1994, increased by a factor of nearly two to 21,661 in 2004, and further to 24,441 in 2006. In 2001, 2004, and 2006, the United States was by far the major destination of Mexican students. In 2001, Spain, the United Kingdom, and Canada were trailing far behind in that order, but in almost equal numbers. However, in 2004, the next four countries were the United Kingdom, France, Germany, and Spain. The colonial connection with Spain seems to have waned, having been replaced by other rationales such as a better life through a better education, and networking on the part of the Mexican students and their families. In 2006, Spain overtook France and Germany. In 2007, Spain was in the second place.[44]

Analysis of policies of every country concerning internationalization of higher education and international student mobility is beyond the scope of this study. A selected number of cases are presented, which are believed to highlight many of the salient features of international student mobility today.

Many of the countries are major host countries for and, at the same time, major countries of origin of foreign students. This clearly shows how truly international student mobility is in today's global knowledge economy. It also indicates how intertwined are the rationales that are driving it at all of the national, institutional, and student–parent levels. Three countries are cases in point.

In terms of total national enrollment at the tertiary level, Norway, with 215,000 students in 2006 (see Table A.1), has a small national system of higher education. On the other hand, with an expenditure of $15,552 per student in 2005 (OECD 2008) and no tuition fees, it is an attractive destination for foreign students. There were 15,826 Norwegian students studying abroad in 2002, and the country was hosting 7,679 foreign students, corresponding to 3.9 percent of the home enrollment (UNESCO 2004). Recently, Norway has been pursuing an active and coordinated internationalization policy in higher education, driven entirely by the skilled migration, mutual understanding, and cultural rationales. In 2001, the Norwegian Parliament passed an extensive reform package to support internationalization and mobility. Norway is now the most advanced country in Europe in complying with the requirements of the Bologna Process, with a degree system based on three cycles and ECTS and the Diploma Supplement (DS; see Section 5.4 and Appendix C). In 2003, the Norwegian Agency for Quality Assurance was established. Founded in 2004, the Norwegian Centre for International Cooperation in Higher Education (*SIU, Senter for Internasjonalisering av Hoyere Utdanning*) is a public agency with the mission of promoting and facilitating international cooperation, standardization, mobility, and the overcoming of cultural barriers to communication and exchange in higher education. The SIU is charged with the task of coordinating national measures according to official Norwegian policy within the field of internationalization, and promoting Norway as an education and research nation. In 2004, Norway hosted 11,060 foreign students, corresponding to 5.2 percent of the total enrollment in the country; the number in 2006 was 14,297 students, corresponding to 6.6 percent of the national enrollment (see Table A.6), and it was 15,002 in 2007. Major countries of origin in 2007 were Sweden, Denmark, China, Germany, Finland, and Iceland.[45]

Total enrollment in Dutch higher education was 580,000 students in 2006 (see Table A.1), and according to UNESCO statistics, the country hosted 18,888 foreign students in 2002, 20,153 students in 2004, and

27,037 students in 2006, which corresponded to 4.7 percent of the national enrollment. With an average per-student expenditure of $ 13,683 in 2005 (OECD 2008), relatively modest tuition fees, and with many degree programs now taught in English and the new bachelor–master degree structure firmly established, Netherlands is an attractive destination for foreign students. International higher education in the Netherlands is coordinated by the Netherlands Organization for Cooperation in International Higher Education (*NUFFIC*). According to *NUFFIC*, the total number of foreign students in the Netherlands in 2008 was approximately 70,000—a figure much higher than those reported by UNESCO. Leading countries of origin were Germany (16,750), China (4,750), Belgium (2,450), Spain (2,000), and France (1,650). Forty-two percent of the foreign students were in universities, and the rest in *HBOs*. Only 54 percent of those enrolled in universities were in bachelor-level programs, whereas that ratio was 96 percent in the *HBOs*.[46]

The Czech Republic is home to the oldest university north of the Alps, Charles University (f. 1347). In 2006, The Czech Republic hosted 21,395 foreign students, corresponding to 7.5 percent of its total higher education enrollment (see Table A.6) Students from central and eastern Europe, mainly from Slovakia, accounted for 81 percent of the foreign enrollment in the Czech Republic (UNESCO 2008, 116). Students enrolled in programs taught in Czech in public institutions do not pay fees, and the share of private institutions is negligible. Nevertheless, the Czech government recently announced an ambitious plan to increase the foreign student enrollment to 10 percent of the total by 2010. According to the Ministry of Education, the new policy is predicated on the need to attract highly talented students and the potential for revenue generation. Many programs currently are taught in English, and the number of such programs is expected to increase (OBHE-BNA, November 8, 2005).

Per-capita income in Thailand is about 50 percent that in Malaysia and 20 percent of that in Singapore (see Table 1.1). The Thai higher education system, which enrolls more than 2.2 million students, is the fourteenth largest in the world, and it is three and nineteen times larger than those of Malaysia and Singapore, respectively (see Table A.1). In 2004, Thailand hosted 4,092 foreign students (0.2 percent of total enrollment), and 23,727 Thai students were studying abroad (1.1 percent of total enrollment), both numbers are significantly lower than those of Malaysia and Singapore. In 2004, the Thai government announced a plan that aims to curb outward student mobility and save revenue as well as making Thailand a regional hub for international education (OBHE-BNA, March 12, 2004; see also Section 4.4.8). Branch campuses, twinning, and franchise arrangements of U.S., Australian, Malaysian, and Singaporean institutions and for-profit providers, and a joint Thai–German Graduate School of Engineering already exist in Thailand. Recently, Chinese institutions and the Egyptian *Al-Azhar* has shown interest in Thailand. The latter has been eyeing the Muslim population of Thailand who go abroad to study in large numbers. How Thailand will fare as a regional hub in competition with Malaysia and Singapore remains to be seen.

It is also worth noting that the post-9/11 period has left Muslim students in a quandary. On the one hand, their preferred choices of destination have traditionally been the United States and the United Kingdom. On the other hand, they are increasingly feeling unwelcome there. Malaysia, Thailand, and the previously mentioned initiatives in Qatar and Dubai thus have the potential to attract students from Muslim countries.

The growth in the number of foreign students in the five major host countries, the United States, Australia, the United Kingdom, France, and Germany, newly emerging major hosts, China, Canada, and Japan, and a number of new hubs, New Zealand, Singapore, and Malaysia have been summarized in Table 6.22 for the period 1997–2008. The total number of foreign students globally has grown 83 percent in this period. Cumulative growth from 1997 to 2008 was fivefold in China, fourfold in Australia and New Zealand, nearly threefold in Canada, more than twofold in Japan, twofold in France, 73 percent in the United Kingdom, 63 percent in Germany, and 36 percent in the United States. Major changes from 2004 to 2008 were as follow:

1. The significant jump in foreign student enrollment in the United States;

2. The moving of Australia into the second place ahead of the United Kingdom, and the taking over of Germany by France for the fourth place, both for the first time;

3. The closing of the distance between China and France and Germany;

4. The declining foreign student enrollment in New Zealand; and

5. The emergence of new hubs like Singapore, Malaysia, South Africa, Czech Republic, the Netherlands, and Norway.

It is now clear that policies and practices of all of the major actors in international student mobility, both as host for and as country of origin of foreign students, are based on combinations of all of the rationales and drivers discussed in Section 5.3.1. This argument is supported by the findings of a recent report by the GAO (2009). The GAO report concludes

Table 6.22. Major Host Countries, 1997–2008

Country	1997	1998	1999	2000	2001	2002	2003	2004	2005	2006	2007	2008
U.S.[a]	457,984	481,280	490,933	514,723	547,867	582,996	586,323	572,509	565,039	564,776	582,984	623,805
UK[b]	198,064	213,264	219,285	224,660	230,870	242,755	275,265	300,050	318,395	330,075	351,470	341,790
Australia[c]	100,383	109,285	119,988	138,381	168,916	193,337	217,646	235,131	255,113	279,989	325,935	389,973
Germany[d]	151,870	158,435	165,994	175,065	187,027	206,141	227,026	246,136	246,334	248,357	246,369	nya
France[e]	125,205[*]	118,433	151,969	160,533	174,557	196,748	221,471	244,335	255,585	265,039	nya	nya
China	39,000	43,084	44,711	52,120	61,869	85,829	77,715	110,844	141,087	nd	162,695	195,503
Japan[f]	51,047	51,298	55,755	64,011	78,812	95,550	109,508	117,302	121,812	117,927	118,498	123,829
Canada[g]	48,763	55,894	65,847	78,764	96,525	110,312	121,635	127,736	130,312	131,269	135,549	nya
New Zealand[h]	9,617	9,272	11,856	16,628	26,236	40,825	47,116	50,442	47,366	42,652	39,942	nya
Singapore	nd	nd	nd	nd	50,000[*]	50,000[*]	50,000[*]	nd	72,000	nya	nya	nya
Malaysia	nd	nd	nd	nd	nd	nd	nd	27,731	66,000	nya	nya	nya
World[i]	1,500,000	nd	1,750,000	1,818,759	1,896,265	2,188,544	2,425,995	2,598,660	2,725,996	2,754,373	nya	nya

Sources: Verbik and Lasanowski (2007).

Report. London: OBHE. September. (Appendix B, 37). and the indicated Web sites

[a]Includes students in associate-, bachelor-, master-, and doctoral-levels, professional degrees (MD, JD, etc.), nondegree, intensive English language (IELP), and optional practical training (OPT) programs. http://www.opendoors.iienetwork.org.

[b]Includes higher education students, both part-time and full-time, who are those students on programs of study for which the level of instruction is above that of Level 3 of the National Qualifications Framework,for example, courses leading to the Advanced Level of the General Certificate of Education (GCE A-levels) and their equivalent. Students enrolled in higher education-level courses leading to various diplomas and certificates offered in further education colleges are included. http://www.hesa.ac.uk. The enrollment value for 2008 is provisional; it is calculated by a new method, which excludes "writing-up" and "sabbatical" students (see Table 6.7)

[c]Includes students, both part-time and full-time, in higher education, vocational and technical education and other postsecondary education programs. Students in English-language programsare excluded. http://www.aei.dest.gov.au/AEI/MIP/Statistics/StudentEnrolmentAndVisaStatistics.

[d]Includes students enrolled in universities, *Fachhochschulen*, and art schools (*Kunsthochschulen*), but does not include graduate students. http://www.wissenschaft-weltoffen.de.

[f]Includes students in universities, IUTs, IUFMs, grandes écoles, tertiary-level institutions affiliated to various ministries, CPGEs, and STSs Values for 1997 and 1998 include universities only. Repères et références statistiques—édition 2006 Les étudiant. http://media.education.gouv.fr/file/42/6/2426.pdf.

[g]Includes students in universities, graduate schools, junior colleges, colleges of technology, special training colleges, and university preparatory colleges. http://www.mext.go.jp

[a]Includes students in universities, nonuniversity vocational institutions (trade), and other postsecondary institutions. Note that the Canadian data reported by Verbik and Lasanowski comprise "student flows," which include only new admissions. Data shown here comprise "student stocks" (i.e., enrollments in a given year). Note also that the student numbers reported here are significantly different from those reported by Savage and Kane (2005). www.cic.gc.ca

[h]Includes students, both part-time and full-time, in universities, institutes of technology, polytechnics, colleges of education, Wananga, and private trainig establishments. http://educationcounts.govt.nz

[i]See Figure 6.1.

Nd, no data available for the year shown; nya, figures not yet available for the year shown.

that the major host countries—the United States, Australia, the United Kingdom, Germany, China, and the EU Commission—use higher education for international students to advance diplomatic, development assistance, economic, and other objectives, often concurrently. These countries and the EU Commission also provide scholarships to support public diplomacy and development assistance goals. Such programs that support public diplomacy goals include Australian Endeavor Awards, Chinese Government Scholarships Programs, EU Erasmus Mundus, DAAD Study Scholarships and Research Grants, the UK Chevenin Program, the U.S. Fulbright Program, are typically merit-based, and mostly for graduate students. Scholarship programs that are used to support development assistance goals include Australian Development Scholarships, Australian Leadership Awards, U.S. Collaborative Research Support, and U.S. Cooperative Association of States for Scholarships, and are also mostly merit-based and at the graduate level (GAO 2009; see also Appendix E for more on EU programs that aim to support international mobility). All major host countries now use marketing practices borrowed from the private sector to promote their higher education systems in the international higher education market. It is interesting to note that these marketing strategies are increasingly using catch-phrases such as "The Appeal of France," "Study in Germany—Land of Ideas," "Study in Australia—Live, Learn and Grow," and "Education UK—Innovative, Individual, Inspirational" (GAO 2009).

6.4. REGIONAL BREAKDOWN OF INTERNATIONAL STUDENT MOBILITY

The policies and practices of the major host countries and the major countries of origin of foreign students are presented and analyzed in the preceding sections of this chapter. Tables 6.23 and 6.24 summarize the global picture in international student mobility in today's world. Table 6.23 shows the regional distribution of students hosted (inbound mobility) and students abroad (outbound mobility) in terms of both the actual numbers and their ratios to the total regional enrollment.

In terms of both actual numbers and as a percentage of the regional enrollment, North America and western Europe is by far the leading region of choice for students who want to study abroad. The region as a whole hosts close to 1.8 million students, which corresponds to 5.33 percent of the regional enrollment and 65 percent of the total number of foreign students in the world. No other region comes close to it.

When outward mobility is expressed in terms of actual student numbers, East Asia and the Pacific is the leading region of origin of foreign students, with North America and western Europe a distant second. On the

Table 6.23. Regional Distribution of International Student Mobility, 2006

Region	Enrollment	Inbound		Outbound	
		Number	%	Number	%
Arab States	7,038,000	80,009	1.14 (0.95)[a]	188,786	2.68 (2.72)
Central and eastern Europe	20,125,000	208,101	1.03 (0.91)	334,201	1.72 (1.56)
Central Asia	1,974,000	51,174	2.59 (1.80)	91,633	4.64 (3.85)
East Asia and the Pacific	43,777,000	507,193	1.16 (0.98)	809,330	1.85 (1.80)
Latin America and the Caribbean	16,247,000	36,803	0.23 (0.25)	154,099	0.95 (1.00)
North America and western Europe	33,752,000	1,798,299	5.33 (5.19)	490,965	1.45 (1.48)
South and west Asia	17,253,000	10,620	0.06 (0.07)	232,256	1.35 (1.26)
Sub-Saharan Africa	3,723,000	62,174	1.67 (1.81)	205,205	5.52 (5.87)
World	143,889,000	2,754,373[b]	1.91 (1.86)	2,754,373	1.91 (1.86)

Source: UNESCO (2008, 116–19).

[a]Percentages shown in parentheses are for 2004.
[b]Includes 247,888 students of unspecified origin.

other hand, when outward student mobility is expressed as a percentage of the total regional enrollment, Sub-Saharan Africa appears as the leading "outwardly mobile" region in the world (5.52 percent), followed by Central Asia (4.64 percent), the Arab States (2.68 percent), and East Asia and the Pacific (1.85 percent).

Table 6.24 shows the regions of origin of foreign students hosted in different regions. Twenty-four percent of the inward student mobility in North America and western Europe is internal. This is mainly due to increased student mobility in Europe, financially supported by EU programs. However, an almost equal percentage of the foreign students in this region (25 percent) originate from the East Asia and the Pacific region, followed by central and eastern Europe (13 percent) and South and West Asia (9 percent).

Table 6.24. Origin of Foreign Students by Geographical Regions, 2006

Host Region	Region of Origin									
	World	Arab States	Central and Eastern Europe	Central Asia	East Asia and the Pacific	Latin America and the Caribbean	North America and Western Europe	South and West Asia	Sub-Saharan Africa	Unspecified
Arab States	80,009	29,442	675	269	1,716	160	2,779	1,970	6,572	36,426
Central and eastern Europe	208,101	10,559	82,118	39,168	10,189	396	15,217	7,694	1,689	41,071
Central Asia	51,174	722	9,045	33,951	2,854	4	133	4,448	25	352
East Asia and the Pacific	507,193	9,446	4,437	2,638	333,701	4,385	34,310	50,391	11,277	56,608
Latin America and the Caribbean	36,803	230	61	35	1,329	30,120	2,009	88	1,899	1,032
North America and eastern Europe	1,798,299	136,570	237,743	15,800	457,823	119,008	435,843	164,640	142,827	88,044
South and west Asia	10,620	1,765	72	132	1,622	24	603	3,010	1,539	1,853
Sub-Saharan Africa	62,174	52	50	—	105	2	71	15	39,377	22,502
World	2,754,373	188,786	334,201	91,633	809,339	154,099	490,965	232,256	205,205	247,888

Source: UNESCO (2008, 116–19).

The Latin America and the Caribbean Region appears as the "least internationally mobile" region in the world. Regionally it hosts only 36,803 foreign students, corresponding to a meager 0.23 percent of the regional enrollment, and is in front of only South and West Asia. Only 154,099 students from the region are studying abroad, which corresponds to a regional outward student mobility of only 0.95 percent, putting the Latin America and the Caribbean region behind South and West Asia (1.35 percent). The international student mobility indicators for the Latin America and the Caribbean region are not commensurate with the population and the comparative income level of this region.

6.5. INTERNATIONAL STUDENT MOBILITY AND MIGRATION

That international student mobility is increasingly linked to international migration in the global knowledge economy has been alluded to in previous sections (see Sections 2.2 and 5.3.1). Brain drain takes place when a person with a good education goes abroad, or does not return, and severs ties with the home country, depriving the country of a global asset.[47] In the case of migrant, unskilled, and semi-skilled workers, remittances in most cases more than compensate for the loss in workforce. In fact, for many countries where investments are low and unemployment is high, exporting of unskilled and semi-skilled workers has not only prevented social unrest, but has also been an economic input; many national economies averted potential balance-of-payment crises by workers' remittances; "better brain drain than brains in the drain."[48]

Literature on international migration and education attainment has emerged very recently (Docquier and Marfouk 2006). However, there is still no study on the relationship between international student mobility and international migration. No published information exists, for example, on the numbers of returnees and their contributions to the countries of origin. A crude attempt is presented here, which combines the data presented in this book with those of Docquier and Marfouk (2006).

With the advent of the global knowledge economy, the demand for skilled labor, defined as workers with at least tertiary-level education, has increased. The total number of migrant workers in OECD countries was 41.9 million in 1990, and this number increased to 59 million in 2000. In the same period, the share of migrants with a tertiary education increased from 29.8 percent to 34.6 percent, and those with a secondary education from 25.3 percent to 29.9 percent. On the other hand, the share of migrants with less than secondary education decreased from 44.9 percent to 36.4 percent. The numbers of migrant workers with at least tertiary education in the five major host countries for foreign students, including Canada and New

Zealand, were as follows in 2000 and 1990 (numbers shown in parentheses): the United States 10,354,285 (6,203,045); the United Kingdom 1,256,892 (570,153); Germany 996,000 (555,735); France 614,598 (300,122); Australia 1,539, 670 (1,109,747); Canada 2,742,090 (1,879,495); and New Zealand 232,296 (194,937).

In 2000, 90 percent of the skilled migrants lived in the OECD member countries. The United States, the United Kingdom, Germany, France, Australia, and Canada hosted 50.7 percent, 6.2 percent, 4.9 percent, 3 percent, 7.5 percent, and 13.4 percent of the skilled migrants, respectively. Like all economic flows, labor migration, too, is driven by wage–price differentials. Skilled labor migrates to those countries, where the return on investment in education is greater.[49]

The figures just given clearly show why the internationalization policies of the major host countries for foreign students are increasingly being based on the skilled migration approach. Starting in the 1990s, the United States, Australia, New Zealand, and Canada introduced "quality-selective" immigration policies. These countries are now giving extra points to foreign students who want to stay after they get their degrees. The United Kingdom, France, and Germany, too, have recently introduced programs aimed at attracting a skilled labor force, particularly in ICT (Hira 2003).

It is interesting to note that the major host countries for foreign students are at the same time the leading destination countries for skilled migrant workers. This shows why the possibility to migrate to these countries and the potential for establishing relationships that will eventually evolve into business networks have emerged as rationales for driving international student mobility on the part of the students and families.

Docquier and Marfouk (2006) also have presented data on the top thirty source countries for skilled immigrants. Sixteen of the top twenty-five countries of origin of foreign students shown in Figure 6.5 are also in this list. India is third with 1,037,000 skilled emigrants in 2000. Mexico is fourth with 922,964; China is sixth with 816,824, followed by Korea with 652,894. Poland is tenth with 449,054; Hong Kong is seventeenth with 290,842, followed by Russia with 289,090; Taiwan is nineteenth with 275,251; Ukraine is twenty-second with 246,218; and Turkey is twenty-seventh with 174,043 skilled emigrant workers.

Emigration of skilled workers is not specific to developing countries. In fact, the United Kingdom tops the aforementioned list with 1,441,307 skilled emigrant workers. Germany is fifth with 848,414; Canada is eighth with 516,471; the United States is ninth with 431,330, followed by Italy with 408,287; France is eleventh with 312,494; and Japan is twentieth with 268,925 skilled emigrant workers.

Docquier and Marfouk (2006) define net brain gain as the number of skilled immigrants minus the number of skilled emigrants expressed as a percentage of the population of working age residents in the source country. The brain gain values for the five major host countries for foreign students, including Canada and New Zealand, in 2000 and 1990 (values shown in parentheses) were as follows: Australia 11.4 percent (10 percent); Canada 10.7 percent (8.3 percent); France 0.7 percent (−1.5 percent); Germany 0.2 percent (0.2 percent); New Zealand 2.9 percent (−0.6 percent); UK −0.5 percent (−1.5 percent) and US 5.4 percent (3.6 percent). The brain gain for the original fifteen members of the EU was −0.5 percent in 1990 and −0.1 percent in 2000.

Thus, brain drain is not specific to developing countries; the EU as a whole is also suffering. In fact, it was the negative values quoted here that prompted countries like France, Germany, and the United Kingdom to change their immigration policies as well as their policies toward foreign students in higher education. Migration of skilled labor from the EU to the United States is a major concern. In particular, the vast majority of the European-born doctoral degree holders from United States institutions want to stay there (Labi 2004). There are an estimated 100,000 European-born academics presently working in the United States, and the EU is trying to lure them back (Blumenstyk 2006). Both the Bologna Process and the Lisbon Agenda are partly driven by the desire on the part of the EU member countries to maintain and expand the European skilled workforce base. The pressures by EU leaders for European universities to modernize all stem from concerns that Europe is losing its technological edge against not only the United States, but also Asia (Labi 2006d, 2006e).

The multiway flow of skilled labor among countries is referred to as "brain circulation" or "brain exchange" (Dassin 2005). This occurs primarily among developed countries. The United States is the clear beneficiary and so too are Australia, Canada, and New Zealand. Recent policy changes in Europe, particularly in the United Kingdom, Germany, and France, concerning foreign students and visa and immigration procedures stem from the desire to make up for the losses in skilled workforce bases of these countries.

Regardless of whether it is expressed in terms of actual student numbers or as percentages of regional enrollments, it is quite clear that the main axis of international student mobility in today's global knowledge economy is from the Asia-Pacific Rim to North America and western Europe. Expressed alternatively, the flow is from "knowledge-user" regions to the "knowledge-producer" regions. As shown in this section, this is also the direction of skilled labor force migration.

Overall, this is creating a win–win situation for both regions. The developed countries are benefiting from the skilled human power, and the rapidly developing countries in the Asia-Pacific Rim are expanding their skilled human resources and improving their knowledge and know-how bases by educating their youth in the most advanced higher education systems in the world. Some of them return home and contribute directly to the development of their countries of origin, and some of those who stay make their contributions indirectly through networks and remittances.

Dassin (2005), too, draws attention to the overall positive effects of "brain circulation," whereby the networks, linkages, and strategic alliances formed between expatriate skilled workers with colleagues, institutions, organizations, and companies back home have contributed to development in source countries. OECD (2004b, 280) cites the recent measures taken by China (see Sections 2.1, 3.2, 3.3, and 6.3.1), as an example of policies that have had some success in reversing the flow. China and India, the two leading countries of origin of foreign students, are clearly benefiting from this paradigm shift in brain drain.

As shown in the previous section, Latin America and the Caribbean is the least outwardly mobile region in the world in terms of foreign student flows. Ozden's results imply that immigrants from countries where English is a common language and expenditure on tertiary education is high perform better in the U.S. labor market. Latin American immigrants, on the other hand, largely have very low levels of education. Moreover, even highly educated immigrants from that region are unlikely to obtain skilled jobs (Ozden 2006). Whether this is part of the explanation for the low level of outward student mobility from that region needs further research.

Brain circulation and brain exchange obviously have positive impact on the global economy. However, underdeveloped countries cannot partake in this process, and the situation is particularly acute in Africa. It is shown in the previous section that Sub-Saharan Africa is the most outwardly mobile region in the world in terms of foreign student flows. Regarding the regional distribution of skilled migration, the most affected country is Africa with skilled emigrants accounting for 10.4 percent of the skilled workforce in the region. If small countries and small territories are excluded, Sub-Saharan Africa is also the region with the highest skilled emigration rate of 12.9 percent in 2000 (Docquier and Marfouk 2006). Once again, any attempt to establish a causal relationship between outward student mobility and skilled emigration rates would be no more than a conjecture at this stage.

SEVEN

CONCLUDING REMARKS

Throughout centuries, scholars and students have moved from one place to another in search of new ideas or to spread their philosophy, religious beliefs, political views, and cultural values, better conditions for doing scholarly work and research, better education that would elevate them to higher positions in the society and better paying jobs, and to flee discrimination and persecution. Institutions have at times recruited students for additional income. Rulers have invited and protected scholars and students to stimulate the local economy, to improve the quality of the local workforce and the intellectual level of their courts, or prohibited them from leaving the country in order to protect the local economy. Mobile students and scholars have almost always taken with them forms of organization, structures, manuscripts, textbooks, teaching material, curricula, structures, and forms of organizations and traditions, which have effectively amounted to mobility of institutions and programs across borders and over intercontinental distances. Spreading of the university and other institutions of higher education to outside Europe, and the diffusion of the British, the French, and the German models, and later the American model to other countries, are examples of such mobility.

International academic mobility has contributed to the development of science and rational, critical human thought, which form the core of today's global civilization. The students and scholars moving across borders have carried ideas, ideologies, and cultural values with them, which have led to the emergence of an internationally shared set of values, including, democracy and respect for human rights, freedom of expression, and freedom of enterprise. This common set of values is now an integral component of the global civilization. Regimes predicated on principles, which are irrational and contradictory to these values, have been evanescent episodes in human history.

International academic mobility has contributed to the formation of the global market, both directly and indirectly. Students and scholars moving from one country to another have introduced goods and services developed abroad to their home countries, developing markets for them. In the process, they have developed acquaintances, which, in time, have evolved into R&D networks, both scientific and technological, business partnerships, and new forms of organization for the production of and trade in goods and services.

International academic mobility has historically been driven by the quest for better education for students, better working conditions for scholars, however they are defined, the desire to promote a certain set of cultural values and political norms, and to generate income. The situation is no different today. However, with the transformation from the industrial to the knowledge society and the emergence of the global knowledge economy, two new drivers of international academic mobility have emerged, the skilled migration approach and the strategic alliances approach, and the relative importance of the revenue-generating approach has increased, all with serious foreign policy implications.

The main characteristics of international student mobility in today's global knowledge economy can be summarized as follows:

1. In 2006, there were 2.75 million foreign students worldwide, up from 110,000 in 1950, corresponding to just under 2 percent of the 144 million students enrolled in higher education, up from 6 million in 1950.

2. The five major host countries were the United States, Australia, the United Kingdom, France, and Germany, which together hosted just over 50 percent of the foreign students in the world.

3. China and India are the two leading countries of origin of foreign students. Students from these two countries account for just under 20 percent of the foreign students worldwide.

4. The United States, the United Kingdom, Australia, Canada, and New Zealand are collectively referred to as MESDCs. Together, they hosted just under 50 percent of the foreign students in the world in 2006; the United States alone hosted nearly 20 percent of them. Thus, demand is mainly for Anglo-Saxon, in particular, American type of higher education provided in English.

5. Higher education systems in the MESDCs traditionally are based on variants of what is today referred to as the "entrepreneurial model," which provides the incentives and the decision-making powers for them to be active in the "international higher education market."

6. The number of foreign students is projected to increase, despite expanding indigenous higher education capacities in the major countries of origin and various forms of offshore delivery.

7. The internationalization of higher education in the United States has been traditionally driven by all four major rationales—the cultural-political approach, the revenue-generation approach, the skilled migration approach, and the strategic alliances networking approach. However, internationalization of higher education in the United States in the past has never been led by policies formulated and implemented at the federal level. With increasing competition worldwide, this is now changing.

8. On the other hand, internationalization of higher education in the United Kingdom, Germany, France, and Australia have always been led by policies formulated and implemented at the central governmental level. French and German policies have traditionally been based on the sociopolitical approach. Policies in the United Kingdom, too, have been based on that approach as well as the revenue-generation approach. However, higher education internationalization policies worldwide are increasingly being based on the skilled migration approach.

9. Many of the major countries of origin of foreign students are transforming themselves into host countries. Malaysia, Singapore, Thailand, the Czech Republic, South Africa, Qatar, and Dubai all are aspiring to become regional hubs for international education. After the recent changes in the governance of Japan's national universities and in the face of declining higher education-age population, Japan is pursuing more aggressive foreign student recruitment policies. China is already one of the major host countries.

10. The quest for a better education for a better life always has been the major rationale on the part of the students for seeking education abroad; this still is the case. However, networking has recently emerged as an almost equally powerful rationale.

The world now seems to be heading toward another bipolar conjuncture, this time economic, rather than ideological and political, with a group of countries largely led by the United States, as "knowledge producers" on the one side, and a second group comprising a large number of countries that are "knowledge users." China is emerging as the major hub for manufacturing goods, and India as that for service production. International student mobility in today's global knowledge economy essentially comprises outward student mobility from knowledge users and inward student mobility to knowledge producers, with student flows from China and India to the United States as its main axis.

A student who returns home after completing studies abroad is a major asset for the home country. However, with increasing international competition for the bright, creative young mind, the best educated now have a wide array of employment opportunities practically anywhere in the world.

The bright, creative young mind is already a most sought after asset; its relative importance as a production factor in the global knowledge economy will increase even more. Attracting students from all over the world to institutions of higher education is increasingly becoming a matter of foreign policy in all developed countries, regardless of the country's demographic profile.

The general direction of international student mobility is the same as the general direction of skilled labor migration, from knowledge users to knowledge producers. It is now almost certain that policies and strategies regarding internationalization of higher education at the national, sectoral, and institutional levels will increasingly be linked to immigration policies. The latter are now much more selective for skilled immigrants, meaning those with at least a tertiary-level degree.

Increasingly squeezed between knowledge-producing countries on the one hand and China and India on the other are a large number of countries, which had just made, or were in the process of making, the transition from a national economy based mostly on agriculture to one with relatively larger and export-oriented service and industrial sectors. This group of countries, including Turkey, Thailand, Indonesia, Mexico, and some of the former Communist bloc countries, can be very negatively affected by the loss of highly skilled workforce. These also are the countries in the politically critical regions of the world. It is in the interests of all to address the issue of the asymmetric flow of skilled people. International mobility of students is an area that has the potential of producing creative solutions to this global problem.

Although the integration of capital and commodity markets is fairly advanced at the present, at least among the industrialized and industrializing nations, globalization will remain incomplete in the eyes of the economists if integration of labor markets does not proceed further than where it now stands—way behind commodity and capital markets. Transnational education, in particular, international student mobility, offers many creative possibilities in this respect, too. The following statement by OECD expresses this view as follows (OECD 2004c, p. 22): "The movement of skilled labor across national borders and new competencies produced by student mobility and internationally oriented qualifications can produce huge benefits for the internationalizing professional labor market."

The major stumbling block is the lack of international frameworks for quality assurance and mutual recognition of qualifications for entry into professions in foreign countries. In many countries, including continental Europe, most academic qualifications also serve as professional qualifications. In Anglo-Saxon countries, on the other hand, entry requirements into many professions, in particular health-related professions, some branches of engineering, legal professions, accountancy, and teaching, are set by professional bodies, and, in general, require qualifications above and beyond academic degrees. An international agreement in this area is highly unlikely to be achieved in the conceivably near future. The Washington Accord for the engineering profession, which was developed in 1989, can possibly set an example for future international agreements covering other professions. Current signatories include Australia, Canada, Hong Kong, China, Ireland, New Zealand, South Africa, the United Kingdom, and the United States. Japan was accepted as a provisional member in 2001, and Germany, Malaysia, and Singapore in 2003. The Accord recognizes "substantial equivalence" of each other's programs in satisfying the academic requirements for the practice of engineering, while not yet formally mutually recognizing professional qualifications (OECD 2004c, 38–39).

The interdependent and intertwined relationship between technology, in particular ICT, globalization, and competition has led to the emergence of new forms of providing higher education, and, in terms of absolute numbers, a historically unprecedented volume of international academic mobility. More than half of the increasing demand for transnational higher education is projected to be met by various types of new providers. The use of ICT is likely to increase in the provision of higher education. There also will be more offshore provision all over the world.

The number of students studying abroad at the tertiary level is likely to increase despite increasing domestic opportunities. China and India, in particular, will continue to have significant unmet demand in the conceivably near future, and the growth of the affluent middle class in these two and other countries will keep fueling international student mobility. The data reported in a recent article in The Economist ("Ready for warfare in the aisles," August 5–11, 2006) show that there presently are 191 million urban households in China, and that this number will increase to 373 million in 2025. Moreover, the share of upper-middle class (annual income 40,000–100,000 yuan), which currently accounts for less than 10 percent of the urban households, will increase to more than 60 percent in 2025, with "global" (annual income more than 200,000 yuan) and "mass" affluent (annual income 100,000–200,000 yuan) households making up more than 10 percent of the total in that year.

Past experience shows that international conflicts and economic crises negatively affect international student mobility. Thus, it is likely that the global economic crisis of 2008 may slowdown international student mobility, and may even lead to declining foreign student numbers in the coming years. This may, however, be more than offset by an increase in other forms of transnational provision. We may in fact see an expansion of offshore programs, double- and joint-degree programs globally.

Institutions of higher education, especially universities, instinctively react negatively to bodies superimposed on them. Furthermore, the academic culture in many countries makes it difficult to establish even national systems of quality assurance, because many academics regard it as an infringement on institutional autonomy and academic freedom. Yet, a measure of quality assurance is definitely needed at the international level so that prospective students at least have an idea about the quality of education they are going to get at a considerable cost to them. Rather than aiming at comprehensive and binding international agreements, which seem rather unlikely to achieve, it is probably more prudent and practical to expand the ERIC-NARIC (see Appendix D) system to all countries that want to take part in transnational education. This should be done in a manner that allows students and employers to readily access transparent and easily understood information on all types of providers worldwide.

It is now clear that the inclusion of education in the GATS in the comprehensive manner in which it is presently envisaged is not being received favorably. Many react negatively to what they perceive to be the "commodification" of education. On the other hand, there are obvious benefits to higher education that may accrue from a balanced and fair competition at the international level, which the GATS may provide if its scope is kept within a generally acceptable limit. At this stage, the future of the GATS negotiations looks uncertain. It may be more prudent to restrict the scope of the GATS that pertains to education to vocational certificate programs, and leave out the degree programs if negotiations start. In that case, a quality assurance mechanism must also be built into the GATS structure. The simplest way of doing this may be by authorizing the ERIC-NARIC in each member country to issue the list of providers registered in that country that comply with the recently adopted OECD-UNESCO Guidelines (see Section 5.6).

The academic community has so far been largely excluded from the GATS negotiations. It obviously is prudent to remedy this if negotiations resume.

Transnational higher education and, in particular, international mobility of students and scholars is an area that has the potential to provide many creative contributions to globalization with benefits to all countries. In the period following World War II, the United States was the main beneficiary of international academic mobility, and still stands as the country that will gain the most from its expansion, politically, culturally, economically and with respect to skilled labor. It is, therefore, incumbent on the United States to play a more effective positive role in this field.

National security is a legitimate concern, and the civilized world should stand by the United States in eradicating terrorism of any kind from the face of the earth. However, United States, as the world leader, should avoid the "isolationist trap"; the United States should never take measures that may produce the unintended result of closing its doors to international academic mobility. The United States is an "international nation." The country's leadership role in global affairs is welcomed by many, including the author, who views the U.S. higher education system as the best in the world, and as the most effective asset in its arsenal of soft power. The United States, however, is advised to refrain from taking stands that may be regarded by many, rightly or wrongly, as hegemonic, rather than exhibiting the attributes befitting of the world leader. The subtle difference between leadership and hegemony, if overlooked, can have very negative repercussions for international student mobility.

As pointed out in Section 2.1, presently, 2.8 billion people are under twenty-five years old. By 2015, the global youth population will reach 3 billion, with 2.5 billion of them living in developing countries. Educating the youth to be productive citizens employable in the knowledge-driven global economy is now a major global challenge. According to estimates by the International Labor Organization, some 500 million jobs have to be created within the next decade to absorb this "youth bulge" ("Why jobs are the critical issue," *Financial Times*, January 25, 2006). There is a complementarity here, with a declining workforce in developed countries and increasing youth populations in developing countries. This can produce mutually beneficial results only if the latter can be educated and trained according to the requirements of the global knowledge economy. Turning the youth into productive, "global citizens" is not only economically sound, but will also contribute to global security by minimizing economic disparities.

Technology now makes it possible to tap into labor resources anywhere in the world without displacing people from one cultural environment to another. In the last decade, China and India have made use of the opportunities provided by trends toward outsourcing and offshoring to develop their people's skills and improve their standard of living. The most significant obstacle they face for further growth is the quality of their higher education systems. This is a common problem for many countries in integrating into the global knowledge economy and sharing its benefits.

Medieval Europe gave humanity the university as, in the words of Perkin (2006), "an intellectual estate." The nation states of the nineteenth and twentieth centuries created national higher education systems, which educated the public servants for state bureaucracies, trained the workforce for the industrial society, and provided opportunities to masses for upward social mobility. The interdependent effects of globalization, technology and competition are now changing lifestyles, forms of social and economic organization and reshaping all aspects of international relations. A global higher education market has emerged that provides a much wider array of choices to today's e-literate youth, the children of parents educated in the past century's massified national higher education systems. The best and the brightest of today's higher education age cohort want and now have opportunities to study in the world's best universities as creative young minds are the most sought after commodity in the global knowledge economy. Thus, there is a complementarity and interdependence that has already created a league of "global universities," and has the potential to evolve into a "global higher education complex" to educate and train the workforce of the global knowledge economy.

Higher education worldwide is now a "global business." It will become even more so in the near future, and competition will become even fiercer. Traditional institutions will have to compete with not only traditional institutions in their own countries, but with those in other countries, and with the new types of providers across the globe.

No country should be disenfranchised from the process of globalization. Education at the tertiary level plays a key role in being an active member of the global knowledge economy, both for individuals and for countries. Ensuring that all peoples feel that they can access the opportunities that exist in transnational higher education is a means to that end. If certain groups of peoples feel unwanted and excluded, they will be susceptible to incursions by rogue elements that are hostile to global peace and security. There are already signs of that occurring in the Middle East, where certain types of institutions and providers are making inroads into transnational higher education.

APPENDIX A

DATA ON ENROLLMENT AND EXPENDITURES IN NATIONAL SYSTEMS AND INTERNATIONAL STUDENT MOBILITY

Table A.1. Characteristics of National Higher Education Systems, Enrollment

Country	Enrollment		GER, %			% 5B 2006	% PRVT[a] 2006
	2004	2006	1999	2004	2006		
China	19,417,044	23,361,000	6	19	22	46	9[b](9)
U.S.	15,312,289[c]	16,611,711[c]	73	82	82	39[c]	27[c]
India	11,295,041	12,853,000	7[d]	11	12	nd	60[d](31)
Russian Federation	8,622,097	9,167,000	nd	68	72	21	15 (15)
Japan	4,091,016[c]	4,091,013[c]	45	54	57	28[e]	80[c](77)
Brazil	3,582,105	4,572,000	14	20	25	5	72 (73)
Indonesia	3,441,429	3,657,000	nd	16	17	26	64 (71)
Korea	3,223,431	3,204,000	66	89	93	37	78 (78)
Ukraine	2,465,074	2,819,000	47	66	76	17	12[f](12)
Philippines	2,427,211	2,484,000	29	29	28	10	67 (75)
Thailand	2,251,453	2,504,000	32	41	50	15	13 (14)
UK	2,369,005[g]	2,469,895[g]	60	60	59	5[g]	100 (<1)[g]
Mexico	2,236,791	2,447,000	18	22	26	3	34 (34)
France	2,256,200[h]	2,283,300[h]	52	56	56	19[h]	13
Egypt	2,153,865	2,594,000	36	29	35	nd	17
Turkey[i]	1,946,422	2,342,898	27	34	43	29	5
Argentina	2,026,735	2,083,000	49	61	64	26	45[j](17)
Italy	1,986,497	2,029,000	47	63	67	1	7 (6)
Poland	1,983,360	2,146,000	44	59	66	1	31 (30)
Iran	1,954,920	2,829,000	19	22	31	26	54[f]
Germany	2,019,465[k]	1,985,765[k]	45	48	nd	15	4 (4)
Spain	1,839,903	1,789,000	55	66	67	13	12
Nigeria	1,289,656	1,392,000	7	10	10	47	nd
Canada	1,192,570	1,327,000	59	57	62	24	nd

Colombia	1,112,574	1,373,000	22	27	32	18	55^i (52)
Taiwan^l	1,299,385	1,317,340	nd	nd	79	44	70^l (72)
Venezuela	983,217	1,381,000	nd	39	52	36	27^l(41)
Australia	944,977^m	984,061^m	66	72	73	5^m	3^m
Bangladesh	877,335	1,054,000	6	7	7	9	58^l (14)
Vietnam	845,313	1,355,000	11	10	16	30	1 (10)
Peru	831,000	952,000	nd	32	35	40	50 (48)
South Africa	717,793	741,000	14	15	15	36	(9)
Algeria	716,422	902,000	14	16	24	10	—
Kazakhstan	664,440	723,000	25	48	51	nd	(47)
Romania	643,911	835,000	22	36	52	3	27 (23)
Malaysia	632,309	697,000	23	29	29	40	29 (39)
Saudi Arabia	573,732	636,000	20	28	30	15	7^f
Chile	567,114	661,000	38	43	47	33	76 (73)
Greece	561,468	653,000	47	72	95	37	—
Myanmar	555,060	nd	nd	11	nd	nd	nd
Netherlands^n	526,767	580,000	50	58	60	—^n	100^m
Pakistan	520,066	955,000	nd	3	5	5	12^f (23)
Belarus	507,360	557,000	52	61	69	27	(15)
Sweden	414,657	423,000	64	82	79	5	6
Iraq	412,545	425,000	11	15	16	17	6^f
Uzbekistan	407,582	289,000	nd	15	10	40	—
Portugal	400,831	367,000	45	56	55	1	25 (26)
Hungary	390,453	439,000	33	52	69	6	14 (14)
Belgium	386,110	394,000	56	63	63	52	58
Bolivia	346,056	346,000	33	41	41	nd	(28)
Morocco	343,599	369,000	9	11	11	24	5^f
Israel	301,326	310,000	48	57	58	18	82 (13)
Finland	291,664	309,000	82	87	93	nd	10

continued on next page

Table A.1. (Continued)

Country	Enrollment		GER, %			% 5B200 6	% PRVT* 2006
	2004	2006	1999	2004	2006		
Czech Republic	287,001	338,000	26	37	50	10	8 (9)
Tunisia	263,414	325,000	17	26	31	19	—
Cuba	235,297	865,000	20	33	109	nd	—
Bulgaria	230,513	243,000	46	41	46	10	15 (16)
Austria	229,802	253,000	54	49	50	9	11
Norway	212,395	215,000	66	80	78	1	13
Kyrgyzstan	205,224	239,000	25	48	43	nd	(7)
Denmark	201,746	229,000	56	67	80	12	2
Switzerland	195,947	205,000	38	47	46	17	8
New Zealand[o]	267,264	270,496	67	72	80	50	14 (9)
Jordan	186,189	220,000	nd	35	39	12	28
Ireland	181,557	186,000	45	55	59	29	8 (7)
Lithuania	167,606	190,000	44	69	76	29	4 (8)
Slovakia	158,089	198,000	26	34	45	1	4 (5)
Hong Kong	155,761	158,000	nd	32	34	46	3[f]
Georgia	155,058	141,000	36	41	37	nd	19[f] (19)
Lebanon	154,635	187,000	36	48	52	14	49[f]
Nepal	147,123	147,000	nd	6	6	nd	nd
Singapore[r]	119,165	140,002	nd	87	85	63	6[c]
Moldova	126,885	148,000	29	32	41	15	20[c] (20)
Azerbaijan	122,770	135,000	15	15	15	nd	14[f]
Croatia	121,722	137,000	31	39	44	33	(3)
El Salvador	120,264	125,000	18	19	21	13	(65)
Ethiopia	172,111	210,000	1	2	3	nd	23[f] (24)

Paraguay	156,000	146,892	13	26	26	10	57 (41)
Honduras	123,000	122,874	14	16	17	9[f]	(20)
Palestine	169,000	121,928	25	38	46	10	58[f]
Latvia	131,000	118,944	50	71	74	14	27 (27)
Mongolia	142,000	108,738	26	39	48	3	32[f] (26)
Kenya	103,000	108,407	nd	3	3	34	(9)
Tajikistan	147,000	108,406	13	16	20	nd	—
Slovenia	115,000	101,458	53	70	83	45	1 (3)
Uruguay	113,000	98,520	34	38	46	24[f]	16[f] (21)
Uganda	88,000	88,360	2	3	3	36	10[f]
Cameroon	120,000	83,909	5	5	7	12	3[f]
Armenia	112,000	79,321	24	26	36	nd	28[f] (27)
Ghana	140,000	69,968	nd	3	6	26	(6)
UAE	77,000	68,182	19	22	23	28	nd
Estonia	68,000	63,625	51	64	65	34	14 (21)
Zimbabwe	nd	55,689	3	4	nd	59	10[f]
Senegal	59,000	52,282	3	5	6	nd	21[f]
Jamaica	nd	45,770	nd	19	nd	56[f]	28[f]
Macedonia	49,000	45,624	22	27	30	6[f]	5 (8)
Cambodia	92,000	45,370	nd	3	5	nd	43[f]
Tanzania	51,000	42,948	1	1	1	17	nd
Madagascar	58,000	42,143	2	3	3	25	8[n]
Oman	69,000	33,807	nd	13	25	12	29[f] (25)
Laos	57,000	33,760	2	6	9	53	22[f]
Mali	51,000	25,803	2	2	4	5[5]	nd
Rwanda	26,000	25,233	1	3	3	35	43[f]
Macao	24,000	24,815	27	69	57	13	67[f]
Mozambique	28,000	22,256	1	1	1	nd	32[f]

continued on next page

Table A.1. (Continued)

Country	Enrollment		GER, %			% 5B200 6	% PRVT* 2006
	2004	2006	1999	2004	2006		
Burkina Faso	18,868	33,000	nd	2	3	24	nd
Cyprus	18,272	21,000	21	32	33	76	—
Mauritius	17,781	17,000	7	17	17	43	nd
Burundi	15,706	17,000	1	2	2	64	32[f]
Iceland	13,342	16,000	40	62	73	2	19
Congo	12,456	nd	4	4	nd	15	8
Namibia	11,788	13,000	nd	6	6	39	nd
Malta	8,946	9,000	20	30	32	14	—
Niger	8,744	11,000	nd	1	1	20	25
Qatar	8,648	9,000	25	18	16	24	nd
World	131,999,450	143,880,000	18	24	25	22	31.5[q]

Note: Unless noted otherwise, data shown in Table A.1 for the years 1999 and 2004 are from UNESCO (2006) and those for the year 2006 are from UNESCO (2008).

[a] Numbers in parentheses show shares of private institutions estimated by PROPHE on the basis of total enrollment in higher education institutions in the period 2001–2007. Data were retrived on March 5, 2009 from www.albany.edu/dept/eaps/prophe/data/international_DATA/PROPHEDataSummaryJAN08.doc.

[b] Value shown is for the year 2001 (Min 2004).

[c] Chronicle of Higher Education Almanac 2003–2004; Chronicle of Higher Education Almanac 2005–2006. Enrollment in 2007 and 2008 were 17,272,044 (Chronicle of Higher Education Almanac 2006–2007) and 17,758,870 (Chronicle of Higher Education Almanac 2007–2008), respectively

[d] OECD (2004a).

[e] Enrollment values for Japan are from: http://www.mext.go.jp/english/statist/, retrieved on March 5, 2009. The lates value available is for the year 2005. Values shown do not include students enrolled in correspondence courses. Total enrollment in such courses was 284,087 in 2005. Shares of 5B programs and private institutions are based on enrollment values that include the latter category of students. GER values shown do not include students enrolled in specialized training colleges; when that category of students are also included, GER value for Japan in 2005 becomes 78 percent (see Figure 1.3.4 on p. 10 in "School Education 2006" by the Ministry of Education, Culture, Sports, Science and Technology).

[f] Value shown is from UNESCO (2004).

[a]Enrollment values for the United Kingdom are from www.hesa.ac.uk/index.php?option=com_datatables&itemid=121&task=show_category&catdex=3, retrieved on March 3, 2009. GER values are from UNESCO (2006, 2008). It should be noted that the shares of ISCED 5B and ISCED 6 programs reported by UNESCO are 22 percent and 4 percent, respectively. Both of these values are vastly different from the values shown based on HESA data. The latest enrollment value available is 2,469,895 for 2007. The only private university in the United Kingdom is Buckingham University. However, many, including PROPHE and UNESCO (2006), consider British universities to be of government-dependent private institutions as indicated in the table.

[b]Enrollment values for France are from http://mediaenseignmentsup_recherche.gouv.fr/file/53/3/2153.pdf and www.education.gouv.fr. Share of ISCED 5B programs was calculated from these data. The latest enrollment value available is 2,254,386 for 2007, retrieved on March 4, 2009.

[c]Enrollment values shown for Turkey are from the Higher Education Statistics for the years 2004 and 2006, annually published by the Student Selection and Placement Center, Ankara. The most recent enrollment value is 2,532,622 for 2008. Shares of ISCED 5B programs and private institutions were calculated from these data. GER values are from Barblan et al. (2008).

[j]Based on university enrollment alone shown in UNESCO (2008).

[k]Enrollment values for Germany are from http://www.wissenschaft-weltbffen.de/. The latest value available is 1,979,043 for the year 2007, retrieved on March 4, 2009.

[l]Enrollment values include students in the two open universities, and are from "Education in Taiwan 2008" by the Ministry of Education available at http://english.education.edu.tw/public/data. The latest enrollment figure available is 1,326,029 for the year 2008. GER for 2006 is from Yung (2008). The percentage of enrollment and in 5B programs and is for the year 2001–2002 from Wang (2003), who gives the total enrollment in that year as 1,008,241.

[m]Enrollment data for Australia are from www.dest.gov.au, retrieved on March 3, 2009. Share of ISCED 5B programs and private institutions are based on these data, and are different from the values reported in UNESCO (2006, 2008). GER data are from UNESCO (2006, 2008). The most recent enrollment figure available from DEST is 1,029,846 for 2007.

[n]The most recent enrollment figures available from NUFFIC are 571,750 and 584,978 for the years 2007 and 2008 respectively, retrieved from: www.nuffic.nl on March 5, 2009. The share of universities of applied sciences (HBOs) was 64 percent in 2008. However, both the HBOs and the universities now offer bachelor-level degrees in compliance with the requirements of the Bologna Process. Thus, enrollment in the HBOs can no longer be considered as ISCED 5B enrollment. This argument is also valid for the Fachhochschulen in Germany. Dutch private universities are of the government-dependent type, and there is little difference in their funding compared to public universities. According to UNESCO (2006), all Dutch universities are private, while all HBOs are public institutions.

[o]Enrollment values shown are Equivalent Full-Time Students (EFTS) obtained from www.educationcounts.govt.nz. Corresponding actual student numbers for 2004 and 2006 are 485,934 and 491,018 respectively. The most recent enrollment value available is 483,743 (269,406 EFTS) for the year 2007, retrieved on March 3, 2009. Private share and ISCED 5B share values were calculated from the indicated enrollment data, and are significantly different from those shown in UNESCO (2008). GER values are from UNESCO (2006, 2008).

[p]Enrollment values shown for Singapore are from www.moe.gov.sg/education/education-statistics-diges/esd-2008.pdf and www.moe.gov.sg/factsheet-2008.pdf. GER values are net enrollment ratios based on student intake. Shares of enrollment in ISCED 5B programs and private institutions were estimated from the data in these Web sites.

[q]UNESCO (2003a).

GER, gross enrollment ratio; %5B, percentage of students in ISCED 5B-level programs; nd, no data available; -, negligible; %PRVT, share of private institutions based on student enrollment.

Table A.2. Institutional Expenditure per Student, $ (ppp)

Country	1990	1995	1998	2000	2001	2002	2003	2004	2005
U.S.	nd	20,207	19,802	20,358	22,234	20,545	24,074	22,476	24,370
Germany	8,459	9,698	9,481	10,898	10,504	10,999	11,594	12,255	12,946
Australia	9,288	13,897	11,539	12,854	12,688	12,416	12,406	14,036	14,579
UK	9,805	10,981	9,699	9,657	10,753	11,822	11,866	11,484	13,506
Brazil	nd	nd	14,618	11,946	nd	10,361	10,054	9,019	9,994
Bulgaria	nd	nd	nd	nd	nd	nd	nd	nd	4,242
Czech Republic	nd	8,785	5,584	5,431	5,555	6,236	6,774	6,752	6,649
Denmark	nd	11,499	9,562	11,981	14,280	15,183	14,014	15,225	14,959
Finland	7,070	10,900	7,327	8,244	10,981	11,768	12,047	12,505	12,285
France	6,601	7,801	7,226	8,373	8,837	9,276	10,704	10,668	10,995
Indonesia	nd	nd	6,840	1,799	1,414	1,296	nd	nd	nd
India	nd	nd	nd	1,831	2,522	2,486	nd	nd	3,601
Latvia	nd	nd	nd	nd	nd	nd	nd	nd	3,582
Lithuania	nd	nd	nd	nd	nd	nd	nd	nd	4,592
Romania	nd	nd	nd	nd	nd	nd	nd	nd	2,655
Spain	3,696	5,654	5,038	6,666	7,455	8,020	8,943	9,378	10,089
Sweden	nd	nd	13,224	15,097	15,186	15,715	16,073	16,218	15,946
Switzerland	16,022	15,802	16,583	18,450	20,230	23,714	25,900	21,996	21,734
Israel	nd	nd	10,765	11,550	11,494	11,295	11,945	11,289	10,919
Italy	7,300	5,621	6,295	8,065	8,347	8,636	8,764	7,723	8,026
Iceland	nd	nd	nd	7,994	7,674	8,251	8,023	8,881	10,468
Japan	nd	9,691	9,871	10,814	11,164	11,716	11,556	12,193	12,326
Canada	11,662	nd	14,579	14,983	nd	nd	16,937	nd	nd
Korea	nd	nd	6,356	6,118	6,618	6,047	7,089	7,068	7,606
Hungary	nd	7,767	5,073	3,223	7,122	8,205	8,576	7,723	6,244

Malta	nd	nd	nd	nd	nd	nd	nd	nd	6,042
Mexico	4,463	4,821	3,800	4,698	4,341	6,074	5,774	5,778	6,402
Portugal	nd	4,664	nd	4,766	5,199	6,960	7,200	7,741	8,787
Russia	nd	nd	nd	892	nd	nd	2,451	2,562	3,421
Slovenia	nd	nd	nd	nd	nd	nd	nd	nd	8,573
Chile	nd	nd	5,897	7,483	6,901	7,023	7,011	6,873	6,620
Turkey	2,696	nd	nd	4,121	3,950	4,267	4,248	4,231	5,598
New Zealand	nd	nd	nd	nd	nd	nd	8,832	8,866	10,262
Greece	nd	3,264	4,157	3,402	4,280	4,731	4,924	5,593	6,130
OECD (ct)	nd	nd	11,720	11,109	12,319	13,343	14,530	14,027	15,559

Sources: OECD (1995)–OECD (2008, Table B1.1a); Turkey 2006: Barblan et al. (2008).

ct, OECD country total average; nd, no data.

Table A.3. Share of Private Sources in Higher Education Expenditures, %

Country	1995	2001	2002	2003	2004	2005
U.S.	62.6	66.0	54.9	57.2	64.6	65.3
Australia	35.2	48.7	51.3	52.0	52.8	52.2
Austria	3.9	5.4	8.4	7.3	6.3	7.1
Argentina	nd	31.5	35.7	nd	nd	nd
Belgium	nd	15.9	14.0	13.3	9.6	9.4
UK	20.0	29.0	28.0	29.8	30.4	33.1
Czech Republic	28.5	14.7	12.5	16.7	15.3	18.8
Denmark	0.6	2.2	2.1	3.3	3.3	3.3
Estonia	nd	nd	nd	nd	nd	30.1
Finland	2.2	3.5	3.7	3.6	3.7	3.9
France	nd	14.4	14.3	18.7	16.1	10.3
Germany	11.4	8.7	8.4	12.9	13.6	nd
Indonesia	nd	56.2	56.2	nd	nd	nd
India	nd	0.2	22.2	nd	nd	nd
Jamaica	nd	56.5	59.9	nd	nd	nd
Spain	25.6	24.5	23.7	23.1	24.1	22.1
Israel	40.8	43.2	46.6	40.7	50.4	51.3
Italy	17.1	22.2	21.4	27.9	30.6	30.4
Iceland	nd	5.0	4.4	11.3	9.1	8.8
Ireland	30.3	15.3	14.2	16.2	17.4	16.0
Japan	54.8	56.9	58.5	60.3	58.8	66.3
Canada	43.4	41.4	nd	43.6	nd	44.9
Korea	nd	84.1	85.1	76.8	79.0	75.7
Norway	6.3	3.1	3.7	3.3	nd	nd
Hungary	19.7	22.4	21.3	21.5	21.0	21.5
Netherlands	19.4	21.8	21.9	21.4	22.4	22.4
Paraguay	nd	40.9	54.3	nd	nd	nd
Peru	nd	43.0	63.6	nd	nd	nd
Philippines	nd	66.9	nd	nd	nd	nd
Mexico	22.6	29.6	29.0	30.9	31.1	31.9
Portugal	3.5	7.7	8.7	8.5	14.0	31.9
Poland	nd	nd	30.3	31.0	nd	26.0
Slovakia	4.6	6.7	14.8	13.8	18.7	22.7
Sweden	6.4	12.3	10.0	11.0	11.6	11.8
Slovenia	nd	nd	nd	nd	24.3	23.5
Chile	74.5	80.4	83.0	84.2	84.5	84.1
Thailand	nd	17.5	nd	nd	nd	nd
Turkey	3.7	4.2	3.9	4.0	10.0	nd
New Zealand	nd	nd	37.5	38.5	39.2	40.3
Greece	nd	0.4	0.4	2.6	2.1	2.9
OECD (cm)	nd	21.8	21.9	23.6	24.3	26.9

Sources: OECD (1995; 2008, Table 3.2b).

cm, OECD country mean average; nd, no data.

Table A.4. Share of Households in Higher Education Expenditures, %

Country	1995	2001	2002	2003	2004	2005
U.S.	nd	33.9	38.9	36.7	35.1	36.1
Australia	20.0	31.0	33.7	34.6	35.6	36.3
Austria	3.9	4.1	6.8	5.9	4.8	5.5
Argentina	nd	27.7	27.3	nd	nd	nd
Belgium	nd	6.0	9.4	8.6	5.1	5.0
UK	nd	17.3	16.6	18.5	19.4	24.6
China	nd	21.0[a]	nd	nd	nd	nd
Czech Republic	3.3	7.7	7.4	7.3	9.2	9.4
Denmark	0.6	2.2	2.1	3.3	3.3	3.3
Estonia	nd	nd	nd	nd	nd	26.9
France	11.8	10.3	10.1	11.8	9.8	10.3
Germany	7.1	nd	nd	nd	nd	nd
Indonesia	nd	49.4	49.4	nd	nd	nd
India	nd	0.2	22.2	nd	nd	nd
Jamaica	nd	50.0	51.7	nd	nd	nd
Jordan	nd	52.0	nd	nd	nd	nd
Spain	19.4	21.5	20.2	19.4	20.8	18.7
Israel	24.3	28.0	33.2	29.6	35.4	34.9
Italy	12.7	16.0	15.7	18.9	18.4	18.0
Iceland	nd	5.0	4.4	11.3	9.1	8.8
Japan	58.0	56.9	58.5	60.3	nd	53.4
Canada	16.7	22.9	nd	20.6	nd	22.3
Korea	nd	58.1	63.8	56.7	55.6	52.1
Hungary	4.8	6.1	5.4	5.3	6.6	6.9
Malaysia	nd	7.0[a]	—	nd	nd	nd
Paraguay	nd	40.9	54.3	nd	nd	nd
Peru	nd	42.0	63.6	nd	nd	nd
Mexico	22.6	28.9	28.5	30.4	30.6	30.6
Poland	nd	17.0[a]	30.3	31.0	nd	26.0
Portugal	3.5	nd	8.7	8.5	14.0	23.4
Slovakia	nd	9.1	6.7	6.0	9.7	9.1
Slovenia	nd	nd	nd	nd	17.3	17.2
Chile	nd	77.8	81.4	83.3	83.7	83.0
Thailand	nd	17.5	nd	nd	nd	nd
Turkey	3.0	4.2	9.9	4.8	10.0	nd
New Zealand	nd	nd	37.5	38.5	39.2	40.3
Greece	nd	0.4	0.4	0.4	0.4	0.4
OECD (cm)	nd	17.1	18.5	nd	nd	nd

Sources: OECD (1995, 2008, Table B3.2b)

[a]Household expenditure shares for China, Malaysia, and Poland are for 1999, quoted in OECD (2004b, 27).

cm, OECD country mean average; nd, no data.

Table A.5. Tuition Fees in Various Countries for Bachelor-Level Programs in Public Institutions, US$ (ppp)

Country	Public			Dual Track
	Low	Medium	High	
Australia (2005, 2004 ppp)	3,500	5,000	5,850	9,500
Austria (2002–2003, 2003 ppp)	800	800	800	na
Canada (2003–2004, 2004 ppp)	1,460	3,170	4,375	na
China (2004–2005, 2003 ppp)	1,640	2,960	3,820	na
Ethiopia (2003–2004, 2003 ppp)	1,559[a]	1,559	1,559	na
Hong Kong (2002–2003, 2002 ppp)	6,060	6,060	6,060	na
Hungary (2000–2001)	0		0	2,400
India (2001–2002, 2002 ppp)	20[b]	85[c]	37[d]	na
Japan (2005, 2004 ppp)	4,060	4,060	4,500	na
Korea (2000–2001, 2000 ppp)	195	1,404	2,927	na
Mexico (1999–2000, 1999 ppp)	178	535	1,159	na
Mongolia (2002–2003, 2002 ppp)	1,125	1,125	1,688	na
Netherlands (2002–2003, 2004 ppp)	1,520	1,520	1,520	Set by institutions
Russia (1999–2000, 1999 ppp)	0	0	0	405
Scotland (2004–2005, 2004 ppp)	3,485	3,485	3,485	na
Singapore (2005–2006, 2003 ppp)	1,340	3,875	4,800	na
South Africa (2004, 2003 ppp)	4,500	7,000	9,300	na
UK (2005–2006, 2004 ppp)	0	1,000	1,900	na

U.S. (2004–2005)	4,350	9,000	12,400	na
Vietnam (2002–2003, 2002 ppp)	0	0	0	410–683

Sources: Johnstone (2006); Marcucci and Johnstone (2007).

[a]Deferred payment; includes room and board and health care as well as tuition.
[b]Central university.
[c]State university.
[d]University or government college.
[e]No tuition fees charged when residual family income is below 22,000 pounds. Some tuition fees charged when income is between 22,010 and 32,742 pounds. Full tuition fees charged when income is above 32,745 pounds.

na, not applicable.

Table A.6. International Student Mobility

Country	Students Hosted				Students Abroad			
	2002	2004	2006 No.	2006 %	2002	2004	2006 No.	2006 %
U.S.[a]	582,996	572,509	564,766	3.4	160,920	191,321	241,791	1.5
UK	242,655[b]	300,050[b]	330,075[h]	13.4	27,715	23,542	16,006	0.6
Germany[c]	206,141	246,136	248,357	12.5	58,700	66,500	75,800	3.8
France	196,748[d]	244,335[d]	265,039[d]	11.6	50,593	53,350	54,046	2.4
Australia	193,337[e]	235,131[e]	279,989[e]	28.5	5,397	6,434	9,833	1.0
Japan[f]	95,550	117,302	117,927	2.9	62,744	60,424	60,225	1.5
China	85,829[g]	110,844[g]	162,695[g]	0.7	181,200	343,126	417,351	1.8
Russia	70,735	75,786	77,438	0.8	25,671	34,473	41,101	0.4
Canada	110,312[h]	127,736[h]	131,269[h]	9.9	35,808	38,847	43,174	3.3
Spain	44,860	15,051	18,206	1.0	26,664	25,691	23,395	1.3
Belgium	40,354	37,103	24,854	6.3	10,407	10,729	10,332	2.6
Switzerland	29,301	35,705	28,016	13.7	8,213	9,545	10,052	4.9
Austria	28,452	31,101	39,329	15.5	12,196	11,679	9,950	3.9
Italy	28,447	40,641	49,090	2.4	41,391	38,544	32,950	1.6
Sweden	22,859	32,469	21,315	5.0	15,260	13,392	13,652	3.2
Netherlands	18,888	20,531	27,037	4.7	11,896	11,440	10,345	1.8
New Zealand	40,825[i]	50,442[i]	42,652[i]	8.7	7,275	6,513	7,355	1.5
Ukraine	17,210	15,622	29,614	1.1	19,723	25,138	25,866	0.9
Malaysia[j]	16,480	27,731	40,029	6.3	37,809	40,884	45,195	7.1
Turkey	16,328[k]	15,298[k]	16,059[k]	0.7	47,382	52,048	34,816	1.4
South Africa	15,494	49,979	53,738	7.3	5,669	5,619	6,638	0.9
Lebanon	15,186	13,930	22,674	12.1	7,853	11,286	12,363	6.6
Denmark	14,480	18,120	12,182	5.3	6,509	6,318	5,374	2.3
Macao	13,080	14,627	11,939	49.7	735	853	1,027	4.3

Romania	11,869	9,730	8,587	1.0	16,332	20,680	21,307	2.6
Hungary	11,783	12,226	14,491	3.3	7,713	7,750	7,160	1.6
Kyrgyzstan	11,291	16,249	27,205	11.4	2,760	3,072	3,512	1.5
Portugal	10,998	15,483	17,077	4.6	11,251	11,213	9,946	2.7
Cuba	10,700	13,705	26,889	3.1	1,061	1,131	1,154	0.1
Czech Republic	9,753	10,338	21,395	6.3	6,012	6,666	7,042	2.1
Ireland	9,206	10,201	12,740	6.8	15,185	17,570	20,254	10.9
Greece	8,615	12,456	16,558	2.5	50,593	49,631	35,033	5.4
Iraq	8,280	3,557	3,557	0.8	2,371	3,134	4,702	1.1
Bulgaria	8,100	8,025	9,361	3.8	17,738	24,619	25,156	10.4
Latvia	7,917	2,390	1,677	1.2	3,072	3,730	3,524	2.7
India	7,791	7,738	7,589	0.06	87,978	123,559	139,459	1.1
Norway	7,679	11,060	14,297	6.6	15,826	14,732	12,943	6.0
Saudi Arabia	7,567	12,199	13,687	2.1	7,831	9,318	11,416	1.8
Poland	7,401	7,608	11,365	0.5	22,333	28,786	30,808	1.4
Finland	6,760	7,361	11,514	3.7	9,868	9,719	6,096	2.0
Kazakhstan	5,982	8,690	11,961	1.7	23,055	27,356	27,858	3.9
Korea	4,956	7,843	22,260	0.7	84,001	95,885	101,913	3.2
Chile	4,883	5,211	1,966	0.3	5,346	5,873	6,162	0.9
Morocco	4,502	6,393	7,029	1.9	50,637	51,503	41,879	11.3
Jordan	4,363	15,816	21,509	9.8	5,646	6,942	8,783	4.0
Thailand	4,092	4,092	nd	nd	22,498	23,727	24,082	1.0
Palestine	4,069	nd	nd	nd	nd	6,875	8,166	4.8
Tajikistan	3,910	2,208	2,829	1.9	1,018	2,233	2,667	1.8
Argentina	3,349	3,261	nd	nd	7,319	8,485	7,934	0.4
Philippines	2,609	4,744	5,136	0.2	5,708	6,974	7,916	0.3
Belarus	2,601	2,428	4,423	0.8	8,181	10,490	12,365	2.2
Tunisia	2,487	2,265	2,338	0.7	10,589	13,983	16,163	5.0
Cyprus	2,472	5,282	5,309	25.3	13,581	17,381	19,081	90.8
Hong Kong	2,355	3,270	6,274	4.0	29,769	34,199	33,598	21.3
Azerbaijan	2,224	1,991	4,286	3.2	5,804	4,202	4,463	3.3

continued on next page

Table A.6. Continued

Country	Students Hosted				Students Abroad			
	2002	2004	2006 No.	2006 %	2002	2004	2006 No.	2006 %
Uruguay	2,100	2,100	nd	nd	1,470	1,873	1,990	1.8
Mexico	1,892	1,892	nd	nd	18,325	21,661	24,441	1.0
Qatar	1,645	1,633	2,487	27.6	1,345	1,105	1,435	15.9
Slovakia	1,641	1,651	1,161	0.6	11,281	14,581	22,338	11.3
Iran	1,304	1,791	2,092	0.07	14,761	17,254	19,720	0.7
Taiwan[l]	nd	7,844	11,035	0.8	32,991	32,525	37,171	2.8
Indonesia	377	432	nd	nd	36,086	31,687	33,904	0.9
Singapore	nd	nd	72,000[m]	51.4	25,078	20,725	20,322	14.5
Brazil	nd	1,260	1,117	0.02	16,362	19,619	19,978	0.4
Algeria	nd	4,677	5,709	0.6	16,136	24,356	23,680	2.6
Pakistan	nd	nd	nd	nd	15,505	18,639	23,795	2.5
Colombia	nd	nd	nd	nd	14,058	16,090	16,290	1.2
Kenya	nd	nd	nd	nd	12,582	14,123	13,879	13.5
Cameroon	nd	1,529	1,606	1.3	11,092	15,129	15,897	13.2
Serbia	nd	nd	nd	nd	10,867	10,038	nd	nd
Vietnam	nd	1,048	2,053	0.2	10,560	15,817	23,160	1.7
Nigeria	nd	nd	nd	nd	9,316	15,138	21,697	1.6
Bangladesh	nd	nd	939	0.09	9,258	13,156	18,687	1.8
Croatia	nd	2,836	1,414	1.0	9,102	9,955	5,499	4.0
Sri Lanka	nd	nd	nd	nd	8,538	9,203	11,266	nd
Israel	nd	nd	nd	nd	8,531	11,974	12,149	3.9
Venezuela	nd	2,472	2,472	0.2	8,022	9,569	9,088	0.7
Albania	nd	nd	483	0.9	7,943	13,214	17,387	32.8
Peru	nd	nd	nd	nd	7,747	9,715	10,517	1.1
Egypt	nd	nd	nd	nd	6,215	6,545	7,244	0.3

Luxembourg	nd	1,137	37.9	nd	6,743	7,041	234.7
Zimbabwe	nd	nd	nd	5,702	16,609	15,940	29.9
Ghana	nd	1,899	1.4	5,275	8,148	8,064	5.8
Lithuania	nd	857	0.5	5,203	6,926	6,793	3.6
Jamaica	nd	nd	nd	4,841	6,833	6,326	14.9
Syria	nd	nd	nd	4,407	10,385	13,211	nd
Georgia	1,056	428	0.3	4,262	6,676	7,538	5.3
Kuwait	nd	nd	nd	4,132	4,959	5,459	14.4
Uzbekistan	nd	148	0.05	3,784	17,163	30,561	10.6
Senegal	nd	nd	nd	nd	11,709	11,696	19.8
Congo	nd	nd	nd	3,514	4,556	4,491	36.6
Armenia	nd	4,239	3.8	nd	2,768	3,746	3.3
Somalia	nd	nd	nd	726	1,139	1,235	nd
Niger	nd	167	1.5	577	1,105	2,123	19.3
Iceland	nd	715	4.5	2,948	3,007	2,429	15.2
World Total	2,108,671			2,455,250	2,754,373		

Note: Unless otherwise noted, by superscripts, the number of students hosted by and the number of students abroad from the countries included are from UNESCO (2004, 2006, 2008), for the years 2002, 2004, and 2006, respectively.

[a] www.opendoors.iienetwork.org accessed on March 7, 2009.

[b] www.hesa.ac.uk accessed on March 3, 2009.

[c] www.wissenschaft-weltoffen.de accessed on March 7, 2009. The value for German students abroad shown under the year 2006 is for the year 2005.

[d] http://media.education.gouv.fr/file/42/6/2426.pdf accessed on March 8, 2009.

[e] http://aei.gov.au/AEI/Statistics/StudentEnrolmentAndVisaStatistics;www.universitiesaustralia.edu; www.idp.com/research/fast_facts/higher_education.aspx accessed on March 8, 2009.

[f] www.jasso.go.jp/statistics/intl_students/data06_e.html#2.

[g] Ross (2004): Atlas of Student Mobility: www.atlas.iie.network.org/?p=53467 accessed on March 12, 2009.

[h] Citizenship and Immigration Canada: www.cic.gc.ca accessed on March 8, 2009.

[i] www.educationcounts.govt.nz accessed on March 5, 2009.

[j] According to Verbik and Lasanowsky (2007, Appendix B, 37), Malaysia hosted 66,000 foreign students in 2005.

[k] The Higher Education Statistics for the years 2002, 2004 and 2006, annually published by the Student Selection and Placement Center (ÖSYM), Ankara. See also Barblan et al. (2008).

[l] "Education in Taiwan." Taipei: The Ministry of Education. http://english.education.edu.tw/public/data.

[m] Verbik and Lasanowsky (2007, Appendix B, 37).

APPENDIX B

DEFINITION OF TERMS
RELATED TO
EVALUATION AND QUALITY ASSURANCE

Source: OECD (2004c, 18–19)

1. Quality assurance refers to a set of approaches and procedures regarding the measurement, monitoring, guaranteeing, maintenance, or enhancement of the quality of higher education institutions/providers and programs, or the processes by which the achievement of education program standards, as established by institutions, professional organizations, government, and other standard-setting bodies, is measured.

2. *Accreditation* refers to the formal approval of a higher education institution/provider or program that has been found by a recognized accreditation body to meet predetermined and agreed standards, through a process of evaluation, which eventually results in the granting of accredited status to that institution/provider or program by the responsible authorities.

3. Recognition of academic qualifications refers to the decision that allows a person to pursue or continue a course of study or confer the right to use a title or degree.

4. Recognition of professional qualifications refers to decisions concerning the evaluation of credentials for entry into and/or practice of a profession and typically involves formal and informal education, work experience, and expertise.

DEFINITION OF TERMS USED BY THE
QUALITY ASSURANCE AGENCY (UNITED KINGDOM)

Source: http://www.qaa.ac.uk/aboutus/heGuide/guide.asp

1. Academic standards are a way of describing the level of achievement that a student has to reach to gain an academic award (e.g., a degree). It should be at a similar level across the United Kingdom.

2. *Academic quality* is a way of describing how well the learning opportunities available to students help them achieve their award. It is about making sure that appropriate and effective teaching, support, assessment, and learning opportunities are provided to them.

3. Institutional audit aims to ensure that institutions are providing higher education, awards, and qualifications of an acceptable quality and an acceptable academic standard, as well as exercising their legal powers to award degrees in a proper manner. It combines scrutiny of internal quality assurance systems at the institutional level, with a more detailed investigation at the discipline level of whether those systems are operating in the manner intended. The process involves audit visits, and heavily relies on the opinions of students, and self-evaluation documents provided by the institutions.

APPENDIX C

THE EUROPEAN CREDIT TRANSFER AND ACCUMULATION SYSTEM AND THE DIPLOMA SUPPLEMENT[1]

THE EUROPEAN CREDIT TRANSFER AND ACCUMULATION SYSTEM

The European Credit Transfer and Accumulation System (ECTS) is a student-centered system based on the student workload required to achieve the objectives of a program, objectives preferably specified in terms of the learning outcomes and competences to be acquired.

ECTS was introduced in 1989, within the framework of the European Community Action Scheme for the Mobility of University Students (ERASMUS), now part of the Socrates program. ECTS is the only credit system that has been successfully tested and used across Europe. ECTS was set up initially for credit transfer. The system facilitated the recognition of periods of study abroad and thus enhanced the quality and volume of student mobility in Europe. Recently, ECTS is developing into an accumulation system to be implemented at the institutional, regional, national, and European level. This is one of the key objectives of the Bologna Declaration of June 1999.

ECTS makes study programs easy to read and compare for all students, local and foreign. ECTS facilitates mobility and academic recognition. ECTS helps universities organize and revise their study programs. ECTS can be used across a variety of programs and modes of delivery. ECTS makes European higher education more attractive for students from other continents.

ECTS is based on the principle that sixty credits measure the workload of a full-time student during one academic year. The student workload of a full-time study program in Europe amounts in most cases to around 1,500 to 1,800 hours per year and in those cases, one credit stands for around twenty-five to thirty working hours.

Credits in ECTS only can be obtained after successful completion of the work required and appropriate assessment of the learning outcomes achieved. Learning outcomes are sets of competences expressing what the student will know, understand, or be able to do after completion of a process of learning, long or short.

Student workload in ECTS consists of the time required to complete all planned learning activities such as attending lectures, and seminars, studying independently and privately, preparation of projects, examinations.

Credits are allocated to all educational components of a study program (such as modules, courses, placements, or dissertation work) and reflect the quantity of work each component requires to achieve its specific objectives or learning outcomes in relation to the total quantity of work necessary to complete a full year of study successfully.

The performance of the student is documented by a local-national grade. It is good practice to add an ECTS grade, in particular in case of credit transfer. The ECTS grading scale ranks the students on a statistical basis. Therefore, statistical data on student performance is a prerequisite for applying the ECTS grading system. Grades are assigned among students with a pass grade as follows: A best 10 percent, B next 25 percent, C next 30 percent, D next 25 percent, and E next 10 percent.

A distinction is made between the grades FX and F, which are used for unsuccessful students. FX means: "fail—some more work required to pass" and F means: "fail—considerable further work required." The inclusion of failure rates in the transcript of records is optional.

An ECTS label will be awarded to institutions that apply ECTS correctly in all first- and second-cycle degree programs. The label will raise the profile of the institution as a transparent and reliable partner in European and international cooperation.

The criteria for the label are an information package/course catalogue (online or hard copy in one or more booklets) in two languages (or only in English for programs taught in English), use of ECTS credits, samples of learning agreements, transcripts of records, and proofs of academic recognition. An application form has been published. The application deadline is November 1, annually. The label will be valid for three academic years. The list of institutions in possession of the label will be published on the Europe Web site.

DIPLOMA SUPPLEMENT

The Diploma Supplement (DS) is a document attached to a higher education diploma providing a standardized description of the nature, level, context, content, and status of the studies that were pursued and success-fully completed by the graduate. The DS should be issued to every student of every type of degree program upon graduation, together with the official diploma, free of charge in a widely spoken European language. The DS provides transparency and facilitates academic and professional recognition of qualifications (diplomas, degrees, certificates).

A DS label will be awarded to institutions issuing the DS correctly to every student, upon graduation, together with the diploma, free of charge, and in a widely spoken European language. Institutions from all Bologna Signatory States may apply for the DS label. Assessment of applications from other countries is not excluded but cannot be guaranteed at this stage. Institutions must provide samples of actual DS as well as public information from the institution explaining that the DS is being issued to every graduate.

NOTE

1. The information in this appendix was condensed from "ECTS Users Guide, European Credit Transfer and Accumulation System and the Diploma Supplement," The European Commission, Directorate General for Education and Culture, August 17, 2004. See also Appendix 11 in Turlington, Naomi, and Porcelli (2002).

APPENDIX D

RECOGNITION OF

QUALIFICATIONS IN EUROPE

(Convention on the Recognition of Qualifications Concerning
Higher Education in the European Region,
Lisbon, April 11, 1997)

"The Convention on the Recognition of Qualifications Concerning Higher Education in the European Region," generally referred to as the Lisbon Recognition Convention, or Lisbon Convention, in short, was adopted at the Council of Europe/UNESCO Diplomatic Conference held on April 8–11, 1997 in Lisbon.[1] As of June 2005, the total number of ratifications/accessions to the Lisbon Recognition Convention was forty, which included thirty-six of the forty-six participating countries in the Bologna Process.[2]

The basic premises of the Council of Europe/UNESCO Convention are the right for a fair assessment of foreign qualifications, recognition if no substantial differences are evident, and mutual trust and information provision. These are embodied in the following points:

1. Holders of qualifications issued in one country shall have adequate access to an assessment of these qualifications in another country.

2. No discrimination will be made in this respect on any ground such as the applicant's gender, race, color, disability, language, religion, and political opinion, national, ethnic, or social origin.

3. The responsibility to demonstrate that an application does not fulfill the relevant requirements lies with the body undertaking the assessment.

4. Each country shall recognize qualifications, whether for access to higher education, periods of study, or higher education degrees,

as similar to the corresponding qualifications in its own system unless it can show that there are substantial differences between its own qualifications and the qualifications for which recognition is sought.

5. Recognition of a higher education qualification issued in another country shall have one or both of the following consequences. (a) Access to further higher education studies, including relevant examinations and preparations for the doctorate, on the same conditions as candidates from the country in which recognition is sought. (b) The use of an academic title, subject to the laws and regulations of the country in which recognition is sought; additionally, recognition may facilitate access to the labor market.

6. All countries shall develop procedures to assess whether refugees and displaced persons fulfill the relevant requirements for access to higher education or to employment activities, even in cases in which the qualifications cannot be proven through documentary evidence.

7. All countries shall provide information on the institutions and programs that belong to their higher education systems.

8. All countries shall appoint a national information center, one important task of which is to offer advice on the recognition of foreign qualifications to students, graduates, employers, higher education institutions, and other interested parties or persons,

9. All countries shall encourage their higher education institutions to issue the Diploma Supplement to their students in order to facilitate recognition.

A special committee was set up in 1999 to oversee the implementation of the Lisbon Recognition Convention. The Lisbon Recognition Convention Committee has members from each party to the Lisbon Recognition Convention, and several other countries and organizations (e.g., the European Union [EU] and the president of the European Network of Information Centers [ENIC]) can participate in the meetings taking place every year. The committee also has the right to approve recommendations related to recognition of qualifications. The Lisbon Convention has become a principal point of reference for conducting UNESCO-European Centre for Higher Education (CEPES) activities related to this strand. This effort is directly related to the fact that along with the Council of Europe, UNESCO-CEPES assures the secretariat of the specialized network–ENIC.

ENIC AND NATIONAL ACADEMIC RECOGNITION
INFORMATION CENTERS

The ENIC Network[3]

To implement the Lisbon Recognition Convention and, in general, to develop policy and practice for the recognition of qualifications, the Council of Europe and UNESCO established the ENIC Network. The Council of Europe and UNESCO-CEPES jointly provide the secretariat for the ENIC Network. The ENIC Network cooperates closely with the National Academic Recognition Information Centers (NARIC) Network of the EU.

The network is made up of the national information centers of the States party to the European Cultural Convention or the UNESCO Europe Region. An ENIC is a body set up by the national authorities.

Although the size and specific competence of ENIC may vary, they will generally provide information on (1) the recognition of foreign diplomas, degrees, and other qualifications; (2) education systems in both foreign countries and the ENIC's own country; and (3) opportunities for studying abroad, including information on loans and scholarships, as well as advice on practical questions related to mobility and equivalence.

The NARIC Network

The NARIC network is an initiative of the European Commission and was created in 1984. The network aims at improving academic recognition of diplomas and periods of study in the member states of the EU, the European Economic Area (EEA) countries and the associated countries in central and eastern Europe and Cyprus. The network is part of the community's program SOCRATES/ERASMUS, which stimulates the mobility of students and staff between higher education institutions in these countries.

All EU and EEA states and all the associated countries in central and eastern Europe and Cyprus have designated national centers, the purpose of which is to assist in promoting the mobility of students, teachers, and researchers by providing authoritative advice and information concerning the academic recognition of diplomas and periods of study undertaken in other states. The main users of this service are higher education institutions, students and their advisers, parents, teachers, and prospective employers.

The ministries of education in the respective countries designate the NARICs, but the status and the scope of work of individual NARICs may differ. In the majority of states, institutions of higher education are autonomous, taking their own decisions on the admission of foreign students and the exemption of parts of courses of study programs that students may be granted on the basis of education undertaken abroad. As a result, most NARICs do not take a decision, but offer on request information and advice on foreign education systems and qualifications.

OTHER INTERNATIONAL CONVENTIONS ON RECOGNITION

The following is the list of other international conventions on recognition of academic qualifications that are related to international student mobility.[4] The texts of these conventions can be accessed on the Web sites of the UNESCO Secretariat for that particular region:

- Regional Convention on the Recognition of Studies, Certificates, Diplomas, Degrees, and Other Qualifications in Higher Education in the African States (1981).

- Regional Convention on the Recognition of Studies, Diplomas, and Degrees in Higher Education in Latin America and the Caribbean Region (1974).

- Convention on the Recognition of Studies, Diplomas, and Degrees Concerning Higher Education in the Arab States (1978).

- Regional Convention on the Recognition of Studies, Diplomas and Degrees in Higher Education in Asia and the Pacific (1983).

For more on UN frameworks and conventions that relate to internationalization and globalization, see UNESCO (2003b).

NOTES

1. The full text and a continually updated list of signatures and ratifications may be found at http://conventions.coe.int; search for ETS 165. See also: http://www.cepes.ro/information_services/sources/on_line/lisbon.htm.
See also Rauhvargers (2004) for more on the Lisbon Convention and its place in the Bologna Process, and Appendix 11 in Turlington et al. (2002).

2. "From Berlin to Bergen," Dr. Per Nyborg, head, BFUG Secretariat, Presentation of the General Report of the BFUG to the Bergen Ministerial Conference May 19–20, 2005. Accessible at: http://www.bologna-bergen2005.no/Bergen/050519_Gen_rep_Nyborg_Per.pdf.

3. Information accessed on July 2005 4, at http://www.enic-naric.net/index.asp?display=About.

4. The list is available under the heading "International Mobility in Higher Education Frameworks, Tools and Trends" on the following Web site, which was accessed on January 2, 2005 at http://www.cicic.ca/mobility/indexe.stm.

APPENDIX E

EDUCATION, TRAINING, AND YOUTH

PROGRAMS OF THE EUROPEAN UNION

Until 2006, the Socrates Program was Europe's general education program for thirty-one countries comprising the twenty-five member states, Romania and Bulgaria, which were then candidates, Turkey, which is still a candidate, and Iceland, Liechtenstein, and Norway. The Leonardo da Vinci Program covered professional education, and the Youth Program focused on informal education and extracurricular activities. In 2007, the new Lifelong Learning Program 2010–2013 replaced these programs, which expired at the end of 2006.[1]

The aim of the new program is to contribute through lifelong learning (LLL) to the development of the community of participating states as an advanced knowledge society, with sustainable economic development, more and better jobs, and greater social cohesion. It aims to foster interaction, cooperation, and mobility between education and training systems within the community, so that they become a world-quality reference.

The Lifelong Learning Program currently comprises four sectoral programs on: school education (Comenius); higher education (European Community Action Scheme for the Mobility of University Student [ERASMUS]); vocational training (Leonardo da Vinci); and adult education (Grundtvig). These sectoral programs are supported by a transversal program focusing on policy cooperation, languages, information and communicaion tecnology (ICT), and dissemination and exploitation of results. Finally, the Jean Monnet program focuses on European integration and support for certain key institutions and associations active in the field. The program budget will be €6,970 million for the total period 2007–2013.

ERASMUS was established in 1987 with the aim of increasing student mobility within the European community. In 1995, it was incorporated into the Socrates Program its sectoral program in higher education, along with four other sectoral programs in school education, adult education, European languages, and ICT in education. It is now one of the four sectoral programs supported under the Lifelong Learning Program.

ERASMUS seeks to enhance the quality and reinforce the European dimension of higher education by encouraging transnational cooperation between universities, boosting European mobility and improving the transparency and full academic recognition of studies and qualifications throughout the European Union (EU). ERASMUS comprises many different activities, including student and teacher exchanges; joint development of study programs (curriculum development); international intensive programs; thematic networks among departments and faculties across Europe; language courses; and support for the implementation of the European Credit Transfer and Accumulation System.

The program is open to all types of higher education institutions in all academic disciplines and at all levels of higher education up to and including the doctorate. Students and staff from the thirty-one participating countries, as well as those from any other country, who are officially recognized by a member state as refugees, stateless persons, or permanent residents are eligible for funding under the program.

In order to participate in ERASMUS activities, higher education institutions have to apply for an Erasmus University Charter. This charter entitles them to apply to the European Commission (EC) for centralized ERASMUS funds and to their National Agency for decentralized mobility funds. Overall responsibility for funding and implementing the program lies with the EC. Only institutions that hold an Erasmus University Charter may send or receive students and teaching staff within this program. Currently, more than two thousand higher education institutions in the thirty-one member countries are participating in ERASMUS. Since its creation in 1987, well over 1.5 million students have benefited from an ERASMUS study period abroad; the goal is to reach 3 million students by 2012.

In 2004, the EU launched the global cooperation and scholarship program, called Erasmus Mundus.[2] The aim of the program is to enhance the quality of European higher education by fostering cooperation with non-EU countries. The basic features of the program include a global scholarship scheme for third-country nationals to enroll in European Union Master's Courses at European universities. These programs involve study at several higher education institutions in different member states, and would be distinguished by their European label. The program funds students from outside the EU participating in master's-level programs in Europe, European students going in the other direction, collaborative efforts to form networks in Europe and partnerships and consortia of these networks with institutions across the globe.

The EC has taken further measures to continuously upgrade the skills and support the mobility of the workforce in Europe. One of these is the Europass, which is designed to encourage mobility and LLL in an enlarged Europe.[3] It aims to help 3 million citizens make their qualifications and skills easily understood throughout Europe by 2010. The Europass brings together into a single framework several existing tools for the transparency of diplomas, certificates, and competences. Helping citizens better communicate and present their qualifications and skills throughout Europe, Europass is intended to promote both occupational mobility, among countries as well as across sectors, and mobility for learning purposes.

The Europass consists of five documents, available in all official EU languages:

1. The Europass Curriculum Vitae is the backbone of the Europass portfolio. It is an improved version of the common European Curriculum Vitae that was defined in the Recommendation of the European Commission in March 2002.

2. The Europass Mobility is the record in a common, simple format of the learning and training experiences of individuals in their home countries as well as abroad, if any. It is filled by the home and host organizations involved. It will replace Europass Training, which has been in operation for five years and was issued to about 100,000 persons.

3. The Europass Diploma Supplement is a personal document developed jointly with the Council of Europe and UNESCO that shows the holder's educational record. The same establishment that issues the diploma provides it. In principle, it should be provided to all new higher education graduates from 2005 on.

4. The Europass Certificate Supplement is a supplement to a vocational education and training certificate, clarifying the professional qualifications of all individuals holding such qualifications.

5. The Europass Language Portfolio is a document in which citizens can record their linguistic skills and cultural expertise. It was developed by the Council of Europe. It is based on the Common European Framework of Reference for Languages that is becoming the European standard to identify the level of language skills.

These documents, and more, are available at the dedicated Europass Portal. Through the Europass Portal, citizens will be able to complete online—with the help of specific guidelines and tutorials—their Europass Curriculum Vitae and their Europass Language Passport—a part of the Language Portfolio where citizens can describe in detail their language skills. The Europass Portal also provides comprehensive information on the other documents that are not completed directly by citizens, but issued to them by the relevant organizations, universities, training centers, and so on.

Because of the huge differences among the national education and training systems, Europass is implemented and promoted largely at the member-state-level. In each country, a National Europass Centre will promote Europass and coordinate all related activities, in cooperation with the relevant organizations, networks and authorities, as well as with the social partners.[4]

1. The material presented in this appendix is based on the information available on the following Web sites:

   — The European Commission: http://europa.eu.int/

   — http://europa.eu.int/comm/education/programmes/socrates/socrates_en.html

   — http://ec.europa.eu/education/programmes/newprog/index_en.html#call

   — The Council of Europe: http://www.coe.int/t/dg4/higher education/

2. For the Erasmus Mundus Program, see OECD (2004b, 110–11), and Borrelli and Teter 2005).

3. The relevant decision was made on December 15, 2004 (2241/2004/EC of the European Parliament and of the European Council of December 15, 2004 on a single community framework for the transparency of qualifications and competences, the Europass). It replaces the old Europass Training that was built on the core concepts of the "European pathway for training" and the "EUROPASS Training" in the decision on the promotion of European pathways for work-linked training, including apprenticeship (1999/51/EC, published in OJ L 17 of 22.1.1999), adopted by the Council on December 21, 1998. Europass now has a wider scope and includes the new member states. See also: http://europass.cedefop.eu.int/, which was accessed on July 4, 2005.

4. For more on the European cooperation programs that are relevant to mobility, see Maiworm (2001), van der Wende (2001a), and OECD (2004b, 89–94).

APPENDIX F

DEFINITIONS OF FOREIGN STUDENTS

Australia: Foreign students are defined on the basis of a combination of variables that can distinguish them from domestic students (residence permit, country of birth, permanent home residence, year of arrival in Australia). The number of foreign students reported comprises only the higher education sector, that is, ISCED 5A/6 and the higher education component of tertiary Type B-level programs. Foreign students enrolled in distance education programs are included. Students in offshore programs are reported separately.

Austria: Foreign students are defined as non-Austrian citizens, thus including permanent residents.

Belgium: Foreign students are defined by nationality rather than citizenship. No distinction is made between resident and nonresident students.

Czech Republic: Foreign students are defined as non-Czech citizens, thus including permanent residents.

Denmark: Foreign students are defined as non-Danish citizens, thus including permanent residents.

Finland: Foreign students are defined as non-Finnish citizens, thus including permanent residents. Foreign students enrolled in distance education programs are included.

France: Foreign students are defined as non-French citizens, thus including permanent residents. Data shown include students in all types of tertiary-level programs.

Germany: Foreign students are defined as non-German citizens, thus including permanent residents. Students with double citizenship are counted as

German students. Data on tertiary foreign students do not include foreign tertiary students enrolled in advanced research programs. Foreign students enrolled in distance education programs are included.

Greece: Foreign students are defined as non-Greek citizens, thus including permanent residents. Data on tertiary foreign students do not include foreign tertiary students enrolled in tertiary Type B-level programs.

Hungary: Foreign students are defined as non-Hungarian citizens, thus including permanent residents, but excluding members of neighboring countries' Hungarian minorities. Data on foreign students in tertiary Type B-level programs include only those enrolled in colleges and universities.

Iceland: Foreign students are defined as non-Icelandic citizens, thus including permanent residents. Foreign students enrolled in distance education programs are included.

Ireland: Foreign students are defined by foreign domiciliary address, thus excluding permanent residents. Data on tertiary foreign students include only full-time enrollments.

Italy: Foreign students are defined as non-Italian citizens, thus including permanent residents. Foreign students enrolled in distance education programs are included.

Japan: Foreign students are defined as non-Japanese citizens, thus including permanent residents.

Korea: Foreign students are defined as non-Korean citizens, thus including permanent residents.

Netherlands: Foreign students are defined as enrolled students with foreign nationality. Data on tertiary foreign students do not include foreign tertiary students enrolled at Open University or in advanced research programs.

New Zealand: Foreign students are defined as noncitizens. However, most Australian students are not counted as foreign students.

Norway: Foreign students are defined as non-Norwegian citizens, thus including permanent residents. Foreign students enrolled in distance education programs are included.

Poland: Foreign students are defined as non-Polish citizens, thus including permanent residents. Data on foreign tertiary students do not include foreign tertiary students enrolled in advanced research programs. Data cover only students enrolled for full curriculum studies or a full academic year, not those enrolled for one or two terms.

Slovak Republic: Foreign students are defined as non-Slovakian citizens, thus including permanent residents. Foreign students enrolled in distance education programs are included.

Sweden: Foreign students are defined as non-Swedish citizens registered in the Swedish population register, thus including permanent residents. Students who are not registered in the Swedish population register (mainly from Nordic countries) are not included. Foreign students in distance education programs are included.

Switzerland: Foreign students are defined as non-Swiss citizens, thus including permanent residents.

Turkey: Only foreigners who come to Turkey for the purpose of study are counted as foreign students. Data on tertiary foreign students do not include foreign tertiary students enrolled in advanced research programs.

United Kingdom: Foreign students are defined by foreign domiciliary address, thus excluding permanent residents. Data reported do not include foreign students enrolled in offshore and distance education programs.

United States: Foreign students are defined as students, who are neither U.S. citizens, nor immigrants (permanent residents), nor refugees, thus excluding permanent residents. These may include holders of F (student) visas, H (temporary worker/trainee) visas, and M (vocational training) visas.

Source: OECD (2004b, 308–11).

APPENDIX G

GENERAL AGREEMENT ON
TRADE IN SERVICES

Services represent the fastest growing sector of the global economy and account for 60 percent of global output, 30 percent of global employment, and nearly 20 percent of global trade.[1] Global trade in services is currently valued at $2.2 trillion annually. The General Agreement on Trade in Services (GATS) is the first and only set of legally enforceable rules governing international trade in services. It was developed in response to the growth in services worldwide and greater potential brought about by the information technology (IT) revolution. It was negotiated in the Uruguay Round, which took place from 1986 to 1994, and entered into force in 1995, together with the revised version of the General Agreement on Tariffs and Trade (GATT), which covers trade in goods, and the Trade-Related Aspects of Intellectual Property Rights (TRIPs).

There are 12 major service sectors and 163 subsectors covered by the GATS, including financial services, energy services, environment services, legal services, transportation, construction, telecommunications, distribution, tourism, entertainment, education, sporting, delivery, and health care. The purpose of GATS is to eliminate barriers to trade in services. Services supplied in the exercise of governmental authority are excluded from the GATS.

Trade in educational services is based on five subsectors of education as categorized by the United Nations Provisional Central Product Classification, including primary education, secondary education, higher education, adult education, and other. Higher education covers postsecondary technical and vocational education services as well as other higher education programs leading to degrees at the postsecondary level, that is, all programs leading to associate-, bachelor-, master- and doctoral-level degrees come under GATS. Adult education covers education for adults outside the regular education system, for example, lifelong learning schemes. Other education covers all education services not classified elsewhere, such as testing, curriculum design, professional development, capacity building, technical assistance, guidance and counseling, and so forth, and excludes recreational education services.

STRUCTURE OF THE GATS

The GATS consists of a set of mutually agreed on rules, binding market access, and nondiscriminatory commitments for services.

The agreement has three core components: the framework of rules that lay out general obligations; annexes on specific service sectors; and the schedules of commitments submitted by each member country on market access and national treatment, which detail its liberalization undertakings by sector and mode of supply.

According to GATS, trade in educational services can occur in one of the following four modes:

Mode 1: "Cross-border supply." This refers to services that cross borders without requiring the physical movement of the consumer or the provider. This is equivalent to movement of programs or program mobility mentioned in Section 4.5, and examples of educational services provided in this category include distance education of all kinds and franchising.

Mode 2: "Consumption abroad." This mode involves the provision of educational services to persons who have moved to another country to receive such services. This corresponds to international student mobility, including trainees as well.

Mode 3: "Commercial presence." Mode 3 occurs when the service provider (institution, organization, or company) establishes facilities in another country to provide the service; this mode of trade in educational services corresponds to institutional mobility mentioned in Section 4.5, and examples include branch campuses and offshore provision.

Mode 4: "Presence of natural persons." This mode refers to persons traveling to another country on a temporary basis to provide educational services, and correspond to the international mobility of teachers and scholars.

The terms *provider* or *supplier* used in the context just provided include all types of institutions of postsecondary education, new types of providers (see Chapter 4), organizations, and companies.

An important rule included in the general framework is the so-called most-favored nation treatment. This means that if a member country allows foreign competition in a certain service sector, it must allow all member countries to compete equally in its market regarding that particular sector. In other words, a country cannot allow only certain countries into that market; either all member countries are allowed or none. Closing the domestic market in a particular sector to all countries is certainly unbecoming to the spirit of the GATS, but complies with the most favored nation treatment. The most-favored nation treatment does not apply to recognition of qualifications.

The second general requirement is the "transparency discipline," which obliges member countries to publish all relevant measures of application that pertain to or affect the implementation of the GATS; to reply promptly to requests by other members for information and to establish enquiry points for this purpose; and to notify the Council for Trade in Services on measures taken by others that they consider affect the operation of the agreement.

The GATS has a flexible negotiating framework. The procedure involves requests by members for other members to open their domestic markets in a certain sector to foreign providers. World Trade Organization (WTO) members are free to choose whether they want to open a particular service sector, or part of a sector, to foreign supply and the conditions under which they are willing to do so. If, however, a commitment is made, it is understood to be a minimum treatment, meaning that a country can subsequently offer better treatment to foreign providers, but not worse.

Under the GATS, WTO members agreed to enter into successive rounds of negotiations to liberalize trade in services. At the conclusion of the Uruguay Round in 1995, forty-three countries and the European Union (EU) had made commitments to education, with twenty-one of them to higher education. Negotiations started in 2000, and by the end of 2001 the United States (December 18, 2000), Australia (October 1, 2001), and New Zealand (June 27, 2001) had submitted proposals outlining their general positions related to commitments in the education sector, and Japan joined them on March 15, 2002. By June 2002, 34 of the then 145, now 149, WTO members had put forward their requests for market access in other countries. The United States had made substantial requests of other countries to remove barriers in higher education, adult education, and other educational services. By March 2003, twenty countries had tabled their offers concerning the conditions under which they would open the education sector in their countries to foreign provision of services and to what extent. Other countries came in later, and these now include Argentina, Australia, Bahrain, Canada, Congo/Zaire, Costa Rica, Czech Republic, the EU, Hong Kong, Hungary, Iceland, Israel, Jamaica, Japan, Korea, Lesotho, Liechtenstein, Mexico, New Zealand, Norway, Panama, Poland, Paraguay, Sierra Leone, the Slovak Republic, Switzerland, Taiwan, Turkey, Trinidad and Tobago, the United States, and Uruguay.

It is not mandatory for countries to publish their requests and offers. The United States has made substantial requests of other countries to remove barriers in higher education, adult education, and other educational services, and Australia, Canada, the EU, Japan, Liechtenstein, New Zealand, Norway, and the United States have publicized their positions.

The request by the United States asked that all WTO members undertake full commitments for market access and most-favored nation treatment in "cross-border supply," "commercial presence," and "presence of natural persons" modes of delivering education services. The United States did not request commitments in primary or secondary education or in public education and subsidies. The following are some of the issues that the United States saw as obstacles to trade in higher education, adult education and training services[2]:

1. Prohibition of higher education, adult education, and training services offered by foreign entities;

2. Lack of opportunity for foreign suppliers of higher education, adult education, and training services to obtain authorization to establish facilities within the territory of the member country;

3. Lack of an opportunity for foreign suppliers of higher education, adult education, and training services to qualify as degree granting institutions;

4. Inappropriate restrictions on electronic transmission of course materials;

5. Economic needs test on suppliers of these services;

6. Measures requiring the use of a local partner;

7. Denial of permission for private-sector suppliers of higher education, adult education, and training to enter into and exit from joint ventures with local or nonlocal partners on a voluntary basis;

8. Where government approval is required, exceptionally long delays are encountered and, when approval is denied, no reasons are given for the denial and no information is given on what must be done to obtain approval in the future;

9. Tax treatment that discriminates against foreign suppliers;

10. Foreign partners in a joint venture are treated less favorably than local partners;

11. Franchises are treated less favorably than other forms of business organization;

12. Domestic laws and regulations are unclear and administered in an unfair manner;

13. Subsidies for higher education, adult education, and training are not made known in a clear and transparent manner;

14. Minimum requirements for local hiring are disproportionately high, causing uneconomic operations;

15. Specialized, skilled personnel (including managers, computer specialists, expert speakers) needed for a temporary period of time have difficulty obtaining authorization to enter and leave the country;

16. Repatriation of earnings is subject to excessively costly fees and/or taxes for currency conversion; and

17. Excessive fees/taxes are imposed on licensing or royalty payments.

The request from Australia described in WTO Document No. S/CSS/W/110 and that from New Zealand described in WTO Document No. S/CSS/W/93, although not as comprehensive and demanding as the U.S. general request, were in favor of liberalization. The Japanese proposal described in WTO Document No. S/CSS/W/137 made specific references to the role of the state, and stressed the need to address the issues of quality assurance, and equivalence of qualifications, all in the context of consumer protection.

The GATS requires WTO members to notify recognition agreements to which they are a party. It does encourage the development of international standards wherever appropriate, but it is envisaged that these standards will be developed not by the WTO, but elsewhere by members working in cooperation with relevant intergovernmental and nongovernmental organizations.

The number of requests made by WTO members of other member countries is not known, because these are not made public. Green (2004) reports that, according to leaks, the United States had also made specific requests of the EU, Mexico, Brazil, Taiwan, Egypt, India, the Philippines, Thailand, El Salvador, Turkey, China, Israel, Japan, South Africa, Greece, Italy, Ireland, Spain, and Sweden to remove specific barriers.

On the other hand, the U.S. offer was the complete opposite of her requests, and underscored:

1. The authority of U.S. institutions in admission policies, setting tuition fees, developing curricula and course content;

2. The granting of U.S. federal or state government funding or subsidies to U.S. schools or citizens;

3. The requirements for regional or specialty accreditation practices; and

4. The conditions for foreign-owned entities to receive public benefits.

NOTES

1. The material presented in this section has been condensed from the following sources: AUCC (2001); Nyborg (2002); Sauve (2002); Knight (2002c, 2003a); Altbach (2004b); Green (2004); OECD (2004b, 33-37; 2004c, 158-166); Robinson (2005); Sorensen (2005); UNESCO (2005); WTO (2005). Some of the requests and offers by WTO members can be accessed on the WTO Web site: http://www.wto.org/english/tratop_e/serv_e/s_propnewnegs_e.htm.

2. WTO Document No. S/CSS/W/23, December 18, 2000. See also: http://ustr.gov./sectors/services/2002-07-01-proposal-execsumm.pdf.

3. Made in March 2003; see http://www.ustr.gov/sectors/services/2003-03-31-consolidated_offer.pdf.

NOTES

ONE: THE GLOBAL KNOWLEDGE ECONOMY AND HIGHER EDUCATION

1. The beginning of rational and scientific thought is generally attributed to the first pre-Socratic philosophers, Thales (c. 624–c. 547 BC), Anaximander (c.610–c.546 BC), and Anaximenes (c. 570–c. 528 BC), who lived in Miletus on the Aegean coast of today's Turkey.

2. For an analysis of the interrelationship among science, technology, and education during the Industrial Revolution and the period that followed, see Mokyr (1990, 81–150, 2002, 28–118, 284–97) and Guagnini (2004).

3. The technological leaders of the Industrial Revolution include Josiah Wedgewood (1730–1795), founder of the Wedgewood pottery manufacturing company; Matthew Boulton (1728–1809), Watt's partner and founder of the Soho Factory in Birmingham, the first of its kind; John Roebuck (1718–1794), inventor of the lead chamber manufacturing process for sulfuric acid, owner of ironworks, and also a partner of Watt's in the earlier stages of the commercial development of the steam engine; and Sir Richard Arkwright (1732–1792), cotton manufacturer, inventor of the spinning-frame, one of the founders of the modern factory system, and the first customer of the steam engine produced by Watt and Boulton for use in his textile factories. Except for Roebuck, who studied medicine in Edinburgh and received his degree from Leiden, and Watt, who only had a secondary-level education, none of these leading industrialists of the Industrial Revolution had formal education, let alone a higher education. Roebuck's educational travel from Edinburgh, where he audited lectures by Joseph Black (1728–1799) and William Cullen (1710–1790), professors of chemistry, to Leiden, where he received his degree in medicine, should be noted as an example of international student mobility. Watt spent a year at the University of Glasgow to learn the craft of a "mathematical instrument maker," assisting Robert Dick, a professor of natural philosophy, and Joseph Black. It also is interesting to look at the educational backgrounds of the three leading names of the so-called Second Transport Revolution that led to the development of railways and steamships, which immediately followed the Industrial Revolution (the First Transport Revolution was the development of seafaring vessels in the late fourteenth and the fifteenth centuries that made the discovery of new lands possible). Richard Trevitchik (1771–1833), who developed the high-pressure steam engine, and the American Robert Fulton (1765–1815), who put the engine on the boat, were self-taught engineers who had no higher education. On the other hand, Robert Stephenson (1803–1859), who had developed the locomotive, was an Englishman

who had studied at the University of Edinburgh, a Scottish university—another example of international student mobility.

4. Mokyr (2002) calls these "the invisible colleges," which provided a platform where scientists, scholars, entrepreneurs, and industrialists met, as well as being an avenue for dissemination of scientific and technical knowledge to the masses through public lectures and demonstrations. The first one was the Royal Society of London founded in 1662, which held its meetings in Gresham College and was presided over by Sir Isaac Newton in its early years. The Lunar Society, founded in Birmingham in 1754, is considered by many to have contributed more to the Industrial Revolution than any other institution. Its members included such scientists as Joseph Priestley (1733–1804), a graduate of the Daventry Academy and a teacher in Warrington Academy, both dissenting academies that educated those who refused to take the oath of subscription to the Anglican Church—a prerequisite for admission to Oxford and Cambridge at the time—and Erasmus Darwin (1731–1802), a biologist himself and the grandfather of Charles Darwin (1809–1882), as well as Watt, Boulton, and Wedgewood. For an account of the Lunar Society, see Uglow (2002).

The second major contributing factor was the existence of a capital market in England, based on a regulatory framework. The East India Company had been founded as a joint-stock enterprise in 1600. The Bank of England, the Bank of Scotland, and the London Stock Exchange were established in 1694, 1695, and 1698, respectively, all by royal charters.

5. The Royal Institution was founded in 1799 to disseminate scientific, technical, and philosophical knowledge. Its first director was Humphry Davy (1778–1829). The mechanics institutes were then transformed into technical schools, which, in turn, became the nuclei of many of today's universities in the region.

6. It is interesting to note that neither Michael Faraday (1791–1867), who pioneered the development of the scientific basis of electrical technologies, nor the two great entrepreneurs, Alexander Graham Bell (1847–1922) and Thomas Alva Edison (1847–1931), who first commercialized much of the scientific developments in electricity to useful products, had any formal education. Faraday was self-trained, but was employed as an assistant by Humphrey Davy, who had recognized his extraordinary talents regardless of his lack of education. Edison was privately educated, and so was Bell, who had also audited lectures in London University and the University of Edinburgh. On the other hand, Augustus Wilhelm von Hofmann (1818–1892) had studied chemistry in the University of Giessen (f. 1607) under Justus von Liebig (1803–1873). He was then appointed as the head of the chemistry department of the Royal College of Science of London University. One of his students there, Sir William Henry Perkin (1838–1907), established one of the first modern industrial research laboratories in his chemical plant at Harrow. Hofmann's relocation from Germany to England is an example of academic mobility in Europe in the nineteenth century, as well as showing the tremendous effects that the German research universities had on the development of science as the bases of new technologies.

7. The research laboratory of BASF was headed by Johann Wilhelm von Baer (1835–1917), who had done his doctoral work at the University of Berlin (f. 1810) under the supervision of Friedrich August Kekule von Stradonitz (1829–1896), a student of Liebig's in Giessen, who had received his doctoral degree in Paris.

8. For the evolution of national research and development systems in the late nineteenth and early twentieth centuries, see Guagnini (2004).

9. This is generally referred to as the second Scientific Revolution; the discovery of x-rays by Wilhelm Conrad Roentgen (1845–1923) in 1895 is considered to be its beginning. Roentgen, the winner of the first Nobel Prize in Physics in 1901, got his doctoral degree from the University of Zurich (f. 1833) in 1867, and later taught at Giessen and Würzburg (f. 1402). Although the first Scientific Revolution was owed indirectly to the university and the institutions of higher education, they were the nuclei for the second.

10. For a description of this dazzling technological transformation, see Friedman (2005, 51–80).

11. For more on these political developments as they relate to globalization, see Friedman (2005, 9, 48–52, 103–104, 114–118, 181–183).

12. The World Development Indicators 2006 comprise a large number of tables, arranged in six sections, in which numerical values are reported for more than two hundred countries covering a wide range of topics. The data is available from the World Bank (2006a), and can be accessed at http://devdata.worldbank.org/wdi/contents/Tablex_y.htm, where x is the section number and y shows the table number in that section.

13. "Source country" also is used instead of "country of origin," and "destination country" also is used instead of "host country."

14. See note 12.

TWO: ENROLLMENT AND INCREASING DEMAND

1. Compilation of statistics on higher education that allows meaningful cross-national comparisons to be made always has been a difficult task due for the most part to lack of standardized definitions and data-collection procedures, such as the Frascati Manual for science and technology indicators. Wide variations in value of the same indicator, even in publications of the same organization are not uncommon. With increasing complexity of higher education worldwide, some of which is discussed in this chapter, this task is becoming even more daunting. Data presented in this chapter are believed to be the latest available values that allow reasonably meaningful comparisons to be made.

A case in point is Trow's classification. Net enrollment ratios should be used to strictly comply with Trow's classification. I have used gross enrollment ratios (GERs) as they are the data that is most commonly available internationally. Hauptman (2009), too, has alluded to the problems associated with using GERs in the context of Trow's classification.

2. Note the difference in the GER values reported by Perkin (2006) and Jarausch (1983) for 1860. The first probably includes only university students. Nevertheless, the values reported by the two sources are reasonably close when one considers the difficulty of collecting reliable higher education data even today.

3. "Education in Taiwan 2008." Ministry of Education. http://english.education.edu.tw.

4. Africa is a continent with fifty-four countries and has a population of close to 800 million with a huge cultural and linguistic diversity—some one thousand languages spoken. For the challenges faced by African countries, see Teferra and Altbach (2003, 2004).

5. Figures were obtained on July 22, 2006 from http://www.unesco.org/iau/onlinedatabases/list.html.

6. This number includes the 3,525,000 so-called self-directed learners, and the number of students is given as 19 million, which is in agreement with the value reported for China by UNESCO (2006). The GER without the self-directed learners is reported as 18 percent by Xie and Huang (2005) for 2003, and is in reasonable agreement with the value of 19 percent reported by UNESCO (2006) for 2004. The foregoing example shows the difficulty of comparing statistics on higher education, a commonly encountered one alluded to in note 1.

7. The International Development Program (IDP) was established in 1969 to promote Australian education in Southeast Asia. Since the mid-1980s, the emphasis of IDP has shifted to building new business in student recruitment worldwide. It now has offices in fifty-six countries and services all sectors of Australian education. IDP's primary focus is on international education, testing, and development services.

8. Quoted in Pearman (2004).

9. Projections by the United Nations Population Division, quoted in Davis (2003, 71), show that the decrease in population in the period 2000–2050 will be 30.3 percent for Russia, 19 percent for Switzerland, 13.6 percent for Japan, and 3.8 percent for Germany. More recent data by the World Bank (2006a, 46–48) show that the population of Germany will decrease from 82.5 million in 2004 to 82.3 million in 2020, that of Japan from 127.8 million to 126.7 million, and that of Russia from 143.8 million to 133.1 million, while that of Switzerland will remain constant in the same period. On the other hand, China will increase from 1,296.2 million people to 1,423.9 million and India from 1,079.7 million to 1,332.0 million.

10. The 1997 UNESCO International Standard Classification of Education (ISCED; UNESCO 1997b; UNESCO 2006, 8–9) provides a global framework for classifying educational programs based on content. Tertiary education comprises ISCED levels 5 and 6. ISCED 5B programs are typically shorter than ISCED 5A programs and are designed so that participants acquire the practical skills and know-how needed for employment in a particular type or certain class of occupations or trades. These programs have a minimum full-time equivalent of two years of study and typically provide graduates with a specific labor market qualification. ISCED 5A programs are largely theoretically based and are intended to provide sufficient qualifications for professions with high skills requirements (e.g., medicine, dentistry, architecture) and for entry into advanced research programs (ISCED 6). Completion at this level involves a minimum full-time equivalent of three years of study. It should be noted that the basis for ISCED classification is not the institutional setting but the program content. This means that not all university education is classified ISCED 5A or 6; that some universities also offer ISCED 5B programs; and that some institutions other than universities offer ISCED 5A programs. Associate-level programs offered in community colleges in the United States and Japan (*tanki daigaku*) and

the regional colleges in Norway (*distrikthogskolar*), as well as the three-year programs offered in the German *Fachochschulen*, the Dutch *HBO* (*hoger beroepsonderwijs*) the Japanese colleges of technology (*koto senmon gakko*) and the ISCED 4-level schools recently upgraded to ISCED 5B-level network of regional colleges in Switzerland (Perellon 2001) are typical examples of ISCED 5B programs offered in non-university institutions, whereas the short-cycle vocational programs offered within universities in Sweden, France (*institut universitaire de technologie*, IUT), Spain (*escualas universitarias*), Italy (Vaira 2003), and Turkey (*meslek yüksekokulu*) are examples of ISCED 5B programs offered within universities. As part of the requirements of the Bologna Process, however, the distinction between ISCED 5A programs in German and Dutch universities as opposed to ISCED 5B programs in the *Fachhochschulen* and the HBOs is being gradually phased out (see Section 5.4 for more on the Bologna Process).

ISCED 4, on the other hand, includes programs that straddle the boundary between upper-secondary and postsecondary education. ISCED 4 programs cannot be regarded as tertiary programs nor are they more advanced than programs at ISCED 3 (upper-secondary level), but they serve to broaden the knowledge of participants who have already completed a program at level 3. Typical examples are programs designed to prepare students for studies at level 5 who, although having completed ISCED level 3, did not follow a curriculum that would allow entry to level 5, that is, predegree foundation courses or short vocational programs. Second-cycle programs can be included as well. An ISCED 4 program has a typical full-time equivalent duration of between six months and two years. The programs offered in the Australian technical and further education and the British further education sectors, the French STS, the private training establishments in New Zealand, and the Japanese *senshu gakko senmon kotei* are examples of ISCED 4 programs. For example, 15,615 of the students in the further education sector were classified as higher education students in the United Kingdom in 2006–2007 (http://www.hesa.ac.uk).

11. The *Observatory on Borderless Higher Education Breaking News* (OBHE-BN) is a monthly news bulletin that summarizes the developments in international higher education and related topics. These are cited in the text as (OBHE-BN, date). Additionally, the OBHE also puts on its Web site "briefing notes," which are cited in the text as (OBHE-BfN, date), "articles," which are cited in the text as (OBHE-A, date), and "key issues," which are cited in the text as (OBHE-KI, date). These can be accessed at the Observatory's Web site: http://www.obhe.ac.uk/news/

12. Docquier and Marfouk (2006) quote the UN statistics, which put the number of international migrants in 2000 at 175 million, up from 154 million in 1990.

13. See Schiff (2006) on the new view on brain drain, which argues that it confers certain benefits, including, in addition to remittances and increased investment due to the general diaspora effect, the skills and knowledge acquired by the returnees and the networks they have established in destination countries. Schiff, however, takes the argument a step ahead, and posits that "brain drain" induces a net "brain gain" in the source country. This happens because when people see the increased wages earned abroad by skilled migrants, demand for and investment in education increases in the source country, which eventually results in net brain gain. In other words, if the return to investment in education is higher abroad

than at home, the possibility of migration increases the expected return of human capital, which, in turn, increases enrollments in the source countries (Docquier and Marfouk 2006).

Migration is a complex issue. Like all economic flows, it is driven by price and wage differentials. It depends on per capita income in and the size of the source country as well as its proximity to destination countries. The increasingly intertwined relationship between international migration and international student mobility is discussed in Section 6.5.

14. The Futures Project was established in 1999 under the leadership of the late Frank Newman to investigate the impact of competition and market-based values on the core values and the public mission of higher education (see, e.g., Futures Project 2000; Newman 2000). The Futures Project closed down on March 31, 2005. The various publications from the Futures Project were accessed at its Web site, which closed on August 1, 2006: http://www.futuresproject.org/.

15. The breakdown of the world total labor force according to education attainment in 2000 and 1990 (numbers shown in parentheses) was as follows: tertiary 11.3 percent (9.1 percent), secondary 29.7 percent (29.4 percent), and primary 59.0 percent (61.5 percent).

THREE: THE RISE OF MARKET FORCES

1. For details on the history of the medieval universities, see Rashdall (1936) and Ridder-Symoens (1992a).

2. The remarks in parentheses are the author's.

3. Bayh-Dole University and Small Business Patent Act, Pub. L. No.96-517, 94 Stat.3015 (1980) (codified as amended at 35 USCA 200–212 (2001 & West Supp. 2003)).

4. According to a news article that appeared in the *Chronicle of Higher Education* ("Licensing revenue and patent activity, 2007 fiscal year." 55(22), January 28, 2009.), twenty-eight U.S. universities had licensing income above $10 million in 2007. At the top of the list were New York University ($791 million), Columbia ($136 million), and the University of California system ($98 million).

5. The institutional spending on institutions values reported in OECD (2004a) are national averages calculated by summing the annual revenues of all types of institutions, unless noted otherwise, from all types of sources and dividing the sum by the total national enrollment in that particular year.

6. Per-student expenditures reported by UNESCO (2003a) for some African and eastern European countries in 2003 were as follows: Senegal $1,495, Russian Federation $670, Romania $570, Cameroon $280, and Madagascar $220.

7. The caveat here is that private universities in the Netherlands and Belgium are government-dependent, and are thus indistinguishable from public institutions.

8. World Bank (1994, 53–54) refers to this scheme as quality-based funding, and considers it as coming closest to a voucher scheme.

9. See Schiefelbein (1990) and Brunner (1993) and for the sweeping reforms introduced in Chile in the early 1980s.

10. "Education heads election agenda." *The Times Higher Education Supplement.* March 2, 2007.

11. The bill passed by a mere five votes despite a government majority of 160 in the British Parliament. In the United States, considered to be the most mature mass higher education system in the world, public institutions are dependent on state legislatures to set fees. Thus, United Kingdom and Australia are now ahead of the United States in terms of the freedom of public institutions to set fees (OBHE-BN, January 2004).

12. Tuition fees were introduced in Hungary in 1995, and were subsequently abolished in 1998, when only foreigners and Hungarian students staying beyond normal periods of study were required to pay fees. In a nationwide referendum as part of the election in 2008, tution fees were abolished. Although the Hungarian Rectors Committee has proposed a new dual track fee structure, it is unlikely that this will materialize in the foreseeable future.

13. a. "Austria faces a boycott of tuition fees." *The Times Higher Education Supplement.* February 9, 2007; b. "End of tuition fees to cost Austria dearly." ACA *Newsletter-Education Europe.* September 2008.

14. Although universities in Ireland do not charge tuition fees, they do charge an annual service fee of 750 euros per year.

15. This is referred to as the "equal-treatment principle," and is based on several decisions of the European Court of Justice, which imply that in all member states students from other European Union countries are treated as domestic students and pay the same tuition fees as national students, but that they are not entitled to the support provided by national governments toward living costs of home students (OECD 2004b, 105).

16. Data fron Program for Research on Private Higher Education (PROPHE) at the University at Albany are shown in parentheses in Table A.1. The PROPHE data are in reasonably good agreement with the UNESCO data.

17. "Plans for private colleges on hold." *The Times Higher Education Supplement.* January 12, 2007.

18. Based on data that was accessed on 23 June 2006 at http://www.hesa.ac.uk for 2004–2005.

19. Nanyang Academy of Fine Arts is the oldest private institution of higher education in Singapore, dating back to 1938. LaSalle College of the Arts was founded in 1984; it offers Open University degrees. The first private university, Singapore Management University, was founded in 2000; it was modeled after the Wharton School. The University of New South Wales founded the first foreign-run institution in Singapore. This also was the country's first privately-funded university and its fourth university (Cohen 2004); it started in 2007.

20. It appears that Vietnamese higher education is headed for more reforms along American lines ("Vietnamese leaders discuss overhaul of higher education during U.S. visit." *The Chronicle of Higher Education* 53[43]: A41, June 29, 2007).

21. In addition to the degree-granting institutions, there are also thousands of noncollegiate institutions in the United States that provide vocational training at the postsecondary level. In 2001–2002, there were 5,059 such institutions, comprising 501 public, 1,018 nonprofit private, and 3,540 for-profit private institutions (Visit: http://nces.ed.gov//programsmdigest/d03/tables/dt005.asp.) These institutions do not award degrees. Those that are for-profit are also commonly referred to as proprietary institutions.

22. "Greece attempts to jump on privatization train." ACA *Newsletter-Education Europe*. August 2008.

23. In the past, the share of private institutions in Russia was reported as high as 41 percent by UNESCO-CEPES (2006). See note 24.

24. According to statistics reported by the European Center for Higher Education, the shares of private institutions in total higher education enrollment in the former Communist countries in central and eastern Europe in the 2003–2004 academic year were as follows: Russian Federation 40.6 percent; Estonia 31 percent; Poland 29.4 percent; Latvia 26.1 percent; Romania 23.2 percent; Belarus 17 percent; Bulgaria 14.4 percent; Hungary 14.2 percent; Macedonia 9.4 percent; Lithuania 7 percent; Slovenia 6.9 percent; Croatia 3.1 percent; Slovak Republic 0.2 percent (http://www.cepes.ro). These are in reasonbly good agreement with the values shown in Table A.1 other than the values for Russia.

25. Unless indicated otherwise, the historical material in this section is based on Rashdall (1936), Ridder-Symoens (1992a, 1996a) and Ruegg (2004b).

26. The dissenting academies were founded in England in the late eighteenth and the early nineteenth centuries by non-Anglicans, who were not allowed as students in Oxford and Cambridge. They were not authorized to award degrees, and eventually disappeared. They did, however, play a key role in the evolution of both the British and the American systems of lay governance.

27. It is interesting to note that Oxford, Cambridge, Durham, and London universities as degree-awarding institutions can be considered as the first quality assurance and accreditation structures, and the University Grants Committee generally is regarded as the first intermediary body between the government and institutions of higher education. Such structures are important elements of modern university governance.

28. Kogan and Martin (2000), too, have used Clark's triangle of coordination for an analysis similar to the foregoing.

29. For definitions of the terms quality assurance and accreditation, and the closely associated terms recognition of academic and professional qualifications, see Appendix B.

30. This is referred to as meta-accreditation or multiple accreditation.

31. According to the data reported in *The Chronicle of Higher Education Almanac Issue 2008–2009*, total financial aid to American students in the 2006–2007 academic year was $149 billion, including loans, grants and various benefits. The breakdown of the total student aid was as follows: $86 billion from federal sources; $9 billion from state sources; $28 billion from private sources; and $26 billion from institutional sources. This was for total annual U.S. higher education budget of approximately $400 billion—found by multiplying the enrollment figure in Table A.1 with the per-student expenditure figure in Table A.3 in 2006.

32. The Hellenic Quality Assurance Agency was established in 2005. It appears that only a few countries are left among the signatories of the Bologna Declaration that do not have a quality assurance organization with statutory powers. Turkey is one of them, but Turkish universities have extensively used the U.S.-based Accreditation Board for Engineering and Technology (ABET) to evaluate engineering programs, and European University Association for institutional evaluation.

33. The New Zealand Qualifications Authority (NZQA) was established in 1990 under the Education Act 1989 to provide an overarching role in quality-assured qualifications and to coordinate qualifications in New Zealand. Only those providers recognized by the NZQA are eligible for government financial assistance (see http://www.nzqa.govt.nz).

34. The new university system (*Shinsei Daigaku*) introduced under American influence in postwar Japan included the establishment in 1947 of the Japanese University Accreditation Association (JUAA, *Daigaku Kijun Kyokai*), a nongovernmental body, to set the standards for new universities (Itoh 2002; Murasawa 2002; Yonezawa 2002). However, in time, because there were no penalties for not seeking accreditation and no rewards for doing so, especially after 1956 when the Ministry set its own standards, the JUAA turned into a voluntary accreditation entity, and as of 2004, only one third of the Japanese universities had been accredited by it (OECD 2004b, 119–29).

35. As noted earlier, it was in fact the large share of private institutions, not the structure of its public institutions that led Clark to depict the Japanese higher education system next to the American system in its responsiveness to market in the triangle of coordination.

36. www.naacindia.org, accessed on March 20, 2009.

37. www.casetrust.org.sg/AccreditationSchemes/CaseTrustforEducation/tab-id/60/Default.aspx www.singaporeedu.gov.sg/htm/stu/stu0109c.htm.

38. More information on the themes of accountability and quality assurance can be found in El-Khawas (2006) and Gürüz (2008). Hauptman (2006) summarized the global trends in higher education finance. Information on the funding schemes currently in place in various countries, albeit changing rapidly, can be found in Forest and Altbach (2006, Pt. 2) and Gürüz (2008).

39. For further analyses and criticisms of the recent developments in American higher education, see Bok (2003), Kirp (2003), Newman, Couturier, and Scurry (2004), and Washburn (2005).

40. The Council of Universities is chaired by the minister of education, and is the national body responsible for the planning and coordination of higher education in Spain. University rectors and education directors of the seventeen autonomous regions are its members.

41. Shanghai Jiao Tong University was one of the nine universities selected in Project 985 to create world-class Chinese universities. The current academic ranking of world universities grew out of the efforts of the president of this university to define the term *world-class university* (N. Liu 2009). The criteria used are grouped into three categories: quality of education, quality of faculty, and quality of research—each measured by quantifiable indicators such as medals and Nobel Prizes won by alumni and faculty, articles published in prestigous journals, patents obtained and highly cited faculty in various scientific fields. These are then expressed on a per-capita basis, www.arwu.org/rank2008/ARWU2008Methodology(EN).htm#M1

42. It should be noted that the two French institutions in the top fifty in the 2008 ranking by *The Times Higher Education Supplement* are both *grands écoles*, and the two Swiss institutions are both federal universities, ETH and EPFL, which have very different governance structures than other institutions in the two countries.

43. Early in 2009, the Indian government announced a new program that aims to create thirty world-class universities, eight new Indian Institutes of Technology, seven new Indian Institutes of Management, and twelve new central universities bringing the total in the latter category to thirty (Altbach and Jayaram 2009).

44. Quoted in Clark (2001, 11). C. Kerr also listed "globalization of economic markets and their impact on the American Economy and on higher education" at the top of his list of items to concentrate on in the twenty-first century (Kerr 2001, 227).

FOUR: NEW PROVIDERS OF HIGHER EDUCATION

1. See also dos Santos (2002) for definitions of the terms used here. The terms *transnational education* and *cross-border education* are used in this chapter without having defined them; their formal definitions are given in Section 5.3.1.

2. "The history of open university," accessed on January 11, 2005 at http://www.open.ac.uk/media/factsheets. Enrollment figures given are for 2006–2007, and were obtained from http://hesa.ac.uk on March 25, 2009.

3. Total enrollment in distance education programs in Turkey in 2007–2008 was 878,000, accounting for 35 percent of the national enrollment.

4. www.wikieducator.org/Handbook_of_Open_Universities, accessed on March 22, 2009.

5. The UK e-University was established in 2000 as a separate institution from Open University, with the aim of exporting domestic higher education provision internationally and increasing national capacity at the same time (OBHE-KI, September 2004; OBHE-BN, November 2004). The government-funded institution was found to be unsustainable and closed in 2004 due to lack of private funding and disappointing enrollment figures. The Danish Virtual University, conceived in 2000, also was shelved (OBHE-BN, November 2003). The U.S. Open University, too, ceased to operate in June 2002 (OBHE-BN, May 2002).

6. Information retrieved on March 25, 2009 from http://www.umuc.edu/ and www.worldwidelearn.com/umuc/index.php.

7. Blackboard and WebCT merged in October 2005 to form Blackboard/WebCT, which is now dominating the LMS market worldwide (Becker and Joikivirta 2007).

8. On March 31, 2001, CRE merged with the Confederation of European Union Rectors' Conferences to form the European University Association.

9. "Guide to 100 Academic Networks World-Wide." *ACA Newsletter-Education Europe*, March 2009.

10. Information retrieved on March 25, 2009 from www.universitas21.com and www.u21global.edu.sg.

11. Information retrieved on May 10, 2009 from www.europace.org/.

12. Information retrieved on March 16, 2009 from www.wun.ac.uk.

13. Information retrieved on March 22, 2009 from www.ocicu.org.

14. Information retrieved on March 22, 2009 from www.iaruni.org.

15. Information available at www.fathom.com.

16. Multiplication of the per-student expenditure value for the United States in 2005, $24,370 in Table A.2 with the enrollment value of 16,611,711 in Table A.1 gives $405 million as the annual higher education expenditure.

17. The Observatory on Borderless Higher Education also has developed the Global Education Index of companies that are publicly traded and deliver education programs and services across borders in the international education market; more than fifty for-profit national companies and international conglomerates are included in the index (Garrett 2005; Garrett and Verbik 2005; Knight 2005a; see also Section 4.5).

18. Information retrieved on January 11, 2005 from www.apollogrp.edu/ http://www.apollogrp.com/ and www.investorguide.com/cgi-bin/stock.cgi?stock=APOL.

19. Information retrieved on May 6, 2005 from www.uopxworld.com/, www.usjournal.com/en/students/campuses/phoenix.html, and www.investorguide.com/cgi-bin/stock.cgi?stock=APOL.

20. Information retrieved on April 12, 2009 from www.apollogrp.edu/Annual-Reports/2008%20Annual%20Report.pdf.

21. Information retrieved on April 20, 2005 from www.careered.com/ and www.investorguide.com/cgi-bin/stock.cgi?stock=CECO.

22. Information retrieved on April 8, 2009 from www.careered.com.

23. Information retrieved on April 8, 2009 from www.cci.edu.

24. Information retrieved on January 11, 2005 from www.devry.com.

25. Information retrieved on April 8, 2009 from www.devryinc.com.

26. Information retrieved on April 20, 2005 from www.edumgt.com/ and www.investorguide.com/cgi-bin/stock.cgi?stock=EDMC.

27. Information retrieved on April 9, 2009 from www.edmc.com.

28. Information retrieved on April 20, 2005 from www.ittesi.com, www.investorguide.com/cgi-bin/stock.cgi?stock=ESI, and on April 10, 2009 from www.ittesi.com.

29. See also Recent developments in for-profit higher education. *Chronicle of Higher Education* 51(11): A28. November 5, 2004.

30. Information retrieved on April 18, 2005 from www.laureateuniversities.com.

31. Information retrieved on April 7, 2009 from www.laureate-inc.com.

32. Information retrieved on April 20 2005 from http://www.strayereducation.com and www.investorguide.com/cgibin/stock.cgi?stock=STRA, and on April 10, 2009 from www.starayereducation.com.

33. Information retrieved on April 21, 2005 from www.listedcompany.com/ir/raffleseducation and www.hartford.com.sg, and on April 10, 2009 from www.raffleseducation-corporation.com.

34. Information retrieved on April 20, 2005 from www.mibt.vic.edu.au.

35. Information retrieved on April 11, 2009 from www.hanseuni.de.

36. Information retrieved on April 20, 2005 and April 11, 2009 from www.wgu.edu.

37. Information retrieved on April 10, 2009 from www.ouw.co.uk/partnerships.aspx.

38. Information retrieved on January 11, 2005 from www.open.ac.uk/media/factsheets.

39. Information retrieved on May 13, 2005 from www.cvu-uvc.ca.

40. The UK Health Service University was closed in 2005. Its demise has been attributed to its politically led nature and the fact that as an organization it contradicted the idea of a university (Taylor, Bell, Grugulis, and Storey 2007)

41. Information retrieved on April 25, 2005 from www.aptech-worldwide.com, and on April 11, 2009 from www.aptech-education.com.

42. The Thomson Corporation is a global conglomerate with 2004 revenues exceeding $8.1 billion, and nearly forty thousand employees in forty countries. It is active in the areas of information and integrated learning solutions for a diverse training and education needs of individuals, businesses, institutions, corporations, and governments. It operates through four groups: Thomson Legal and Regulatory, Thomson Learning, Thomson Financial and Thomson Scientific and Healthcare (information retrieved on May 5, 2005 from www.thomson.com/corp, hed.thomson-learningco.uk/, and www.prometric.com.

43. Information retrieved on April 11, 2009 from www.cengage.com and www.thomsonreuters.com.

44. Information retrieved on May 9, 2005 from http://www.iccp.org/iccpnew/council.htm.

45. Information retrieved on April 12, 2009 from www.pearsoned.com.

46. Information retrieved on April 25, 2005 from www.university.barnesnoble.com.

47. Information retrieved on March 23, 2005 from www.onlineuc.net.

48. Information retrieved on April 24 2005 from www.universityalliance.com.

49. Information retrieved on May 13, 2005 from www.onlineuniversityguide.org.

50. Information retrieved on 5 May 2005 from www.unext.com.

51. The name Cardean was taken from Cardea, the Roman goddess of portals that possesses the power to open what is shut and shut what is open (www.cardean.edu).

52. See note 42.

53. See note 50.

54. Information retrieved on April 11, 2009 from http://cardeanlearninggroup.com.

55. Information retrieved on May 13, 2005 from www.ola.edu.au.

56. Information retrieved on April 12, 2009 from www.open.edu.au.

57. Foundation programs are postsecondary qualifications, often of a vocational nature, designed to meet labor shortages and provide one to two years of further education opportunities. They also allow graduates the possibility of gaining access to university-level studies, and it is in that capacity that they are now becoming an instrument of international higher education marketing (OBHE-BN, June 2004). Similar programs also are offered to foreign students intending to enter British institutions who lack the necessary admission qualifications. In June 2004, Chinese authorities signed deals with the International Development Program Education Australia, the Scottish Qualifications Authority, and the Canadian Institute of Management to open foundation programs in China that would provide alternative pathways for Chinese students to enter higher education (OBHE-BNA, June 3, 2004).

58. See also Krieger (2008).

59. Excerpt from *Open Doors* 2007 at www.opendoors.iienetwork.org/file_depot/0-10000000/0-10000/3390/folder/69364/BranchCampus2007Analysis.pdf.

60. HESA Press Release no. 133, April 16, 2009.

61. Information retrieved on January 14, 2005 from www.studymalaysia.com/is/education12.shtml.

62. The Singapore campus of the University of New South Wales was closed in May 2007, only months after it started operating. Lack of interest, rising costs and difficulties with Singapore Economic Development Board were cited as reasons.

63. See Section 3.3 for UniSIM, through which the Singapore University of Management started offering degrees in 2005.

64. Quoted in British Columbia Center for International Education, News and Views, Spring 2004. Retrieved from www.bccie.bc.ca.

65. Information retrieved on March 29, 2009 from www.nottingham.edu.cn.

66. There is relatively little information on foreign education activity in Latin America and the Caribbean. The material I have summarized here has been condensed from Aupetit and Joikivirta (2007).

FIVE: GLOBALIZATION AND INTERNATIONALIZATION OF HIGHER EDUCATION

1. International academic mobility did not take place in the West alone. Klineberg (1976, 21, 144) cites the large exchange of scholars between China and India, which was focused on the transfer and spread of Buddhism from India to China. Between 206 BC and 905 AD, 736 Indian scholars visited China, and in the period 307–689, 166 Chinese scholars visited India. Many Buddhist texts were translated from Indian to Chinese.

2. Nakayama (1984, 73–82) provides an analysis of why Chinese tradition based on the works of Confucius (551–479 BC) did not go beyond the accumulation of routine knowledge and consequently did not evolve into a central position in the development of modern science, as did those of Greek philosophers. Among the reasons he gives is the rather limited international mobility of scholars in a region isolated at the eastern end of the Eurasian landmass.

3. See Stanton (1990) and Rubenstein (2003) on the transmission of the Greco-Roman intellectual heritage to the West by Muslim scholars.

4. Ridder-Symoens (1992b) refers to the translation center in Toledo as a school for translators, attracting students from all over Europe, and cites it as an example of earlier academic mobility in Europe.

5. The material presented in this section has been condensed mainly from Ridder-Symoens (1992b).

6. The irony is that the works of the Muslim scholars cited here never became a part of the curricula in the madrasa. Consequently, as the university evolved into a central institution of the global civilization, the madrasa decayed into a bastion of fundamentalism, eventually becoming the breeding ground for the Taliban.

7. Oxford, for example, was staffed by masters (teachers) and scholars (students) of the Sorbonne, who, following a tavern brawl and the ensuing riots, accepted the invitation of the English king, Henry III, in 1229. Cambridge, in turn, was founded by masters and students who fled Oxford following the arrest and execution of students. It was, however, the developed region of northern Italy that was

the scene for early academic mobility, with students and teachers leaving one city to found a university in a rival city, such as Padua being founded due to migrations from Bologna (Verger 1992).

8. The material presented in this section has been condensed mainly from Ridder-Symoens (1996b).

9. For the new structures of knowledge that emerged then, see Schmidt-Biggemann (1996).

10. Philip Melanchton (1497–1560), professor of Greek at Wittenberg University and the founder of Marburg University, regarded as the intellectual leader of Protestantism, is referred to as the "Teacher of Germany" (praeceptor germaniae).

11. See, for example, R. Porter (1996) and also Section 1.2.

12. For more on the topics in this section, see Neave (2003) and Perkin (2006).

13. Unless otherwise indicated, the material presented in this section is based on Charle (2004) and Shils and Roberts (2004).

14. In Altbach's (2004a, 4) words: "Much of the non-Western world had European university models imposed on them by colonial masters. Even those countries not colonized by Western powers—such as Japan, Thailand, Ethiopia and a few others—adopted the Western academic model. This is the case even where, as in China, well-established academic traditions already existed. The basic structure of the institution and the orientation to teaching, for example, characterize universities internationally and are derived from the medieval European tradition." To Altbach's list of countries that were not colonized, had their own traditions of teaching, and adopted the Western model of higher education, Turkey should be added. One of the earliest laws that was enacted by the young Turkish Republic in 1928 was Law No.1416, which laid out the procedures, rules, and regulations for the selection and the financing of students to be sent abroad for training on government scholarships.

15. Ringer (2004) reports the female participation rate in a number of European countries in the period c. 1900–c. 1930. In the years c. 1900, there were female students only in France (3 percent), Sweden (3 percent), the Netherlands (7 percent), Great Britain (17 percent) and Switzerland (20 percent). Germany started to allow female students after 1900; the female participation rate had increased to 18 percent in Germany by c.1930. Figures for other European countries for those years were as follows: Spain (7 percent), Switzerland (12 percent), Italy (15 percent), Austria (17 percent), the Netherlands (18 percent), and France and Great Britain 26 percent each.

16. The College Entrance Examination Board was founded in 1900. The first Scholastic Aptitude Test was given in 1926, and the first Graduate Record Examination in 1926. The first automatic test reader was developed by IBM in 1936. The Educational Testing Service was established in 1948 to prepare and administer such tests nationwide. For more on the development of admission tests to U.S. institutions, see Lemann (1999).

17. For the history of the Institute of International Education, Deutscher Akademischer Austausch Dienst, and the British Council visit:

http://www.iie.org/Content/NavigationMenu/About_IIE/History_of_IIE.htm.
http://www.daad.de/portrait/en/1.4.2.html.
http://www.britishcouncil.org/history-when-1930s-2000s.htm.

18. For the proceedings of the first Conference of Foreign Student Advisers, held in Chicago on April 28–30, 1947, see IIE (1947). The 57th NAFSA annual conference was held in Seattle on May 29–June 3, 2005; the total number of participants was 6,771, with 1,995 foreign participants from ninety-five countries.

19. For more on the history of the International Development Program, visit http://www.idp.com/ aboutidp/article7.asp.

20. See also Barber (1992) for the determinants of international student mobility in the 1980s, when the new rationales started to appear with the advent of globalization.

21. Bohm et al. (2004) also include personal security and lifestyle among the key attributes affecting student choice of destination country.

22. See Corbett (2005) for the historical background to and the politics behind the Bologna Process and van der Wende (2000); OECD (2004, 94–97), Reichert and Tauch (2004) for more on its structure and aims.

23. The Lisbon Agenda should not be confused with the Lisbon Convention. The Lisbon Agenda refers to the objective set forth in the meeting of the European Union (EU) heads of states and governments in March 2000, which aims to make EU "the most competitive and dynamic knowledge-based economy in the world capable of sustainable economic growth with more and better jobs and greater social cohesion." To this end, the EU heads of states and governments set the EU-wide target for research and development spending as 3 percent of the gross national product, reduced red tape for innovation and more employment. For more on the Lisbon Agenda, see OECD (2004b, 97–99).

24. "Realizing the European Higher Education Area-Achieving the Goals," Conference of European Higher Education Ministers, Contribution of the European Commission, May 19–20, 2005, which can be accessed at http://www.bologna-bergen2005.no/.

25. "Towards the European Higher Education Area: responding to changes in a globalized world," which can be accessed at http://www.enqa.eu/newsitem.lasso?id=128.

26. Information retrieved on April 15, 2009 from www.eqar.eu.

27. "The Bologna Process into the next decade." ACA Newsletter-Education Europe, April 2009.

28. See, for example, Amaral and Magalhes (2004).

29. "Mobilizing the Brainpower of Europe: Enabling Universities to Make Their Full Contribution to the Lisbon Strategy." Communication from the Commission of the European Communities, COM (2005) 152 final, April 20, 2005.

30. Focus on the structure of higher education in Europe 2006/2007: National trends in the Bologna Process." EURYDICE. http://eacea:ac.europa.eu/portal/page/portal/eurydice/showpresentation?pubid=086EN. See also van der Wende (2001b).

31. Data retrieved on March 30, 2009 from www.wissenschaft-weltoffen.de and http://ec.europa.eu/education/erasmus/doc920_en.html.

32. Information retrieved on March 30, 2009 from http://ec.europa.eu/education/programmes/mundus/projects_en.html.

33. The basic sources of information on the General Agreement on Trade Services (GATS) as it relates to higher education are "An overview of higher education and GATS," August 2002. The American Council on Education. It can be accessed at

http://www.acenet.edu/AM/Template.cfm?Section=Topics&Template=/CM/HTMLD-isplay.cfm&ContentID=5851; "US update on GATS: January 2004," The American Council on Education. It can be accessed at http://www.acenet.edu/AM/Template.cfm?Section=Intl&Template=/CM/HTMLDisplay.cfm&ContentID=5852; "Trade in higher education and GATS." It can be accessed at the basics portal of UNESCO: http://www.unesco.org/education/studyingabroad/highlights/global_forum/gats_he/basics_he_trade_main.shtml.

The following page on the ACE Web site is dedicated to GATS: http://www.acenet.edu/AM/Template.cfm?Section=Intl&Template=/CM/ContentDisplay.cfmCONTENTID=15605.

34. See also "Sharing Quality Higher Education Across Borders" at http://www.acenet.edu/AM/Template.cfm?Section=Intl&CONTENTID=16437&TEMPLATE=/CM/CONTENTDisplay.cfm.

35. See also "The great GATS scandal," by Aileen Kwa in *Focus on the Global South*, November 2, 2005, which can be accessed at http://www.focuswb.org.

36. Ibid.

37. In what appears to be a move to make use of the proposed "plurilateral" approach to negotiations, New Zealand has already taken the initiative to form a "Friends of Private Education Exports Group." It is interesting to note that this is an initiative taken by a labor government (OBHE-BNA, November 15, 2005).

38. See note 34.

39. Visit the International Council for Open and Distance Education Web site at http://www.icde.org/

40. Information retrieved from http://portal.unesco.org/education/en/ev.phpURL_ID=4070&URL_DO=DO_TOPIC&URL_SECTION=201.html, and on May 16, 2009 from www.inqaahe.org.

41. Altbach (2006) has referred to the role of the governments of the United States and Australia in advocating the interests of the for-profit providers in the World Trade Organization (WTO) as a new "neo-colonialism." The role of UNES-CO, on the other hand, is generally perceived as a multinational organizational response to WTO/GATS (Eaton 2005). Vlk (2006, 108-110 underscores the role of UNESCO in advocating the right to education and development in connection with GATS.

42. For a more on quality and recognition issues in transnational higher education see Knight (2008, 123–36).

SIX: INTERNATIONAL STUDENT MOBILITY

1. Similar data can be found in Cummings (1991) and Barber (1992) for the 1980s and before.

2. The UNESCO convention of citing the later year when the data reported are spread over two years is adhered to in this study also.

3. *Agence Campus France's* booklet, dated January 2009, entitled "Programs Taught in English" lists hundreds of full-degree programs taught in English in French institutions (www.campusfrance.org). According to an article that appeared in *NRC Handelsblad* ("English becomes Lingua Franca at Dutch universities" March 20, 2009,

English is almost the second official language of instruction in Dutch institutions. (www.spiegel.de/internationalization/world/0,1518,614572,00.html#ref=nlint).

4. Sixty-seven percent of the students hosted in South Africa are from Sub-Saharan Africa, and the rest are of unspecified nationality—quite probably also from neighboring countries. Eighty-five percent of the students hosted by Cuba are from the Latin America and the Caribbean region. Similarly, 81 percent of the students hosted by the Czech Republic are from the central and eastern European region (UNESCO 2008, 115–20). In a conference entitled "Higher Education in Cuba" at Ankara University in Turkey on March 4, 2009, Ruben Zardoya, the rector of the University of Havana stated that Cuba's target was to host 100,000 students. It appears that Cuba's internationalization policy is driven by the political rationale, whereas the Czech policy is based on the cultural rationale.

5. The figure for Cyprus does not include the enrollment in the Turkish side of the island, which grew from 11,710 students in 1998 to 30,505 in 2006, with students from Turkey accounting for close to 90 percent of the foreign enrollment (private communication from the Turkish NARIC).

6. Data for United States are from the annual *Open Doors* reports by the Institute of International Education available in CD-ROM for the years 1948–2004, and online for the years 2005–2008 at www.opendoors.iienetwork.org.

7. *Open Doors* 1948–1949, p. 21.

8. China, however, meant different things in different years. In 1949, Republic of China included students from Hong Kong, Formosa (today's Taiwan) and Macao. In 1965, China covered those students who declared their country of citizenship as China, but many of whom were domiciled in other counties. It was after China joined the UN in 1971 that statistics started include Peoples Republic of China and Taiwan separately.

9. In those years, many small colleges were dependent on tuition fee revenue from Iranian students. According to an article that appeared in *The New York Times* ("Iranian Plight Puts a Spotlight on U.S. Colleges," February 20, 1979, p. C.4), the small Windham College in Vermont depended on Iranians for 30 percent of its enrollment and went out of business when these students were unable to make tuition payments. Quoted in Bound et al. (2009, 22).

10. Two thirds of the world's most "highly cited scientists" are working in the United States. American scientists have won more than half of the scientific prizes since the 1930s (Institute of Scientific Information data accessed at http://www.in-cites.com/countries/2002allfields.htm; National Science Foundation, "International Mobility of Scientists and Engineers to the United States-Brain Drain or Brain Circulation," NSF 98–316, November 10, 1998; Nobel Prize data accessed at http://www.nobel.se/index.html, quoted by Paarlberg (2004).

11. In a recent report, Bound et al. (2009) argue that the representation of a large number of students born outside the United States among the ranks of doctorate recipients from U.S. universities is one of the most significant transformations in U.S. graduate education and the international market for highly trained workers in science and engineering in the last quarter century. They quote the following figures in support of their arguments. Students from outside the United States. accounted for 51 percent of PhD recipients in science and engineering fields in 2003,

up from 27 percent in 1973. In the physical sciences, engineering, and economics, the representation of foreign students among PhD recipients is yet more striking; among doctorate recipients in 2003, those from outside the United States. accounted for 50 percent of degrees in the physical sciences, 67 percent in engineering, and 68 percent in economics.

12. *Soft power* is a term coined by Nye (2004), which means obtaining outcomes the United States wants through co-option and persuasion rather than coercion. The latter relies on the use of hard power, which includes military and economic means, whereas soft power relies on cultural and ideological influences through various means including educational.

13. See for example, "No Longer Dreaming of America" in the *Chronicle of Higher Education*, October 8, 2004, and "Editorials and Opinion Pieces in Support of International Education" in IIE Interactive, at http://opendoors.iienetwork.org/?p=53075.

14. See "Foreign Students: Uncle Sam Wants You" in *Chronicle of Higher Education*, January 20, 2006; OBHE-BN, January 2006, June 2006.

15. HESA Press Release 133, April 16, 2009.

16. HESA Press Release 120, March 19, 2008, and HESA Press Release 97, March 13, 2006.

17. HESA Press Release 97, March 13, 2006.

18. Ibid.

19. Based on data retrieved on May 25, 2009 from UKCOSA (recently renamed UKCISA, UK Council for International Student Affairs) Web site: www.ukcosa.org.uk.

20. Ibid.

21. Further education data supplied by the British Council office in Turkey.

22. Data for Germany are from the *Deutscher Akademischer Austausch Dienst (DAAD)* Web site, www.wissenschaft-weltoffen.de.

23. *Bildungsinlaender*: Secondary-school diploma from a German school; *Bildungsauslaender*: secondary-school diploma from a school outside of Germany.

24. Information was retrieved from the DAAD Web site: www.daad.de/portrait/en/1.1html.

25. EduFrance Newsletter Key Figures, Special Edition 2, November 2004.

26. Data for 2005 from "International students: It's a buyers market." By N. Clark and R. Sedgewick, World Education News and Reviews, Feature August 2005. Data for 2009 from: www.campusfrance.org.

27. Data from: AEI Research Snapshot No. 42, November 2008, and AEI Research Snapshot No. 45, March 2009.

28. Quoted in the following Web site, accessed on January 15, 2005 at http://www.hothousemedia.com/etm/etmbackissues/janetm0 5/janetm05news.htm.

29. Citizenship and Immigration Canada "Foreign Students in Canada 1980–2001." Accessed on January 10, 2005 at http://www.cic.gc.ca/english/research/papers/foreignstudents/students.html.

30. Breakdown of foreign student enrollment by countries of origin for 2002–2004 is from Savage and Kane (2005), and for 2003–2004 from http://aei.dest.gov.au/AEI/PublicationsAnd Research/Snapshots/03SS05_pdf.pdf.

31. "Students head for Ireland," accessed on January 15, 2005 at http://www.hothousemedia.com/etm/etmbackissues/janetm05news.htm.

32. Data on Chinese students abroad were taken from UNESCO (1963)–UNESCO (2008). The data on Chinese students represented only students from Taiwan until 1971, when China became a member of the UN. Davis (2003, 79) gives the number of Chinese students abroad in 2000–2001 as 120,486.

33. Among the Chinese students who studied overseas in the period 1978–1999, 75 percent did not return, including 85.9 percent who studied in the United States, 62.6 percent in Japan, 55.1 percent in Australia, 53.2 percent in the United Kingdom, and 52.4 percent in France. The average stay rate of Chinese doctoral recipients in science and engineering fields four to five years after graduation increased from 65 percent in 1992 to 96 percent in 2001 (OECD 2004b, 78–279).

34. "More than 100,000 Chinese students who have studied abroad return to China." Chinese Education and Society 33(5), 2000. Quoted as related article in Mooney and Neelekantan (2004).

35. See also Atlas of Student Mobility: www.atlas.iienetwork.org/?p=53467, accessed on May 26, 2009.

36. Ibid.

37. Retrieved on 4 August 4, 2006 from http://english.people.com.cn/200606/13/eng200606/3_273485.html., quoted at http://atlas.iienetwork.org/.

38. See also www.atlas.iienetwork.org/?p=53608, accessed on May 26, 2009.

39. The most recent figure reported by the Atlas of Student Mobility is 18,594, with Iran as the leading country of origin. This is vastly different from the enrollment values reported by UNESCO. Ibid.

40. See also www.atlas.iienetwork.org/?p=48038, accessed on May 26, 2009.

41. There are four for-profit universities and one public university in northern Cyprus. Recently, Middle East Technical University, the premiere institution of higher education in Turkey, opened a branch campus. Total enrollment in 2006 reached 38,850 students, up from 16,842 in 1998. Students from Turkey currently number 25,700, up from 10,744 in 1998. These, however, do not show up in the UNESCO statistics because UN does not recognize the Turkish Republic of Northern Cyprus (private communication with the Turkish NARIC).

42. See www.wissenschaft-weltoffen.de/daten/2007/1/2/3, accessed on April 28, 2009.

43. Information on Singapore was retrieved on March 14, 2009 from www.spring.gov.sg and www.business.gov.sg. For more on international education in Singapore, see "Can Singapore become the Boston of Asia?" Singapore Business Review, October 2004, and visit http://moe.gov.sg.

44. See www.atlas.iienetwork.org/page/97988/ accessed on May 26, 2009.

45. "Facts about education in Norway: key figures 2007." Oslo: Statistics Norway.

46. Information retrieved on April 12, 2009 from: www.nuffic.nl/international-organizations/docs/keyfigures/KeyFigures2007.pdf.

47. First coined by the British Royal Society to describe the migration of scientists and technology experts from Britain to the United States and Canada in the 1950s and early 1960s, the term brain drain has come to be associated with a

one-way, definitive, and permanent migration of skilled people from developing to industrial countries (Dassin 2005).

48. The statement is attributed to Rajiv Gandhi, quoted in "Brains business," (*The Economist*, September 8, 2005). See also note 13 in Chapter 2 for the new view on brain drain.

49. According to data reported in article in *USA Today*, "Recent Arrivals Better Educated," on February 22, 2005, the education attainment of immigrants to the United States is increasing. Moreover, adult children of immigrants are exceeding their parents' income and educational levels.

BIBLIOGRAPHY

AIEA. 1988. Action for international competence: Recommendations by the AIEA. June 3. Washington, D.C.: AIEA.

———. 1995. A research agenda for the internationalization of higher education in the United States: Recommendations and report of the AIEA working group based on the August 10–11 meeting. Washington, D.C.: AIEA.

Allen, I. E., and Seamann. J. 2006. Making the grade: Online education in the United States 2006. Sloan Consortium. www.sloan-c.org/publications/survey/pdf/making_the_grade.pdf.

Altbach, P. G. 1999a. Private higher education: Themes and variations in comparative perspective. *Prospects* 29 (3): 311–23.

———. 1999b. Comparative perspectives on private higher education. In *Private Prometheus: Private higher education and development in the twenty-first century*, ed. P. G. Altbach, 1–14. Newton, Mass: Boston College Center for International Higher Education. Rep. 2003.

———. 2001. The rise of the pseudo-university. *International Higher Education* 25 (Fall): 2–3. (Note: All articles in *International Higher Education* can be accessed at http://www.bc.edu/bc_org/avp/coe/cihe/newsletter.)

———. 2004a. Globalisation and the university: Myths and realities in an unequal world. *Tertiary Education and Management* 10: 3–25.

———. 2004b. GATS redux: The WTO and higher education returns to center stage. *International Higher Education* 37 (Fall): 5–7.

———. 2006. Globalization and the university: Realities in an unequal world. In *International handbook of higher education*, pt.1 (2 pts.), ed. J. J. F. Forest and P. G. Altbach, 121–39 (2 parts). Dordrecht, The Netherlands: Springer.

Altbach, P. G., and Jayaram, N. 2009. India's effort to join 21st-century higher education. *International Higher Education* 54 (Winter): 17–19.

Altbach, P. G., and Teichler, U. 2001. Internationalization and exchanges in a globalized university. *Journal of Studies in International Education* 5 (1): 5–25.

Alvarez-Mendiola, G., and de Vries, W. 2005. Public universities in Mexico: The politics of public policies. *International Educator* 14 (3): 10–12.

Amano, I. 1997. Structural changes in Japan's higher education system: From a planning to a market model. *Higher Education* 34:125–39.

Amaral, A., Jones, G., and Karseth, B. 2002. Governing higher education: Comparing national perspectives. In *Governing higher education: National perspectives on institutional governance*, ed. A. Amaral, G. A. Jones, and B. Karseth, 279–98. Dordrecht, The Netherlands: Kluwer Academic Publishers.

Amaral, A., and Magalhes, A. 2002. The emergent role of external stakeholders in European higher education governance. In *Governing higher education:*

National perspectives on institutional governance, ed. A. Amaral, G. A. Jones, and B. Karseth, 1–22. Dordrecht, The Netherlands: Kluwer Academic Publishers.

Anandakrishnan, M. 2001. Inaugural address. In *Internationalization of Indian higher education*, ed. K. B. Powar, iv–vii. New Delhi: Association of Indian Universities.

Anderson, S. 2004. The multiplier effect. *International Educator* 13 (3): 14–21.

Askling, B. 2001. In search of new models of institutional governance: Some Swedish experiences. *Tertiary Education and Management* 7:197–210.

Asonumo, A. 2002. Finance reform in Japanese higher education. *Higher Education* 43:109–26.

AUCC. 2001. Canadian Higher Education and the GATS. AUCC Background Paper. Accessed on January 2, 2005 at http://64.233.161.104/search?q=cache: ZbvFjiMwQAoJ:www.aucc.ca/_pdf/eenglish/reports/.

Aupetit, S.D., and Jokivirta; L. Foreign education activity in Latin America and the Caribbean: Key issues, regulation and impact. OBHE Report, June. London: OBHE.

Barber, E. G. 1992. Student mobility (international). In *The encyclopedia of higher education*, vol.2 (4 vols.), ed. B. R. Clark, and G. Neave, 1020–28. London: Pergamon Press.

Barblan, A. 2002. Academic co-operation and mobility in Europe: How it was and how it will be. *Higher Education in Europe* 27 (1, 2): 31–58.

Barblan, A., Ergüder, Ü., and Gürüz, K. 2008. *Higher education in Turkey: Institutional autonomy and responsibility in a modernizing society—Policy recommendations in a historical perspective*. Case Studies, Observatory for Fundamental University Values and Rights. Bologna: Bononia University Press.

Bashir, S. 2007. *Trends in international trade in higher education: Implications and options for developing countries*. Washington, D. C.: World Bank

Becker, R., and Joikivirta, L. 2007. Online learning in universities: Selected data from the 2006 Observatory survey. OBHE Report, November. London: OBHE.

Beckmeier, C., and Neusel, A. 1990. Decision-making process in French and German universities. *Higher Education Management* 2 (1): 7–19.

Billing, D. 2004. International comparisons and trends in external quality assurance of higher education: Commonality or diversity? *Higher Education* 47:113–37.

Birchard, K. 2006. Canada eases rules for foreign students. *Chronicle of Higher Education* 52 (36): A46. May 12.

Blight, D. 1995. *International education: Australia's potential demand and supply*. Canberra: IDP Education Australia.

Blumenstyk, G. 2005a. For-profit education: Online courses fuel growth. *Chronicle of Higher Education* 51 (8): A11. January 7.

———. 2005b. Investments growing in education firms. *Chronicle of Higher Education* 51(30): A39. April 1.

———. 2005c. For-profit outlook. *Chronicle of Higher Education* 52(14): A14. November 25.

———. 2005d The Chronicle index of for-profit education. *Chronicle of Higher Education* 52(12): A31. 11 November.

———. 2006. European Union beckons expatriates home. *Chronicle of Higher Education* 52(45): A36. July 14.

———. 2007a. The Chronicle index of for-profit education. *Chronicle of Higher Education* 54(11): A27. November 9.

———. 2007b. The Chronicle index of for-profit education. *Chronicle of Higher Education* 53(23): A25. February 9.

———. 2007c. The Chronicle index of for-profit education. *Chronicle of Higher Education* 53(36): A31. May 11.

———. 2008a. Economic downturn brings prosperity and opportunities to for-profit colleges. *Chronicle of Higher Education* 55(17): A13. December 18.

———. 2008b. The Chronicle index of for-profit education. *Chronicle of Higher Education* 54(25): A27. November 9.

———. 2008c. New nonprofit online university has unusual corporate beginnings. *The Chronicle* daily-news archives. August 22.

Bockstaele, P. 2004. The mathematical and the exact sciences. In *Universities in the nineteenth and early twentieth centuries (1800–1945)*, ed. W. Ruegg, vol. 3 (3 vols.) of *A history of the university* in Europe, gen. ed. W. Ruegg, 493–518. Cambridge: Cambridge University Press.

Bohm, A., et al. 2004. Vision 2020: Forecasting international student mobility: a UK perspective. Report commissioned by the British Council, Universities UK and IDP Australia. London: British Council.

Bok, D. C. 2003. *Universities in the marketplace: The commercialization of higher education*. Princeton, N.J.: Princeton University Press.

Bollag, B. 2004a. Degrees of separation. *Chronicle of Higher Education*, 51(8): A36. October 15.

———. 2004b. Wanted foreign students. *Chronicle of Higher Education* 51(7): A37. October 8.

———. 2004c. Enrollment of foreign students drops in the US. *Chronicle of Higher Education* 51 (13). November 19.

———. 2006a. America's hot new export: Higher education. *Chronicle of Higher Education* 52 (24): A44. February 17.

———. 2006b. Proposed visa change would make it easier for foreign students to stay in US after graduation. *Chronicle of Higher Education* 52(32): A45. April 14.

Bonk, C. J. 2004. "The perfect e-storm: Part 1; storm #1 and #2." OBHE-Report. London: OBHE. June.

Borrelli, V, and Teter, W. 2005. Erasmus Mundus and the new European dimension to higher education. *IIE Networker* (Spring): 46–49.

Bound, J., Turner, S., and Walsh, P. 2009. Internationalization of U.S. doctorate education. Working Paper 14792. Cambridge, MA: National Bureau of Economic Research. www.nber.org/papers/w14792.

Brender, A. 2004a. In Japan, radical reform or same old subservience. *Chronicle of Higher Education* 50(27): A39. 12 March 12.

———. 2004b. Japan recognizes US and other foreign universities on its soil. *Chronicle of Higher Education* 51(8): A38. October 15.

———. 2006. South Korea overhauls higher education. *Chronicle of Higher Education* 52(28): A50. March 17.

British Council. 2003. Positioning for success. London: Education UK.

Brunner, J. J. 1993. Chile's higher education: Between market and state. *Higher Education* 25: 35–43.

Brunner, J. J., and Tillett, A. 2006. Chile. In Pt.2 of *International handbook of higher education*, eds. J. J. F. Forest and P. G. Altbach (2 pts.), 647–66. Dordrecht, The Netherlands: Springer.

Bush, V. 1980. *Science: The endless frontier; three centuries of science in America.* Washington, D.C.: National Science Foundation.

Bushan, S. 2006. Foreign education providers in India: Mapping the extent and regulation. OBHE Report, March. London: OBHE.

Cai, Y. 2004. Confronting the global and the local: A case study of Chinese higher education. *Tertiary Education and Management* 10:157–69.

Calero, J. 1998. Quasi-market reforms and equity in the financing of higher education. *European Journal of Education* 33 (1): 11–20.

Carlson, S. 2005. The net generation goes to college. *Chronicle of Higher Education*, 52 (7): A34. October 7.

Carnegie Foundation. 1982. *The control of the campus.* Princeton, N.J.: Princeton University Press.

Casanova-Cardiel, H. 2006. Mexico. In Pt.2 of *International handbook of higher education*, eds. J. J. F. Forest and P. G. Altbach (2 pts.), 881–98. Dordrecht, the Netherlands: Springer.

Ceaser, M. 2004. Chile moves toward voluntary accreditation. *Chronicle of Higher Education* 51 (8): A39. October 15.

Charle, C. 2004. Patterns. In *Universities in the nineteenth and the early twentieth centuries (1800–1945)*, ed. W. Ruegg, 33–81 in vol. 3 (4 vols.) of *A history of the university in Europe* (3 vols.), gen. ed. W. Ruegg. Cambridge: Cambridge University Press.

Chellaraj, G., Maskus, K. E., and Mattoo, A. 2006. Skilled immigrants, higher education and US innovation. In *International migration, remittances & the brain drain*, ed. C. Ozden and M. Schiff, 245–59. Washington, D.C.: World Bank and Palgrave Macmillan.

Chevaillier, T. 2002. University governance and finance: The impact of changes in resource allocation on decision making structures: In *Governing higher education: National perspectives on institutional governance*, ed. A. Amaral, G. A. Jones and B. Karseth, 87–98. Dordrecht, The Netherlands: Kluwer Academic Publishers.

Chevaillier, T., and Eicher, J. C. 2002. Higher education funding: A decade of change. *Higher Education in Europe* 27(1–2): 89–99.

Clark, B. R. 1983. *The higher education system: Academic organization in cross-national perspective.* Berkeley and Los Angeles: University of California Press.

———. 1998. *Creating entrepreneurial universities: Organizational pathways of transformation.* London: Pergamon Press. (Published for the IAU Press.)

———. 2001. The entrepreneurial university: New foundations for collegiality; autonomy and achievement. *Higher Education Management* 13 (2): 9–24.

Clark, N., and Sedgwick, R. 2005. International students: It's a buyer's market. *World Education News & Reviews* 18(4), August. Retrieved from: http://www.wes.org/ewenr/05July/feature.htm.

Cohen, D. 2004. Singapore to get its first foreign-run university. *Chronicle of Higher Education* 50 (36): A42. May 14.

———. 2006a. Carnegie-Mellon plants the US flag in Australia. *Chronicle of Higher Education* 52(35): A49. May 5.

———. 2006b. Growth of foreign-student enrollments slows in Australia. *Chronicle of Higher Education* 52(29): A53. 24 March 24.

Corbett, A. 2005. *Universities and the Europe of knowledge*. New York: Palgrave Macmillan.

Cowley, W. H. 1980. *Presidents, professors and trustees: The evolution of American academic government*. San Francisco: Jossey-Bass.

Cummings, W. K. 1991. Foreign students. In *International higher education: An encyclopedia*, ed. P. G. Altbach, 107–25. New York: Garland Publishers.

CVCP (Committee of Vice-Chancellors and Principals). 1985. Report of the steering committee on efficiency studies in universities. London: CVCP. March 29.

CVCP-HEFCE. 2000. The business of borderless education: UK perspectives. Summary report. London: CVCP-HEFCE. March.

Daniel, J. S. 1996. *Mega universities and knowledge media*. London: Routledge.

Dassin, J. 2005. Brain gain, not drain, fosters global development and security. *International Educator* 14 (3): 20–25.

Davis. T. M. 2003. *Atlas of student mobility*. New York: IIE.

de Boer, H. 2002. Trust, the essence of governance? In *Governing higher education: National perspectives on institutional governance*, ed. A. Amaral, G. A. Jones and B. Karseth, 43–61. Dordrecht, The Netherlands: Kluwer Academic Publishers.

de Boer, H., and Goedegebuure, L. 2001. On limitation and consequences of change: Dutch university governance in transition. *Tertiary Education and Management* 7:43–61.

de Boer, H., Maassen, P., and de Weert, E. E. 1999. The troublesome Dutch university and its Route 66 towards a new governance structure. *Higher Education Policy* 12:329–42.

de Groof, J., Neave, G., and Svec, J., eds. 1998. *Democracy and governance in higher education*. Vol. 2 in the Council of Europe Series on Legislating for Higher Education in Europe. The Hague, The Netherlands: Kluwer Law International.

Dobson, I. R. 2001. How has massification changed the shape of Australian universities? *Tertiary Education and Management* 7:295–310.

Docquier, F., and Marfouk, A. 2006. International migration by education attainment, 1990–2000. In *International migration, remittances & the brain drain*, ed. C. Ozden and M. Schiff, 151–99. Washingto, D.C.: World Bank and Palgrave Macmillan.

dos Santos, S. M. 2002. Regulation and quality assurance in transnational education. *Tertiary Education and Management* 8:97–112.

Doyon, P. 2001. A review of higher education reform in modern Japan. *Higher Education* 41:443–70.

Duckett, S. J. 2004. Turning right at the crossroads: The Nelson Report's proposals to transform Australia's universities. *Higher Education* 47:211–40.

Eaton, J. S. 2005. Quality and international higher education space. *International Higher Education* 40 (Summer): 3–4.

Eicher, J. C. 1998. The costs and financing of higher education in Europe. *European Journal of Education* 33 (1): 31–39.

Eicher, J. C., and Chevaillier, T. 2002. Rethinking the financing of post-compulsory education. *Higher Education in Europe* 27 (1, 2): 69–88.

Enders, J. 2004. Higher education, internationalization and the nation-state: Recent developments and challenges to the governance theory. *Higher Education* 47:361–82.

El-Khawas, E. 2006. Accountability and quality assurance: New issues for academic inquiry. In Pt. 1 of *International handbook of higher education*, eds. J. J. F. Forest and P. G. Altbach (2 pts.), 23–37. Dordrecht, The Netherlands. Springer.

Espinoza, O. 2000. Higher education and the emerging markets: The case of Chile. In *The emerging markets and higher education*, ed. M. S. McMullen, J. E. Mauch, and B. Donnorumm, 171–98. Abingdon, UK: Routledge Falmer.

Fanelli, A. M. G. 2006. Argentina. In Pt.2 of *International handbook of higher education*, eds. J. J. F. Forest and P. G. Altbach (2 pts.), 573–86. Dordrecht, The Netherlands: Springer.

Fazackerley, A., and Worthington, P., eds., 2007. British universities in China: The reality beyond the rhetoric. An AGORA Discussion Paper. December.

Federal Ministry of Education Science and Culture. 2002. University Organisation and Studies Act (Universities Act 2002), University Organisation Amendment Act and Universities of the Arts Organisation Act, No. 120/2002/9 August, 2002. DVR 0064301. http://www.bmbwk.gv.at.

Feng, G., and Gong, S. 2006. Sino-foreign joint ventures: A national, regional and institutional analysis. OBHE Report. August. London: OBHE.

Flexner, A. 1932. The universities of America: American universities as institutions of Learning. In *The university in a changing world*, eds W. M. Kotsching and E. Prys, 121–24. Oxford: Oxford University Press.

Forest, J. J., and Altbach, P. G. (eds.) 2006. *International handbook of higher education*. (2 pts.). Dordrecht, The Netherlands: Springer.

Friedman, T. L. 2005. *The world is flat: A brief history of the twenty-first century*. New York: Farrar, Straus & Giroux.

———. 2006. The exhausting race for ideas. *Newsweek* (special edition: The knowledge revolution). December 2005–February 2006.

Frijhoff, W. 1996. Patterns: In *Universities in early modern Europe (1500–1800)*, ed. H. de Ridder-Symoens, vol. 2 (3 vols.) of *A history of the university in Europe*, gen. ed. W. Ruegg, 43–113. Cambridge: Cambridge University Press.

Fulton, O. 2002. Higher education governance in the UK: Change and continuity. In *Governing higher education: National perspectives on institutional governance*, ed. A. Amaral, A. Jones and B. Karseth, 187–212. Dordrecht, The Netherlands: Kluwer Academic Publishers.

The Futures Project. 2000a. Policy for higher education in a changing world. Briefing on demographics. June. Retrieved from http://www.futuresproject.org (Web site no longer available.)

———. 2000b. Policy for higher education in a changing world. Briefing on workforce skills. July. Retrieved from http://www.futuresproject.org (Web site no longer available.)

————. 2000c. Policy for higher education in a changing world. Briefing on for-profit higher education. October. Retrieved from http://www.futuresproject. org (Web site no longer available.)

————. 2002. An update on new providers. June. Retrieved from http://www.future-sproject.org (Web site no longer available.)

Gallup-Black, A. 2004. International student mobility: Project Atlas. *International Higher Education* 37 (Fall): 10–11.

————. 2005. International student mobility in Europe. *IIE Networker* (Spring): 20–24.

Gamage, D. T., and Mininberg, E. 2003. The Australian and American higher education: Key issues of the first decade of the twenty-first century. *Higher Education* 45:183–202.

GAO (Government Accountability Office) 2009. Higher education: Approaches to attract and fund foreign students in the United States and abroad. Report No. GAO-09-379. Higher Education: Washington, D. C.: GAO. April.

Garcia-Guadillo, C., Aupetit, S. D., and Marquis, C. 2002. New providers, trans-national education and accreditation in Latin America. IESAL-UNESCO. http://www.iesalc.unesco,org.ve/programas/internac/n_provedores/general/pro-vee_gral_in.pdf.

Garrett, R. 2002. E-Libraries: Adoption and business models. OBHE Report. July. London: OBHE.

————. 2003. Mapping the education industry Part 2. Public companies-Relation-ships with higher education. OBHE Report. February. London: OBHE.

————. 2004. Foreign higher education activity in China. *International Higher Education* 32 (Winter): 21–23.

————. 2005. The rise and fall of transnational higher education in Singapore. *International Higher Education* 39 (Spring): 9–10.

Garrett, R., and Verbik, L. 2004a. Transnational delivery by UK higher education, Part 1: Data and missing data. OBHE Briefing Note No. 18. London: OBHE. July.

————. 2004b. Transnational higher education, Part 2: Shifting markets and emerg-ing trends. OBHE Briefing Note. 15 December. London: OBHE.

————. 2005. Global Education Index 2005, Part 1: Public companies—Share prices and financial results. OBHE-BfN 25, September: London: OBHE.

Gates, B. 2006. The new road ahead. *Newsweek* (special edition: The knowledge revolution). December 2005–February 2006.

Gellert, C. 1997. Higher education in Western Europe. In *Transforming higher educa-tion*, ed. M. Green, 114–30. Phoenix, Arizona: Oryx Press.

Gerbod, P. 2004. Relations with authority. In *Universities in the nineteenth and the early twentieth centuries (1800–1945)*, ed. W. Ruegg, vol. 3 (3 vols.) of *A history of the university in Europe*, gen. ed. W. Ruegg, 83–100. Cambridge: Cambridge University Press.

Gevers, L. and Vos, L. 2004. Student movements. In *Universities in the nineteenth and the early twentieth centuries (1800–1945)*, ed. W. Ruegg, vol. 3 (3 vols.) of *A History of the University in Europe*, gen. ed. W. Ruegg, 269–362. Cambridge: Cambridge University Press.

Gieysztor, A. 1992. Management and resources. In *Universities in the middle ages*, ed. H. de Ridder-Symoens, vol.1 (3 vols.) of *A history of the university in Europe*, gen. ed. W. Ruegg, 108–43. Cambridge: Cambridge University Press.

Gonzalez, L. E. 1999. Accreditation of higher education in Chile and Latin America. In *Private Prometheus: Private higher education and development in the twenty-first century*, ed. P. G. Altbach, 65–82. Newton, Mass.: Boston College Center for International Higher Education (Reprinted 2003).

Goodman, R. 2005. W(h)ither the Japanese university? An introduction to the 2004 higher education reforms in Japan. In *The "Big Bang" in Japanese higher education: The 2004 reforms and the dynamics of change*, ed. J. S. Eades, R. Goodman, and Y. Hada, 1–31. Melbourne, Australia: Trans Pacific Press.

Government of India 2003. *Selected educational statistics 2000–2002.* New Delhi: Government of India.

Green, M. 2004. GATS update. *International Higher Education* 37 (Fall): 3–5.

Green, M., Eckel, P., and Barblan, A. 2002. The brave new (and smaller) world of higher education. Washington, D.C.: American Council on Education (ACE) and European University Association (EUA). (See also *International Higher Education* 29(Fall): 2–3.)

Guagnini, A. 2004. Technology. In *Universities in the Nineteenth and Early Twentieth Centuries (1800–1945)*, ed. W. Ruegg, vol. 3 (3 vols.) of *A History of the University in Europe*, gen. ed. W. Ruegg, 593–636. Cambridge: Cambridge University Press.

Guangqui, X. 1999. The ideological and political impact of US Fulbrighters on Chinese students: 1997–1998. *Asian Affairs: An American Review* 26 (3): 139–58.

Gupta, A. 2004. Divided government and private higher education growth in India. *International Higher Education* 35 (Spring): 13–14.

———. 2005. Judicialization of education: The fee cut controversy in India. *International Higher Education* 38 (Winter): 19–20.

———. 2001. *Higher education in the world and in Turkey.* Pub. No. 2001–4. Ankara: Student Selection and Placement Center (in Turkish).

Gürüz, K. 2001. *Higher education in the world and in Turkey.* Pub. No. 2001–4. Ankara: Student Selection and Placement Center (in Turkish).

———. 2008. Quality assurance and funding systems. Workshop on Norms for Financing and Managing the Operation of State-Supported Universities Organized by the Hellenic Quality Assurance Agency. 31 March 2008, Athens. Paper available at www.hqaa.gr/files/Guruz_paper.pdf.

Guri-Rosenblit, S. 2005. Eight paradoxes in the implementation process of e-learning in higher education. *Higher Education Policy* 18:5–29.

Hammerstein, N. 1983. University development in the seventeenth and eighteenth centuries: A comparative study. *CRE Info* 62:81–88.

Hatakenaka, S. 2005. The incorporation of national universities: The role of missing hybrids. In *The "Big Bang" in Japanese higher education: The 2004 reforms and the dynamics of change*, ed. J. S. Eades, R. Goodman, and Y. Hada, 52–75. Melbourne, Australia: Trans Pacific Press.

Hauptman, A. M. 2006. Higher education finance: Trends and issues. In Pt. 1 of *International handbook of higher education*, eds. J. J. F. Forest and P. G. Altbach (2 pts.), 83–106. Dordrecht, The Netherlands: Springer.

———. 2009. Taking a closer look at the OECD tertiary statistics. *International Higher Education* 55(Spring): 19–21.

Hayhoe, R., and Zha, Q. China. In Pt. 1 of *International handbook of higher education*, eds. J. J. F. Forest and P. G. Altbach (2 pts.), 83–106. Dordrecht, The Netherlands: Springer.

Hewitt, D., and Liu, M. 2006. The campus craze. *Newsweek* (special edition: The knowledge revolution). December 2005–February 2006.

Hezel Associates. 2005. "Global e-learning opportunity for U.S. higher education." http://www.hezel.com/globalreport/.

Hira, A. 2003. The brave new world of international education. *World Economy* 26(6): 911–31.

Hochstettler, T. J. 2004. Aspiring to steeples of excellence at German universities. *Chronicle of Higher Education* 50(47): B10. July 30.

Holroyd, C. 2006. Canada missing opportunity in the booming China education market. *Canada Asia Commentary*. No. 40. January. (Available at the Asia Pacific Foundation of Canada Web site: http://www.asiapacific.ca/analysis/pubs/pdfs/commentary/cac40.pdf.)

Hore, T. 1992. Nontraditional students: Third-age and part-time. In *The Encyclopedia of Higher Education*, vol. 2 (4 vols.), ed. B. R. Clark and G. Neave, 1666–74. London: Pergamon Press.

Horie, M. 2002. The internationalization of higher education in Japan in the 1990s: A reconsideration. *Higher Education* 43:65–84.

Huang, F. 2003. Policy and practice of the internationalization of higher education in China. *Journal of Studies in International Education* 7 (3): 225–40.

———. 2005. Qualitative enhancement and quantitative growth: Changes and trends of China's higher education. *Higher Education Policy* 18:117–30.

Huang, J. 2005. Two paradoxes of the seller's market of Chinese higher education. *Higher Education Policy* 18:169–77.

Huang, P. L., and Fry, G. W. 2004. Universities in Viet Nam: Legacies, challenges, and prospects. In *Asian universities: Historical perspectives and contemporary challenges*, ed. P. G. Altbach and T. Umakoshi, 301–33. Baltimore: Johns Hopkins University Press.

IDP. 2002. Global student mobility 2025: Forecasts of global demand for higher education. Canberra: Australian Universities International Development Program (IDP) Education Australia.

———. 2007. "Global student mobility: An Australian perspective five years on." Canberra: Australian Universities International Development Program (IDP) Education Australia.

Institute of International Education (IIE) 1947. The conference of foreign student advisers. News bulletin, special issue, June 1.

Iram, Y. 2006. Israel. In Pt. 2 of *International handbook of higher education*, eds. J. J. F. Forest and P. G. Altbach (2 pts.), 793–810. Dordrecht, The Netherlands. Springer.

Itoh, A. 2002. Higher education reform in perspective: The Japanese experience. *Higher Education* 43:7–25.

Jadot, J. 1980. Survey of the state-of-the-art and likely trends of university management in Europe. Paris: OECD-CERI.

———. 1984. University structures: An instrument for shaping the future. In the *Proceedings of the Eighth General Assembly of the Conference of Rectors, Presidents and Vice-Chancellors of European Universities (CRE) 9–14 September, Athens*, 249–99. Geneva: CRE.

Jarausch, K. H. 1983. Higher education and social change: Some comparative perspectives. In *The transformation of higher learning 1860–1930*, ed. K. H. Jarausch, 9–36. Chicago: University of Chicago Press.

———. 1995. American students in Germany, 1815–1914: The structure of German and U.S. matriculants at Göttingen University. In *German influences on education in the United States to 1917*, ed. H. Geitz, J. Heideking, and J. Herbst, 195–211. Cambridge: Cambridge University Press.

Jeliazkova, M., and Westerheijden, D. F. 2002. Systematic adaptation to a changing environment: Towards a next generation of quality assurance models. *Higher Education* 44:433–48.

Johnstone, D. B. 1986. *Sharing the costs of higher education*. New York: College Entrance Examination Board.

———. 1991. The costs of higher education. In *International higher education: An encyclopedia*, vol.1 (2 vols.), ed. P. G. Altbach, 59–90. New York: Garland.

———. 1992. Tuition fees. In *The encyclopedia of higher education*, vol.1 (4 vols.), ed. B. R. Clark and G. Neave, 1501–1509. London: Pergamon Press.

———. 1993. The costs of higher education: Worldwide issues and trends for the 1990s. In *The Funding of higher education*, ed. P. G. Altbach and D. B. Johnstone, 3–23. Garland.

———. 2004. The economics and politics of cost sharing in higher education: Comparative perspectives. *Economics of Education Review* 23:403–410.

———. 2006. *Financing higher education: Cost sharing in international perspective*. Rotterdam: Sense Publishers.

Johnstone, D. B., and Arora, A. 1998. The financing and management of higher education: A status report on worldwide reforms. Prepared for the World Bank for the UNESCO World Conference on Higher Education, Paris. October 5–9.

Johnstone, D. B., and Marcucci, P. N. 2007a. Worldwide Trends in Higher Education Finance: Cost-Sharing, Student Loans, and the Support of Academic Research. This paper was commissioned by the UNESCO Forum on Higher Education, Research and Development. Available from ICHEFAP: www.gse.buffalo.edu/org/IntHigherEdFinance.

———. 2007b. Tuition fee policies in a comparative perspective: Theoretical and political Rationales. *Journal of Higher Education Policy and Management* 29(1): 25–40.

Jones, G. A. 2002. The structure of university governance in Canada: A policy network approach. In *Governing higher education: National perspectives on institutional governance*, ed. A. Amaral, G. A. Jones and B. Karseth, 213–34. Dordrecht, The Netherlands: Kluwer Academic Publishers.

Jongbloed, B. 2003. Marketisation in higher education: Clark's triangle and the essential ingredients of markets. *Higher Education Quarterly* 57 (2): 110–35.

Kaneko, M. 1997. Efficiency and equity in Japanese higher education. *Higher Education* 34:165–81.

Karmel, P. 2003. Higher education at crossroads: Response to an Australian ministerial discussion paper. *Higher Education* 45:1–18.

Kelo, M., Teichler, U., and Wachter, B. 2006. Toward improved data on student mobility in Europe: Findings and concepts of the Eurodata study. *Journal of Studies in International Education* 10 (Fall): 194–223.

Kerr, C. 2001. *The uses of the university.* Cambridge, Mass.: Harvard University Press.

Kerr, C., and Gade, M. L. 1985. *The guardians.* Washington, D.C.: Association of Governing Boards of Universities and Colleges.

Kirp, D. L. 2003. *Shakespeare, Einstein and the bottom line: The marketing of higher education.* Cambridge, Mass.: Harvard University Press.

Klineberg, O. 1976. *International student exchange: An assessment of its nature and its prospects.* New York: Mouton.

Knight, J. 1994. Internationalization: Elements and checkpoints. Research Monograph No. 7. Ottawa: Canadian Bureau for International Education (CBIE).

———. 1999. A time of turbulence and transformation for internationalization. Research Monograph No. 14. Ottawa: CBIE.

———. 2002a. GATS-Higher education implications, opinions and questions. In Proceedings of the First International Forum on International Quality Assurance, Accreditation and the Recognition of Qualifications of Higher Education, 137–51. Paris: UNESCO. October.

———. 2002b. Trade creep: Implications of GATS for higher education policy. *International Higher Education.* 28 (Summer): 5–7.

———. 2002c. Trade in higher education services: The implications of GATS. OBHE Report: London: OBHE. May.

———. 2003a. "GATS, Trade and Higher Education *Perspective* 2003– *Where are we?*" OBHE-Report. London: OBHE. May.

———. 2003b. Updated internationalization definition. *International Higher Education,* 33(Fall): 2–3.

———. 2004. Internationalization remodeled: Definition, approaches and rationales. *Journal of Studies in International Education* (Spring): 5–31.

———. 2005a. New typologies for cross-border higher education. *International Higher Education* 38 (Winter): 3–5.

———, 2005b. International race for accreditation stars in cross-border education. *International Higher Education* 40 (Summer): 2–3.

———. 2006a. GATS: The way forward after Hong Kong. *International Higher Education* 43 (Spring): 12–14.

———. 2006b. Internationalization: Concepts, complexities and challenges. In *International handbook of higher education,* pt. 1 (2 pts.), ed. J. J. F. Forest and P. G. Altbach, 207–28. Dordrecht, The Netherlands: Springer.

———. 2008. *Higher education in turmoil: The changing world of internationalization.* Rotterdam: Sense Publishers.

————. 2009a. Double- and joint-degree programs: Double benefits or double count-
     ing? *International Higher Education* 55(Spring): 12–13.
————. 2009b. Internationalization: Unintended consequences? *International Higher
     Education* 54(Winter): 8–10.
Kogan, M., and Marton, S. G. 2000. The state and higher education. Chp. 4 in
     Transforming higher education: A comparative study, eds. M. Kogan, M. Bauer,
     I. Bleikle, and Henkel, M., 89–107. London: Jessica Kingsley Publishers.
Krieger, Z. 2008. Desert bloom. *The Chronicle of Higher Education* 54(29):B7. March
     28.
Kuder, M., and Obst, D. 2009. Joint and double degree programs in the Transatlantic
     context: A survey report. The Institute of International Education and the
     Freie Universitat Berlin. January.
Labi, A. 2004. Europe strives to keep its scientists at home. *Chronicle of Higher
     Education* 51(2): A1. September 3.
————. 2005a. English U.'s invoke power to raise tuition fees. *Chronicle of Higher
     Education* 51(31): A.38. April 8.
————. 2005b. Plan would create "excellence clusters" of German universities.
     Chronicle of Higher Education 51(46): A22. July 22.
————. 2005c. German court gives lift to universities by overruling tuition ban.
     Chronicle of Higher Education, Today's News, January 27. Available at http://
     chronicle.com/daily/2005/01/2005012705.htm
————. 2006a. Germany moves closer to restructuring its university system. *Chronicle
     of Higher Education* 52(22): A47. February 3.
————. 2006b. Program will allow Chinese graduates to work in Britain. *Chronicle
     of Higher Education* 52(33): A50. April 21.
————. 2006c. Britain expands foreign student recruitment. *Chronicle of Higher Edu-
     cation* 52(34): A55. April 28.
————. 2006d. European higher education falling behind. *Chronicle of Higher Educa-
     tion* 52(29): A52. March 24.
————. 2006e. EU leaders press for modernization. *The Chronicle of Higher Education*
     52(38): A49. May 26.
————. 2007. Bologna conference highlights pogress and limits of Europe's new
     degree cycled. *Chronicle of Higher Education* 53 (39): A36. June 1.
Le, N. M., and Ashwill, M. A. 2004. A Look at non-public higher education in
     Viet Nam. *International Higher Education* 36 (Summer): 16–17.
Lee, M. N. N. 2006. Higher education in Southeast Asia in the era of globaliza-
     tion. In *International handbook of higher education*, ed. J. J. F. Forest and P. G.
     Altbach, 539–56 in Part 2 (2 parts). Dordrecht, The Netherlands: Springer.
Lenton, P. 2007. Global value: The value of UK education and training exports-an
     update. London: The British Council.
Lemann, N. 1999. *The big test: The secret history of the American meritocracy*. New
     York: Farrar Straus Giroux.
Leslie, L., L., and Brinkman, P.T. 1988. *The economic value of higher education*. New
     York: American Council on Education/MacMillan Series on Higher Educa-
     tion.

Levy, D. C. 1986. Alternative private–public blends in higher education finance: International patterns. In *Private education: Studies in choice and public policy*, ed. D. C. Levy, 195–213. Oxford: Oxford University Press.

———. 2009. For-profit versus nonprofit private higher education. *International Higher Education* 54(Winter): 12–13.

Lewis, L., Snow, K., and Farris, E. 2000. Distance education at degree-granting post-secondary institutions: 1997–98. NCES 2000013 Washington, D. C.: USDE NCES Institute of Education Sciences.

Lin, J. 2004. Private higher education in China: A contested terrain. *International Higher Education* 36 (Spring): 17–18.

Liu, M. 2006. High-tech hunger. *Newsweek* (international edition.), accessed at http://www.msnbc.msn.com/id/10756796/site/newsweek/page/2/.

Liu, N. C. 2009. The story of academic rankings. *International Higher Education* 54 (Winter):2–3.

Longman, P. 2004. The global baby bust. *Foreign Affairs* (May/June): 64–79.

Luyendijk-Elshout, A. M. 2004. Medicine. In *Universities in the nineteenth and early twentieth centuries (1800–1945)*, vol. 3 (3 vols.) of *A History of the University in Europe*, gen. ed. W. Ruegg, 543–92. Cambridge: Cambridge University Press.

Maassen, P. 2000. The changing role of stakeholders in Dutch university governance. *European Journal of Education* 35 (4): 448–64.

———. 2002. Organisational Strategies and Governance Structures in Dutch Universities. In *Governing higher education: National perspectives on institutional governance*, ed. A. Amaral, G. A. Jones and B. Karseth, 23–42. Dordrecht: The Netherlands: Kluwer Academic Publishers.

MacLeod, D. 2005. Numbers up for overseas students. *Education Guardian*, April 5.

Maiworm, F. 2001. ERASMUS: Continuity and change in the 1990s. *European Journal of Education* 36 (4): 459–72.

Makdisi, G. 1981. *The rise of colleges: Institutions of learning in Islam and the West*. Edinburgh, Scotland: Edinburgh University Press.

Marginson, S. 1996. University organisation in an age of perpetual motion. *Journal of Higher Education Policy and Management* 18 (2): 117–23.

———. 2002. Nation-building: Universities in a global environment; the case of Australia. *Higher Education* 43:409–28.

Marginson, S., and Rhoades, G. 2002. Beyond national states, markets, and systems of higher education: A glonacal agency heuristic. *Higher Education* 43:281–309.

Maruyama, F. 2005. Latest developments in higher education financing in Japan. *IAU Horizons* 18(1): 5.

McBurnie, G. 2001. Globalization: A new paradigm for higher education. *Higher Education in Europe* 26 (1): 11–26.

McCormack, E. 2006. Foreign applications to graduate schools rise after 2-year drop. *Chronicle of Higher Education* 52(30): A47. March 31.

McDaniel, O. C. 1996. The paradigms of governance in higher education systems. *Higher Education Policy* 9 (2): 137–58.

McNeill, J. R., and McNeill, W. H. 2003. *The human web: A bird's-eye view of world history*. New York: Norton.

Meek, V. L. 2002. On the road to mediocrity? Governance and management of Australian higher education in the market place. In *Governing higher education: National perspectives on institutional governance*, ed. A. Amaral, G. A. Jones and B. Karseth, 235–60. Dordrecht, The Netherlands: Kluwer Academic Publishers.

Meister, J. C. 1998. *Corporate universities: Lessons in building a world-class work force.* New York: McGraw-Hill.

———. 2001. The brave new world of corporate education. *Chronicle of Higher Education.* 47(22): B10. February 9.

Mendivil, J. L. I. 2002. The new providers of higher education. *Higher Education Policy* 15: 353–64.

Mignot-Gerard, S. 2003. Who are the actors in the government of French universities? The paradoxal victory of deliberative leadership. *Higher Education* 45:71-89.

Min, W. 2004. Chinese higher education: The legacy of the past and the context of the future. In *Asian universities: Historical perspectives and contemporary challenges*, ed. P. G. Altbach, 53–83. Baltimore: Johns Hopkins University Press.

MinEduNZ (Ministry of Education of New Zealand) 2003. Export education in New Zealand: A strategic approach to sector; an overview. Retrieved on January 6, 2005 from http://www.minedu.govt.nz/index.cfm?layout=documentid=6093&indexid=666.

———. 2004. New Zealand's offshore public tertiary education programmes. Retrieved on April 20, 2005 from http://www.minedu.govt.nz/index.cfm?layout=document&documentid=6876.

———. 2005. The New Zealand international education sector: Trends from 1999 to 2004. December. Retrieved on July 11, 2006 from http://www.minedu.govt.nz/web/downloadable/dl10947_v1/nz-ie-trends-report-1999-2004.pdf.

———. 2008. International student enrollments in New Zealand 2001–2007. International Division. May 16.

Mock, J. 2005. American universities in Japan. In *The 'Big Bang' in Japanese higher education: The 2004 reforms and the dynamics of change*, ed. J. S. Eades, R. Goodman, and Y. Hada, 183–98. Melbourne, Australia: Trans Pacific Press.

Mohrman, K. 2005. World-class universities and Chinese higher education reform. *International Higher Education* 39 (Spring): 22–23.

Mok, K. 1999. Education and the marketplace in Hong Kong and Mainland China. *Higher Education* 37: 133–58.

Mokyr, J. 1990. *The lever of riches: Technological creativity and economic progress.* Oxford: Oxford University Press.

———. 2002. *The Gifts of Athena: Historical origins of the knowledge economy.* Princeton, N.J.: Princeton University Press.

Mollis, M. 2006. Latin American university transformation of the 1990s: Altered identities? In *International handbook of higher education*, ed. J. J. F. Forest and P. G. Altbach, 503–16 in Part 2 (2 parts). Dordrecht, The Netherlands: Springer.

Mollis, M., and Marginson, S. 2002. The assessment of universities in Argentina and Australia: Between autonomy and heteronomy. *Higher Education* 43:311–30.

Mooney, P. 2004. Asian students flock to China for education. *Chronicle of Higher Education* 51(9): A52. October 22.

Mooney, P., and Neelekantan, S. 2004. No longer dreaming of America. *Chronicle of Higher Education* 51(7): A41. October 8.

Mora, J, and Vidal, J. 2000. Adequate policies and unintended effects in Spanish higher education. *Tertiary Education and Management* 6:247–58.

Mora, J-G. 2001. Governance and management in the new university. *Tertiary Education and Management* 7:95–110.

Morey, A. I. 2004. Globalization and the emergence of for-profit higher education. *Higher Education* 48:131–50.

Murasawa, M. 2002. The future of higher education in Japan: Changing the legal status of national universities. *Higher Education* 43:141–55.

Murphy, D., Zhang, W-Y, and Perris, K. 2003. Online learning in Asian open universities: Resisting content imperialism. OBHE Report. June. London: OBHE.

Musselin, C., and Mignot-Gerard, S. 2002. The recent evolution of French universities. In *Governing higher education: National perspectives on institutional governance*, ed. A. Amaral, G. A. Jones and B. Karseth, 63–86. Dordrecht, The Netherlands: Kluwer Academic Publishers.

Nakayama, S. 1984. *Academic and scientific traditions in China, Japan, and the West.* Tokyo: University of Tokyo Press.

NAFSA. 2003a. In America's interest: Welcoming international students. Report of the Strategic Task Force on International Student Access. January 14. Washington, D.C.: NAFSA.

———. 2003b. Securing America's future: Global education for a global age. Report of the Task Force on Education Abroad, Washington, D.C.: NAFSA.

NASULGC (The National Association of State Universities and Land-Grant Colleges) 2004. A call to leadership: The presidential role in internationalizing the university. Washington, D. C.: NASULGC. October.

NCES (The National Center for Education Statistics) 2004. The condition of education: 2004 in brief. USDE Institute of Education Sciences NCES 2004-076, June. Available at http://nces.ed.gov.

NPEC (The National Postsecondary Education Cooperative). 2004. How does technology affect access in postsecondary education? What do we really know? NPEC 2004-831, prepared by R. A. Phipps. June. Available at http://nces.ed.gov/npec.

Neave, G. 1986. The all-seeing eye of the prince in Western Europe. In *Standards and criteria in higher education*, ed. G. C. Moodie, 157–70. London: The Society for Research into Higher Education.

———. 1988a. The making of the executive head: The process of defining institutional leaders in certain European countries. *International Journal of Institutional Management in Higher Education* 12 (1): 104–14.

———. 1988b. On the cultivation of quality, efficiency and enterprise: An overview of recent trends in higher education in Western Europe 1986–1988. *European Journal of Education* 23:7–23.

———. 1997. On living in interesting times: Higher education in Western Europe 1985–1995: In *Higher education in Europe*, ed. P. Darvas, 33–52. New York: Garland.

————. 1998. The evaluative state reconsidered. *European Journal of Education* 33 (3): 265–83.

————. 2002. Anything goes: Or, how the accommodation of Europe's universities to European integration integrates an inspiring number of contradictions. *Tertiary Education and Management* 8:181–97.

————. 2003. Perspectives on higher education in North America. *Higher Education Policy* 16:1–7.

————. 2005. The marketeers and the marketizing: The American eagle and the Chinese dragon. Editorial. *Higher Education Policy* 18:83–86.

Neave, G., and van Vught, A. 1994. Government and higher education in developing nations: A conceptual framework. In *Government and higher education: Relationships across three continents*, eds. G. Neave, and F. van Vught, 1–21. London: Pergamon Press.

Neelekantan, S. 2006a. India rejects plan for overseas campus. *Chronicle of Higher Education* 52(21): A49. January 27.

————. 2006b. India gives go ahead to campuses abroad. *Chronicle of Higher Education* 52(25): A41. February 24.

Newman, F. 2000. Saving higher education's soul. The Futures Project. 10 July.

Newman, F., and Couturier, L. 2001. The new competitive arena: Market forces invade the academy. The Futures Project, June.

Newman, F., Couturier, L., and Scurry, J. 2004. *The future of higher education.* San Francisco: Jossey-Bass.

Newman, F. and Scurry, J. 2001. Higher education in the digital rapids. The Futures Project. June.

Niklasson, L. 1996. Quasi-markets in higher education: A comparative analysis. *Journal of Higher Education Policy and Management* 18 (1): 7–22.

Norwegian Council for Higher Education 2002. Report to the European University Association, December 13. Oslo: Norwegian Council for Higher Education.

Nuna, S. 2001. Internationalisation of higher education: Australian experiences. In *Internationalization of Indian higher education*, ed. K. B. Powar, 33–47. New Delhi: Association of Indian Universities.

Nyborg, P. 2002. "GATS in higher education." Norwegian Council for Higher Education. April 23. Available at: http://www.uhr.no/internasjonaltsamarbeid/utskrifter/.

Nye, J. S. 2004. The decline of America's soft power. *Foreign Affairs* May/June: 16–20.

Oblinger, D.G., Barone, C.A., and Hawkins, B.L. 2001. Distributed education and its challenges: An overview. Available at: http://www.acenet.edu/bookstore.

OECD. 1990. *Financing higher education: Current patterns.* Paris: OECD.

————. 2003a. Review of financing and quality assurance reforms in higher education in the People's Republic of China. CCNM/EDU (2003) 2. October 14. Paris: OECD.

————. 2003b. Changing patterns of governance in higher education. In *Education Policy Analysis*, 59–75. Paris: OECD.

————. 2004a. *Education at a glance 2004.* Available at http://www.oecd.org/edu/eag2004.

———. 2004b. *Internationalisation and trade in higher education: Opportunities and challenges.* Paris: OECD.

———. 2004c. *Quality and recognition in higher education: The cross-border challenge.* Paris: OECD.

———. 2005. *Education at a glance 2005.* Available at http://www.oecd.org/edu/eag2005.

———. 2006. *Education at a glance 2006.* Available at http://www.oecd.org/edu/eag2006.

———. 2007. *Education at a glance 2007.* Available at http://www.oecd.org/edu/eag2007.

———. 2008. *Education at a glance 2008.* Available at http://www.oecd.org/edu/eag2008.

OECD-UNESCO. 2005. Guidelines for Quality Provision in Cross-Border Higher Education. Paris: OECD.

Ogawa, Y. 2002. Challenging the traditional organization of Japanese universities. *Higher Education* 43:85–108.

Ohmori, F. 2004a. Japan and transnational higher education. *International Higher Education* 37 (Fall): 13–15.

———. 2004b. Japan's policy changes to recognize transnational higher education: Adaptation of the national system to globalization. OBHE-Report. September. London: OBHE.

Okada, A. 2005. A history of the Japanese university: In *The "Big Bang" in Japanese higher education: The 2004 reforms and the dynamics of change*, ed. J. S. Eades, R. Goodman, and Y. Hada, 32–51. Melbourne, Australia: Trans Pacific Press.

Olsen, A. 2003. E-Learning in Asia: Supply and demand. *International Higher Education* 30 (Winter): 8–9.

Osaki, H. 1997. The structure of university administration in Japan. *Higher Education* 34: 151–163.

Osborne, M. 2003. Increasing or widening participation in higher education? A European overview. *European Journal of Education* 38(1): 5–22.

Overland, M. A. 2006. Private: No longer a dirty word in Vietnamese higher education. *Chronicle of Higher Education* 52(40): A37. June 9.

Ozden, C. 2006. Educated migrants: Is there brain waste? In *International migration, remittances & the brain drain*, ed. C. Ozden and M. Schiff, 227–44. Washington, D.C.: World Bank and Palgrave Macmillan.

Ozden, C., and Schiff, M. 2006. Overview. In *International migration, remittances & the brain drain*, ed. C. Ozden and M. Schiff, 1–17. The World Bank and Palgrave Macmillan.

Paarlberg, R. L. 2004. Knowledge as power. *International Security* 29 (1): 122–151.

Palandt, K. 2003. Universities as foundations: The new model of Lower Saxony. Private communication.

Parsad, B., and Lewis, L. 2009. Distance education at degree-granting postsecondary institutions: 2006–07. NCES 2009-044 Washington, D. C.: USDE NCES Institute of Education Sciences.

Paulsen, M. B., and Smart, J. C., eds. 2001. *The finance of higher education: Theory, research, policy & practice*. New York: Agathon Press.

Pearman, G. 2004. International education: New Zealand; a case study. *Continuing Higher Education Review* 68 (Fall): 37.

Perellon, J. F. 2001. The Governance of Higher Education in a Federal System: The Case of Switzerland. *Tertiary Education and Management*, 7: 211–24.

Perkin, H. 2006. History of universities. In *International handbook of universities*, pt. 1 (2 pts.), ed. J. J. F. Forester and P. G. Altbach, 159–206. Dordrecht, The Netherlands: Springer.

Persell, C. H., and Wenglinsky, H. 2004. For-profit post secondary education and civic engagement. *Higher Education* 47:337–59.

Pickering, J. 2001. International education in New Zealand: The drivers and the driven. *International Education-EJ* 5 (3). Accessed at http://www.canberra.edu.au/education/crie/2000-2001/ieej19/forum19.html.

Porter, M. E. 1990. *The competitive advantage of nations*. New York: The Free Press.

Porter, R. 1996. The scientific revolution and the universities. In *Universities in early modern Europe*, ed. H. de Ridder-Symoens, vol. 2 (3 vols.) of *A history of the university in Europe* (3 vols.), gen. ed. by W. Ruegg, 531–64. Cambridge University Press.

Post, D., Clipper, L., Enkhbaatar, D., Manning, A., Riley, T., and Zaman, H. 2004. World Bank okays public interest in higher education. *Higher Education* 47:213–29.

Postiglione, G. A. 2005. China's global bridging: The transformation of university mobility between Hong Kong and the United States. *Journal of Studies in International Education* 9 (1): 5–25.

Powar, K. B., and Bhalla, V. 2001. International providers of higher education in India. *International Higher Education* 23 (Spring): 11–13.

Psacharopoulos, G. 1992. Rate-of-return studies. In *The encyclopedia of higher education*, vol. 2 (4 vols.), ed. B. R. Clark and G. Neave, 999–1007. London: Pergamon Press.

Psacharopoulos, G., and Patrinos, P. 2002. Returns to investment in education: A further update. World Bank Policy Research Working Paper 2881, September. Washington, D.C.: World Bank.

Ramirez, F. O., and Riddle, P. 1991. The expansion of higher education. In Vol.1 of *International higher education: An encyclopedia*, vol.1 (2 vols.), ed. P. G. Altbach, 91–106. New York:. Garland.

Rashdall, H. 1936. *The universities of Europe*. Repr. edited with an introd. and notes by F. M. Powicke and A. B. Emden (3 vols.). Oxford: Clarendon Press, 1987.

Rauhvargers, A. 2004. Improving the recognition of qualifications in the framework of the Bologna Process. *European Journal of Education* 39 (3): 331–45.

Reed, M. I. 2002. New managerialism, professional power and organisational governance in UK universities: A review and assessment. In *Governing Higher education: nationalperspectives on institutional governance*, ed. A. Amaral, G. A. Jones and B. Karseth, 163–86. Dordrecht, The Netherlands: Kluwer Academic Publishers.

Reed, M. I., Meek, L. V., and Jones, G. A. 2002. Introduction. In *Governing higher education: National perspectives on institutional governance*, ed. A. Amaral, G. A. Jones and B. Karseth, i–xxxi. Dordrecht, The Netherlands: Kluwer Academic Publishers.

Reichert, S., and Tauch, C. 2004. Reforming Europe's higher education area: As the fog clears, new obstacles emerge. *International Educator* 13(1): 34–41.

Rektorkollegiate (The Danish Rectors Conference) 2003. Report to the European University Association. Ref. 2003-4100 SB. January 14. Copenhagen: Rektorkollegiate.

Ridder-Symoens, H. de, ed. 1992a. *Universities in the middle ages.* Vol.1 of *A History of the university in Europe* (3 vols.), gen. ed. W. Ruegg. Cambridge University Press.

———. 1992b. Mobility. In *Universities in the Middle Ages*, ed. H. de Ridder-Symoens, vol.1 (3 vols.) of *A History of the university in Europe*, gen. ed. W. Ruegg, 280–303. Cambridge: Cambridge University Press.

———. ed. 1996a. *Universities in early modern Europe (1500–1800)*, vol. 2 (3 vols.) of *A History of the university in Europe*, gen. ed. W. Ruegg. Cambridge: Cambridge University Press.

———. 1996b. Mobility. In *Universities in early modern Europe (1500–1800)*, ed. H. de Ridder-Symoens, vol. 2 (3 vols.) of *A history of the university in Europe*, gen. ed. W. Ruegg, 416–51. Cambridge: Cambridge University Press.

Ringer, F. 2004. Admission. In *Universities in the nineteenth and early twentieth centuries (1800–1945)*, ed. W. Ruegg, vol. 3 (3 vols.) of *A history of the university in Europe*, gen. ed. W. Ruegg, 233–64. Cambridge: Cambridge University Press.

Rizvi, F. 2004. Offshore Australian higher education. *International Higher Education* 37 (Fall): 7–9.

Roberts, J., Cruz, A. M. R., and Herbst, J. 1996. Exporting models. In *Universities in early modern Europe (1500–1800)*, ed. H. de Ridder-Symoens, vol. 2 (3 vols.) of *A history of the university in Europe*, gen. ed. W. Ruegg, 256–82. Cambridge: Cambridge University Press.

Robinson, D. 2005. GATS and OECD/UNESCO guidelines and the academic profession. *International Higher Education* 39 (Spring): 6–7.

———. 2006. GATS and education services: The fallout from Hong Kong. *International Education* 43 (Spring): 14–15.

Ross, M. C., 2004. China's universities look outward. Published previously in the print version of the Fall 2004 issue of *IIE Networker*. See http://www.iienetwork.org/?p=Ross.

Rubenstein, R.E. 2003. *Aristotle's children.* New York: Harcourt.

Ruegg, W., ed. 2004a. *Universities in the nineteenth and the early twentieth centuries (1800–1945)*, vol. 3 (3 vols.) of *A history of the university in Europe*, gen. ed. W. Ruegg, Cambridge: Cambridge University Press.

———, 2004b. Themes. In *Universities in the nineteenth and the early twentieth centuries (1800–1945)*, ed. W. Ruegg, vol. 3 (3 vols.) of *A history of the university in Europe* (3 vols.), gen. ed. W. Ruegg, 3–32. Cambridge: Cambridge University Press.

Ryan, Y., and Stedman, L. 2002. The business of borderless education: 2001 update. Canberra, Australia: Commonwealth Department of Education Science and Training.

Sachs, J. 2005. *The end of poverty*. The Penguin Press.

Salmi, J. 2009. *The challenge of establishing world-class universities*. Washington, D.C.: World Bank.

Sarotto, A. 2004. Ringing an alarm on the state of science and research in the US. *The Federalist Debate* 27 (2) (new series): 27–29.

Sauve, P. 2002, Trade, education and the GATS: What's in, what's out, what's all the fuss about. Washington, D.C.: OECD/US Forum on Trade in Educational Services, May 23–24.

Savage, C., and Kane, M. 2005. The national report on international students in Canada 2002. Ottawa: The Canadian Bureau of International Education.

Scardino, L., Brown, R. H., Caldwell, B. M., Cournoyer, S., Dreyfuss, C., Marriott, I., Maurer, W., and Young, A. 2004. Gartner on Outsourcing, 4Q04. Stamford, Conn.: Gartner Inc. Research ID Number: G00125258. December 4.

Scardino, A., Crichton, J., and Papademetre, L. 2006. "A framework for quality assurance in the development and delivery of offshore programs in languages other than English." OBHE Report, December. London: OBHE.

Schiff, M. 2006. Brain gain: Claims about its size and impact on welfare and growth are greatly exaggerated. In *International migration, remittances & the brain drain*, ed. C. Ozden and M. Schiff, 201–26. Washington, D.C.: World Bank and Palgrave Macmillan.

Schiefelbein, E. 1990. Chile: Economic incentives in higher education. *Higher Education Policy* 3(3): 21–48.

Schmidt-Biggemann, W. 1996. New structures of knowledge. In *Universities in early modern Europe (1500–1800)*, ed. H. de Ridder-Symoens, vol. 2 (3 vols.) of *A history of the university in Europe*, gen. ed. W. Ruegg, 489–530. Cambridge: Cambridge University Press.

Schramm, C. F. 2004. Building entrepreneurial economies. *Foreign Affairs* 83 (4): 104–15.

Schuetze, H. G., and Slowey. M. 2002. Participation and exclusion: A comparative analysis of non-traditional students and lifelong learners in higher education. *Higher Education* 44:309–27.

Schwarz, S., and Rehburg, M. 2004. Study costs and direct public student support in sixteen European countries-Towards a European Higher Education Area? *European Journal of Education* 39(4): 521–32.

Scott, P. 1996. Unified and binary systems of higher education in Europe. In *Goals and purposes of higher education in the 21st century*, ed. A. Burgen, 37–53. London: Jessica Kingsley.

———. 1998. Massification, internationalization and globalization. In *The globalization of higher education*, ed. P. Scott, 108–29. Buckingham, UK: Open University Press.

———. 2000. Globalisation and higher education: Challenges for the twenty-first century. *Journal of Studies in International Education* (Spring): 3–9.

———. 2002. Reflections on the reform of higher education in Central and Eastern Europe. *Higher Education in Europe* 27(1, 2): 138–52.

Segal, A. 2004. Is America losing its edge? *Foreign Affairs* 83 (6): 2–8.

Selingo, J. 2006. Two companies plan to buy a chain of for-profit colleges for $3.4 billion. *Chronicle of Higher Education* 52(28): A39. March 17.

Sharma, G. D. 2001. Internationalisation of higher education: Status and policy suggestions. In *Internationalization of Indian higher education*, ed. K. B. Powar, 121–35. New Delhi: Association of Indian Universities.

Shils, E., and Roberts, J. 2004. The diffusion of European models outside Europe. In *Universities in the nineteenth and the early twentieth centuries (1800–1945)*, ed. W. Ruegg, vol. 3 (3 vols.) of *A history of the university in Europe*, gen. ed. W. Ruegg, 163–232. Cambridge: Cambridge University Press.

Shivkumar, V. 2001. Relevance of Indian higher education to foreign students. In *Internationalization of Indian higher education*, ed. K. B. Powar, 176–79. New Delhi, Association of Indian Universities.

Singh, S. J. 1991. Higher education and development: The experience of four newly industrializing countries in Asia. *Prospects* 21 (3): 386–400.

Sizer, J., and Howells, L. 2000. The changing relationship between institutional governance and management in the United Kingdom: A Scottish Higher Education Funding Council perspective. *Tertiary Education and Management* 6:159–76.

Slantcheva, S. 2005. Legitimating the goal of educating global citizens. *International Higher Education* (Winter): 8–10.

Smolentseva, A. 2003. Challenges to the Russian academic profession. *Higher Education* 45: 391–424.

Sorensen, O. 2005. GATS and education: An "insider" view from Norway. *International Higher Education* 39 (Spring): 7–9.

Spinelli, G. 2005. Mobility and admission of graduate students across the Atlantic: New challenges with the Bologna Process. *IIE Networker* (spring): 43–44.

Stanton, C. M. 1990. *Higher learning in Islam.* Savage, Md.: Rowman and Littlefield.

Stella, A. 2002. Institutional accreditation in India. *International Higher Education* 27 (Spring).

Stella, A., and Gnanam, A. 2004. Quality assurance in distance education: The challenges to be addressed. *Higher Education* 47:143–60.

Stetar, J., Panych, O., and Bin, C. 2005. Ukrainian private universities: Elements of corruption. *International Higher Education* 38 (Winter): 13–15:

Sussex Centre. 2004. International student mobility. Falmer, Brighton, UK: The Sussex centre for Migration Research, University of Sussex, and the Centre for Applied Population Research, University of Dundee, Issues paper, July 2004/30.

Taylor, S., Bell, E., Grugulis., and Storey, J. 2007. The institution that wasn't: The British National Health Service University. OBHE Report, December. London: OBHE.

Taylor, S., and Paton, R. 2006. Corporate universities. OBHE Report, July. London: OBHE.

Teferra, D. 2005. "African higher education: Challenges and prospects." Lecture given at the Boston College Center for International Higher Education, May 9, Newton, Mass.

Teferra, D., and Altbach, P. G. 2003. *African higher education: An international handbook*. Indiana University Press.

———. 2004. African higher education: Challenges for the twenty-first century. *Higher Education* 47:21–50.

Teichler, U. 1991. Western Europe. In vol.1 (2 vols.) of *International higher education: An encyclopedia*, ed. P. G. Altbach, 607–42. New York: Garland Pub.

———. 1996. The changing nature of higher education in Western Europe. *Higher Education Policy* 9 (2): 89–111.

———. 1997. Higher education in Japan: A view from outside. *Higher Education*, 34:275–98.

———. 2001. Mass higher education and the need for new responses. *Tertiary Education and Management* 7:3–7.

———. 2004. The changing debate on internationalization of higher education. *Higher Education* 48:5–26.

Tilak, J. B. G. 1989. Education and its relation to economic growth, poverty and income distribution: Part evidence and further analysis. Washington, D.C., World Bank discussion paper no.46.

———. 1991. The privatization of higher education. *Prospects* 21 (2): 227–39.

———. 1999. Emerging trends and evolving public policies in India. In *Private Prometheus: Private higher education and development in the twenty-first century*, ed. P. G. Altbach, 111–35. Newton, Mass.: Boston College Center for International Higher Education (Reprinted 2003).

———. 2005. Global trends in the funding of higher education. *IAU Horizons* 11(1): 1–2.

Trow, M. 1972. The expansion and transformation of higher education. *International Review of Education* 18 (1): 61–83.

———. 1984. The analysis of status: In *Perspectives on higher education*, ed. B. R. Clark, 132–64. Berkeley and Los Angeles: University of California Press.

———. 2003. In praise of weakness: Chartering the University of the United States, and Dartmouth College. *Higher Education Policy* 16:9–26.

———. 2006. Reflections on the transition from elite to mass to universal access: Forms and phases of higher education in modern societies since WWII. In Pt. 1 of *International handbook of higher education*, eds. J. J. F. Forest and P. G. Altbach (2 pts.), 243–280. Dordrecht, The Netherlands: Springer.

Turlington, B., Naomi, F.C., and Porcelli, M. 2002. Where credit is due: Approaches to course and credit recognition across borders in US higher education institutions. Washington, D.C.: American Council on Education (ACE), Center for International Initiatives.

Uglow, J. 2002. *The lunar men: Five friends whose curiosity changed the world*. New York: Farrar, Straus and Giroux.

Umakoshi, T. 1997. "Internationalization of Japanese higher education in the 1980s and early 1990s." *Higher Education* 34: 259–73.

UNDP. 2001. *Human development report 2001*. New York: UNDP.
UNESCO. 1963. *Statistical yearbook 1963*. Paris: UNESCO.
———. 1970. *Statistical yearbook 1970*. Paris: UNESCO.
———. 1971. *Statistics of students abroad: 1962–1968*. Paris: UNESCO.
———. 1972. *Statistical yearbook 1972*. Paris: UNESCO.
———. 1974. *Statistical yearbook 1974*. Paris: UNESCO.
———. 1975. *Statistical yearbook 1975*. Paris: UNESCO.
———. 1978–79. *Statistical yearbook 1978–1979*. Paris: UNESCO.
———. 1980. *Statistical yearbook 1980*. Paris: UNESCO.
———. 1982. *Statistics of students abroad: 1974–1978*. Paris: UNESCO.
———. 1985. *Statistical yearbook 1985*. Paris: UNESCO.
———. 1990. *Statistical yearbook 1990*. Paris: UNESCO.
———. 1994. *Statistical yearbook 1994*. Paris: UNESCO.
———. 1995. *Statistical yearbook 1995*. Paris: UNESCO.
———. 1996. *Statistical yearbook 1996*. Paris: UNESCO.
———. 1997a. *Statistical yearbook 1997*. Paris: UNESCO.
———. 1997b. International standard classification of education: ISCED 1997. November. Paris: UNESCO.
———. 1998a. Higher education in the twenty-first century: Vision and action. UNESCO Working Document ED-98/CONF, 202/CLD.23. Prepared for the World Conference on Higher Education, Paris, October 5–9, 1998.
———. 1998b. *Statistical yearbook 1998*. Paris: UNESCO.
———. 1999. *Statistical yearbook 1999*. Paris: UNESCO.
———. 2003a. Meeting of higher education partners: Synthesis report on trends and developments in higher education since the World Conference on Higher Education; (1998–2003). Paris, June 23–25.
———. 2003b. "*Higher education in a globalized society.*" Education Position Paper. Paris: UNESCO.
———. 2004. *Global education digest 2004*. Montreal: UNESCO Institute for Statistics. Available at http://www.uis.unesco.org.
———. 2005. *Trade in higher education and GATS*. Accessed on July 20, 2005 at: http://www.unesco.org/education/studyingabroad/highlights/global_forum/gats_he.
———. 2006. *Global education digest 2006*. Montreal: UNESCO Institute for Statistics. Available at http://www.uis.unesco.org.
———. 2007. *Global education digest 2007*. Montreal: UNESCO Institute for Statistics. Available at http://www.uis.unesco.org.
———. 2008. *Global education digest 2008*. Montreal: UNESCO Institute for Statistics. Available at http://www.uis.unesco.org.
UNESCO-CEPES 2006. Statistical information on higher education in Central and Eastern Europe 2003–2004. Accessed on April 10, 2006 at http://www.cepes.ro/cepes/Default.htm.
Vaira, M. 2003. Higher education reform in Italy: An institutional analysis and a first appraisal 1996–2001. *Higher Education Policy* 16:179–97.
———. 2004. Globalization and higher education organizational change: A framework for analysis. *Higher Education* 48:483–510.

van Damme, D. 2001. Quality issues in internationalization of higher education. *Higher Education* 41:415–41.

van der Wende, M. C. 2000. The Bologna Declaration: Enhancing the transparency and competitiveness of European higher education. *Higher Education in Europe* 25(3): 303–10.

———. 2001a. Internationalization policies: About new trends and contrasting paradigms. *Higher Education Policy* 14:249–59.

———. 2001b.The international dimension in national higher education policies: What has changed in Europe in the last five years. *European Journal of Education* 36 (4): 431–441.

———. 2002. The role of US higher education in the global e-learning market. Research and Occasional Paper Series CSHE. 102, University of California Berkeley. Available at http://cshe.berkeley.edu/publications/papers/papers/ROP.WendePaper1.02.pdf.

Veld, R., Fussel, H. P., and Neave, G., eds. 1996. *Relations between state and higher education*, Vol. 1 in the Council of Europe series on Legislating for Higher Education in Europe. The Hague, The Netherlands: Kluwer Law International.

Verbik, L. and Lasanowski, V. 2007. International student mobility: Patterns and trends. OBHE Report, September. London: OBHE.

Verbik, L., and Merkley, C. 2006. The international branch campus—Models and trends. OBHE Report, October. London: OBHE.

Verger, J. 1992. Patterns. In *Universities in the Middle Ages*, ed. H. de Ridder-Symoens, vol. 1 (3 vols.) of *A history of the university in Europe*, gen. ed. W. Ruegg, 31–76. Cambridge: Cambridge University Press.

Villareal, E. 2001. Innovation, organisation and governance in Spanish universities. *Tertiary Education and Management* 7:181–95.

Vossensteyn, J. J. 1999. Where in Europe would people like to study? The affordability of higher education in nine Western European countries. *Higher Education* 37:159–76.

Walts, L., and Lewis, L. 2003. Distance education at degree-granting postsecondary institutions: 2000-01. NCES 2003-017. Washington, D. C.: USDE NCES Institute of Education Sciences.

Washburn, J. 2005. *University Inc.: The corporate corruption of higher education*. Basic Books.

Weidner, W. W. 1962. *The World role of universities*. The Carnegie Series in American Education. McGraw-Hill.

Welch, A. R. 1997. The peripatetic professor: The internationalization of the academic profession. *Higher Education* 34:323–45.

Westerheijden, D. F. 2003. Accreditation in Western Europe: Adequate reactions to Bologna Declaration and the General Agreement on Trade in Services? *Journal of Studies in International Education* 7(3): 277–302.

Wittrock, B. 1993. The modern university: the three transformations. In *The European and American university since 1800*, ed. S. Rothblatt and B. Wittrock, 303–62. Cambridge: Cambridge University Press.

Woodley, A., and Wilson, J. 2002. British higher education and its older clients. *Higher Education* 44:329–47.

World Bank 1994. *The lessons of experience*. Washington, D.C.: World Bank.

———. 1995. *Priorities and strategies for education*. Washington, D.C.; World Bank.

———. 2000. *Higher education in developing countries: Peril and promise*. The Task Force on Higher Education and Society. Washington, D.C.; World Bank.

———. 2002. *Constructing knowledge societies: New challenges for tertiary education*. Washington, D.C.: World Bank.

———. 2003. *Lifelong learning in the global knowledge economy*. Washington, D.C.; World Bank.

———. 2006a. *06 World development indicators*. Washington, D.C.: World Bank.

———. 2006b. *World development report 2006: Equity and development*. Washington, D.C.; World Bank.

WTO. 2005. Services: rules for growth and investment. Accessed on July 20, 2005 at http://www.wto.org/english/thewto_e/whatis_e/tif_e/agrm6_e.htm.

Xie, Z., and Huang, R. 2005. Research on the macro-regulation model of China's Mainland post-secondary education expansion. *Higher Education Policy* 18:145–62.

Yang, R. 2000. Tensions between the global and the local: A comparative illustration of the reorganization of China's higher education in the 1950s and the 1990. *Higher Education* 39:319–37.

Yonezawa, A. 2002. The quality assurance system and market forces in Japanese higher education. *Higher Education* 43:127–39.

Zastrocky, M., Yanosky, R., and Harris, M. 2004. E-learning in higher education: A quiet revolution. Gartner. June 9. Available at http://www.gartner.com/DisplayDocument?doc_cd=121312.

Ziguras, C., and Law, S. F., 2006. Recruiting international students as skilled migrants: the 'global skills race' viewed from Australia and Malaysia. *Globalisation, Societies and Education* 54 (1): 57–76.

INDEX

413